A CULTURAL TOUR ACROSS CHINA

By

Qiu Huanxing

Translated by Harry J. Huang

NEW WORLD PRESS   BEIJING, CHINA

First Edition 1993
Cover design by Gao Donghui

ISBN 7-80005-192-7

Published by
NEW WORLD PRESS
24 Baiwanzhuang Road, Beijing 100037, China

Distributed by
CHINA INTERNATIONAL BOOK TRADING CORPORATION
35 Chengongzhuang Xilu, Beijing 100044, China
P.O. Box 399, Beijing, China

Printed in the People's Republic of China

CONTENTS

Hakkas' houses in Jiaoling, Guangdong Province
A farmer's earthen caves in Northern Shaanxi

A village castle in Minle, Gansu Province

Earthen caves in Gong County, Henan Province

A farmer's house in Gong County, Henan Province

A Spring Festival flower market in Guangzhou

Celebrating Tiancang Festival on the 20th of the first lunar month in Xun County, Henan Province

Purchasing festival goods before the Spring Festival in Dongliao, Jilin Province

The newlywed bride returning to her mother's home with her husband by a one-wheel cart in the Yimeng mountainous areas, Shandong Province

Firing firecrackers in celebration of setting up the upper beam of a new house in Suzhou, Jiangsu Province

Carrying the bride's dowry to her new home in Zigui, Hubei Province

A papermaking workshop in Jiajiang, Sichuan Province
A cow cart, a means of transportation in northeastern China, in Jilin Province

The sheepskin raft owner is waiting for a passenger in Gansu Province

Hakkas "second burial" ceremony in Jiaoling, Guangdong Province

Hui'an women in Fujian Province

A typical man with a white sheep's belly towel on head of Northern Shaanxi

Slippery poles in Sichuan Province

CHAPTER I

SHAANXI — Seat of the Early Chinese Empires

STONE CAVES

A Unique Peasant House

On a freezing winter's day warmed by the sun we arrived at the peasant house of six stone caves which was our goal in Northern Shaanxi Province on the vast loess plateau. In the courtyard stood several leafless jujube trees hung with bright yellow corn ears. On one side of the arched door were strings of red chilis — on the other, jade white gourds. The clucking of the hens as they pecked grain from the ground added life to this quiet country house.

"This would make a gorgeous New Year woodcut!" exclaimed my companion, press photographer Lu Huang. He had graduated from the Beijing Institute of Fine Arts two years before and he couldn't resist making a composition of everything he saw.

Ma Jinxi, the official of the county government who was showing us around, added, "You should have seen it in the fall when the threshing grounds were covered with different kinds of grain and the jujube trees were green and thick with dates, like so many agates."

We were in Suide County 400 kilometers north of Xi'an, Shaanxi's capital. Northern Shaanxi is the part of the province which includes among its more than twenty counties and cities Yan'an, the revered cradle of the Chinese revolution. Back in the Qin Dynasty over two thousand years ago, Suide was an important town in the frontier area. In today's capital

1

of the county, are the tombs of Crown Prince Fu Su and General Meng Tian of the Qin Dynasty. It was Meng Tian who helped the first emperor of Qin build the Great Wall. He also may have invented the Chinese writing brush.

Entertaining Visitors on the Warm *Kang*

Our host Wang Shuhou emerged to greet us in a sheepskin coat, a white towel tied around his head. A tall, rugged man of 57 with a deeply lined sunburned face and bushy eyebrows, he looked every inch the hard-working peasant he was. As he led us to the arched doorway, insisting on carrying our luggage, he gestured toward the three caves to the east, explaining that these were his quarters while the rest were occupied by his nephew. Now Mrs. Wang drew aside the door curtain and motioned us inside and onto the *kang*.

Inviting visitors to take their ease on the *kang* goes back a long way among the peasants of north China. A multi-purpose piece of furniture if ever there was one, the *kang* serves as a bed, a place for members of the family to sit and talk among themselves, a sewing center, a desk for the children to do homework, a place to entertain visitors. Always adjacent to the stove, it is usually built of mud bricks or stone slabs with a fire passage inside. The left-over heat of the cooking fire passes under the *kang* before it goes out the chimney at the roof of the cave. The *kang* not only helps save firewood—it keeps the air fresh indoors.

Sitting on the *kang* with our legs crossed warmed us in more ways than one. The felt blankets helped, but the Wangs' spirit of welcome produced the stronger glow.

First our host set a small short-legged table in the middle of the *kang* on which he put a plate of apples and a large bowl of peanuts and wine-saturated dates, simple enough fare to be sure but delicious and meaningful. Wang pointed out that there was little to offer guests in these remote mountains, but "these are the products of our village and it's our pleasure to share them with you."

We were to be offered these wine-saturated dates everywhere we went in Northern Shaanxi. You can make them your-

2

self quite easily. Here's how: you clean and dry however many you want to preserve, put them in jars, and after spraying them with a bit of white spirits, seal the mouths of the jars and put them away for a couple of weeks. They have now expanded fully; they are plump and lovely to look at and even better to taste — deliciously sweet and fragrant with the scent and flavor of wine. The locals here swear that these red dates invigorate one's spleen and benefit the kidneys. Moreover, they say, since they have no side effects, you can eat as many as you like. Lu Huang and I made the most of our opportunity, leaving only a couple in the bowl.

All the villagers here plant jujube trees around their houses, and the red ones of Northern Shaanxi are well-known throughout China. The local people keep a sack or two of dried dates for themselves to send to friends and relatives, give to children, or keep for folks like us passing through. For festivals, weddings and elderly people's birthday celebrations they make date cakes that look like pagodas.

After consuming all those dates and peanuts I was suddenly quite thirsty, but neither Mr. nor Mrs. Wang saw fit to offer us tea and I asked Ma Jinxi how come. He explained that tea drinking was a habit that somehow had never penetrated this area and that if I wanted any I'd have to ask for it. "But," he pointed out, "fruit can quench your thirst just as well now, can't it?" And he passed me a nice fat apple.

The Stone Caves

As we were chatting idly back and forth, I was measuring the cave with my eyes since I had come to understand that this was where we were going to be spending the night. It was about seven meters long, 3.3 high and the same wide. Thanks to the door and the window built right up to the roof, it was bright inside. In full view of the window was the warm *kang*, three meters long and two wide, connected to the stove. Next to the stove against the east wall was a row of tables covered with bowls, ladles, plates, pots and other cooking utensils. Facing the door was a cupboard holding an alarm clock, a mirror, a tea set, vases, winebowls and pots. On both sides were

3

trunk stands, on which were placed wooden trunks for clothes. Along the west wall stood a washstand, three jars of pickled cabbages and carrots, a water vat, a vat of pig feed next to a neat pile of pumpkins, and a sewing machine.

A painting on the back wall was drawn from the fairy tale, "Sun Wukong Subdues the Whiteboned Demon" from the classic novel, *A Journey to the West*. Apparently any monkey who was capable of subduing demons and devils was a good bet for the job of being protective god of the caves. The east and west walls were both covered with New Year pictures and the window with all kinds of papercuts. Over the wall against which the *kang* rested were affixed all sorts of pictures of flowers and plants known as "*kang*-side pictures." The Wangs had also drawn a design in the shape of a shrine on the wall over the stove with characters saying "High Positions and Great Wealth" written above it. We Chinese seldom miss a chance to invite luck into our lives.

Each time we finished our meal, Cailian, Wang's daughter, would scrub the stone range and the wall around the stove until they shone. It was customary here for the hostess of the family to clean thoroughly all the pots and pans, bowls and ladles, plates and dishes to win the praise of the other women of the village.

When our host was showing us around the yard, to my amazement I caught sight of two jujube trees and an electric pole standing right on the two-meter-thick roof of one of the caves. Seeing my reaction, he explained to me that caves built of stone could withstand heavy pressure. So long as there was no leak in the roof, the heavier the pressure was, the more solid the cave would be. He pointed to the stone roller on the roof and said, "Two or three years from now when the surface becomes more weathered, we'll have to shovel it off and spread new earth over it. And we will also have to roll over it until it becomes really solid."

Very often people traveling in the loess plateau of Northern Shaanxi are unaware that they are walking in the lanes or threshing grounds of a village until they hear people's voices, hens clucking and dogs barking, or see smoke curling into the sky.

No wonder the poet has given us the line: "Carts and horses can run across the roofs."

Traditional cave dwellings are found all over the provinces and autonomous regions of the upper and middle valleys of the Yellow River, which cover 600,000 square kilometers and have a population of 40,000,000.

Three types of cave dwellings are found in Northern Shaanxi. Besides stone caves, there are those built of bricks and those dug directly into the cliffs. Known as "earthen caves," these are ready for use right after the doors and windows are in place. From a mechanical point of view, stone and brick caves are the most solid, but the earthen ones are certainly firm enough because the loess cliffs are solid, the air in the Northwest is dry, and the inhabitants usually cook indoors — which helps to "cure" the walls and ceilings and keep the inside dry. It is said that after withstanding 1,300 years of severe weather, the cave dwelling of famous General Xue Rengui (a native of Hejin County on the bank of the Yellow River) of the early Tang Dynasty is still in good condition.

However, after long years of use, the facades of the caves can become damaged. This happens most often during the rainy season, and the villagers have developed ways of meeting this problem. Some simply cut off the facades and dig the caves farther into the cliffs. Prosperous families build eaves covered with tiles along the edge of the roof, which effectively prevents rain from running over the facade, the door, and the windows.

Cave dwellings that have thick solid roofs are never cold in winter or hot in summer, their natural insulation protecting them against such highs and lows. And since they can easily be built of materials within easy reach, they don't cost much. Nor do they destroy the configuration of the earth, being mostly built inside cliffs, and they don't occupy farmland. With all these advantages, they have attracted the attention of architects throughout the world, not to mention environmentalists who are impressed at their ecological soundness.

Outsiders often find it difficult to understand the intensity of cave dwellers' passion for their homes, their readiness to declare that they wouldn't trade their cave for any apartment or "spacious" modern home anywhere, including Beijing. Ma Jinxi, our escort, stated his unwavering loyalty to the cave frankly, "I'd rather stay home in my cave than in these modern buildings in Beijing!"

It must be said, though, that not all these caves are ideal dwelling places. In fact, some of the old ones are not only low-ceilinged and narrow but dark and dreary because of too small doors and windows. Meanwhile, however, living standards of the peasants are clearly rising—and as this happens, they are building more beautiful and more comfortable caves. Doors are getting larger, windows wider and higher, walls taller and thinner. Old caves were built with roofs that arched too much so that furniture had to be placed away from the walls. Since today arches don't start until a considerably higher wall is built, large pieces of furniture like wardrobes can be put against the wall, with much more usable space being the result. In addition, modern builders fix fanlights above the windows, which means fresher air indoors.

Local Peasant Food

Before Mrs. Wang set to cooking for us she asked us what we would like.

The food of the villagers during winter in particular is simple. Generally they eat cabbages and radishes cooked with mutton and a large portion of a peasant family's time is spent in some aspect of preparing staple food. According to Ma Jinxi, there are at least twenty to thirty different kinds of staple food here but the emphasis is on millet, steamed bread and noodles. Millet, which is boiled and dredged up with a bamboo strainer, was the primary food of the Chinese Communists during the '30s and '40s when they were holed up in the caves of Yan'an. Using the slogan "millets plus rifles," Chairman Mao honored it for the great contribution it had made to the success of the Chinese revolution.

The local daily fare is made up of "*qianqian* porridge" and "getuo." Ground peas and cowpeas mixed with corn and millet cooked together becomes *qianqian* porridge. *Getuo* results when you put little lumps of dough into the left

6

hand and then press them into bowl-shaped thin pieces with the right thumb.

The villagers have three ways of making noodles: they roll them into thin ones using rolling sticks, pull them into fine long ones with their hands, or press them into thick round ones with a mold. Hearing that *hele* noodles were easy to make and especially filling, I made them my choice.

Mrs. Wang selected a china basin to hold the flour she would fetch from the "cold cave" and asked if I would like to come along for a look. The Wangs' home consisted of three caves — the central one of which they lived in while their two daughters occupied the one in the east. We set out for the one in the west: the storeroom. It was certainly fully occupied.

On the *kang* next to the window were corn ears, bamboo baskets, sieves and any number of such household articles. Along the east and west walls were rows of jars of various sizes containing wheat flour, soybeans, small red beans, mung beans, peas, black beans, soybean paste, soy sauce, vinegar, brown sugar and other foodstuffs. Everything except for the brown sugar had been produced by the Wangs themselves.

When Mrs. Wang lifted the covers of the jars to reveal their contents, I noticed that these lids were either woven of *gaoliang* stalks or carved from whole slabs of stone. In this stone-rich area nearly everybody can function as a mason, saving a considerable amount of money that might otherwise have to be laid out for materials and labor. Stone lids provide an extra measure of safety since the mouse or rat has not been born that could find its way past such a barrier!

As I got around the village later on I found that it was a common practice to use stone slabs to cover pots during cooking. But what about the extra work they required? Each such cover weighed about fifteen kilos and it seemed to me that the cook would have to lift them up at least a dozen times a day. And then I found out why they might have considered it worth the effort.

It turned out that even though there were obvious advantages in building the *kang* adjacent to the stove, the practice also posed dangers. Small children needed to be watched lest

7

they climb onto the stove. But the risks to them were considerably increased if the stove held pots with unstable covers. Slabs too heavy for a child to move minimized dangers of scalding. (In places where stone is not available, wooden fences are erected between the *kang* and the stove to keep children at a safe distance). Another advantage of the slab covers is their function as ovens on which villagers often bake dry beancurd shreds and potato slices and dry wet clothes. I also learned that I needn't have worried about the poor cooks getting exhausted from all that heavy lifting of covers since they almost never did it. They simply shoved them around when they wanted to spoon something out.

In front of the "cold cave" was the Wang granary of four stone "cabins." Wheat, sorghum, millet and corn were separately stored inside. Such simple stone cabins or silos, being proof against dampness, make ideal granaries, and the average peasant family in Northern Shaanxi has two rows of them. A few families prefer a storage cabin which is rigged up with planks and sticks. Before the Spring Festival when they slaughter pigs and sheep and cannot finish all the meat in a short time, they hang it up inside the stone cabins. This way they can have fresh meat with which to entertain visitors throughout the whole festival season.

Many hands were needed in the making of the *hele* noodles. After kneading the dough and stewing the cabbages with mutton, Mrs. Wang brought out all the ingredients that would be required: sesames, chopped green onions, radish shreds, sesame oil, soy sauce and vinegar. Meanwhile her daughter was blowing air into the stove with the bellows to boil the water, and Wang Shuhou himself was setting up the *hele* mold above the cooking vessel. The mold was made of a log with a round hole dug through it at the bottom of which was a round piece of bronze covered with small holes. The top round hole was first filled with dough which was pressed down with a stick until noodles ran out from the small holes. They were chopped off when they reached the desired length and dropped into the boiling water.

With an itch to try, I offered to try my hand at it. It had looked easy but I began to sweat in no time. Wang pushed me aside with the face-saving comment: "How can we let our guest do our work for us!"

These noodles we had made with our own hands were quite wonderful. Because it was the first time I had ever had noodles like them, I gobbled down two large bowls, winning recognition as the number one eater there.

Like people in other parts of north China, during festival seasons or when they have visitors, people in Northern Shaanxi also make *jiaozi* (dumplings) which they call *bianshi* (oblate food). Nearly all the local *jiaozi* are filled with carrot stuffing mixed with mutton. The way they make them is their own. They separate out a little mass of dough, shape it into an oblate (flattened at the poles or ends) ball, put it into the left palm, then seize it with the right thumb and forefinger and keep turning it around until it becomes a small bowl to wrap around the filling. This takes a fraction of a second. When I tried it, it took me many minutes of struggle until I produced something that was far from presentable. By contrast the clever hostess put three oblate balls in her hand at once and turned out three wrappers in the twinkling of an eye.

The White Towel

After supper we sat around crosslegged on the *kang* talking about this and that as we munched on wine-saturated dates and cracked melon seeds and peanuts when we were treated to a visit by a village official by the name of Wu Keyu. Except for the white towel known as a "white sheep's belly towel" tied on his head and the overcoat made of old sheepskin draped over his shoulders (exactly the garb worn by our host as he stepped forth to greet us) he was all in black: black cotton-padded shoes, black trousers, a black cotton-padded jacket. I asked him to explain this standard outfit.

First of all, raising sheep is the main form of animal husbandry practiced in Northern Shaanxi. It not only provides the people with their own food and clothing, it's the main source of their livelihood. Each household of this village, for example, raises ten to twenty head a year.

9

Wu told us that the sheepskin overcoats villagers wear are almost always made from the skins of their own animals. When the sheep are slaughtered, they strip off the skins and send them to town for processing. The making of an overcoat, including the processing of the skin and all the tailoring, costs only about ten *yuan*. With such a heavy, durable overcoat, they don't have to worry about fierce wind or snowstorms when traveling outdoors, working in the fields, or tending sheep in the mountains. And sometimes the coats do double duties as blankets or quilts.

But about the towel now: why the name "white sheep's belly towel"?

"Maybe because the woolly towel looks like the belly of a sheep," guessed Wu.

But why always wear it? There are so many other kinds of head gear available. Why not switch off?

"Ah, to us farmers our head towel is indispensable all year round — we can't do without it!" Wu declared and with a flourish pulled off his towel and proceeded to show the different ways of using it much as if he were a magician in a traveling troupe. First he tied it loosely and bowed this way and that. "This is for spring and autumn." he pointed out, "Very useful in keeping off the dirt." Now he tightened it and hunched his shoulders to fend off imagined cold. "Winter is something else again," he said, "and we farmers do a lot of outside work. But, we don't want to freeze our ears and so...." He slipped the towel down to cover them. "And then there's the summer when we work in the fields and mind the sheep in the blazing sun." He wrapped the towel around his head loosely rather like brides do their heads and faces with scarves. The sun's rays can't penetrate but it's loose enough for the air to circulate underneath. "Then when the sun is so bright it hurts your eyes, you do this," said Wu as he rolled the towel into a thick rope to tie above his forehead. It was apparent that it could be a most effective shield.

"Unfortunately, young people nowadays like to follow the fashion," Wu said sadly, shaking his head. "They complain that the towel is out of date and refuse to use it at all."

10

At this point Mrs. Wang told her daughter to make some pumpkin soup for "the visitors," and half an hour later a steaming pot and bowls for each of us were brought to the *kang* table. As a special favor to me, Mrs. Wang picked out two large ruddy pieces and plopped them into my bowl with the promise that the local soup would moisten my throat.

Pumpkins have been a long-standing staple in this area. In the past when they were short of grain, the people ate millet gruel mixed with pumpkin every day. Since today there is plenty of grain, they don't have to stretch it, and so pumpkin has become more of a snack food than a staple, beloved for its sweetness. It is said that pumpkin has the effect of moistening the lungs. Since in winter the air throughout the Northern Shaanxi plateau is invariably dry, drinking a bit of pumpkin soup before going to bed at night can help prevent colds.

Caves for Growing Vegetables in Winter

At daybreak I was awakened by the cocks crowing. I had had a very sound sleep, probably because I had drunk pumpkin soup the night before! I'd been told that sleeping on a heated *kang* had the effect of promoting blood circulation and clearing the nasal passages. I decided it was true, for I felt wonderful when I got up. All the fatigue of my journey, which had been with me for several days, had simply vanished overnight.

At half past six the loudspeaker that hung on the caves' front wall began to send forth news from Beijing. Thanks to the cable broadcasting system of the county, people in the remote villages were quite well informed of what was going on at home and abroad.

I'd decided to take a ramble along the cliffs and was glad I did: most invigorating! Nothing like fresh mountain air! The caves were already teeming with life both inside and out. Through the windows I could see cooks over their stoves, others working the bellows; there were water carriers, chicken feeders, food fetchers, yard sweepers. "Get up early to sweep the courtyards" is a Chinese saying and also habit.

A group of boys and girls carrying buckets of water on their shoulders in more or less single file came up to where I

11

was taking my stroll, laughing merring. Tracing their path over the cliffs facing the brook, I saw a rectangular stone well about a meter deep, its clear water having nearly risen to the level of the earth so it was easy for the fetchers to scoop up water.

Wells in this area were unique. None had a platform and each was built beneath the cliffs with a protective cave over it, effectively preventing pollution of the water. This well was only three hundred meters away from the Wangs' home. They were certainly lucky in this respect. Villagers we visited later on our tour often had to cross hills or mountains to carry water with the help of donkeys from wells two and more kilometers away.

A world of caves, not only human beings dwelled in caves in the area— so did nearly all their domestic animals, their lavatories, their vegetables, farm tools and household articles, and of course their wells, as we have seen. Ma Jinxi took me over to the Wangs' vegetable cellar for a look. He said, "You see, we have had to use our ingenuity to have fresh vegetables throughout the year. So we not only store our vegetables in cellars but also plant them inside caves too." And he beckoned me to follow.

This I had to see and so I fell in step behind him. We stopped on the cliffs near the local primary school where there were a large number of neat cellars, the entrances to which were sealed with thin stone slabs. Since these doorways were very short, you had to bend over to go inside. When he removed the slab from the opening, I thrust my head into the cave and discovered that inside this earth cave of about ten square meters were big autumn cabbages planted close to one another. Every family here had one or two caves of this type in which they could store enough cabbages to last until the next spring.

So that's how they did it! Cabbages were recycled in a way by replanting them in caves. But how was this done? "When you harvest the cabbages in autumn, you pull up everything, including the roots," Lao Ma explained. "You dry them in the shade for a day or two to reduce some of the water inside, which will prevent their getting rotten in the caves. Before you store them, you cut off the dry and yellow leaves, tie

12

up each cabbage with a straw string, and cut off most of the roots. Planted inside the warm caves this way, their small living roots will keep the cabbages alive throughout the winter without needing any nutrient.'' Ma Jinxi seemed to be enjoying enormously my fascination. "You know, these cabbages are a lot like hibernating animals,'' he told me. "But we can't just put them in the caves and let them be. We have to regulate the temperature. When it's still warm in early winter, we move the slab doors to one side in the daytime and put them back at night. In mid-winter the slabs are kept in place, but loosely so that a little bit of air can circulate.'' And thus ended that lesson.

Farming on the Loess Plateau

One day when I was helping with the meal preparation by pulling the bellows, I noticed the array of tools leaning against the wall: plows, hoes, shovels and other such implements. What intrigued me was that all their handles were extremely short. How come, I wanted to know. Would it not be tiresome to work in the fields with tools that had such short handles? I would ask my host about it.

The answer lay in the slope of the land. Everything was on a slant in this hilly, mountainous place. Obviously it cost less effort to work upward, and tools with long handles would be clumsy to use. And certainly in the digging of caves the tools would have to be short-handled.

Unfortunately right now was their slack season and my curiosity to see the farmers using their tools could not be satisfied. But I could at least walk the fields, so I asked Wang Shuhou if he'd lead the way. He'd be delighted. We ended up on the top of a mountain after climbing several slopes. The climb had left me winded, but I might have been breathless anyway standing on that summit looking down on that vast yellow land, that universe of loess. The slopes and villages lying nearby and far off; the endless rolling hills; the gullies that had been left behind by floods down through the ages — all of it, *all*, was covered with loess. It was awesome — but also desolate, monotonous.

Soil erosion is a serious problem in this region, the aver-

13

age loss per year per square kilometer going as high as 18,000 tons. Nonetheless, as the saying has it: "Hard it is to leave one's hometown," and the Northern Shaanxi peasants are legendary for their loyalty to their native place. The plots of land in various sizes look from the distance like so many yellow rags hanging from the mountain ridges. But year after year, generation after generation, the villagers have been plowing those "rags" with their donkeys, spreading manure over the soil again and again. During the very short spring rainy season they plant drought-enduring crops: rice, millet, potatoes, legumes. When fall comes they carry back what they have harvested to the threshing grounds, either on the backs of donkeys or on their own shoulders, where they are husked, sunned or otherwise prepared for storage and year-round consumption.

The local people over the years have developed ways of improving the thin clay soil they have to work with, reducing the ravages of erosion and increasing their crop yields. They have opened up terraced fields across the hills where they grow apple trees along with ground crops. Over steeper slopes they dig level drills instead. They even build stone dikes in some of the gullies to stop the washing away of soil during the rains.

As my gaze traveled over this intricate maze of terraces and patchwork fields, I caught sight of some small touches of green here and there on the edges of cliffs. In the dead of winter? Naturally I had to know what and how. I asked my host.

With roots that go deep into the earth, these *ningtiao* (*Caragana Korshinskii*) plants, as I learned they were called, survive droughts, sandstorms, frigid temperatures, and grow all in a rush, allowing them to play an important role in the conservation of soil and water. In addition, their twigs and leaves make fine fodder as well as excellent fertilizer and when dry they can be used for firewood. So it's easy to see why the villagers in Northern Shaanxi call *ningtiao* "lifesaving grass."

"I suppose it grows wild," I said, noting the patches fringing a sheer cliff in the distance.

"No, it's all planted," said Wang, "every bit of it."

"But it's so steep," I protested. "How can you climb up there?"

14

Wang shook his head. "You don't climb up there and you don't have to. All you have to do is throw up lumps of mud with seedlings wrapped inside. After a rain, the seedlings that are stuck on the cliffs with the mud will take root and start to grow."

It was my turn to shake my head, but for different reasons. I'd never heard of a method of planting remotely similar.

The Laying of the Closure Stone

Winter was the logical time for the building of new cave dwellings and courtyards, and the third day of our visit to the village happened to be the one set aside for the laying of the "closure stone" of Wang Shiyou's new cave — as ceremonious an event as the setting up of the central beam of a new house can still be in villages elsewhere.

According to the old traditional idea, the way a cave is built determines the life of the descendants: happy and prosperous or poor and miserable. That's why the villagers used to ask geomancers to select the spots for their caves. But that superstitious practice has been replaced by practical considerations like how much sunshine is available, convenience to transportation, freedom from windstorms, proximity to drinking water. And in this particular region where soil erosion is such a problem, the place to look for is a spot by a firm cliff safe from floods and mud-rock avalanches.

Once the location is picked, the villagers usually open up a flat spot off the hill which will serve as the work site and later be turned into a courtyard. Next they dig out an earth mold of the same size as the cave-to-be against the hill and after ramming in the base, start to build up the cave on the mold. (If they were to have built their cave house on a level piece of land, they would have instead set up a wooden mold in advance.) When the laying of slabs is completed, they cover the roof with a two-meter-thick coat of soil, continuing to ram it tight and press it flat as soil is brought up. Finally, when the earth mold is removed, the new cave is completed.

Wang Shiyou was preparing dinner for everybody when we arrived to witness the ceremony, but he stopped what he was

15

doing to welcome us and explain the whole process, adding that our presence there was the crowning touch to the event and sure to bless his new home with good fortune now and in the years to come.

What had been designed for the closure stone was in fact an opening right in the middle of the roof into which the precut stone could be easily fitted and at that moment mark the completion of the new cave. In the old days, when superstitious villagers feared evil spirits that might be lying in wait to rush in and take over the new cave, they used to cut out the hearts of three small animals or birds — perhaps a rabbit, a cock and a pheasant — and place them in the tiny holes that had been cut around the opening. In this way they hoped to drive away all evils and devils and improve their chances to lead a happy life in the new home. For good measure they also hung on the two sides of the closure stone a pair of red chopsticks, a Chinese writing brush, an ink stick, an almanac, colored cotton strips, silk threads, and a red bag filled with wheat, rice, sorghum, corn and millet. Every one of these items had its own meaning, but in summary what they were trying to insure for the future were family harmony, thriving animal husbandry, abundant harvests of all crops, and sufficient food and clothing.

At twelve o'clock, the hour for the closure stone ceremony, the stonemason and Wang Shiyou climbed onto the roof and ceremoniously fitted the previously cut stone into the opening and hung up the chopsticks and other items where they belonged.

"The roof is completed!" shouted the villagers, who were immediately drowned out by the firecrackers.

Amid the din Wang began to throw out the gifts that the owner was expected to provide for his neighbors to scramble for, the excited villagers began to fight for whatever they could get hold of, a bun, a sewing kit, some coins or some of the five types of grain. Through this ceremony called "Throwing the Buns," outcomes associated with the various items were expected or at least hoped for. Naturally, a coin catcher improved his chances to get rich and have good luck; a sewing kit receiver could look forward to becoming a skilled embroiderer. And so on.

On either side of the two doors of the completed cave had been placed two couplets written on red paper, one of which read:

> Life in the past was rather hard —
> Days to come will be very bright.

A horizontal scroll read: "Sweetness comes after bitterness." Both this and the door couplet were in sharp contrast to sentiments posted elsewhere, all of which stressed only the positive — for example: "The closure sees good luck everywhere" or simply: "Everlasting peace." It's also true that it's much more typical on this and similar occasions when posting is traditionally done to stick with the upbeat. So I was curious about these hints of a dark side and asked my host about it later that day.

"Well, that's not easy for me to talk about," Wang admitted, peering into the depths of his cup — one of many he had downed that afternoon as the redness of his face attested. He told me how in the past his family of twelve people had been limited to a decrepit old dwelling with only three caves. Yes, life had been more than "rather hard," to hear him tell it. His parents had been too old to work while his four sons and four daughters went off to school one after another, and his wife had her hands full with the house. He had been the only one to carry the burden of supporting all those people. For ten successive years he had been heavily in debt to the production team, to the point where it seemed he'd never be clear of it and any thought of building a new cave was out of the question. He expressed some doubt that he'd even be here to tell the tale if it hadn't been for the production team. Of course now his children had all grown up and were able and willing to add to the family income, so their debts had long since been paid off. In fact, just that year they had contracted for eighteen *mu* of farm land from the village, and Wang could report proudly on a harvest of ten tons of sweet potatoes which they had sold for 1,200 *yuan*. They had also sold two pigs which had brought them another 300 *yuan*.

17

When he talked about the present Wang was all smiles. "To tell you the truth today is really my second son's 'closure day,' not mine. And the work site of a new cave dwelling for my eldest son has already been leveled. It will be ready in a few days. And that isn't all. Five days later my third son will be getting married. Hey, look, don't forget to come to his wedding and join in the fun and feasting, eh?" I assured him I wouldn't dream of missing it.

The appropriateness of the "sweetness comes after bitterness" sentiment was clear.

A COUNTRY WEDDING

The wedding day of Wang Mingzhong was at hand. A "happy shed" — a temporary kitchen — had been set up in the courtyard of his parents' home, where a constant stream of helpers came and went. Some were involved in the butchering of pigs and sheep for the feast; some were making soft millet cakes and steamed buns; others busied themselves cutting designs and characters meaning "double happiness" from red paper.

Coming to congratulate the family on their "happy event," we found Mingzhong's father grinding flavorings with a mill. "You couldn't have come to our village at a better time," he told us. "You really must stay for the wedding feast the day after tomorrow. Say 'yes' right now and I won't have to knock on your door with an invitation card."

The delivery of the invitation cards is called just that formally in China, with a "happy" added to describe them. What happens is that the members of the host family go to the elders or leaders of the village with large red invitation cards as well as pastries and perhaps a collection of other small gifts such as toys, various home-made items and other foods. The cards are expensive and thus are reserved for persons who command respect because of their position or age. The usual method for relatives, friends and neighbors is casual. But not to make a point of specifically asking would be considered insulting, even though everyone in the village is expected to be there.

18

Stuck on the two sides of the door was a couplet which read:

> Clever chefs prepare succulent meats—
> Skilled hands present delectable feasts.

Above the door was pasted the statement: "All rejoice."

The preparatory work was being done in systematic fashion. The "List of Helpers" on the wall detailed the specific titles and/or duties of each and the names of those assigned. "General Director, Receptionists, Kitchen Workers, Keepers of the Ceremonial Chamber and the Feast Chamber; Carriers of Dishes, Rice Buckets, Water; Boilers of Water; Errand Runners, etc. Sometimes assignments overlapped — that is, one person's name might appear several times. All helpers were from the village. As the saying goes: "A happy event of one family cheers up the whole village."

The Bride's Escort

At dawn a three-gun salute was fired in the village followed by drumbeats, and the troop whose job it was to fetch the bride set off.

"The bride's leader" — here, as is usually the case, the wife of the bridegroom's eldest brother — was the commander. They all were fortified with the red bean porridge they had dutifully consumed to conform to custom and were carrying the bride's wedding clothes and two long loaves of yellow millet cake called "departure cake." Once these were in the bride's hands she would know it was the moment to leave her mother.

For three days the bride had been sequestered indoors with her mother, sewing, gossiping, hearing advice on how to behave to please her husband and be a dutiful wife, and exchanging the last affectionate words she would with her mother as still a girl.

With drumbeats announcing the approach of the escort, the bride emerged and offered the troop "happiness noodles," as is customary at this point. Her own escort was gathering also, people from her family, except that neither parent nor a younger sister could be part of it and the number had to equal that of the bridegroom's side.

Rules also demand that the bride enter the bridegroom's house at noon. If he lives too far away to make meeting such a schedule feasible, then she and the escorting parties must arrange for an overnight stay. Such troops may request lodging from any villager, whether they know each other or not, and the hosts are expected to be hospitable. Indeed, they consider it an honor.

The Wang courtyard was overflowing with wedding guests long before the noon hour struck, all of them eager to greet the procession and admire the bride. The young women crowded together gossiping and giggling, most of them holding a curious or sleepy child. "It's such a beautiful day," they kept saying. "The bride must be particularly virtuous!" They were speaking out of a superstition passed down through the ages in Shaanxi. Brides whose wedding fell on a fine day were clever and chaste, while those who were so careless as to marry on a cloudy day were muddleheaded. And if it rained, watch out! Bad luck lay in wait right around the corner. I thought to myself that it was lucky Northern Shaanxi was a dry region and weddings usually fell in the wintertime — a season of fine weather. Not only was a whole lot of gloom and doom thus averted, but just consider the wives that escaped with their reputations!

Drumbeating was heard from the ridge of the western mountain and there came the troops of escorts in slow descent. They had to make their way on foot all the way to the bridegroom's home because it was all mountain paths here. Such walking would never do in the past. Custom had it that the bride must be seated in a sedan chair or at the very least on a donkey. A rich family would provide a sedan not only for the bride but one for the "bride's leader" as well.

Naturally there were many poor families who could not possibly afford a bridal sedan. But they had a way out. They could turn a square table upside down and tie two bamboo poles on two sides. Then they would fix two shoulder poles at the ends of the long poles. When this basic bridal sedan was readied, the women would wrap red cloth around the legs and stretch it the length and breadth of the table, thus creating an enclosed space for the bridal passenger. Next they tied on a red cloth roof. Meanwhile, perhaps two or three of the attending women would cover the sedan floor with wheat straw and then bedding. Now the bride could be hoisted aloft and carried with as much style as if she could afford a "real" sedan.

When the bride was carried to the home of the bridegroom, a master of ceremonies — the villager most glib of tongue — would walk around the bridal sedan with a jujube branch in hand singing the wedding song:

> A table is turned upside down
> Draped in red and blue but never brown,
> Fixed with a red roof and held with green belts,
> Laid with wheat straw and then cotton felts.
> A Diao Chan is seated inside.
> The four bearers grin with special delight
> Since they know that soon they'll be within sight
> And that this is a maiden's last ride.

The image of Diao Chan, heroine of the classical Chinese novel, *The Romance of the Three Kingdoms*, is often called up by villagers in Northern Shaanxi to personify the perfect bride — e.g., pure, selfless, submissive, beautiful. Legend has it that Diao Chan was a native of Mizhi in Northern Shaanxi, known for its beautiful women.

Nowadays brides no longer arrive either in sedans or on the backs of donkeys. Since roads have been opened up across the village which are joined with the highways, escorts going to fetch the bride and accompany her to her new home most often travel by automobile, by tractor, or in several carts pulled by donkeys. There are also the escorts who go by bicycle to transport the bride, her dowry and perhaps the "bride's leader" on bicycle carriers. There are very few walking escorts anymore — the Wang party to the contrary notwithstanding — and fewer still walking brides.

Let's look again at those Wang nuptials. The escorts of both sides had now arrived at the village. Immediately two young men carrying a new bed sheet tied to bamboo poles ran toward them. For all the world like the flag-bearing leaders of a parade, they fell in step ahead of the escorting troops holding aloft the "happiness sheets" fluttering at the tops of the bamboo poles. And now came the grand strains of music accompanied by drumbeats.

Suona (woodwind instrument) horners, one pointing his instrument to the sky, the other to the earth, heralded the approach of the bride, their cheeks bulging with the effort of producing that high, piercing melodic line. Firecrackers arranged to go off in a chain greeted the bride as she entered the yard.

Traditional Practice After the Bride's Arrival

Graceful 21-year-old Ma Yufang and handsome Wang Mingzhong at twenty-three made a handsome pair. Observing local custom, they bowed in thanks to the sky and earth, then carried into their chamber a *dou* (rice dipper) as a way of improving their chances of experiencing abundant harvests and conjugal happiness. Filled with grains, the dipper was placed in front of a mirror, the rod of a scale, and a ruler. The mirror in this instance was a "demon detector" with the function of heading off evil spirits that might be lurking about, while together the ruler and arm of the scale — with its special units of measurement in Chinese, *fen* and *cun*, which combined stands for a sense of propriety — in this context symbolize a code of marital ethics or manners that will make for harmony in the marriage.

But don't forget that customs of the Han people are not the same everywhere. There can be differences even within the same geographical area. For example, in Luochuan County, also in Northern Shaanxi, brides who have entered the yards of their bridegrooms do not bow in thanks to the sky and earth but to a pair of Chinese characters " 雁 " meaning wild geese instead.

Behind this practice lies a romance. It emerged from the belief that a wild goose and gander who have mated protect and stay close to each other for life. If one of the pair gets lost or dies, the survivor will mourn and refuse to eat until it also dies. Thus the wild goose in some parts of China has become the symbol for true love.

But we left Ma Yufang in the bridal chamber, did we not? We must get back to her!

No sooner had the bride stepped into that room than many of the men pressed around the door. Part of the fun of a wedding throughout China is the license to peek and listen — especially later when the bride and groom are alone — and then to gossip and report to others what one has seen or heard (or imagines that he has) and tease the groom with it. In this instance a few naughty boys even climbed onto the windowsill and peeked into the room, first poking holes in the newly pasted window paper. It is out of bounds for strangers to participate in such goings on, so we observed it all from some distance. I had been told that there were several ceremonies for the bride to perform in the bridal chamber.

First of all, she must wash her face. In the old days, before a young woman was married she had the fine hair on her face removed with silk thread in a rite which was called "opening the face" to mark the beginning of true womanhood. But nowadays for the most part a symbolic washing of the face has been substituted.

Next, the bride combs her hair ceremonially. In the past when a man reached the age of twenty, to declare to the world that he had become a man, his family would sponsor a ceremony in which his hair would be tied on the top of his head in a ritual called "tying the hair." A girl's womanhood was seen to arrive the moment of marriage so that her "hair coiling ceremony" came at that time. She coiled it on top of her head and inserted hairpins, thus making manifest her married status. Today's hair combing is simply a reenactment of an ancient custom.

Ma Yufang, having completed her face washing and hair combing, was now an official member of her new family and eligible to take her place on the *kang*. But she was not finished with her ceremony — far from it! Her mother-in-law had placed two long, fully stuffed pillows embroidered with designs appropri-

23

ate to the occasion on the edge of the *kang*. On each pillow was embroidered a tiger and a white rabbit tied together by a red thread. The powerful tiger stood for the bridegroom and the gentle white rabbit for the bride while the red thread was a symbol of love and marriage. (The legend goes that the old man under the moon who unites a couple in marriage ties lovers separated by geography with red threads. That is why we have the saying that "the marriage thread ties persons far away from each other together as loving couples.") The bride's mother-in-law had done the preliminary work in preparation for the couple's performing the ceremony of plumping and embracing the pillows to declare to the world that theirs was to be a harmonious marriage.

At this moment two walnuts were placed in the middle of the *kang*. No sooner had the bride and bridegroom seated themselves on the *kang* than they seized the walnuts and threw them away. In the local dialect a walnut or *gedan* is a homophone of the word "quarrel." Therefore, by throwing away the walnuts together, the couple pledged that they would never quarrel but would always respect each other.

When the walnuts were thrown away, the mother-in-law brought over a bowl of *jiaozi* (dumplings) to her daughter-in-law and as Ma Yufang ate asked, "*Sheng ma?*"

"*Sheng,*" answered the bride shyly.

In Chinese *sheng* means "undone" and also "give birth to a child." The mother-in-law was pleased at Yufang's answer, never mind that tradition allowed no other reply. It meant that she could anticipate a healthy grandchild in a year. In addition, *ma* in Chinese is an auxiliary word with grammatical function of mood in questions.

Ever since ancient times, most Chinese, especially in the countryside, have considered a large family desirable and a sign of prosperity. But today, with a population of close to a billion and a half, that is changing. Everyone in China knows about the government's policy of population control and most support it. So, as I was told, some brides while eating the *jiaozi* answer, "Yes (*sheng*) but only one." I was also told that this answer usually wins the warm applause of those present.

24

In Luochuan County, after taking her seat on the *kang*, brides participate in a game called "Uncovering Dishes." A tray holding four covered bowls, containing respectively coins, salt, bran or fried dough sticks, is presented to the bride for her to take her pick. If she uncovers the one filled with coins, she will be praised as one who will be industrious, thrifty and resourceful in helping the family acquire wealth. If she uncovers the one containing bran, she will also be considered a financial asset to her new family, since "bran" and "fortune" are homonyms in Chinese. But woe unto the bride who happens to choose the fried dough sticks, for those present will despise her for the greedy woman that has been thus exposed even though no one would, of course, dare speak out such thoughts.

One day while we were in Luochuan County we saw a bride by the name of Zhao Fangling uncover the dish of salt, whereupon the room resounded with laughter and called-out comments. "A marriage made in heaven!"— "Meant for each other, that's plain!"— "A born couple!" were some of the sentiments expressed. The reaction made clear that the dish of salt had been a lucky choice. "Salt" and "happy marriage" are homophones in the Northern Shaanxi dialect, as it turns out.

The function of this game is to help lay the foundation for a favorable future. Perhaps the main point of the game, however, is simply to add to the fun. No one I ran across had ever heard of a bride so silly as to choose the dish with fried dough sticks in it, which surely suggests collusion. The tray bearer, in other words, apparently tips off the bride with a subtle gesture or meaningful look as to which dish *not* to pick!

Later on I challenged Zhao Fangling. "Be honest," I said. "Didn't you get a hint beforehand?"

"Oh, no," she insisted. But her red face spoke louder than her words.

Teasing Games in the Bridal Chamber

Ma Yufang, at last liberated from the "tortures" of the bridal chamber, was able to join the bridegroom in toasting with the guests. As one of these, I was asked to sit at a table on the *kang* to enjoy the wedding feast—a sumptuous meal of four cold dishes and eight hot courses prepared by local cooks.

Once the banquet was done with, the master of ceremonies was heard from. "It's time for the young couple to meet the old and the young," he boomed. Masters of ceremonies, here as elsewhere, were required to have loud voices. So the bride and bridegroom were beckoned to the "table of etiquette" to meet the older contingent.

Accompanied by the ceremonial singing of the master of ceremonies, the young couple bowed low to their grandparents, uncles and aunts; then brothers and sisters-in-law and the other relatives in accordance with ancient custom. Then the master of ceremonies proposed another toast to each of these important relatives on behalf of the young couple.

And now it was gift-giving time. The bride presented "first meeting gifts" to those who fit that category: to the men, small embroidered bags suitable for carrying money and a few other small items; and to the women, embroidered sewing kits. This done, she had become part of the community in "relationships by means of connection."

Those who received her gifts were expected to give her something in return, usually money. At this moment some of the onlookers from the village had to have their little joke. "How can the grandpa be so stingy with the bride?" they taunted. Thus trapped, the grandfather had to pull out his wallet and fatten the collection. However, nobody could go overboard in that there were rules that governed the proportions of each gift. That is, the grandparents should give the largest amounts followed by the parents, while contemporaries gave the smallest sums. Among the relatives, the uncles (brothers of the bridegroom's mother in this instance) were expected to give the most significant amounts. It would be considered a breach of etiquette for a junior to offer the bride a sum larger than that of any of these elders.

Once the bride had met all the family members and relatives, the guests began to leave. As the escorts of the bride's family set off for home, the bridegroom accompanied them with a pot of wine in one hand and a bowl in the other, offering and joining in toasts and bowing to them over and over until they were well on their way.

After night had fallen, the teasing and games began in earnest. Everybody, except for the bride's parents-in-law and married brothers-in-law, were eligible to join in. Laughter resounded through the mountain valley until the games had run their course and it was time to leave the newlyweds in peace.

This custom of "fun and games in the bridal chamber" again goes way back in history and until recent years was essential in breaking the ice that kept the couple at a frozen distance from each other. In the old society, when marriages were arranged by parents and matchmakers, the bride and bridegroom hadn't laid eyes on each other before the wedding day. Such teasing activities in the bridal chamber helped the bride and bridegroom overcome their shyness and eased the way toward the intimacies to come. Of course there is more to consider than simply the relationship between the bride and groom but relationships of all the family members, relatives and friends to the newly united couple and to each other. The festive atmosphere promotes closeness and good will among all the family members and the community beyond.

In Jia County, when all the guests have left after the wedding night games are over, the mother-in-law enters the bridal chamber with an apron full of red dates, peanuts and "buns for young ones" and drops them in a shower on the seated couple, who spread them all over the *kang*. As they attempt to cover every bit of the *kang*'s surface, the mother-in-law sings:

> Just like my rolling dates and buns,
> On the *kang* children will jump and run.
> All the boys must be good sons
> Who will in future wear long gowns
>   (a sign of a successful man)
> And our girls must all have clever hands
> To make papercuts that are good ones.

The dates, of course, are a symbol of fertility, and the buns stand for children. It is said that this custom of assuring a

27

fecund union by spreading dates and buns on beds originated at the wedding of Emperor Hanwu and a Madam Li over two thousand years ago.

On the second day after their wedding, the newlyweds returned to the home of the bride's parents. It was their turn to host a banquet, and her family's chance to get back at the groom for the merciless teasing the bride had had to endure. And so the moment the bridegroom walked in the door he was set upon by his young sister-in-law, who blackened his face with soot before he could fend her off. And when he bit into the *jiaozi* she had put in his hand, he found it filled with nothing but chili powder and pod shells. A broad grimace telling her that her trickery was working, his new sister-in-law grinned in smug satisfaction. "Serves you right," she crowed. "You mistreat my sister and you have all of us to answer to!" And she made a sweeping gesture that took in the crowd of people filling the room. But his mother-in-law was more compassionate. She came forward with another bowl of *jiaozi* stuffed with a succulent meat filling.

It was obvious that this bit of mischief did nothing whatsoever to diminish the happy atmosphere. Quite the contrary, it seemed to loosen everyone up for another day of celebration.

PAPERCUTS, DOUGH FIGURINES AND YANGKO DANCE

Papercuts — Art of Decoration in Caves

Papercuts decorate the lattices of windows and doors of almost all the cave dwellings on the loess plateau of Northern Shaanxi, most of them the work of the women who live inside.

Li Xiufang, a countrywoman of Ansai County, is especially skilled at the craft, as we saw for ourselves when we paid her a visit. Her scissors snips through colored paper to free barnyard animals, pomegranates, peaches, lotuses and all varieties of wild flowers and those that the local people plant and nurture. What's more, she produces complex illustrations of folktales, some from antiquity, others from more recent history. She showed me some of her works filed in an old magazine, some of whose titles were "White Rabbits Eating Radishes," "A Mouse Steals Eggs," "Fighting Cocks," and "An Eagle Seizes a Rabbit," all depicting countryside realities.

Chinese peasants have always measured time by the lunar calendar, numbering the years in the order of the twelve animals— or *shengxiao* in China: the Rat, Ox, Tiger, Rabbit, Dragon, Snake, Horse, Sheep, Monkey, Rooster, Dog and Boar. This way of numbering the years is found only in a few Asian countries besides China, Japan being one.

Li Xiufang is not unique. The twelve animals are favored subjects of innumerable countrywomen in Northern Shaanxi. Just before the Spring Festival each year, peasants in north China are in the habit of replacing their old papercuts with new ones, affixing them to newly pasted snow-white window papers. Among all the colorful subjects, you are sure to find the animal that symbolizes the year. When we visited, it was the Year of the Boar and the villagers had pasted scissor-fashioned boars on trunks, walls, mirrors, wardrobes and vases as well as their doors and windows, hoping thus to insure an abundant harvest— the particular job of this unglamorous animal. But despite the beast's lack of sex appeal, Li was able to produce fat piglets— or ones resembling the clumsy, honest Zhu Bajie from the classical Chinese novel, *A Journey to the West*— which could only be called lovely.

Papercutting as a folk art is not confined to Shaanxi— it is everywhere, its styles varying from region to region. In Jiangsu, Zhejiang and other places that lie in the lower valley of the Yangtze River, because it is usually rainy and wet, the local people don't paste papercuts in windows but create them to be parts of lanterns or as patterns for embroidery, using burins as well as scissors. After cutting out the designs, they refine them carefully so that the smooth final lines vividly reflect the local scenery. In Foshan, Guangdong Province, papercuts are done even more delicately. The designs are first cut out of gold paper, then painted in detail, and finally affixed to other colorful paper with results that are dazzling.

Since Northern Shaanxi is an area without much rain, papercuts pasted on doors and windows are safe for a long time — that is, they can be kept secure from winds. So that they can resist strong winds, the women scissor out bold lines which are joined one with the other. In this way a vigorous, dashing style has developed here.

In Ansai I visited Bai Fenglan, sixty-nine, the artist who had created "Cattle Plowing the Field" and "Monkeys Eating Peaches," whose short, strong lines put one in mind of the stone inscriptions found in the Han Dynasty tombs excavated in Suide County in Northern Shaanxi. Bai began to learn papercutting at eight. Because her family was too poor to afford paper, she practiced on leaves plucked from trees in front of her house. And actually this is just how the folk art originated, cutting shapes out of the leaves of trees. In his *Historical Records*, Sima Qian tells how the King Zhou Chengwang cut out a tung tree leaf in the design of an elongated pointed tablet of jade (ancient rulers held such tablets on ceremonial occasions) and gave it to his younger brother Jiyu as he granted him the duke-dom of Tang State (today's southwestern Shanxi) at the beginning of the Western Zhou Dynasty (1100-771 B.C.). This could have been the very first papercut.

Before papercutting was invented, there had of course been those tree leaves, but also gold foil, silver and bronze sheets, silk, leather, bamboo and wood all playing their role as precursors of paper. Like the first paintings that were done on silk, papercuts were first scissored out of gold and silver foil or thin, tough silk. As is revealed in *Chronicles of Chu State*, on the first day of spring during the Liang Dynasty (A.D. 502-557), wealthy women in the area that comprises the Hunan and Hubei of today would welcome the arrival of the season by cutting out of colored silks and gold foil finches which they would pin in their hair. But it was only when paper became cheap and widely available that papercutting could develop as a folk art.

In Northern Shaanxi, mothers-in-law usually paste the figure of a tiger on the door when their daughters-in-law give birth, believing that baby-snatching devils will thus be scared off. A prolonged rain during summer harvest will also provoke papercutting, in this case of figures with brooms who will be hung up in front of the house or pasted on nearby trees in the hope that the paper broom wielders will sweep away the clouds so that the sun can come out and dry their wheat.

Nowadays the number of people who really believe in the supernatural power of the papercuts keeps shrinking. Nonetheless, since the local people love papercuts so much, they continue to play an important role in daily life. Li Xiufang's home, which consisted of five caves, was covered with papercuts from floor to ceiling. With the furniture and all indoor objects beautifully ornamented, the rooms put together had become a gallery.

I was told that in Northern Shaanxi men rate skill at papercutting and embroidery high on the list of assets they look for in a wife. No wonder that as we traveled through there we often saw young girls of seven or eight sitting in groups practicing papercutting.

Xintianyou — **Folk Songs Resounding Through the Loess Plateau**

In the capital of Ansai County we were introduced to affable He Yutang, forty, a local folk singer whose straightforward friendliness made him a pleasure to be around.

"My father and both grandfathers all love to sing," he smiled. "They began teaching me to when I was ten." He was born with a superior instrument; one could tell that as soon as he opened his mouth. There was melody when he spoke as well as when he sang in his pure lyric tenor. He was quick to respond to our request for a song:

> My lad is now well on his way
> And here I sit alone and cry
>
> For the mountains are high and he's beyond them.
> I can see him no more for the tall peaks hide him.
>
> Over rivers larks safely fly;
> How I wish I could share their sky.

But when we two meet again some day
We'll pour out all we want to say.

Here a wife sees off her husband, who will be away for a long time, in a song of the form known locally as *xintianyou*, which is characterized by both formalism and spontaneity. In each line there are supposed to be seven Chinese characters, a rule that is generally followed. The upper line of each couplet describes scenery or objects while the lower one expresses the singer's feelings. Again, this convention is usually observed, but in folk songs in a sense anything goes — or can. Spontaneity is the main ingredient of *xintianyou*. The singers can burst into song as the spirit moves them, whenever and wherever they please, using words of their own choice made up on the spot. They can be working in the fields, herding sheep in the hills, cutting firewood in the woods, carrying coal with the help of their donkeys, weaving cloth, doing embroidery, cooking dinner, feeding the livestock — you name it. When sung, such songs are typically highly melodic and resonate with images of the loess plateau.

There are many types of folk songs native to Northern Shaanxi. Besides *xintianyou*, there are *sijige* (four-season songs), *wugengdiao* (five-watch songs), *jiuge* (toasting songs), *yangko* or *yangko* (work songs), *tanjiadiao* (returning home melodies), among others. "The East Is Red" composed in the '40s by Li Youyuan, a peasant of Jia County, actually belongs to the category of *tanjiadiao*. Because this song, which expressed the people's love for Chairman Mao Zedong and the Communist Party, was melodic and easy to sing, and because of its timing, it swept China.

However, of all the songs that He Yutang sang that day he gave us a concert in his cave, only one example of the *sijige* form was included and that one concerned farmers' activities in the four seasons. All the rest were love songs. He explained that in the old society, because young people had no freedom of choice in love, they expressed their resentment against arranged marriages and their strong desire to make their own choice in song — that being the only outlet available to them.

Life for the local peasants was extremely hard in the old days. To help support their families, many of the men organized themselves into gangs and went to find work in far away places where they would stay for years without returning home even once. Meanwhile their wives, whenever they were especially lonely, would sing melancholy songs in a low voice as they spun cotton into yarn at their spinning wheels or gathered together outdoors. Their songs are among the most touching of the Northern Shaanxi folk songs. Here is a sample:

> Small flowers hang on every pea vine—
> Sewing here I long for you, sweetheart of mine.
>
> I yearn to see you but cannot do so;
> Sweet sugar's bitterly hard to swallow.
>
> Fish cannot breathe if they leave water for land—
> Just so I need walk with you hand in hand.
>
> A pair of larks fly into the vast sky—
> How I yearn to see you standing by, standing by.

During the dark days of the Cultural Revolution songs' lyrics which took as their theme the devotion of countrywomen to their loved ones were condemned by the Gang of Four as decadent and were accordingly banned. Similarly, for some years young people were not allowed to sing their own folk songs.

"Now we are singing *xintianyou* again," said He Yutang, the presiding judge of the People's Civil Court of Ansai County. When the court must tend to affairs in rural areas, he and his colleagues are apt to climb to the ridges of mountains when they take a break. Looking down at the vast loess plateau below often inspires them to sing the old songs. Their voices echo in the valleys and often inspire antiphonal singing in response.

In these days of the reform, land in the countryside has been divided among the peasants, each of whom is now responsible for one share. Naturally with the breaking up of the communes and the assignment of plots of land to individual farmers, they end up working in smaller groups, which can lead to boredom. Yet their living standards are steadily improving and you only have to look at their faces to know it. No gloomy countenances these. They sing more often, too — songs like this:

> The sun comes out and magpies chatter now;
> Contracted land has come to every house.

> Blooming lilies redden the mountain slopes,
> With our sweat we bring up bountiful crops.

Dough Figurines: the Sculpture of Countrywomen in Northern Shaanxi

Dough figurines, or *mianhua*, as the local people call them, are in fact small animals, fruits and flowers molded from fermented dough — yet another folk art.

When we were visiting Li Zhengfu's family in Shanjiagou, Mizhi County, we found Mrs. Li and her relatives making dough figurines. To us strangers watching them work was an experience of the first order — more of a treat than eating them could possibly be — for they were true artists, no doubt about that. They first cut off a little lump of dough and kneaded it a bit, shaping it into the body of a bird in no time. Then they lifted from the dough a short noodle, pressed it flat, stuck it onto the dough in the shape of a cross and then imprinted feathers on the "body" with deft pats of a comb. After molding a bill on the head that emerged under practiced fingers, they cut it open with a pair of scissors. Before you knew it, we had before us a mini flock of sparrows with heads up chirping to the sky.

The most interesting feat of all was Mrs. Li's sculpting of a little monkey squatting on the table with its arms hugging its legs. She turned to us and said humorously, "It's cold, so don't you think we should give him something to keep his head warm?" Answering her own question, she fashioned a tall hat like the ones worn by clowns in a circus and placed it on the

34

monkey's head. Finally she inserted two grains of millet as its eyes — and presto, we saw before us a life-like little monkey.

I had kept track of the time. It had taken her four minutes to make a bird and five to make a monkey.

Separating out another small mass of dough, Mrs. Li said, "Let's make a snake coiled around a rabbit," and proceeded to shape from a thick noodle a plump little body with a bullet head and floppy ears. A thinner noodle she twisted into a snake wound around the rabbit, finally scissoring out scales on the body of the snake.

I had to admire such skill and speed, but the rabbit's plight made me uneasy. Having run across snakes entwined around rabbits in other Shaanxi designs, I felt impelled to ask how come.

"There's a saying around here — that you will be rich when snakes twist around rabbits," Mrs. Li explains.

"But isn't it a pity that the rabbit should have the life twisted out of it by a snake?" I persisted.

Mrs. Li reassured me. "No such thing," she said. "They just stick together. It is said that men are just like snakes — quick and clever — and they should find women who prefer to stay in their homes, like rabbits who venture forth mainly to find food for their babies. Don't you think that a family with a smart man who can bring in the money while the woman is industrious and thrifty in managing the household stands a good chance of getting rich?" I had to agree that what she said sounded convincing — certainly in terms of the local people's outlook on life. These villagers knew well the living habits of animals. Through such comparisons they express their own hopes and dreams.

When I asked her about the origins of dough figurines, she was at a loss. She only knew that the making of them had been passed down through the generations. Research has shown that their origins had something to do with ancient ceremonies surrounding burials and offerings of sacrifices. In the slave society of the Shang Dynasty, slaves were buried alive with their deceased masters. But under feudalism, wooden and pottery figurines took the place of living slaves. Still later, things were

35

even further simplified when the common people came to bury dough figurines with their dead. During the Qingming Festival, people in Northern Shaanxi still observe the ancient custom of splashing the tombs with purified water and offering large steamed buns with birds molded at their tops known as *zitui* dough figurines. How did these particular dough figurines come to be? They were named for Jie Zitui, a minister of Jin State during the period of the Warring States, who loyally followed Prince Zhong'er into self-imposed exile at a time of imperial court intrigue. Jie Zitui stuck with his prince through the bitterest of hardships, at one point going so far, according to legend, as to cut off a piece of flesh from his own thigh to save Zhong'er from starvation.

After the passage of nineteen years, the way was cleared for Zhong'er to return to his homeland and succeed to the throne as King Jin Wengong. But when the newly installed monarch rewarded and promoted those who had shared his hard lot, he forgot Jie Zitui. The ex-minister thereupon left the imperial court, carrying his mother on his back, for a hermit's life in the Mianshan Mountain.

When word of Jie Zitui's quitting the capital reached him and he realized how deeply he had wounded his faithful friend, Jin Wengong immediately led a party to the foot of Mianshan Mountain where he stood for three days calling for Jie to come down from the mountain. But there was no reply, no Jie Zitui, no sign of life at all.

Finally Jin Wengong ordered a fire to be set, thinking thus to force the loyal minister and the filial son down the mountain where he would find his old friend determined to make up many times over for having slighted him.

When the fire strategy didn't work, a search party was dispatched which found Jie's charred body over that of his mother under a big tree. Obviously he had been trying to protect her from the flames. Overhead flew a flock of birds as if in mourning or seeking to protect the now dead pair.

Denied the opportunity to set things right and now bearing a double burden of guilt, Jin Wengong was overcome with grief. He immediately named Qingming (Pure Brightness, 5th of the fourth lunar month) a memorial day for Jie Zitui and ordered that there be no fire anywhere on the day before or on the day of his death. And in Northern Shaanxi, Shanxi and other places that once belonged to the ancient Jin State, there developed the custom of using as offerings to ancestors *zitui* dough figurines adorned with birds. However, today's dough figurines are used primarily as holiday decorations for the cave dwellings or gifts on special occasions.

In Luochuan County where we were visiting Wu Jincang, whose son had just gotten married, he showed us the oversized dough figurines he had put away in trunks and barrels for safekeeping. Those made in the design of a dragon or phoenix were labeled "The Dragon and Phoenix Bring Good Luck." Those made in the shape of the Chinese longevity locket were meant to point the young couple toward a long life of conjugal bliss. There were also ones called "A Carp Leaps Through Lotuses," which carried the implication that the young couple would produce wonderful children one after another.

Describing the scene, our host told us that the moment the master of ceremonies shouted, "Now for the presentation of gifts," a procession led by the brothers of the bridegroom's mother led the way to offer their dough figurines and other gifts on trays. Eighteen families of relations presented as many pairs of dough figurines. Naturally all the guests present compared them and fussed over them adding no end to the fun and fascination of the day's doings.

As local practice dictated, the young wife was expected to bring some dough figurines to her parents at her first visit to them from her new home. The dough rings presented to her parents and elder relatives carried the blessing of the young that the elder's lives were, or would be, like a ring and just go round and round without stopping. Decorative bats and deer on the ring meant "happiness" and "good fortune" respectively, the latter being a homophone for, first, the *bat* and then the *deer*. So *happiness* and *luck* were being wished for these elders for many long years ahead.

The dough rabbits and tigers for the children that were

37

gifts of the bride's family carried the expectation that the boys would be as brave and vigorous as tigers and the girls would be as lovely and home-loving as the white rabbits. The dough birds that were part of the special food and folk art were meant to help make singers of the children. Meanwhile, what the children were interested in was something good to eat rather than symbolism. Their mouths began to water at first sight of the dough figurines hung above the *kang*, and the moment the adults went out of the cave they began a mad scramble for a bird or a tiger.

To eat or just to look was the dilemma of any guest from afar. A group of French visitors to Luochuan County, for example, could only stare at the meal of dough figurines as it was set before them. Finally the host demanded why they didn't try one. "Don't you like this kind of food?" he wanted to know.

The foreign friends explained that the figurines were just too beautiful to make disappear! "We want to take them home as souvenirs," they confessed.

The villagers were relieved. "Don't worry," the host reassured them. "There're lots more where they came from. Eat all you want and still take away souvenirs when you go. You can have it both ways!"

Only then did the French guests dig in with relish.

Exciting *Yangko* and Drum Dances

Since they have few farming chores in the winter, the young men and women of the villages begin rehearsing on the 15th of the last lunar month for the *yangko* dance performance that will be part of the ceremonial activities of the Spring Festival and the Lantern Festival (the 15th of the first lunar month).

On Spring Festival, the first day of the first lunar month, right after finishing their first meal of *jiaozi* (filled dumplings) of the new year, the villagers begin to call on each other and exchange festival greetings. Meanwhile, the dancers have started up accompanied by *yaogu* (waist drums).

Research has revealed that the *yangko* originated at the Spring and Autumn Period over two thousand years ago. Originally a religious ritual through which the dancers welcomed the

38

arrival of gods among them and drove away evil spirits, it is now simply a form of holiday entertainment.

According to the local practice, a "director" holding an umbrella leads the *yangko* dancers as they visit from door to door. When they arrive at each house, the host must entertain the dancers with wine and cigarettes. Then when the "leading umbrella" sings new year greetings with extravagant sentiments like "may bumper harvests of all crops cheer your household and your granaries burst with grains worth their weight in gold," this is the cue for the dancing team to perform its lively dance in the courtyard. As the dancers finish their final stamp and leave in a crescendo of drumbeating and the clang of gongs, the host sets off firecrackers to thank them. It's a wild moment for this normally sleepy courtyard.

Now comes the "main event" with *suona* horns, drums and cymbals accompanying the dancers to the village square. Dressed as different opera characters — colorful fans, handkerchiefs and silk scarves in hand — the dancers throw out their arms as they begin their patterned light steps, forward and then back half a pace, leaning from left to right in turn as they dance the time-honored *yangko* movements. The most conspicuous figure is the clown. Dressed in white with red dates hanging from his ears and a string of red chilis suspended from his neck, he moves in a rolling gait, swinging from left to right with a broom in hand. From time to time this consummate buffoon jumps out of formation and runs through the crowd like a naughty boy. The focus of the audience frequently strays to the clown, conditioned as they are to expect amusement from this source.

Most impressive of all are the drum dancers. Dressed in black or solid colored outfits, red or yellow scarves tied around their heads, tube-like drums tied to their waists with silk ribbons fluttering from their drum sticks, they beat out a rhythmic accompaniment to their own vigorous dancing. To us they personified the high spirits and boldness of the Northern Shaanxi villagers.

Drum dancing differs from place to place, but there are two major schools: *wen* (gentle) and *wu* (military). The *wen* school

39

is refined and uses more drumbeats and lighter, quicker dance movements than the *wu* school, which is majestic and forceful in style. Here the dancing drummers keep leaping high in the air as they shout "Hai! Hai!" — their dancing raising a thick cloud of dust that swirls about the performers.

Drums have been traced as far back as the Shang Dynasty over three thousand years ago. In 1935, archaeologists excavated ancient drums made of wood and boa skin at Yinxu (Yin Dynasty ruins), Anyang, Henan Province. In ancient times, they were used at funerals, among other ceremonial occasions; on marches and in actual battles; also to broadcast warnings, to report the hours, and as part of informal entertainments. From the fact that *The Book of Changes*《易经》 recorded *guzhiwuzhi* (鼓之舞之: drum and dance) we can see that *gu* (drum) and *wu* (dance) were closely related two thousand and more years ago. Ever since, the expression *guwu* (inspire) in the context of trying to persuade others to aim high.

Descriptions of waist drums have come down to us from the Tang Dynasty, though these were said to have smaller necks than ends, differing from those found in Northern Shaanxi today. From the glorious dances of the Tang Dynasty painted on the walls of the Mogao Grottoes in Dunhuang, Gansu Province, one can also see waist drums attached to dancers of the time.

As to the origin of the local drum dance, some people believe that the waist drum was a tool for the soldiers guarding the frontiers, who used it to deliver warnings and other signals. The cavalrymen, for example, as they galloped struck their waist drums and shouted during an attack. Later, when these soldiers retired from military service and returned to their home villages, they doubtless brought their drums with them, which led to the development of today's waist drum dance. This theory is supported by the fact that the drum dance is mostly found along the Great Wall or in frontier areas and that the dancers dress as soldiers and mimic ancient battle formations.

Another theory holds that it was the shepherds of Northern Shaanxi who invented the instrument, fashioning drums from dug-up tree stumps in which they carved out holes that they then covered with sheepskin. Thus the herdsmen whiled away lonely hours. Later, together with other percussion instruments, the drum was used to accompany prayers for favorable weather and for many healthy children and domestic animals.

When the *yangko* dancers finished their last dance turns in their own village, they would go to perform in neighboring villages. Such special seasonal calls naturally helped to promote friendship between villages. Families, too, became intertwined as young people met, fell in love and chose mates.

CHAPTER II

GANSU — A Province of Strategic Importance on the Silk Road

ALONG THE SILK ROAD

Gansu Province lies across the ancient Silk Road in northwest China. Traveling there, I took a sheepskin raft on the Yellow River and rode a camel around the barren deserts.

Taking a Sheepskin Raft on the Yellow River

Lanzhou, the capital of Gansu Province, is the center of transportation of the Northwest. Four trains from Beijing stop here every day.

The Yellow River flows right through the city. Pontoon bridges built of wooden boats across the river date back to 1376. Research proves that travelers on the Silk Road over one thousand years ago were not able to cross the river here; they could only take the northern route and ferry the river in Jingyuan County located in the northeast of Lanzhou, or take the southern route and cross the river through the "No. 1 Bridge in the World" in Yongjing County situated in the southwest of the city. The old bridge is said to have been built in the Eastern Jin Dynasty (A.D. 317-420). We can see from the grottoes of Bingling Temple that this was an important passage through which Buddhists, businessmen and travelers carried out their various activities.

Reaching the site of the bridge, we found that the old bridge which used to make transportation so much easier for businessmen at home and from abroad had long since disappeared. It turned out that in 1974 a huge hydropower station,

42

the Liujia Gorge Hydropower Station — the largest in China up till now — was built here in Yongjing County, its dike being 147 meters high. The dike turned this section of water, 76 kilometers in length, into a long, narrow artificial lake. That day we also boarded a pleasure boat for sightseeing. Unexpectedly, after three hours' sailing we caught sight of seven or eight sheepskin rafts moored at the ferry as we neared Bingling Temple. One of the raftsmen was sunning his raft on the bank with his wooden oar supporting it from underneath.

After going ashore, we asked the middle-aged raftsman how he had made his raft. "Shear all the wool off the sheep when you kill it," he began. "Slit its neck and hind hips and take the whole skin off. Let it dry in the shade, rub it with salt and sesame oil until it becomes soft, then coat it with tung oil which is waterproof and antiseptic. Leave only one front leghole for blowing air in and tie tight the neck and the other holes with strings. That's it: the sheepskin becomes a bag now. Finally, you tie a sufficient number of bags neatly to a frame of willow bars to form a rectangular raft. Blow the bags full, tie the air holes tight, and there it is, ready to take you across the river."

Could I try it? He answered by putting his oar into the water with one hand and helping me onto the raft with the other. After kneeling at the front as he grasped the wooden bar, he started to row.

I felt rather frightened. I asked the raftsman how many persons it could hold and if we would get wet. "It must be your first adventure on a sheepskin raft, eh?" he answered me. "Don't worry. We could handle three or four more people." He was right. My shoes were dry as a bone when we got to the other side.

The average sheepskin raft on the Yellow River consists of ten bags. However, there are also large ones made up of six hundred bags, twelve meters long and seven wide. A raft of this size, which requires six men to row, can carry twenty to thirty tons of wool, medicine, or any number of other items. Sailing with the current, it covers over two hundred kilometers per day. But as the local saying goes, "Downstream you take the

43

raft, upstream the raft takes you;'' on the surging river the raft moves with the current, never against it. That is why the raftsman has to take an oblique route by going some distance upstream whenever he wants to cross the river.

In 1958, on the bank of Taihu Lake in Wuxing County of Zhejiang Province, archaeologists excavated New Stone Age wooden oars and pendants, from which we conclude that boats came into existence in China about 4,700 years ago. When did the raft come into being? History records that Emperor Guangwu of the Han Dynasty had his soldiers cross rivers in "leather boats" (sheepskin rafts) when fighting in the South.

But why should rafts still be in use today when ships are sailing everywhere and strong bridges have been built at strategic locations to connect the two sides? "Perhaps we just don't want to give them up," the raftsman conjectured after thinking it over for long moment. He pointed out that there could not be that many modern bridges and ferries in the countryside. Like people in the cities who ride bicycles, the peasants find the rafts very convenient. When they want to call on their friends and relatives on the other side of the river or ferry grains or manure, they need only tote the raft, which weighs no more than twenty kilograms, and blow air into it by the river; before long they will find themselves reaching the other side. Besides, the making of a raft does not cost much since sheep are raised by every household. I learned that quite a few families are still using the sheepskin rafts left to them by their dead elders.

I personally found the sheepskin raft very safe. Situated in the northwestern highlands, the upper reaches of the Yellow River are all rapids and shoals. Since the handy raft is elastic, it usually rebounds without getting torn when it runs into rocks while sailing across the river. Even if one or two of the sheepskin bags are torn, the raft can still sail well and will not sink. Incidentally, the one I took actually hit a reef, which caused the air to go out of one bag on the right side. I couldn't help but be at least a little worried then, but the raftsman showed not the least concern. When we got to the shore, he blew more air into it until it was full again and continued his ferrying operation.

Mid-Autumn Festival Celebrations at Wuwei

Wuwei, or Liangzhou, as it was known in ancient times, is an important town on the Silk Road two hundred kilometers north of Lanzhou. In 115 B.C., after General Huo Qubing conquered the region west of the Yellow River, Emperor Hanwu established four prefectures there: Wuwei, Jiuquan, Zhangye, and Dunhuang. It happened to be the Mid-Autumn Festival when I was at Wuwei. I found it a particularly pleasant experience to celebrate the Festival here, watching the glowing full moon with the peasants.

Zhongqiu, or mid-autumn, originated from the Chinese lunar calendar. In ancient times, a year was divided into four seasons and one season into three sections — *meng* (first month), *zhong* (second month), and *ji* (third or last month). The eighth lunar month is also the second month of autumn, and the fifteenth falls right in the middle of the month. That is why the fifteenth of the eighth month finally came to be known as "mid-autumn."

Autumn is a golden season when bumper harvests are being expected and vegetables and fruits compete for attention in the market. The weather is comfortable and the moon is exceptionally bright on the night which marks mid-autumn. It is believed that this very night sees the brightest moon of the year. Traditionally, when the "mid-autumn" night falls, every family places in the courtyard a table of fruit and mooncakes to enjoy at this time of reunion. Observers usually watch the bright full moon and exchange good wishes as they munch on fruit and mooncakes. The Mid-Autumn, Spring, Lantern, and Dragon Boat Festivals are the four major festivals in China.

Watching the full moon on the mid-autumn night is a common practice throughout China which dates back to the Zhou Dynasty more than two thousand years ago. As recorded in classical books, King Zhou welcomed the coming of spring on the mid-spring day by presenting offering sacrifices accompanied by music, and made sacrifices on the mid-autumn night in order to welcome the coming of the cold season, praying for abundant harvests all over his land. It was only

45

after Emperor Li Shimin of the Tang Dynasty designated the fifteenth of the eighth lunar month as "Mid-Autumn Festival" that this once palace practice of offerings began to spread among the people.

As for the custom of eating mooncakes, a popular folk tale traces it to a rebellion against the cruel rulers of the late Yuan Dynasty (1271-1368). The story details that the rebels put in the mooncakes a message written on a piece of paper informing each other of their rebellion on the fifteenth of the eighth month. They exchanged mooncakes and reminded one another to act at the same time, hoping to overthrow the rulers.

But in fact, people began to make mooncakes as early as the Tang Dynasty, though they did not become really popular until the Song Dynasty. Eating houses of the Tang's capital Chang'an, or Xi'an in Shaanxi Province today, were making *Wanyue* (enjoying moonlight) cakes then, which were served as one of the special foods of the holiday season. The lines written by Su Dongpo (1037-1101) of the Song Dynasty: "The little cake is like the moon / It is crisp inside with maltose" describes the mooncake.

Research proves that the ancestors found roundness appealingly beautiful because of their worship of the sun and their naive belief that "the earth is square and the sky round." They not only used round things such as pottery jars, copper coins and spinning wheels in their daily lives but also worshipped roundness. For example, the haloes on the heads of the statues of immortal beings and Buddhas were round, and their symbol of reunion was roundness. That is why eating round things on holidays gradually became a custom. In the Lantern Festival season, for example, people eat *yuanxiao* whose shape and pronunciation are both *yuan* (round); in the Mid-Autumn Festival season they eat cakes that look like a full moon, which express good wishes for family reunions and happiness in general.

China is said to have more than 150 kinds of mooncakes at present. They vary from one region to another because of differences in ingredients and ways of making them. Mooncakes from Jiangsu are known for their crisp crusts and various layers of filling while those made in Beijing are known for their vegetable ingredients. Mooncakes from my hometown in Guangdong are unique in color, flavor and shape and are filled with bits of fruit like shredded coconut or lotus seeds, which are special products of the South. Besides, yolks, baked chicken and ham are also used as fillings.

Liangzhou's mooncakes are different from any of these. In the first place, they are almost always steamed at home, and they are exceptionally big. On Mid-Autumn Festival we were invited by Xiao Wu, a driver, to celebrate the Festival with his family. Upon our arrival we saw his wife and mother making mooncakes that were as big as straw hats. We were told that some became as big as a meter in diameter. According to custom, the number of mooncakes a family makes should correspond to the number of family members. Large families can use as much as fifty kilos of flour in the making of mooncakes consumed over a period of fifteen to twenty.

The final difference in their mooncakes lay in their designs. While those of the cities and towns are similarly molded, the local mooncakes greatly differed in design from one household to another: they certainly did look like "one hundred flowers blooming."

We were relishing the large mooncakes at Xiao Wu's when Lao Lü, a local official, came calling. He especially loved having company and insisted on having us spend the evening in his house. So we went. Entering his house, we noticed that his 80-year-old mother was making beautiful mooncakes as she enthusiastically instructed her granddaughters and granddaughters-in-law in how to make colorful dough wings that looked like petals and stick them around the cakes. Finally she placed on this "One Hundred-winged Mooncake" a little white rabbit and a monkey she had kneaded herself.

A fairy tale about these festival foods tells how Chang'e became Goddess of the Moon. On earth she had been the wife of Houyi, who had shot down nine suns and thus freed the peasants of droughts. One day Chang'e swallowed the elixir stolen from her husband and could not help floating up to the moon herself. The little white rabbit on the mooncake represented one she had brought along. What about mooncake's monkey? That was Sun Wukong from the classical novel *A Journey to the West*, an infinitely resourceful creature where every somersault covers 54,000 kilometers. Lao Lü's mother wanted Sun Wukong to take her mooncake to Chang'e up in the Moon Palace!

After night fell, Lao Lu's family set up two tables in the courtyard, placing on them mooncakes, apples, grapes, pears, peaches, watermelons, and Chinese crabapples. Later I learned that the Mid-Autumn Festival was a time for people to show off their abundance and cooking skills. The richer their tables looked, the prouder they would feel. Women of the village would even visit each other to find out who had made the best mooncakes.

"The moon rises now!" shouted the children. The hostess lit the candles and joss sticks; they had always kept the old custom of offering sacrifices to the moon.

Seeing the moon begin to go west, Lao Lü finally said, "OK now!" And in a twinkle the children crowded around the tables, waiting for their shares of fruit to be handed out by the elders. A clever child of about ten immediately seized the little monkey on the "One Hundred-winged Mooncake" and tucked it into his inner pocket. This upset the grandmother, who exclaimed, "You must never eat it! Never eat it!"

The Mid-Autumn Festival, as we have seen, is a day of reunion in China. In most places, it is the elders who cut the mooncakes after their moon vigil and pass out pieces to every member of the family as a symbol of reunion. But the practice in Liangzhou is quite the opposite. People here believe that since the mooncake is a symbol of the full moon in the sky and reunion on the earth, they must not eat the round cakes until the next day when the moon begins to lose its roundness.

This practice is said to have originated from the history of Liangzhou. As an important town by the Silk Road, Liangzhou was a place which armies always tried to occupy and a place where exiled officials and banished criminals stayed. Wang Han, a poet of the Tang Dynasty, left these lines to express the poor morale of soldiers who had to serve there:

48

Stars shine on the cup of sweet wine I can't drink—
The *pipa*'s (Chinese guitar) been struck and we
  soldiers must go;
Laugh at me not who lie drunk in the field,
Who's now left alive I hardly know.

On the Mid-Autumn Festival every year, the home-leavers and the soldiers would feel even more homesick, recalling Li Bai's lines:

To watch the shining moon I raise my head,
Lowering it I dream of the town of my birth.

Since everybody was anxiously looking forward to an early reunion with his family, nobody dared to touch the mooncake that symbolized reunions.

Castle-like Houses

After visiting Wuwei, we traveled one hundred kilometers northward to tour around Minqin County. There we saw many "country castles." By "country castles" I refer to the country houses with courtyards all over this county. One afternoon an official of the county's cultural museum, a man with considerable knowledge of local history and customs, took us to a country castle in Dongzhen District. The ten-meter-high house, had a huge arch over its gateway and four strong watchtowers at the four corners with walls of yellow mud two to three meters thick. "It looks like an ancient castle!" I exclaimed.

Entering the arched door of the wall, we noted that the country castle measured about forty meters from east to west and sixty from north to south and that it faced south. The eastern part of the large front yard was for carts, farm tools and sorghum stalks while the western part was a stable. Entering the castle, we got a glimpse of the first row of rooms, the second, and the wing-rooms on both sides. We went up the stairs to the room occupied by different household sundries and noticed many holes for weapons in the arch over the gateway and the watchtowers. The various doors were not only about half a foot thick but also nailed with iron sheets. Obviously, this well-protected castle had been built by a rich family wary of bandits.

Scholars have in recent years studied the traditional castles and concluded that such old buildings were also built to keep out winds and sand. This belief is supported by the fact that the average peasant compound is surrounded by tall thick walls, although without arches over gateways or watchtowers.

Minqin County covers 16,000 square kilometers, two-thirds of which are deserts. With three sides surrounded by deserts, this county may see as many as 124 windy days a year, thirty of which are truly stormy. Such winds usually blow up thick sand all over the place, darkening the sky and making it impossible for you to see anything lying several steps ahead. When you pour water into a bowl outside, you will find a layer of sand in the bowl immediately afterwards. Since the winds are so fierce, it is only natural for the peasants to build houses with tall walls that can keep out some of the sand and wind.

For a dwelling place on the "isolated island" of the desert, the villagers dig deep into the earth for a sort of yellow soil and ram it with water in two boards to make the walls, tier upon tier. The builders are usually divided into two teams, one working from the north wall to the east one and the other from the east to the north. They sing a work song as they build the walls; one team sings the first line and the other the next. Their work song not only synchronizes the rise and fall of the stone pestle, but also reduces the hardship of their labor.

It is said that only through this way of ramming can the four walls be well joined and can they withstand winds and storms. Later when we visited the Jiayu Pass of the western Great Wall, we also found the peasants working in the same way when they were mending the Wall. We were even told that the tall walls of the country castles were no less stronger than the Great Wall that has stood for thousands of years.

After the founding of the People's Republic of China, bandits disappeared, and as the society became more and more peaceful, people stopped investing large sums of money in building castles that could keep out robbers and looters. Tall walls are not necessary, for they shade the house from the warm sun in winter. As for protecting themselves from the winds and sand, they believe it is better to accomplish this by planting trees around the houses. Trees not only keep out the sand blown up by winds, but provide timber. That is why the villagers are beginning to build quadrangles instead of castles. However, perhaps it is because they are observing the old tradition, since they still tend to build their enclosing walls somewhat higher than those seen in other places.

Peasants' Quick Meal — Buns Steeped in Watermelon Juice

When we learned that a young man in Yongfeng No. 4 Village of Shoucheng District was going to get married, we immediately got on the bicycles our guide had borrowed for us and headed for his village. We were eager to see a local wedding. The dirt roads were rugged and rough and before long I was sweating all over. Seeing me left behind, our guide shouted to me, "Come on! We'll take a break in the village ahead."

The moment we entered the village, our guide pushed open the door of a peasant's house by the road, and a spry old man with a silvery beard came to greet us. Though he was eighty-three years old, he still had sharp ears and eyes and walked steadily. As soon as he learned that we were from Beijing, he invited us indoors.

Seeing we had all taken seats, his son of about sixty presented us with a plate of steamed buns and three huge watermelons. "Have some watermelon, please; they're just like water," he said. With this he lightly pinched the melons all the way around with his thumbs and tapped the areas pressed until it fell apart into neat halves! Following local custom, we presented our elderly host what we had been given, but he protested, "There's nothing to entertain you with here, so do try our watermelons."

For a moment I felt intimidated by this huge half melon and then our guide picked up his chopsticks and said, "Come on, try some buns soaked in watermelon juice and see how you like this Minqin flavor!" He stirred the pulp from left to right and right to left. When the pulp had turned into liquid he put in pieces of buns and began to eat them when they became soft in the juice. I did it in exactly the same way, but my chopsticks just would not work. I could only manage to cut my pulp into uneven pieces, though I had stirred it for what seemed a very long time. Eager to sample its flavor, I started to eat now, one mouthful of bun with one piece of watermelon, but not buns soaked in juice.

After my fast bicycle ride I felt hot and hungry. We really could not expect anything better than such buns steeped in watermelon juice. I said it was the best melon I had ever tasted and our host smiled happily. Stroking his beard, he nodded. "You are right. Watermelons produced in Minqin aren't bad at all."

Minqin is the oasis of this desert, with a soil and climate particularly good for melon growing. Truly, watermelons and *bailan* melons produced here are regarded as a rare species, being both big in size, thin of skin and thick with pulp. They are also exported thanks to their fine quality.

Entertaining guests with buns steeped in watermelon juice in summer is a tradition in Minqin. Every household here grows watermelons. Apart from those for sale, the average family usually stores one or even two tons in their well-ventilated rooms. Visitors, be they old friends or new, expected or unexpected, will be treated to buns soaked in watermelon juice, our own record coming up to five treats in one day. Of course, in winter and spring when watermelons have run out, the host can only offer his visitors hot tea with buns and apologize for having no more melons. However, whatever time of year it is, buns are a "must." Should you treat your visitors to tea alone, the whole village would laugh at you derisively.

Later we discovered that almost all the young shepherds over the grassland and women threshing sunflower seeds or aniseeds on the threshing grounds and people going to the market or the cinema carried some buns and watermelons on their backs. Whenever they felt hungry they broke the melons into halves and steeped the buns in the juice for a quick snack.

When we asked how this meal came into existence, our guide explained that the peasants often went to work in places two to ten kilometers from home, with the deserts even further away; therefore, they all carried food with them when leaving home. In summer, it is blazing hot in the daytime, and with water hard to find, buns soaked in watermelon juice make a perfect quick meal.

Children whose schools are far away from home all carry two bags, one of buns and one of ready food with full round watermelons in it. I even saw with my own eyes two greedy children eating their melons with spoons on their way to school. Before they had even got there, they had already finished half of their lunches.

Buffoons Tease the Bride on Her Wedding Day

Saying good-bye to our aged host, we hurried to Yongfeng No. 4 Village for the local wedding. It was already past twelve o'clock, so we were lucky that the bride had not arrived yet. Then we saw two tractors decorated with huge blossoms coming closer and closer. One carried the bride, the other her dowry. Following close behind was a train of bicycles carrying those who were seeing her to her new home and those who had come to receive her on behalf of the bridegroom's family.

People here used to receive brides in small decorated box wagons and feast invitees in big carts laid with red carpets which rode easily in the deserts because they had huge wheels with a diameter of about two meters. But nowadays young people do not like carts pulled by oxen since they are slow and jouncey as well as old-fashioned; they like trucks and tractors instead.

But what was this? As the troop that had been accompanying the bride reached the bridegroom's house, it suddenly stopped and its members crowded around the main entrance. Wasn't it twelve o'clock after all? I elbowed forward to find out and saw that the clowns had tied a rope across the gateway, refusing to let the bride in!

One of the clowns wore a torn paper hat and a shabby fur coat turned inside out with two chilis hung from his earlobes. The other wore a sunflower atop a watermelon skin upside down on his head and a printed sheet on his body. Spots of red and blue had been painted on their heavily powdered faces. Now they smiled foolishly at the bride as they reached out, seeming to ask for something. Why the clowns?

Minqin has always viewed it as essential that on public occasions the old must look serious and the young be well-behaved and polite. Then what should they do to make their weddings lively and prepare the shy bride and bridegroom for the festivities and bridge the gulf between them? Probably following the example of ancient operas, no clown with a made-up face has to be prim and proper. Here, as the world over, anything goes—so is the clowns that bring liveliness and a spirit of fun to a wedding.

In this case the clowns were the bridegroom's own brothers. Following their traditional practice, they stopped the bride at the entrance demanding the present she was supposed to offer on her arrival at the bridegroom's house, an embroidered seal box. The tiny box covered with embroidery was something a man used to carry with his seal in it when he left home on a business trip or had a long journey on camelback. Then it also became a love token a young girl would give her sweetheart or a gift a bride would present.

The moment they entered the courtyard, they were stopped by a group of people who brought up a saddle and placed it on the ground as the master of ceremonies intoned: "Now the bride and bridegroom straddle the saddle. May their life always be joyous!" And the young couple did as directed. In Chinese *an* in *ma an* (saddle) is a homonym for *an* in *ping an* (peace). With this homonym people here express their best wishes to brides and bridegrooms.

Now the bride's sister-in-law presented a wooden tray on which bridal garments and a pair of embroidered shoes had been placed, asking the bride to change. Traditionally, the bride must not enter the nuptial chamber until she has put on the clothes and shoes provided by the bridegroom's family and thus becomes a member of her new family.

Later, although she had changed, she found the door of the bridal chamber tightly bolted and unyielding against the best efforts herself and her bridegroom. Then they saw the clowns and several other young men thrusting their hands out

54

the window. Here was yet another trick designed to free the couple from their shyness and bring all members of the two families closer together. Finally, having no other way out, the bride had to surrender another seal box to buy her way into the bridal chamber.

However, that was only the ritual of the bride's entering her new home. The wedding ceremony itself was formally held at three o'clock the same afternoon. The attendants formed a kind of circle with chairs and benches, putting all the presents in the middle. The elders, relatives and friends took their seats according to their status, but the new couple just would not come out no matter who called for them. At last, the two clowns appeared again, one holding a broom and the other a torch, pushing the shy bride and bridegroom in front of the audience. We could see the important role that the clowns performed.

In the northern countryside, after the bride enters the bridal chamber her mother-in-law showers her with dates, chestnuts and longans, which symbolizes the birth of a promising son as soon as possible. In some families it is the father-in-law who throws cigarettes all over the *kang*, meaning there will always be burning joss sticks, or there will always be children from generation to generation. Both the mother-in-law and the father-in-law have the same wish— more and more children for a thriving family far into the future.

Minqin does not produce dates, chestnuts, or longans (produced in the South only). Instead, the local people use big radishes and round buns to stand for lovely fat babies. At dawn the day after the wedding two little brothers of the bridegroom came to knock at the door of the nuptial chamber, "Dear Bride and Bridegroom, do open the door; we've brought you a big-headed child." No sooner had the bride opened the door than two radishes flew toward her bosom. Soon after, her mother-in-law came as well to throw two black buns at her bosom as she prayed, "From here I throw my buns; next year I'll have a grandchild to carry in my arms."

That was also a day when the bride could show all her cooking skills. She cut up the onions and chopped up the ginger

55

to make the sauce. When the noodles were cooked, she presented them on a plate to her father- and mother-in-law, "Dad, please try the soup!" ("soup" here refers to the noodles she had made). In return, the mother-in-law left to her a piece of cloth for a dress and some money on the wooden plate.

As part of the wedding ceremony, the young couple were expected to fetch water from the well. Accordingly, as soon as the couple entered the yard, the two clowns suddenly appeared again and began to throw stones into their buckets, wetting the bride from head to foot. Why did they play such a mischievous trick? Because *chenshi* (sinking stones) has nearly the same pronunciation as *chengshi* (honest) in Chinese. In other words, they expected them to be honest with each other.

CARAVANS IN THE DESERT

Camels have long been known as "boats in the desert." Two thousand years ago, camels carried to the western countries, by way of the ancient Silk Road, Chinese silk, steel, tea, pottery and porcelain and back home jade, pearls, medicines and perfumes from Central Asia and items from Arabic and European countries. Today, such trade caravans, which once contributed a great deal to the cultural exchanges between China and foreign countries, are being replaced by trains, trucks and planes. However, when I visited Minqin County, I still found herds and herds of camels drinking water from the ditches or wandering on the grassland.

Preparations Before the Camel Caravan Set Out

As noted, Minqin is an oasis in the desert, with three of its four sides surrounded by the Tenger Desert and the Badinjaran Desert. Traditionally, apart from farming, many of the villagers here raise camels. In summer they milk the camels and shear their coats. They not only get food and material for clothing from the camels, but also use them as a means of transportation so as to increase their incomes. Such families are called "camel households."

The caravans do not transport goods in all seasons, for the animals cannot endure hot weather. In mid-summer, the deserts become intensely hot in the blazing sun, and even eggs will easily be baked, I was told, if buried in the sand. Camels can never go out in such hot weather. Only when the Mid-Autumn Festival is spent and the weather becomes cool and comfortable, will set out from Minqin. Some caravans carry local products such as medicines and furs to Baotou, the commodities center in Inner Mongolia. They take the eastern route through the Tenger Desert, the Wulanbuhe Desert and the Kubuqi Desert, and usually return with cloth, tea, sugar and other goods. Others go westward to Urumqi in Xinjiang through Badinjaran Desert and then the Jiayu Pass. This round trip, which covers about three thousand kilometers, takes at least three months.

After traveling a long distance, the camels normally become exhausted and their humps sink. Then the cameleers have to stop and let them recover. In the 1950s, when the railways connecting Baotou, Jiayu Pass and Urumqi were completed, trains began to take the place of the caravans to and fro the central areas of the Badinjaran Desert and the Tenger Desert, sending the Mongolian herdsmen there foods, tea, cloth and other daily necessities.

As our caravan was due to set out that afternoon, cameleers Li and Ma drove back their camels that had been grazing in the field.

"Cao, cao!" they shouted continuously and the two- or three-meter-tall animals obediently knelt on the sand dune. Then the villagers all came out to help put together the packs and place them on the camels' backs, turning the dune behind the village into a bustling place.

First they tied on the 1.7-meter-long saddles, then moved up all the packs and tightened them with ropes. The camels took the increasing loads comfortably. One of the cameleers patted his animal on the hairy back as he told me that the strongly built camel could walk for two or three days continuously with a load of two hundred kilograms on its back. Soon the villagers brought out the tents, grain sacks, stoves and other cooking utensils, loading them all on the leading animal in the front according to their normal practice.

Finally, they loaded on the buckets and the "water turtles" both filled with water, which is vitally important to the desert travelers. The oval "water turtle," with a mouth on the top and four rings on the sides through which a rope can go, looks exactly like a soft-shelled turtle. It holds no more than seven kilograms of water because it is not very big. The oblate bucket, however, holds seventy kilograms. On the top there is a hole through which water is filled, and at the bottom a spout tightly corked. When they need water, the travelers simply pull off the stopper to let it flow out. Nevertheless, the water is only prepared for the cameleers. It is impossible and unnecessary to store water for the camels, for they drink far too much. One animal can drink a hundred kilograms of water all at once, so that one large bucket is not even enough for one animal!

The cameleers handle the water problem of the camels this way: ten days before they set out they not only keep the animals from drinking but also shorten the usual hours of grazing in order to lessen the amount of water they may obtain from the green grass. That is called "water control" and "food control," the purpose of which is to keep the camels fit and sturdy to avoid the wearing out of their hoofs which may result from overmuch moisture. The camels will drink their fill only when they are ready to set out. Thus fortified, they can travel two to three weeks without drinking water.

When everything was ready, the cameleers teamed up the camels by tying the second one's nose to the front one's saddle. As the seven camels were teamed up (in the Hui nationality a team consists of eleven camels while in Inner Mongolia fifteen) the owner just led the first one. Thus this caravan, made up of the four owners' twenty-eight camels, set out. According to the local custom, they had to burn two piles of wood before they got on the road, doubtless a superstitious practice started by their ancestors. In the past, they encountered all sorts of difficulties and dangers on their long trips, from storms, droughts and water shortages to bandit and wild animal attacks and diseases. Unable to avoid all misadventures, the cameleers elected to pick lucky days and hours for departures — the even days of the lunar calendar being considered lucky — and prayed to the immortal beings for blessings as well. They believed that the fires could drive away evils and assure them of a peaceful journey.

The Long Days and Nights We Spent in the Desert

Sitting on the back of one camel, I watched the "desert boats" walking on the barren land briskly and rhythmically and was somehow reminded of the graceful movements of dancers on the stage. I was rocked back and forth as the camel continued forward, and the monotonous bell soon brought me into a state of drowsiness.

After covering about forty kilometers, we reached green grass and water. There we stopped for a rest. The cameleers unloaded the cargo and the saddles, allowing the animals to drink and graze on the grassland. In the beginning, I did not understand why the caravan started out at four in the afternoon and why they would not stop traveling until midnight. But before long I learned that camels were vulnerable to the summer heat. It was cool in the morning and at night. Only during these hours would the grass be cool and healthy for the camels.

Then the cameleers pitched their tents and lighted a fire to cook supper in the dark. Their food was simple: they nearly always had noodles and millet gruel. Noodles with dried mutton (long pieces dried in the shade) slices added would count as the best meal. Fresh tender greens were never available, and root vegetables like potatoes were also rare. But this does not mean that the deserts are totally grassless. Sometimes they offer the travelers some edible wild vegetables. There is a herbaceous plant that looks like chives, whose leaves curl into the shape of an onion stalk. Since it grows in the desert, it is named "desert onion stalk" by the local inhabitants. We were lucky that day to be able to taste the fresh tender "desert onion stalks" collected by the veteran cameleers. Fried with salt and oil, they went perfectly well with our food. The left-over "onions" were salted and kept for later use.

Watching the cameleers cooking, I was impressed by their unique utensils: the sacks containing flour and millet were knit of threads spun from camel hairs. The sacks with alternating black and yellow lines in design seemed crudely made, yet they were airtight. In a windstorm in the desert, fine sand can easily find its way into cotton grain sacks through the seams, so that airtight sacks certainly come in handy.

Their stove was also unique. Around the usual triangle iron stand was fixed an iron strap with punches, which could prevent the fire from being blown from left to right and maintain its heat, thus saving on firewood, which is had to find in the desert. Dry camel excrement is used for campfires more frequently than wood.

Right after supper the cameleers retired to their low tents for the night. Their bedding was simple indeed: first they spread on the sandy ground their blankets knit of long camel hairs as a mattress and then wrapped themselves in their fur coats. In the daytime, though the sun was scorching hot, they still wore these heavy coats which almost touched the ground. Were they not uncomfortably warm in the heat of the day. Not at all— for the white fur reflected the rays of the scorching sun. At night when turned inside out, with the fur against the skin, it kept the wearer warm and yet caught no sand.

Thinking of the unwritten rules and laws of different places, I asked Lao Li, "Are there rules that the camel caravans observe?"

"Yes," he answered. "When two teams meet on the road, an unloaded team must make way for the loaded one."

"There is another rule," added Lao Ma. "When caravans pass by the Mongolian *Aobao* (a pile of stone standing as a road sign, often worshipped as a god by various minorities as well as Mongolians), the cameleers are supposed to add oil to the lamps burning in front of the Buddha, burn incense, and offer paper money. Also, sometimes owners walk their camels around the *Aobao* once to pay their respects and pray for blessings."

"Do you believe in Lamaism?"

"No. But once we enter the Mongolian areas we must

observe their customs. Besides, the lamps on the *Aobao* that burn around the clock are also our 'streetlights.'''

The tall *Aobao*s used to function as road signs on the Mongolian prairies; built of stone they were marked by flagpoles and tree branches to direct the camel riders in the vast prairies. Later the *Aobao* became a place where the local people made their offerings to gods and celebrated their festivals and other important events as well as a spot for lovers to meet.

Why Does the Camel Bell Keep Ringing?

The camel bell has long been a familiar theme for poets, painters and musicians. Before I came to Minqin, I took it or granted that it was decorated and delicate like the small bells hanging from the necks of farmers' mules and horses. But on seeing a real camel, I was quite amazed to see the equivalent in size of a metal bucket! It was hung on a stick inserted into the saddle of the last camel but never on the animal's neck, and there was only one bell per team. As the camels plodded along, the striker constantly hit the bell, which in turn rang loudly and rhythmically during each day's journey.

So what was the bell for anyway?

One theory is that since the cameleers must get lonely during their long days of trudging on the endless desert, the jingling of the bell can bring them a kind of musical diversion, and there is probably some truth in this explanation. I was told that in the old days whenever they felt melancholy, the cameleers would sing to the rhythm of the camel bell a gloomy folk song:

> We set out with the camels,
> Trudging beyond the Great Wall;
> Reaching the Jiayu Pass
> To find our eyes still moist.

However, the main purpose of the camel bell, I learned, was to prevent the camels from getting lost. Even though each camel is tied through its nose with an eight-foot-long rope, there is still the danger it will run wild should it come across a running hare, for example. To assure that the scared camel will not tear its nose when running wild, the cameleer ties only slipknots to the stick placed through its nose so that a frightened camel can run away at any time.

Normally, the front cameleer either leads the first camel or sits on it. If he hears no jingle from behind, he will immediately know that some of his camels have gone astray and he will stop in time to get them back. Because of their long years of traveling with camels, the cameleers are so sensitive to the bell that once the jingling stops they will wake up immediately no matter how sound asleep they may be in the saddle.

At times the bell signals the whole caravan into action. In old China the Silk Road was by no means a safe route: bandits lay in wait along its length watching out for travelers to rob. Once they entered these unsafe places, the experienced cameleers would tie up the striker of the bell. That is known as "hanging the camel bell upside down." When the familiar dingdong disappeared, the clever camels at once understood that their owners wanted them to be silent. Therefore, all the animals would cooperate, walking quietly through the dangerous places.

The camel bell is also an alarm. In the tranquil desert its clear sound is heard within a distance of over two kilometers. Hearing the constant jingling, foxes, hares, desert rats and the like that are looking for food will run back to their dwelling places and hide themselves. As for the wolves, they have learned to beware of the caravans armed with shotguns. Should a camel grazing alone run into a wolf, it will immediately become brave and even aggressive instead of timid and obedient and wage its own form of warfare against this enemy.

But how can the camel defend itself since it has no sharp teeth or strong claws?

Once the camel catches sight of a wolf running in its direction, it will immediately lie down with its back against a bush or a sand dune, freeing itself from any possible attack from behind. Then it holds up its head, ready to fight. We all know the camel is a ruminant animal. When it fights back, it spits out at the wolf the fodder stored in its stomach and its gastric juice, which is foul smelling as well as corrosive. It is believed that if a wolf is attacked in this way, it will develop an inflammation which will soon fester. Wolves must have learned from bitter experience these effects. Otherwise why would they be at pains to keep their distance from a camel when it lies down to fight with them? Of course, the battle is seldom joined. The wolf most often gives the camel a wide berth.

Cameleers' Affection for the Camels

There is a Chinese saying "An old horse knows the way." To those whose path lies through the desert, the camel is certainly a most faithful friend and a good guide.

"Desert weather changes as fast as a baby's face" is another oft-repeated expression among cameleers. A blue sky may suddenly be darkened by a windstorm with thick sand blowing everywhere. Then it is impossible to identify the directions and one may easily lose his way. An experienced cameleer will lose no time in driving his camels together and making them lie down one by one; he will then squat between two animals, thus avoiding the wind.

The long years of desert life have also enabled the camels to smell water within a distance of seven kilometers. Lao Shi, one of the cameleers, told me the following story: They were trudging in the Badinjaran Desert, which is well known for its high sand dunes and severe shortages of water among the twelve deserts and gobis in China that cover 1,280,000 square kilometers. For seven days and nights they were not able to find water. Then they came to Tabeyalada, a place which once provided them with drinking water and looked for the well all over the place to no avail. The disappointed cameleers were about to leave when they noticed the camels sniffing a sand dune they were circling. Try as they might, the cameleers could not act the animals to move away from the dune. Could it be that the camels had found the well? The cameleers set about digging and soon came upon a camel saddle with under which they found the well filled with water. It turned out that when the Mongolian herdsmen had passed this way, there had been a heavy windstorm. To prevent the well from being filled with sand in the storm, they covered it with a saddle which had stopped the blowing sand and allowed for the formation of the dune that hid it. It had been the sensible camels that had discovered the well and rescued the cameleers from their water shortage.

The cameleers also praised their camels for keeping them safe from the cold. Sometimes because there are too many people on the caravan, the tent becomes too small for all of them. When this happens, some will have to sleep in the open, wrapping themselves in their fur overcoats and covering up with a blanket to keep out the frost and the dew. At midnight when they find the cold too much for them, they will drive two camels together and make them lie down face to face and then sleep under the long hairs of their necks. With their owner curled up between them, the sympathetic camels will not move their necks even a trifle until the sleeper wakes up.

Because the weather in the desert changes quickly, the camels fall ill easily if the cameleers do not graze them properly. When the animals do not want to get up after crouching on the ground, their owners will immediately know that they have caught cold. With their companions ill, the cameleers always become anxious. In the past when there were no veterinarians, they treated the camels with their own recipes. They would first unload the camels and tie their forelegs together, then bring out their acupuncture needle of over two inches long and burn it over a fire after dipping it in some oil. When the needle was hot enough, they drove it into the camel's body, at the acupoints on the head, neck, back, legs and other parts. After this treatment, which effectively dispelled the cold, the ill camel normally would get up and continue its journey.

The cameleers have a whole set of folk recipes for camels' common diseases such as "febrile disease due to summerheat evil," itchiness and dermatitis. No wonder that even though Lao Li and Lao Ma had brought along quantities of brick tea, sugar, and Chinese herbal medicines, I never saw them make tea or porridge with these ingredients for themselves, reserving such for the camels. If a camel eats hot grass at noon, it will accumulate heat in the body and lose its appetite gradually until it only wants to lie down on the ground. Its hair and body become unhealthy as well. At this point the cameleer needs only boil some *Dahuang* (Rheum palmatum) and brick tea with sugar and pour it into the ill camel's mouth. Usually one or two prescriptions are sufficient to rid the animal of ill effects.

The cameleers who are aware how much the camels mean to them well know that though their companions can travel many kilometers in the desert, they will easily wear out their hoofs if they walk on hard roads full of stones. For this reason, the cameleers always forgo dirt roads with stones even if they are much shorter than the desert routes. When they have no choice but to travel at least part of the way on tar or dirt roads, they will have to put shoes on their camels: pieces of soft sheepskin tied under each camel's hoofs.

CUSTOMS OF DUNHUANG

We decided to trace the roots of some of Dunhuang's customs that have been practiced from generation to generation. Dunhuang, a fortress on the Silk Road more than two thousand years ago, lies about a thousand kilometers west of Minqin. Driving across the vast desert plains, we suddenly caught sight of an oasis. There appeared our long-dreamed-of Dunhuang— a treasure trove of classical Chinese art. We were high with excitement— our fatigue all but forgotten.

Ancient and Current Customs Revealed in the Mogao Murals

Since A.D. 366 when the first cave of the Mogao Grottoes was dug, thousands of grottoes have been dug here. As an art center of Buddhism, its surviving painted statues, over 2,400 in number, are naturally related to Buddha, Heavenly Kings and Mighty Warriors. Most of the 45,000 square meters of murals also reflect Buddhist lore.

Nevertheless, arts always reflect social realities. Beneath the Buddhist cloak, one discovers all types of human activities. Displayed on the magnificent murals are earthly scenes of the west valley of the Yellow River of different dynasties, showing farming, harvesting, lumbering, hunting, horseback riding, cattle grazing, grain milling, caravan traveling, butchering, cooking, distilling, dancing, game playing, weddings, funerals, entertaining guests.

What the artists of the No. 445 Grotto of the Tang Dynasty painted is the Sukhavati, but from the murals one can easily get a clear picture of work and life of the local farmers. The plow pulled by two oxen, harvesting with sickles, threshing on the ground, winnowing with wooden spades, in fact, reveal nothing but the peasant activities of the time that are shown.

One of the murals showed a country wife sweeping on the threshing ground with a gray broom made of *jiji* grass, as it is called in Chinese, a wild plant growing all over the northwest desert. The leaves and stems of this plant turn white in the strong autumn winds. Therefore, it is also known as "white grass." Cen Shen, a frontier poet of the Tang Dynasty, once wrote:

> The white grass bends when sweeping north winds blow,
> The autumn desert's soon covered with snow.

The fluffy *jiji* grass, the stems of which are strong, smooth and springy, is widely used. It is said that over two thousand years ago, Zhang Qian, who was made prisoner by the Huns after being sent to Mobei on a diplomatic mission, wove straw shoes of *jiji* grass when he was herding cattle for his captors. The making of straw clothing, however, is recorded in *A Handbook of the Han Dynasty*. The straw clothes made of "white grass" were light but strong and arrow-proof so that they were even used by the frontier soldiers as armor in those days. And from the broken arms of damaged Buddhist statues in the Mogao Grottoes we conclude that the ancient sculptors even bound the frames of these clay statues with *jiji* grass.

Today, like willow twigs in the North and cane and bamboo in the South, the plentiful *jiji* grass is still used in the making of many things by the Mobei people. Mats and baskets of this fiber material are white and beautiful. Rope strands of softened *jiji* grass are lasting and strong enough for tying oxen to carts. If a layer is laid in the middle of a roof, the roof becomes much firmer and keeps out the cold effectively. Besides, chopsticks made of strong stems of this plant look like ivory.

Among the books found in Dunhuang's Scripture Storecave is *Anecdotes of Dunhuang*, which carries a "Marriage Message." From the message we discover that "worshipping eagles" was once an important part of the wedding ceremony during the Tang Dynasty. When the bridegroom came to the bride's home to take her to her new home, the bridesmaid would present him with an eagle whose mouth and body were wrapped in colorful silk. The bridegroom's task was to set it free. If they had no eagle, they would make one with colorful silk and simply throw it into the sky to fulfill this part of the ceremony.

Why did they worship eagles? According to Gao Guofan, an expert in Dunhuang studies, during those years the local people were under the control of the Tufan slaveholders and the releasing of the eagles symbolized their yearning for freedom. At the same time it was a fine wish for the bridegroom: they expected him to fly as high as the eagle — in other words, have a glorious future.

The painters of various dynasties showed wedding ceremonies many times over in works of the Mogao Grottoes. The ceremony taking place in the Tang Dynasty shown in the No. 445 Grotto in particular is interesting: We see cloth curtains hung in the courtyard, with guests sitting with legs crossed on the left and right sides of the tables covered with steamed buns and other foods. But the enclosure created by the curtains was not wide enough to include all the attendants, some of whom had to stand outside. When the ceremony started, the young couple, accompanied by music and dancing, kowtowed to a pair of wild geese. But when the bridegroom knelt down, the young bride stopped moving altogether. The Tang custom of the bridegroom kowtowing alone is still practiced in some remote villages today.

Nowadays both eagles and geese have disappeared from the wedding ceremonies held in the west valley of the Yellow River. Nonetheless, the villagers of Luochuan County, over a hundred kilometers north of Chang'an, the capital of the Tang

Dynasty, or today's Xi'an, still observe the custom. There they make a circle within the courtyard with chairs and benches as a place to gather. Here the bride and bridegroom will bow to a pair of wild geese cut out of paper, or two Chinese characters for *yan* (wild goose) written on a piece of red paper. When asked about the original intention in holding this ceremony, the villagers said that the male and female wild geese always kept each other company wherever they were and never parted. Thus the fidelity of geese came to symbolize everlasting love among humans.

A Night at Yangguan Village

The Yangguan Pass, which was described by Wang Wei, a poet of the Tang Dynasty, in his "Ode to Weicheng," is seventy kilometers south of the Yumen Pass. It is named "Yangguan" merely because ancient Chinese called "south" *yang*. The two passes, both built during the Han Dynasty, were known far and wide, for they were the north and south passages of the Silk Road. I learned that the remains of the Yangguan Pass were near Yangguan Village, 66 kilometers southwest of Dunhuang. After a two-hour drive across the desert we arrived at Yangguan Village.

Driving another three kilometers westward from the village, we found on the ridges of hills the remains of thick walls, around which were ancient ditches, farmland and kilns as well as copper coins, arrowheads and pottery of the Han Dynasty. All this evidence strongly suggests that the Yangguan Pass stood right here during the Han Dynasty.

At nightfall we sought lodging in this village of about two hundred households. The cottages, all lying against the sand dunes, formed a straight line from north to south. Our guide Lao Wang led us to the Zhang household. But as the host was still working in the field, the hostess offered us cigarettes and watermelons on his behalf once we were introduced.

Dunhuang has always been known for its hospitality. In ancient times tradesmen traveling along the Silk Road would miss the local inn from time to time and turn to a private household. Even if such an individual needed— accommodations for a week or two, he would invariably be warmly received by any household. Indeed, the hosts usually would not allow a single lost tradesman to continue his journey until another group of travelers or a caravan came which could accompany him.

The Zhangs were a family of five living in a small compound consisting of four principal rooms facing east, four wingrooms on the left and another four on the right. In addition, there were two more storerooms in which they put their carts, farm tools, fruit and other foodstuffs and household articles. At the southwest corner outside the back gate were the pens and the toilet. The well-designed compound was spacious and comfortable.

What we found particularly interesting was that every household built with tree branches a shelter over its roof, something rarely seen in other places. Our hostess told us that because the village lay right next to the dunes and was easily covered with sand in a wind, the shelter was built as a barrier. Besides, the house became intensely hot in the blazing summer sun, and the shelter would naturally reduce the heat. She also pointed out that the villagers all grew large numbers of trees around their compounds and the plentiful branches pruned off every autumn made good material for the shelter. The fresh branches replaced the dry ones that in turn could heat the *kang* in winter.

Peasants in the North usually build their *kang* next to the stove so that the cooking fire can do double duties, but here the *kang*s and stoves are separate from one another, with the stoves' pipes fixed at the foot of the back wall. Thus the villagers heat the *kang* directly with firewood. Though the beds are more easily heated this way, people in other places consider them wasteful of firewood, and point to the excess of unwanted ashes. But our hostess explained that this doesn't matter much; we rebuild our *kang* every year anyway.

The real reason is that because their earth contains so much sand bricks do not hold up well. That is why every summer they dispose of the used *kang* and build a new one. Fortunately, the remains of the used one are still useful as fertilizer for the crops.

With regard to the building of their compounds, the bricks have to be solid and firm. The villagers usually dig clay out of the ancient farmland covered with grit and carry it back with their carts. Then they add a proper amount of sandy soil and make bricks out of the mixed material. When the walls are built, they coat them with whitewash. Even so, the walls still will not be able to stand the desert weather for more than a score of years. Because the walls have to be rebuilt regularly, villagers over sixty have usually lived in three or four different houses.

When a house is being rebuilt, the owner's neighbors and other villagers come to help as they are needed. Traditionally, the owner provides the helpers with food but no payment. That is why the reconstruction of a house does not cost much.

At dusk, our host Zhang Hongshou returned from the fields with his son — an obviously capable man of about forty-five with sunburned face and bright eyes. With the help of his fellow villagers, he had harvested five tons of onions, planning to sell them in the oil fields of Qinghai Province. We learned that the local soil produced onions well-known throughout the desert areas for their long thick leaves.

The standard supper in the Northwest is "hand-pulled noodles." They put some soda into the dough and wait until it becomes soft and springy. Then with their fingers they pull it again and again until it turns into noodles. That evening we had two other accompanying dishes, spinach and potato shreds fried with onions. Simple though the meal was, the newly picked vegetables made it a tasty one.

We chatted with the host after supper, learning that he had from his thirteen *mu* of land harvested three tons of wheat, half a ton of corn, half of castor beans, nearly a quarter of soybeans, and varying measures of watermelons, cabbages, onions, and other crops. With a net income of one thousand *yuan* through their vegetable sales alone, these earnings alone were equal to a whole year's wages of a skilled worker in Beijing.

The Tradition of Growing Trees

I rose early in the morning to take a few deep breaths of

the fresh air of this oasis by the irrigation ditch in front of the compound. On both sides of the dike were two neat rows of soaring poplars, which looked like two lines of soldiers in gray armor and green helmets guarding the ditch and the crops in the fields day and night. Walking around, I found all over the village and even along the roads and ridges of the fields rows and rows of pear, apricot, and plum trees. Their Liguang Apricot, which was named after the famous General Li Guang of the Han Dynasty, yielded large sweet fruit which was well received everywhere.

Planting trees has been a tradition of the inhabitants of Dunhuang and places around it ever since ancient times. Classical books from the Scripture Storecave record: "When you plant trees, you should plant nine peach trees in the east, nine poplars in the west, nine jujubes in the south, and nine elms in the north. Trees planted this way are good for your descendants and will bring great fortune." "Dreaming of trees and grass growing in the doorway means wealth and rank." "Dreaming of fruit trees and eating their fruit means much good luck." "Dreaming of cutting down trees means any wish you make will come true."

The ancients of this place well understood that planting trees and protecting water were a matter of primary importance if they wanted to settle in a desert oasis. So with the help of the occult book, *The Explanation of Dreams*, they encouraged the farmers to plant trees by promising fortune and wealth. The previously mentioned "nine" in fact refers not only to the specific number of nine peaches or nine poplars but to "many," as is the case with so many Chinese expressions.

Elms are seen all over Dunhuang. As I was told, when the fruit is ripe in the third lunar month, every family will pick some from the trees. Then they wash the seeds and soak them in water, after which they mix them with wheat flour and steam the mixture. Fried with oil, salt and chives, it is most delicious. This food is usually available to the average family once or twice a year.

Today, in answer to the government's call to "plant trees everywhere and dress the country in green," the villagers

71

make still greater efforts to plant as many trees as they can. Our host in particular planted over two hundred poplars in front of his house last year and has planted six hundred more this year behind the house or along the ridges of the fields. Poplars live easily and grow rapidly; it takes only ten years for them to grow into useful lumber. This also brings a decent income to the villagers.

Nevertheless, the main purpose of their growing trees is to protect themselves from the fierce desert winds. Upon my arrival here, I could not understand why their houses were built so close against the dunes. Did they intend to keep off the sandy winds this way? But in a few days I came to know why.

When a house is built, a ditch must first of all be dug, and trees must be planted around the house. Even so carefully cultivated is the shelter belt behind the house, which consists of tall white poplars soaring skyward, then shorter trees such as narrow-leafed oleasters, and finally brambles and other low plants growing over the dunes. This shelter belt protects the village and its fields, beautifying the nearby small dunes with green plants. In due time when their children grow up and need to build more houses, they can move to the green land behind the village.

Washing Away Sand Dunes and Village Rules of Irrigation

After lunch we took our host's cart to Wowa Lake, one kilometer south of the village, which stored the water of several underground springs. There was a dam by the lake known as "Huangshui Dam" built by the ancestors of the villagers. As their farm work was not busy at moment, every household of all the villages sent one person with a cart, as was their rule, to carry stone and earth to reinforce the dam.

At present this lake provides all the water for the peasants, animals, crops, trees, fish ponds and power stations of Yangguan Village and three other villages. No wonder that all the villagers regard it with awe.

The farmers also told me that with the help of its water they had turned many small dunes as well as big ones, into farmland of more than a thousand *mu*.

Their method of "washing away sand dunes" is widely used in opening up new fields: first they build a waterproof terrace around the dune, then channel water from the ditches and let it run around the dune until it becomes an even plot. When the water is all absorbed, a piece of land is silted up.

But such land contains too much sand and too little soil, causing it to absorb fertilizer and water too rapidly. Obviously, it must have soil added into it. But where can they find soil in the desert?

The Chinese saying goes, "Those living on a mountain live off the mountain, those living near the water live off the water." Is it possible to find soil for the new land? Yes, it is. They build terraces between the dunes to store any soil that is washed down upon them by rains. When the mud dries and cracks, the villagers carry it to the sandy field in carts.

The desert is not a place devoid of green plants. The villagers have discovered that the fallen leaves of the red willows covering the dunes will together with the sand turn into humus after a certain period of time. Therefore, they collect it wherever it is available for the improvement of the sandy land.

Luxuriant reeds cover the sides of the lake, and of course the lake is rich in fertile mud. Whenever the dry season comes, the villagers move the reeds with turf attached to the sandy land and burn them after piling them into a pyramid. When the reed roots of the turf become ashes, it is transformed into good fertilizer.

People in Dunhuang have traditionally considered water as their lifeblood; they have had strict rules for planned water consumption and water conservancy ever since ancient times. Documents discovered in the Scripture Storecave of the Mogao Grottoes record that back in the Tang Dynasty specific rules and regulations were issued for the use of Dunhuang's rivers and its thirty-seven big ditches. For instance, the apportionment of workdays for digging ditches and building terraces according to the amount of land involved, and regular dredging the purpose of which was to prevent the overflowing of water and possible damaging of the dikes — were clearly stipulated. A professional keeper was assigned to every ditch. From the 3rd till the

9th lunar months every year when the fields were irrigated, the local government provided the keepers with horses so that they could patrol along the ditches and channel the water into the farmland. Besides, the specific dates of watering and the principle of watering lower fields first and higher land second were also made clear in the documents.

These rules and regulations are still being observed today. For example, Yangguan Village elects 13 impartial ditch keepers every year. When the busy season of spring sowing comes, all the land must be irrigated within four or five days. Any delay will bring about poor harvests. During this period, the land is irrigated according to the order fixed in advance. The land tillers will count the time of the irrigating, with twenty minutes of watering five *mu* costing 40 *yuan*. Should the water escape because of the tiller's negligence, his fields will not be irrigated again. Anyone who steals water or lets into his land more water than is needed will be fined forty *yuan*.

The Antique Sands

The Antique Sands are two kilometers west of Yangguan Village. Strong winds often blow away the sand, exposing ancient bricks, coins, pearls, agates and pottery. That is how it got its name.

Walking on the Antique Sands, I asked myself, "How can there be antiques in this gravel place?" Then I asked the guide and learned that in the Han and Tang dynasties Yangguan Pass stood in the west while the prosperous Shouchang Town lay in the east. These sands, however, were a vast open land where fallen frontier soldiers, citizens of Shouchang Town, and tradesmen of the Silk Road were buried.

The superstitious ancients believed that after their deaths people still needed food and money as they did on the earth. Therefore, the dead were buried here with valuables and things they had used in life. Such customs provide rich relics through which the living can acquire a better knowledge of history.

Later, due to droughts and wars, and because too much ground was opened, the local inhabitants could no longer live here. Then a sandstorm in the Ming Dynasty buried all the farmland, graves, and Shouchang Town itself. Only when grave robbers later tried to dig for the buried objects, and when high winds began to blow away much of the sand on the surface, did the antiques start to show up.

I picked up the topic of the Antique Sands with my host that night. He said that within the first half of the first lunar month— from the Spring Festival till the Lantern Festival— all the villagers, old and young, men and women, will put on their holiday best, get on their carts and go to find treasures over the Antique Sands. Those who have picked ancient coins, strings of pearls, earthen jars, or even bricks, feel extremely happy, for it is said that such people will have good luck throughout the new year. Those who cannot find anything are believed to be unlucky.

After the founding of the People's Republic of China, the Chinese government passed laws to protect relics which are today well established. So people do not take as much interest as before in going to the Antique Sands during the holiday seasons. And if a lucky individual happens to come upon a treasure, he will voluntarily send it to the government, which will reward him for his honesty.

Last year the museum of Dunhuang County, which has a rich collection of relics, received a china basin from the Han Dynasty. According to the owner from Yangguan Village, it has magic powers: though the weather be blazing hot, food kept in it will remain fresh for at least three days. After he learned that the county's museum was collecting relics, he generously presented to the museum this rare artifact handed down to him from his forefathers.

Here is a demonstration of the way in which social change alters local customs.

CHAPTER III

JILIN — A Province in Northeast China

SPRING FESTIVAL CELEBRATIONS AT A NORTHEASTERN VILLAGE

In China the Spring Festival is much more ceremonious than New Year's Day. In the cities, people working for the government and factories have only one day off for New Year's Day but three for Spring Festival. In the countryside, however, there is hardly any holiday atmosphere surrounding New Year's Day while the Spring Festival season lasts more than a month.

The Spring Festival is in fact the lunar New Year of over three thousand years ago. It was in 1912, one year after "the Revolution of 1911," that China adopted the Gregorian calendar and began to refer to the first of January as New Year's Day while the Chinese New Year was renamed Spring Festival.

The traditional ways of celebrating the Spring Festival are more or less the same throughout China. My experience with the peasants at mountain village in Jilin Province was typical.

The Last Lunar Month — a Month of Preparations

Because we started off quite late that month, by the time we got to Fulu Village of Weijin, a mountain village of thirty-six families in Dongliao County, it was already the 28th of the last lunar month. We saw people busy with preparations all along the way. Many households had already finished or were in the process of decorating their doors with pine branches and large red lanterns. Marketers were toting back heavy sacks of all sorts of different sizes by cart. Though the school had closed for the holidays, its playing field was still in a bustle with young men and women accompanied by drums and gongs practicing their *yangko* dance and walking on stilts.

Liu Yongtian invited us to celebrate the Spring Festival with his family of six — which included his mother, his wife, three boys and himself — in his spacious home of five principal rooms facing the south. When we arrived, his mother was busy making steamed buns stuffed with bean paste, a standard northeastern food every family prepares for the festival season. Made of a type of well-kneaded yellow millet dough and thoroughly pounded steamed red bean paste, the buns were steamed after being placed on fragrant perilla leaves. They were then frozen outside the windows and whenever you wanted to have some, you simply brought them in and reheated them.

Every family made so many buns, which were supposed to last for a whole month, that it couldn't manage the job alone. An unwritten law of the village had it that "whichever family is making buns, the neighbors should give a hand." All the neighboring women, old and young alike, would come to help whenever they were needed. They would crowd onto the *kang*, catching up on gossip as they worked, and soon finish the otherwise tedious work. At the Liu's home where I was stopping there was one particular old woman among the helpers who was a practiced storyteller. The young women listening were so riveted that they often forgot to stuff the buns. But when the hostess asked everybody to try one, they all pronounced them tender and delicious.

As the saying goes, "Busy is the twelfth month." Starting from the first day of the last month of the lunar year, the villagers all began to prepare for the important Festival. Lao Liu told me that the first event was the meal of *laba* porridge (*laba* means the eighth of the twelfth month) — a mixture of rice, millet, glutinous rice, husked *gaoliang* (Chinese sorghum), red beans, peanuts, dates, and finally walnuts cooked with sugar. Originally, *laba* porridge was an offering the villagers made to Sakyamuni in the Buddhist temples, but it has come to symbolize abundant harvests in the coming year. On that same day, according to their custom, the villagers also

77

poured some porridge into the roots of the pear, believing that the tree would yield more fruit after "drinking" the porridge.

With the eighth day celebrated, the villagers began to slaughter pigs for the Festival in turn. Any household that had a pig slaughtered would invite the neighbors to a simple meal of "stirred blood in pork intestines." Fresh pig blood mixed with water and several ingredients was filled into thoroughly cleaned intestines, which were then tied tightly. The stuffed intestines were stirred with large slices of pork and pickled cabbages. Cut into fine slices and mixed with garlic sauce and vinegar when served, they were uncommonly tender and tasty. Thus, thanks to the frequent dinners of the various families, their days passed quickly. Soon came the "Minor Spring Festival."

On the "Minor Spring Festival," which falls on the 23rd of the month, the villagers sent the god of the kitchen up to the heavens. In the old days, whoever got married and had a family of his own, be he rich or poor, would put up a picture of the kitchen god above the brick stove. On the two sides of the picture they would paste up this antithetical couplet:

> Tell the Jade Emperor nothing ill
> Bring us humans but more bliss still

This picture was worshipped as the "king of the house" that controlled the destiny of the whole family. The ceremony of making offerings to the kitchen god, one of the five worshipped — originated from the Shang Dynasty, about three thousand years ago. The kitchen god was said to be invented by an old woman at that time. As the local legend goes, the god of the kitchen was in fact the third brother of the Jade Emperor up in the heavenly palace. On the 23rd of the twelfth month every year, he returned to his brother to report to him what the family had done during the year. Based on this report, the emperor would decide whether to commend the family members for their good deeds or punish them for their wrongdoings.

On the very day when the kitchen god returned to the heavens, every family set up tables in their courtyard, burned incense and served the kitchen god buns and other foods. The

78

women also made a corn stalk horse for him to ride on. Then the master of the house prayed, "O Kitchen God, when you see the Jade Emperor in the heavens, tell him nothing but our fine deeds." With this, the picture of the kitchen god that had been dirtied by their daily smoke was burned up and a new one put in its place. Still they could not relax: they offered the God the local malt candy which meant sealing up his mouth lest words of criticism slip out in the heavens and bring harm to them.

After the 23rd, the villagers become even busier. Their daily activities are clearly revealed through the popular local doggerel:

> Clean your house on the 24th,
> Make your bean curd on the 25th,
> Get your liquor on the 26th,
> Kill your chickens on the 27th,
> Leaven your dough on the 28th,
> Paste your incense burner (paper one
>   as sacrifice) on the 29th.

The second day after our arrival at the village was the 29th. Early in the morning, Lao Liu busied himself in the killing of chickens and ducks. His two boys, however, were concentrating all their attention on the pasting of their lanterns. Standing by the range, Liu's mother was kneading the dough with which she would make date buns to offer to the ancestors. Mr. Lu and I wanted to help but did not know how, so out of politeness we tried to express a kind of sympathy, or rather comfort, to her. But she answered, "We are busy because life is getting better and better. Busy, busy, the busier we are, the better we like it!"

Putting Up Spring Festival Couplets

On the eve of the Spring Festival, all the households put up Spring Festival couplets. The three boys of our host, one carrying the paste, one holding the couplets, another doing the posting, worked from the inner room to the outer ones. First they put in the eastern room occupied by their grandmother the following couplet:

> Each passing year brings you longevity—
> Every spring fills our house with happiness.

Then they went to the west room where their parents slept and put up:

> Fine weather and fertile land bless our family—
> A heavy spring snow begins another year of
>   bumper harvests.

Moving to the courtyard, they posted "Abundant harvests of all crops" in the eastern grain room while "A seed sown in spring / Tons of grains in the fall" in the western storeroom. On the large cart they pasted up

> Travel far and near—
> Be blessed everywhere.

In the stable they put up:

> Buffalo stronger than mountain tigers—
> Horses sturdier than ocean dragons.

The pigsty was dressed with:

> Crowded with grown hogs year by year—
> Filled with young pigs month after month.

Of course, they would not forget the chicken coop: "Golden hens crowd the coop...." A flourishing population with an increasing number of domestic animals and a bumper harvest of all crops are always the first wishes of the villagers before the new year begins.

Finally, the three brothers deliberately posted the huge Chinese character *fu* (happiness) upside down to surprise passers-by who would unknowingly utter *Fu dao le*, which means that the character *fu* is posted upside down, or: there pours happiness — since *dao* means "upside down" as well as "pour": To their minds a perfect beginning for the new year.

Spring Festival couplets originated from *taofu* (peach wood charms against evil) over two thousand years ago. Believing that peach wood could drive away ghosts, the ancient Chinese hung two boards of it on the sides of the main gate of a house so as to keep away evils. In A.D. 964, Emperor Meng Chang of the Later Shu Dynasty wrote on the peach boards:

> The New Year arrives and the dead are remembered
> The joyous festival starts a long spring.

This might have been the first Chinese couplet. Nevertheless, peach wood charms were not named Spring Festival couplets until after Zhu Yuanzhang became emperor in the Ming Dynasty. It was he who ordered that every family in the country, rich and poor alike, put up couplets on the Chinese New Year's Eve to celebrate peace in the nation. Thereafter, the posting of couplets became a custom observed throughout China every year.

When night fell that day, all the families of Fulu Village hung up lighted lanterns on lantern poles, the twinkling lights in the evening sky adding to the atmosphere of festivity. Hanging lanterns on poles in the courtyards was a custom practiced in the villages of this district only. Meanwhile, they decorated the tops of the poles with green leaves, red flags, pinwheels and wooden planes. Believe it or not, the villagers used to fix wooden fish there to pray for a surplus of grains and money. The word for "fish" in Chinese is *yu*, a homonym of "surplus." But nowadays they have fallen in love with planes instead, believing that the plane symbolizes a prosperous family!

We climbed the hills in the west of the village to take a few shots of this charming northern village and to our surprise saw that several villagers had also come up. We soon figured out that they had come to invite their dead elders back home for the festival feast. When the couplets had been posted and the liquor warmed, when everything was ready and dinner about to start, they had thought of their dead elders who had worked hard all their lives but were now lying in their isolated graves.Why not invite them back for the Spring Festival? So they had put up their family tree with their ancestors' names on it in the center of the north wall of the central room and placed offerings such as buns, cake, a whole fish, and dishes of different food before it. After that they went to the hills with joss sticks, candles and firecrackers. When the offering ceremony was repeated before the graves they invited the dead back home to share the Spring Festival.

As for those who were buried faraway, the villagers were not able to go to their graves to invite them back home for the Spring Festival, but they still held a ceremony, that of "watching the sky." They uttered their prayers at the crossroads in front of their village, made a "parcel" by putting a wad of "paper money" into a "bag"— a large envelope with the specific names of the dead receivers on it, then burned it up. Although the "posting" of fake money to guarantee their ancestors a happy festival was a superstitious activity, their act of honoring and remembering their dead was both impressive and moving to us.

A Family Reunion Dinner on the Spring Festival Eve

When the ancestors were "served," the whole family crowded onto the warm *kang*. Then Lao Liu ordered his second son, "Boy, fire the crackers now!" And so amid the popping of firecrackers their dinner started and they began to drink to their reunion. Since those who worked away from home usually returned for this dinner, it was also known as "family reunion dinner."

For everyone this was the richest dinner of the year. Every family served all the dishes that had been prepared over the past few days, most of which could boast a fine name. For example, a course of fish was a "must," since the word for fish, *yu*, is a homonym for "surplus" in Chinese, as we have seen, and naturally all farmers want more than enough of all their crops. A bowl of fried meatballs (meaning "round" or "reunion" in Chinese) symbolized the reunion of the whole family; a basin of *fuyong* (fortune forever) cake stood for everlasting good fortune.

In the past, the people of Fulu Village and the neighboring villages never ate chicken on Spring Festival or on the Eve. When I asked why, the host told me with a smile: "*Ji* (chicken) is a homonym of 'starvation.' Because the villagers often starved in the past, they're afraid that eating chicken is inviting famine." Then he put a piece of chicken into the boiling pot and added, "Now we don't follow this convention anymore. With six tons of grains at home, do I have to worry about famine?" Last year, the Lius harvested from their forty *mu* of farmland over twenty tons of corn, peas, millet, sorghum and rice. Selling off fourteen tons, they kept the rest. The storeroom in the house was too small for so much grain, so they had to build a free-standing barn in the open.

Because it is cold in the Northeast, villagers there are in the habit of eating "*huoguo*" food or food prepared in chafing dishes. They also have their own way of boiling the food: "flyers" in the front, "walkers" at the back, fish on the left, shrimps on the right and vegetables gently spread all over. In the front part of the boiler that faces the visitors, they drop in tender fowl, behind which are pork, beef, mutton and other meats of walking animals. After they have put fish on the left and shrimps on the right, they gently spread over pickled vegetables and vermicelli. That day we had not only fish and shrimp, but also crabs. They were very tender, fresh and delicious.

Fragrant Smells Filling the Air Far and Wide — Staying There Through New Year's Eve

The Spring Festival Eve dinner being over, the children were now waiting for their "lucky money." It is said that in ancient times "lucky money" was copper coins strung together with colored threads placed beside the beds or pillows. Later, as customs changed, the elders gave the children money directly with two purposes: to wish them a long life and to allow them to buy candy, firecrackers, and picture books to enhance their enjoyment of the festival season. Because Lao Liu's children had all grown up, he gave money only to the nephews and nieces who were visiting. Seeing the excited children receiving their money and then running out into the yards to fire their crackers, I thought back to my own boyhood and how anxiously I waited for that gift of "lucky money" — so anxiously, in fact, that I could not enjoy or even taste my festival dinner.

In the eyes of the grandmother, everything in her house was an intelligent being like her grandchildren. Having given "lucky money" to the little ones, she put some coins beneath the sauce pans, water vats, straw mats on the *kang*, and the incense burners. This way she hoped to insure long life to these household necessities.

Nobody went to sleep that night, for it is the custom in families to wait together for the arrival of the lunar New Year. A typical scene in the past Northeast might find the grandparents cracking melon seeds on the warm *kang* as they told their little grandchildren stories. The middle-aged people would play mahjong or cards while the bigger girls played *galaha*, a game of the Manchu nationality which used a thoroughly cleaned kneecap of a pig or sheep that had been dyed red. The boys, of course, would have the hardest time sitting still. They would walk out into the courtyard with their lanterns from time to time to light firecrackers. Things were somewhat different the night I was there, for besides the traditional activities, something new had been added— TV. It was somehow a very special treat in this remote mountain village sitting on a warm *kang* watching programs from Beijing on Festival Eve.

Su Dongpo (1037-1101), a poet of the Song Dynasty, wrote in one of his poems "Waiting for New Year's Day":

> The young ones tried to stay away from beds,
> To join the ringing laughter of New Year's Eve.

The little nephew of our host could basely keep his eyes open after playing hard all day, but far from sending him off to bed,

Lao Liu allowed him only a nap with his clothes on.

"Let him have a good sleep," I urged.

"Oh, no," Lao Liu shook his head firmly. "It would be most disrespectful of our ancestors if after inviting them back home to celebrate with us, we left them alone and went to sleep ourselves."

Most Chinese nationalities welcome the arrival of the lunar New Year, but their ways of celebrating and the meaning it carries for them can differ markedly. Though both belong to the minority nationalities of the Northeast, people of the Dawoer nationality sing and dance wildly through the night while Olunchun young men politely present flowers and propose toasts to their elders. In the South, people of the Tujia and the Buyi nationalities await New Year's Day sitting around a bonfire. But Tujia people like to sit on the grass, hoping that their sitting will help make the wild grass grow in the fields, while Buyi girls will try to carry the first two buckets of water which symbolize happiness from the river.

Welcoming New Year's Day with Firecrackers

When it was nearly twelve o'clock that night, the popping of firecrackers filled the air of Fulu Village. The flames of fireworks shooting into the air turned the cold night sky into a riot of color. Now my host moved their table of candles, joss sticks and offerings from the central room to the yard next to a fire. After making his prayer by the table, Lao Liu, with a lantern and burning incense in his hands, strode out of the courtyard to welcome the god of the kitchen, the god of wealth and the god of happiness who were returning to the earth. As the firecrackers went off, the family opened all the doors wide to let in the returning gods.

With regard to the origin of firecrackers, there is an old folk tale.

Once upon a time there was a fierce animal called a *nian*, who was even bigger than a camel and ran like the wind, devouring any human being or animal within sight. Then, the god of heavens locked it up in the high mountains, allowing it to come out only once a year. It was on New Year's Eve that the *nian* came out. So with their grains stored and rich foods prepared, human beings would fight with the *nian* with sharpened swords and heavy sticks. During their fights with this animal, they discovered that the creature feared the color red, bright lights and loud noise. So from then on every family put up red paper on their doors, kept a fire in their yard, beat drums and gongs, and burned bamboo. Because gunpowder had not yet been invented, they could only burn bamboo until it crackled. Thus the *nian* was frightened away, returned to its cave and there starved to death. After that people were free to live a peaceful life. But the custom of posting red couplets, keeping a fire, and setting off firecrackers has been practiced ever since.

On New Year's Day Lao Liu soon came in from the yard — his face flushed with excitement. "We're going to have a year of bumper harvests," he exclaimed. When I asked how he knew this, he said, "Because the sky is covered with stars and there isn't any wind at all. A north wind would mean just the opposite."

What he said reminded me of the poem "New Year's Day in a Peasant' House" written by Meng Haoran of the Tang Dynasty:

> From the weather the peasants all predict:
> A bountiful harvest will be theirs this year.

So we know that such prognostication dates at least from the Tang Dynasty.

Praying for rich harvests was always an important activity in agricultural China during the festival season in ancient times. The Qinian Hall of the Heavenly Temple in Beijing was the place where the emperors of the Ming and Qing dynasties regularly sought celestial intervention to bring good harvests to the whole country. Though the word *nian*, or "year," became a unit of time in the Zhou Dynasty of three thousand years ago, people have always associated it with good harvests. The expression *you nian* in "When all the five cereals are ripe, it is a *you nian*;" clearly stands for good harvests.

A Two-Year-Old Meal of Dumplings

The hostess was cooking *jiaozi*, or dumplings, as firecrackers resounded in the courtyard. The dumpling consists of a thin round wrapper rolled out of a small ball of dough and some meat stuffing. With the stuffing placed in the center of the rolled-out dough, it is wrapped into the shape of a new moon. Back in 1968, a bowl of dumplings, looking exactly like today's, was excavated from a tomb of the Tang Dynasty in Turfan, Xinjiang. From this we can see that by the Tang Dynasty, *jiaozi*—a food of the Han nationality—had already been introduced to the minority nationalities in the western regions.

Believing the dumplings were ready, the host shouted toward the west room, "Are the dumplings 'earned' now?"

"Yes, 'earned' now," answered his wife.

"That's good."

The Spring Festival season, people are cautious about words with negative connotations, such as "dead," "bad," and "worn." When the dumplings burst in the boiler, they should say they are "earned," meaning earning money. It was clear that the dialogue between husband and wife was designed to encourage good luck.

The hot dumplings were laid on the table shortly before the clock struck twelve. Dumplings served on the night which links two years together they refer to as the "two-year-old meal."

Everybody was busy eating when Liu's second boy suddenly shouted, "Money!" He had bitten into a coin wrapped in one of the dumplings.

"The New Year has just begun and you've already bitten into a coin. You're sure to make big money this year!"

"Congratulations!"

"When you get the money for it, how about a color TV?"

Lao Liu was obviously enjoying the hubbub. "It seems we're on our way to becoming a Fulu Village ten-thousand-*yuan* household this year!"

It turned out that while making the dumplings, they usually

wrap in one and sometimes three clean coins. Some people, wrap in dates, peanuts and sweets instead of coins. With peanuts (also named "longevity nut"), dates and sweets (happiness) they express the wish for a long and happy life.

Of course, people in different places eat different foods on this special eve. Southerners, in particular, have *hun tun* (won ton) which is a homophone of "full grain bins" in Chinese, hoping thus to have much grain to spare. Those praying for longevity eat noodles, but those hoping for family reunions have *tang yuan* — round dumplings made of glutinous rice flour and sweet stuffing.

Paying New Year Calls

When the "two-year-old meal" was over, the Lius in turn began to kowtow to the family tree on the wall. The aged grandmother started the ceremony, finally taking her place on the *kang*. Next came the second generation — Lao Liu and his wife — who knelt to pay their respects to both their forefathers and the grandmother. Finally came the grandchildren. The youngest child naturally was the last and busiest one. When he was kowtowing and saying "Happy New Year!" respectively to his grandmother, father, mother, and then brothers, his smiling grandmother interrupted him with "Yes, Happy New Year! May everybody have a Happy New Year! But now stop the kowtowing and save your head for further growing!" And she reached into her pocket for some money wrapped in red paper.

Dawn was just breaking when we followed the Lius in their round of New Year calls to the eldest people of the village. Troops and troops of visitors were swarming into the houses of the elders at the same time. For good measure they exchanged greetings amongst themselves, wishing each other a Happy New Year as they made a hand bow: one hand clasped over the other. I was told that New Year calls carried a certain magic power, so that those who had had a falling out in the past year could easily make up once they had exchanged a New Year greeting with a hand bow.

According to folklore, the custom of paying New Year

calls originated from the expelling of the monster *nian*. The day after the creature had been driven away, people got up and opened the doors of their houses, each relieved to see others safe and sound. For the first time on New Year's Day they felt overjoyed, so that they began to exchange congratulations and good wishes with one another.

This custom continued until the Song Dynasty when some scholars decided that paying such calls was too time-consuming. Since they could not visit in person friends and relatives living far away from them, somebody hit upon the idea of sending New Year greetings through the mail. Thereafter, many people began to send "flying cards" as they were called at that time. The sender wrote on a piece of letter-writing paper, three inches long and two inches wide, the name of the receiver, his greetings and his own name and address and asked his servant or the postman to deliver it to his friend, relative, or to a member of his family. This might be the origin of today's New Year cards.

It was a beautiful sunny morning as we strolled through the village when we heard the sudden beating of drums and clanging of gongs.

"The stilt walkers! The stilt walkers!" shouted the young boys as they bounded toward them. It was a troop of over twenty persons, the drum and gong beaters leading the way—the men and women dancers following behind. Waving colored fans and silk kerchiefs and dressed in traditional stage costumes, they swung their bodies forward on one-meter-high stilts that had been tied to their feet. During the Spring Festival the different teams representing the *yangko*, lion, and dragon dance, and the land oars and stilt walking acts that go from one village to another not only bring entertainment to the villagers, but also promote friendship among the villages. So these activities in a way are inter-village New Year calls. Wherever the stilt group went, its singers were able to produce a ditty appropriate to each family they visited. One such was:

We beat gongs and see you all smiles,
Your family thrives like gold mines:

Fair fowl and cattle form long lines,
Silver dollars ascend in high piles.

The "long-legged" visitors were dancing with swinging bodies around the yard. In one minute, they formed a circle — in another they arranged themselves in a figure "8." The clown attracted the most attention — in one moment flopping to the ground and then springing up to jump over the table; in the next moment leaping over the ladder carried by his fellow dancers. The applause told the story. He was everybody's favorite.

WINTER FOODS, CLOTHES, HOUSES, AND TRANSPORTATION

I had heard about the five so-called "strange things" of the Northeast long before I came to Jilin:

Thatched cottages with wattled walls,
Chimneys built away from gables,
Window paper pasted outside,
Babies always kept in cradles,
Big girls' [tobacco] pipes known far and wide.

Lying in the east of the Shanhai Pass of the Great Wall, the three northeastern provinces of Liaoning, Jilin and Heilongjiang are generally known as the "East of Shanhai Pass." After visiting these places in person, we came to know that outsiders found the so-called "strange things" strange merely because northeastern ways of life differed from those of other places. Perhaps that is why we often say in Chinese — "The less you see, the more you will wonder."

Houses Built with *Kangs* Against All Walls

After the Spring Festival, we left Fulu Village for nearby Dadao Village of Shiyi District. Though the freezing winter had passed, the vast land of the North was still covered with snow. Early spring was nearly as cold as winter: on our way to the village, we saw our moist breath turn to frost as we exhaled.

90

Also, the brims of our hats and our collars, eyebrows and beards were covered with frost.

Houses in Dadao Village were markedly different from the desert compounds, and that of our host family was typical of the style: surrounded by a wattle fence about two meters high. Wang and his son answered our knock with a welcoming smile and eagerness to relieve us of our heavy baggage. A yellow dog shared their enthusiasm at the sight of a pair of new faces, which he showed by vigorous tail wagging and characteristic running about. We were waved to the warmest seats, as befitted our status as guests, at the head of the *kang* in the west room. In a moment we felt surges of warmth from head to foot and our frozen bodies lost the rigidity they owed to winter's chill.

Peasants in north China all sleep on a heated *kang* in winter. In the North and Northwest, the average room has only one *kang*, but the room we stayed in had been built with three. There was a *kang* below the south window and a north *kang* opposite it. Built against the west wall was another, the fire passage of which was designed in the shape of the Chinese character "卐" (*wan*). Thus, all the walls, except the one with the door, were built with a *kang*. The north room occupied by Wang Liyou's son and his daughter-in-law also had two *kang*s — a big one and a small one.

A kitchen connected the west and north rooms, its hot smoke passing through the flues of the five *kang*s and gathering inside the west *kang* of the west room before it went out through the chimneys built outside the walls. With this particular design they can make the best use of the leftover heat to warm the house. Thanks to the heat-proof double doors, they are able to insulate themselves against a cold season that lasts for six long months whose coldest weather drops to minus 30°C.

A means they have devised of meeting the cold's challenge is their special ways of building chimneys, counted as one of the five "strange things" by those living inside Shanhai Pass. Some slant upward from the gables, looking rather like camel necks and therefore called "camel-neck chim-

91

neys.'' Some smoke passages are built underground connected to round chimneys that look like pagodas three or four feet away from the walls. In order to strengthen them, the villagers build an arched bridge between the chimneys and the main structure of the house. These chimneys look like an arched door in the shape of a new moon, so they are called "Bridged Chimneys and Moon-like Doors.''

The Wangs' house consists of three small rooms, which were remarkable for their orderliness. The diligent hostess had placed her cabinet against the west wall near the north *kang* and the wardrobe adjacent to the south *kang*. The box on the third *kang* of the same room which was also meant for clothes, however, was seldom used, so later it became a container for pots, cups, glasses and other odds and ends. The small room with the three *kang*s was a marvel of neatness — its glass windows spotless. As for the "strange thing" — "window paper pasted outside," — it was not to be seen since the present houses had been fixed with double glass windows.

Most of the villagers in China paste paper over the lattices of their windows from inside. When I asked our host why they had ever followed the custom of pasting their paper from outside, he answered simply that there was no other way in a land of such fierce winds. Paper pasted outside and thus supported by the window lattices could not be blown off that easily, neither would it be torn by naughty children. At the same time it also prevented snow and dirt from gathering at the lattices, guaranteeing the house the best possible sunshine in winter. So it was a custom born out of the conditions of real life here.

Houses with Straw Walls

A quiet man in his late fifties, our host was a most industrious and versatile man. During the slack seasons in farming, he worked as a bricklayer, building houses and *kang*s for other villagers.

Describing the ways they built their houses, he pointed out that "the cold here can freeze up more than three feet of the water in the rivers!" Therefore, the foundations of the houses had to be over two meters deep, so as to avoid the frozen earth surface. In the past they had just built the walls on the rammed ground. Consequently, the foundation sank in the rainy summer but rose up in the freezing winter. Because of this the walls cracked easily and often had to be rebuilt. That is why they later built the foundation with sand and stone instead: they first laid a layer of sand in the troughs and rammed it until it was firm enough, then built on the sand a foundation of stone, and finally built up the walls with bricks.

Remembering the saying that "A house built on sand will not last long," I asked, "Is it solid enough?"

"It certainly is!" he replied confidently.

Then I learned that foundations built of sand and stone would neither be affected by water nor crack in the cold of winter. And since the layer of sand was never thick, these houses were never like those "built on sand."

In winter when they do not have much farming to do, the women of the village often weave straw into baskets, and the villagers even build walls from straw, calling it "weaving walls of straw." Adopting this method, the villagers first plant wood poles into the foundation, one at every other foot. Then they weave onto the poles straw ropes that have been soaked in slurry, after which they cover the two sides of the unfinished walls with mud from bottom to top and smooth them. When the walls are finished, they set the beams and the purlins and then lay the wicker and smooth it with mud. Finally they cover the roof frame with a layer of grass half a foot thick, and the house is ready for habitation.

Our host himself had spent his childhood in a house of this type. Thanks to the warm straw in the middle of the walls, he told us, such houses were very warm in winter. Within the structure consisting of wood poles, straw and mud, the poles and straw could be compared to the bars of reinforced concrete, and the mud the cement. "I still remember what painstaking efforts were involved in pulling down the straw house when we were rebuilding this new one," he recalled.

Nonetheless, the making of the ropes is enormously costly in terms of time and straw. Besides, it is all too easy for mice to dig holes and stay inside the straw walls, which are also most untidy in appearance. Thus in recent decades, straw walls have gradually been replaced by brick ones. But the custom of covering the roofs with warm grass has never changed.

When a new house is built, a special beam is set above the warm *kang* where later mothers can hang their boat-shaped cradles. The cradle, when gently pushed by the mothers, can easily send the babies into sweet slumber, setting the mothers free for work. Also, the *kang* is still hot in summer; babies sleeping in the cradle instead of on the *kang* do not fall ill that easily. Perhaps this is why the local people insist on keep babies in cradles!

With regard to another "strange thing"— "big girls' pipes known far and wide,"— pipe smoking was a practice resulting from the special environment of the Northeast. In the old days women endured at home the endless cold season with nothing to do. Usually they sat idly on the *kang* cracking sunflower seeds or munching popcorn. They feel into the habit of filling strong Northeast tobacco into the bowls of the long pipes and smoking by the fire. When I was traveling in the area, I still saw a few old women smoking pipes as they chatted with one another. But nowadays, girls do not smoke anymore, for they have all gone to school and know smoking is harmful to one's health. Besides, they now have plenty of recreational activities throughout the winter.

An "Indoor Hothouse"

Host Wang's mother and her daughter-in-law began busying themselves preparing dinner for us the moment we arrived at their house. An hour later, they brought in from the kitchen a great variety of dishes covering every inch of space on the round *kang* table. In the middle of it was a fish braised in soy sauce surrounded by large dishes of stewed chicken, quick-fried mutton with onions, pork fried with dried bean curd, and quick-fried cabbage with vinegar.

When everyone was seated, the host raised his cup. "We're overjoyed at the coming of our guests," he toasted. "Their visit brings us much happiness in this Spring Festival season. All cheers!" And he downed his first cup of white spirits.

94

The custom followed here demands that once the host has offered a toast, all present must drink down three cups in succession. Only when the third cup is drunk are the diners free to eat and drink at as slow a pace as they please. Seeing all of them drinking cups upon cups of white spirits, I could not help saying to myself, "These people know how to drink— that's sure!"

Villagers in the Northeast are well-known as heavy drinkers, which perhaps can be partly explained by the fact that liquor can warm one up in winter. The habit may contribute also to their liking of visitors and their reputation for being outspoken. Whenever they have visitors, they will without fail slaughter chickens and be sure to have sufficient liquor on hand. As a regular practice, they use big cups for drinking and large bowls for dining. The more the guests drink, the happier the host will be. Only when they are clearly inebriated are they considered to have drunk their fill, and only then will the host believe his treat is successful. In Beijing when we invite someone to our homes we usually say, "Come over and have a chat." But the villagers here will say, "Do stop by for a drink." And they won't take "no" for an answer.

I raised my cup high up to propose a toast to our host, but when we were clinking cups, I noticed he was holding his lower than mine, which made me feel uncomfortable. What I didn't know was that he was simply being polite and deferential. So said our guide Lao Wan when I asked him about it. After my toast I took a little sip and tried to put down my cup on the table. They wouldn't have it! "You can't do that." I was told. "It's against the rules. Once you've clinked your cup, you have to drink it up!" But I protested that I was an amateur as a drinker, and my host took pity on me and allowed me the freedom to drink it in more than one gulp and to have food with it as well. But no way was I to be permitted the further privilege of putting down my cup before I had drunk it up.

During the Spring Festival we had fish and pork every day, and naturally we got tired of both. But when the hostess brought out a dish of fried green peppers, our appetite got a boost. "Green peppers grown in hothouses are so tender and fresh," I commented.

"We don't have a hothouse," she answered. "These are from the vegetable cellar."

In the Northeast, every family has a large vegetable cellar about two or three meters deep where cabbages, potatoes, radishes and onions are stored. Thanks to the earth's temperature the vegetables do not get frozen or rotten and can last for the whole winter. The way they store green peppers in particular is very special. In autumn, choice peppers are alternately laid in a big jar with stove ashes — ending with a layer of the ashes as the seal. Peppers kept in this way remain fresh till spring and can be used to produce a variety of courses in the freezing festival season.

At present, the villagers have not set up hothouses for vegetable production during the cold season. Yet when we visited the Langs that day, we saw that our host had built a vegetable bed with wood planks on a *kang* in his west room where green garlic bulbs were growing healthily. When I praised the bed, Lao Lang joined in proudly, "This little bed serves two purposes: it beautifies at the same time that it produces food ingredients. When I have visitors, I pull up a handful of them and can quickly make shredded meat fried with garlic or dumplings with garlic-flavored stuffings.

Of course the daily vegetable fare available to the peasants in the winter are fresh and pickled cabbage and dried bean curd. The making of pickled cabbage is actually quite easy. When the cabbages are harvested, you first dry them in the sun for two days and cut them into halves, then wash them in boiling water for one second, put them into jars and add clean water. The sour pickles you end up with taste not only fresh but also tender.

After eating fresh and pickled cabbage for half a year, everybody is sick and tired of them. So when May comes and the earth is covered with edible green plants like dandelions, shepherd's purses, and plantains, all the women and children go out to the fields to collect whatever they can. Back home they cannot wait one minute longer but just wash the plants, dip them in thick sauce and begin to eat them without even cooking them.

Dogskin Hats and *Wula* Shoes

After dinner I went for a stroll in the village which lay at the foot of the hills with a river running before it. Covering the hills behind the village was an oak forest where tussahs (silkworms that produce coarse silk) were raised in summer and autumn. A group of village boys and girls were skating on the frozen river wearing special wooden skates— shoe-shaped wooden boards tied to their feet with two thick wires. As the boys chased one another, their flushed faces were alive with glee under their dogskin hats.

In the Northeast, men as well as boys wear dogskin hats whenever they go out. Compared with other headgear, dogskin hats are warmer, more comfortable and longer. They also represent a kind of manly agility and bravery. All the villagers in the Northeast raise dogs who watch their houses for them and provide skins when killed that can not only be made into hats but bedding and clothing as well.

The traditional hat of the villagers in this area is known as the "four-tiled hat" because from its four sides droop pieces of fur which look like tiles. Though it is not stylish and not much appreciated by youngsters, the aged still like it, for with its four "tiles" it does a good job of warming the ears and forehead in freezing temperatures.

Indoors the villagers only need wear cotton-padded coats and trousers. For the outdoors they slip on another overcoat, and that is quite enough. The cart drivers, however, who are out from morning till night, have to wear much more. Normally, they wrap their necks in a scarf outside the hat, put on leather trousers over the cotton-padded ones, and wear *wula* shoes. Since the Northeast is a place of heavy snow, it's important to protect your feet from frostbite when traveling outdoors.

During our visit to Lang Dianjia's, we asked the grandfather of the family to explain *wula* shoes to us. He immediately told his daughter-in-law to fetch a pair of *wula* shoes which had been out of use for many years. Each shoe was made from a single piece of cattle skin. To close it up, a row of pleats had been sewn into the instep. Higher up were six holes for the shoelaces. The elderly host began to put on the shoes now. But before he did so, he tied up his trouser legs and then put on his cotton socks. Next he wadded some soft *wula* grass into the shoes and tied the laces. Finally he put on the puttees.

Now he walked back and forth, "*Wula* shoes are light and comfortable. With them on you won't slip on ice or snow. The *wula* wads inside are as soft as cotton fluff and toasty warm."

Of course, *wula* shoes also have drawbacks. For one thing it takes at least twenty minutes every time you put them on or take them off. Their soles, which are very thin, usually wear out in two to three years. Besides, they are certainly not attractive. For all these reasons they were replaced as soon as cotton shoes with rubber soles and leather shoes with large insteps came into use.

Nevertheless, the old still show deep affection for the *wula* shoes once they are mentioned. They even consider them to be one of the three treasures of the Northeast, the other two being ginseng and mink. Popular stories about these shoes have spread far and wide. The following tale is about *wula* grass:

Long long ago, two brothers lost their way in the woods where they wandered for fifteen days without a clue as to a way out. As death seemed at hand, the elder brother thought he would rather help his brother get out of the woods alive than for both to die together of starvation in the cold. So he left next to his brother his last handful of rice and took off his cotton-padded coat and covered the sleeping form with it. Then he noted that his shoes as well as his brother's had already worn out. What now? Suddenly he remembered that hair could keep the body warm too, so he cut off his own hair and wadded it into his brother's shoes. When the younger man woke up he felt comfortably warm but to his sorrow found the frozen body of his brother under the pine! With tears in his eyes he buried the body there in the woods, using the hair he had put in his shoes as a marker for the grave. The next year when he returned from the home he had finally found to seek the grave of his elder brother, the hair had disappeared, but he found instead long, thin, hair-like grass growing there. Believing that this might mean that his brother was still worried that his feet might get frozen and that he was therefore growing the grass for him, he cut it and put it into his *wula* shoes where it made for comfort as well as warmth. When this news spread around, the local people all wadded *wula* grass into their shoes in the same way. Thus the shoes got their name.

The Cart and the Sleigh

The earth was still frozen solid in early spring and working the fields was impossible. Thus the villagers did not start to get ready to farm until after the Lantern Festival— the 15th of the first lunar month. Women wove baskets inside the house, young men dug loose the muckheap with picks and carried it on their carts to the farmland in front of the village while the old men fixed the farm tools.

The horse-drawn cart is an important means of transportation in the northeast plains of China, and it is an essential in their spring sowing and autumn harvesting. It transports grains and goods; it takes the villagers to market and to visit their friends and their relatives.

Originally pulled by an ox, the cart is believed to have been invented by Huangdi in about 2600 B.C. Then during the Xia Dynasty (about 2200 to 2100 B.C.-1700 B.C.) a man by the name of Xi Zhong began to break horses for cart pulling. In the Spring and Autumn Period (770 B.C.-476 B.C.) and the Warring States (475 B.C.-221 B.C.), the armored cart became an important battle weapon. In 1980 exquisite bronze carts and horses were excavated from a tomb subordinate to the tombs of Emperor Qinshihuang in Lintong County, Shaanxi Province. But those were carts with single shaft. In the early years of the Han Dynasty, the cart was improved through the design of the double shafts. Now much firmer, the improved cart could carry much more weight, and it has been used ever since.

Nearly every one of the families in Dadao Village raises two or three draft animals. The villagers love the animals as they do their own lives, taking the most tender care of them all year round. The high point, however, occurs just before and after the Spring Festival. On the 24th of the twelfth lunar month when they do their annual thorough cleaning, the riders first clean the stables, then comb the animals with brushes. On the eve of the Spring Festival they not only paste couplets on the carts and the stables but also feed the animals particularly fine fodder. "It's Spring Festival now, and you should have some better food too," they tell their animals. Before they make their first trip after the Spring Festival, the carters burn incense and set off firecrackers next to the stables, seeking the gods' blessings for the whole year.

However, Dadao Village is a mountain village whose roads are narrow and usually covered with thick snow in the cold season, so that it is by no means easy or safe for the carts to carry their muck in the sloping fields. At this time then the carters use sleighs instead.

Our host has three sleighs of different sizes. The big one, when fixed with side boards, can hold large baskets. Pulled by the draft animals, it is usually used to carry mud and muck. When the farmers go to gather firewood in the hills they do not fix on the side boards but simply tie the wood onto the sleigh so that it can move faster. The grandmother and her daughter-in-law use the small ones to carry their grains and vegetables easily and safely.

The sleighs used in the snow fields are ever so simple. Gifted with a pair of clever hands, our host can make one in just a day. In the beginning, I sort of looked down on this primitive means of transportation, not appreciating its value until I climbed the Changbai Mountains.

The day we were driving up the mountains, the roads were covered with a layer of snow one meter thick. As we were taking a turn, the car suddenly slipped and just would not go an inch farther. Fortunately, we had brought some picks, with which we all dug hard, finally managing to push the vehicle forward. Within a short distance of five kilometers we had to dig the wheels out of the snow four times, a total of one whole hour! Later we had to change to the sleighs. Pulled by a caterpillar known as "Climbing Tiger," we traveled forty kilometers without any trouble in the vast forests covered with thick snow. I was told that people of the Hezhe nationality who live along the Wusuli River use sleighs pulled by dogs instead. On the frozen river with a thick layer of ice, their sleighs run as fast as a plane.

While we were climbing the Changbai Mountains, I jumped off the sleigh into the thick snow. Before long, snow permeated my hats and cotton-padded trousers, and as it melted I felt wet and cold and miserable. Lao Lang blamed me. "Why didn't you tie up your trousers and wrap up your legs before you got off?" he demanded.

"A fall into the pit, a gain in your wit." Later, whenever I went outdoors into the snow, I would wrap my legs exactly the same way the northeastern peasants did.

Wonderful Corn Towers

At sunset, I climbed the hills behind the village to enjoy the enchanting beauty of this northern village, whose thatched cottages, storerooms and corn towers were bathed in the golden glow of the evening sun.

The corn tower is a special storeroom which is found only in the villages of the Northeast where corn is one of the staples. Whoever has just been married and set up a family of his own will build one outside his house, first planting four wooden poles and covering them with planks and then fencing it up with wickers and topping it off with willow screens and straw.

When I asked my host about the origin of the corn tower, he told me that grains used to be hoarded in badly ventilated round barns, which led to moldy corn due to the moisture inside. Every household in the sparsely populated northeastern territories had thirty to forty *mu* (1 *mu* = 0.1647 acre) of farmland. When the harvest season in autumn came, the villagers became very busy, cutting rice, millet and sorghum, digging sweet potatoes and picking corn. Soybeans, in particular, would burst and spread all over the fields if they were not harvested in time. Crops carried to the threshing grounds could be buried under a heavy snow if they were not promptly threshed. In order to get everything threshed before the coming

101

of the cold season, the villagers simply moved the ears of corn into the barns without threshing them. As time went on, the corn often got rotten. Then somebody hit upon the idea of building the present corn tower, and before long this tower was seen all over the northeastern villages.

The whole corn tower is well ventilated, so the ears dry gradually inside and will not get moldy for many years. Besides, because the ears are shelled only when they are needed, the flour ground from them is always deliciously fresh.

"The tower hangs about one and a half meters above the ground. Neither chickens nor pigs can reach the grains. So you don't lose a bit when you store them up there," our host said.

Thinking of the grain stealer — the mouse — I could not help asking, "Won't mice get in and eat the maize?"

"Mice? No way!" And he led me to the richly stored corn tower in front of his house. Pointing at the old basins that had been fixed upside down on the poles, he said, "Look, these have long been fixed here to keep the mice away." There, with the slippery enameled basins fixed upside down on the poles, no mice would ever be able to climb up no matter how sharp their paws might be.

Later I discovered that other villages had different ways of keeping away the mice. For example, some villagers wrapped the pillars with plastics. Climbing slippery plastic also rendered mice totally helpless.

In our present world mice cause great damage everywhere. Certain experts have calculated that the world's ten billion mice destroy one-fifth of our grains. That is why the World Organization of Grains and Agriculture has called on every country to declare war on mice in order to save grains. I personally believe that the corn tower provides an answer, at least a partial one. It's a simple structure that could be introduced throughout the world.

WOODSMEN, HUNTERS, AND GINSENG DIGGERS

The saying "The Northeast mountains produce three treasures — ginseng, martens, and antlers" points up the specialities and wealth of the Northeast forests.

Wooden Walls, Wooden Tiles, and Wooden Chimneys

Leaving Dongliao County, we boarded a train heading east for Fusong County, the well-known home of ginseng. As we drove deep into the mountains, we found ourselves surrounded by thick forests that covered the mountain ranges on all sides. Different from the scenery in autumn when the forests are a riot of color, the branches of Korean pines and firs were drooping with heavy snow, while the aspens, lindens, pineapples and chinaberries whose leaves had long since fallen looked fragile in the cold wind. Only the white birches seemed in their glory in the snow.

The snowfall of the previous night had covered the woodland with a top layer of soft snow. Our car was running on the highway through which logs were being transported, leaving behind two deep tracks that stretched ahead of us. After passing a col, we soon caught sight of Changsong Village, which was our destination.

There were 90 families in the village, all of whose houses were built with wooden fences and gateway arches either at the foot of the mountains or by the river. Since these houses, including the storerooms and stables, were all built of wood, the village was simply a "kingdom of wood"! Led by Lao Sun, the local official who was showing us about, we went to visit Gao Wenzhi's family. At first glance, the three principal rooms of the Gaos looked exactly like those of brick houses we had visited, with their smooth white walls. But, looking at them closely, we noticed projecting logs at the four corners, and we learned that the walls were built of logs with joints at both ends. But for the sake of tidiness, and to protect the logs from weathering and cold winds from getting into the house through the seams, the villagers covered both sides of the walls first with mud, then with lime paste. With their smooth surfaces, they looked just like brick walls.

The Gaos were cooking when we arrived. Their smoky chimneys had looked strange from the distance. Getting closer, we found that the chimney outside the west wall was a wooden one, and so was the one outside the east wall.

"Won't they catch fire?" I asked.

"No, the smoke first goes through the *kang*, and by the time it reaches the chimneys its sparks have long been extinguished," Lao Sun explained.

But I had another puzzle: how could they manage to make the holes through the four- or five-meter-long round logs?

Lao Sun smiled. "That's not hard. You simply burn them," he said.

I was told that the inner part of weathered dead old trees that were rotten usually burned more easily than the harder outer part. Therefore, the mountain villagers lighted the rotten part from the bottom and let it char through slowly to the top. How clever of them to make use of the holes this way!

Unlike thatched cottages in the Northeast Plains, houses here are covered with wooden tiles. Seeing the weather-stained wooden tiles I was wondering how much manpower they had to invest in sawing out those tiles. I asked Lao Sun, but he answered smilingly, "They were split with the ax." Split tiles are smoother and more durable because they do not hold rain water. Sawed tiles, on the other hand, cost much more energy, and as their surface is rough and holds water, they do not last longer than three or four years.

It was the season for wood splitting. I saw the young wood splitters piling up a mountain of firewood. Trees felled in winter become brittle when the water inside freezes. Neat bars of ice fall off the logs the moment they are axed. In summer, such logs become dry and tough and are far more difficult to split.

Houses built of wood are warm and earthquake-resistant as well. Yet they might easily catch fire; besides, they cost too much wood. That is why, in recent years, the government has been encouraging the mountain villagers to build brick houses instead.

104

Delicacies from Mountain — Weicai and Mushroom

Our host Gao Wenzhi did not return home from the woods where he had been working until it was nearly noon. A tall thin man of fifty-four with deep-set eyes, Gao was the picture of the intrepid mountaineer with his path-clearing ax rakishly aslant in his waist band.

Our hospitable hostess was an excellent cook. She prepared for us a full table of delicious food with rare mountain ingredients: *xianggu* mushrooms stewed with chicken, sliced pork fried with *mu'er* (an ear-like edible fungus growing on rotten tree trunks), and braised *weicai*. It was my first time sampling *weicai*, in color yellow and greenish at the same time, a most refreshing dish said to have the effect of preventing cancer because of its combination of vitamins. I ate a lot, to the delight of Lao Gao, who confided that he hadn't expected me to like it. He asked his wife to bring in another dish.

Adding foods from time to time is a custom practiced in the Northeast when they entertain guests. The hospitable Northeast folks always prepare large pots and bowls of food and will not feel at ease until their visitors have eaten and drunk their fill. Knowing that I liked *weicai*, after lunch my host fetched from his storeroom a bag of this dry plant made into balls and said, "This is more of what we've just eaten."

Weicai is one of the wild plants in the Northeast mountains. In early summer every year when their curly buds have grown to be as big as a fist, the villagers, both men and women, go in groups with large baskets to the gullies covered with *weicai* and collect this wild plant as they enjoy the beautiful scenery of the mountains. Returning home, the women boil large pots of water in which they wash their *weicai* quickly as they parboil the plants. Taking them out of the pots and dry them in the shade. When the yellow hairs over the new buds are picked, the boiled buds become edible.

There are many ways of eating *weicai*: dipped in thick sauce, it is tasty and crisp. Fried with shredded meat, it is delicious and refreshing. It is also a good ingredient for dumplings and stuffed buns. However, since the villagers have large baskets of them, they cannot eat them up within a short time.

That's why they pickle them so that they can consume them any time they like. Nonetheless, most of their processed *weicai* is sold to outsiders, primarily to neighboring Japan.

As the Chinese saying goes, "Those living on a mountain live off the mountain." Apart from collecting *weicai* the villagers here also pick mushrooms in their spare time. Large numbers of thick tender mushrooms grow out of the decaying logs and the grass from the beginning of summer till the end of autumn. These rare mountain mushrooms seem inexhaustible. As soon as "Jade Emperor Mushrooms," "Tree Chicken Mushrooms," "Blue Mushrooms" and "Earth Spirit Mushrooms" are picked, "Preserved Egg Mushrooms" come up, which will be followed by "Hazel Mushrooms," "Round Mushrooms," "Color Cloud Mushrooms" and "Monkey Head Mushrooms," among others.

What frightens the mushroom pickers most is the possibility of running into black bears or getting lost in the deep forests. That is the reason why they have to go in groups and carry weapons such as axes. The mountain villagers are good at telling directions thanks to the help of the sun, the moon and the stars. But even though they have no trouble in telling east from west and north from south, they still break branches behind them as they go deep into the thick forests. The broken branches hanging on the trees become road signs not only for themselves but also for other villagers who have lost their way.

"What would you do if you really lost your way in the mountains?" I asked.

"If this happens, you must be calm and should not run around wildly like a frightened animal. The simplest thing is to go down from the mountains. If you can find a stream and follow it down the mountains, you will surely find people."

Stumps Worshipped as Mountain Gods

Now we heard Lao Gao's neighbors calling him. The four of them were going together to bring in logs by sleigh from the forests. So we followed them.

Lao Gao urged the Mongolian gazelles that were hauling our sledge to go faster by shouting at them while telling me that the Changbai Mountains were one of the major forestry bases in China. It was now icy cold and trees that had all stopping growing were very brittle and easy to fell. Thanks to the thick snow accumulating in the past months, sledges carrying logs could go easily. Surely that could count as the golden season of the year for tree felling. However, the villagers were not going to carry trees that had been felled, but overgrown ones that had been swept down by winds. They would then saw them into logs and send them to the state-run tree farms.

As it was my first trip to the forests, I became dog-tired and began to pant after a few hours trudging along the narrow paths covered with heavy snow. Then no sooner had I seen trees blown down by winds lying by the roadside than I swept off the snow clinging to them and sat myself down.

"Sitting on these trees is all right," Lao Gao said. "But you must never sit on stumps because they are seats belonging to the mountain gods."

And who were these mountain gods then? Lao Gao explained.

In the old days, the lumberjacks were superstitious, believing that the forests were controlled by mountain gods whom they accordingly worshipped with total devotion, although these protecting gods had neither temples nor statues. In those days, the lumberjacks were usually escorted to the forests by the owners of the tree farms. Wherever they set up their temporary camps (they dug a pit of two meters deep in a dry place, then walled and topped it with logs), the farm owner, as a rule, would find three planks or stones with which to build a tiny cottage by the camp.

Of the three stones the middle one represented the "tiger god" — who would reward worshippers by protecting them against fierce tigers. The left and right stones were believed to stand for the *wudao* (five-direction) god and the god of earth respectively. The mountain god was actually the tiger. At times when they could find no planks or stones, they would simply cut a little house in a large tree, having it serve as a temple and stand for the gods as well.

107

Then the lumberjacks would cut two pine torches as candles and a handful of grass as joss sticks and plant them in front of the "temple." When all the offerings such as buns, cakes, liquor and meat were placed properly, the farm owner would take the lead and together with the lumberjacks kneel down and pray to the gods: "Mighty gods of the mountains, we woodsmen here kowtow to you. May you keep us from all mishaps and disasters." With the offerings thus made, they would burn the grass and pine branches, letting them crack loudly as if they were firecrackers. Thus, their worshipping turned out to be nothing more than praying for the safety of the woodsmen.

In the old days, it was dangerous to work in the forests. Lumberjacks could easily be injured or killed by falling trees or withered branches if they did not exercise the utmost care. The fellers might also be hurt by their own cutting tools while the carriers might injure themselves through slipping, and they were also subject to attack by tigers and bears. As a result, the lumberjacks began to fear the forests so much that they turned to worship of the mountain gods instead.

On the lunar New Year's Day the lumberjacks followed the custom of "cutting the first tree of the year" to predict their fortunes in the new year. After their first breakfast of the year and when the mountain gods were worshipped, the lumberjacks would gather before the "first tree," — a healthy, solid, straight Korean pine that had been carefully selected. It had been partially cut the day before, and the ceremony commenced with the owner of the farm saying his prayers. After a few cuts "the first tree of the year" fell toward the foot of the mountains with a crack. As expected, it was unimpeded by neighboring trees and none of its branches fell off to hurt the woodsmen. Once this was done, all the woodsmen felt relieved, reassured that with the "first tree" cut they could expect a year of safety.

Nowadays, the lumberjacks of the state-run farms all wear safety helmets to protect themselves from falling branches. Since machines are widely used in logging, the number of accidents has greatly decreased. The superstitious custom of worshipping the mountain gods, of course, is no longer observed. But to this day the mountain villagers avoid sitting on stumps or felling trees that are cut in the pattern of a temple.

At dusk, I followed Lao Gao to the timber ground which was piled high with logs sending forth the pungent aroma of rosin. No sooner had the cattle taken a few steps forward as Lao Gao untied the ropes than the one ton load of wood fell off the sledge. The liberated animal cut loose and headed at a trot back toward the mountain village.

Mysterious Customs Practiced by Ginseng Diggers

Manjiang, eight kilometers west of Changsong Village, is a land of hunting and the home of ginseng as well. There I was lost in fascination as Wang Chengwu, a man in his sixties, regaled me with tales about the customs practiced by the local ginseng diggers.

Jilin's ginseng is a rare and valuable medicinal herb widely appreciated at home and abroad. The first Chinese pharmacopoeia, *Shen Nong Scripture of Materia Medica*, written in the first century, records, "It nourishes the five internal organs, relieves uneasiness of the body and calms the mind, rids [it of] evil that causes pathology, sharpens the eyes, cheers the heart, benefits intelligence, strengthens *yin* and invigorates *yang*...." The latest research shows that ginseng can even check cancer cells — the secret of its effectiveness being its special pharmacological composition: ginseng glucoside.

Wild ginseng, known as the "king of herbs" mainly grows in the shade of Korean pines in natural forests. It requires soft humus soil and plenty of rain in summer; it's dormant in winter. It is said that a wild ginseng plant of real medicinal value takes fifty summers and fifty winters to mature. In the case of the artificial ginseng garden, a crop is planted every thirty years, or even less often!

In summer the year before our visit, when such valuable wild plants were bearing red seeds and were easy to identify, Lao Wang led four young men into the forests to search for ginseng. They brought with them axes, saws, swords, wooden choppers, deerhorns and other digging tools, carrying sufficient food for half a month and all the utensils they would need. When they set out for the mountains on an auspicious day settled on in advance, each carried a path-beating stick with a red thread around it to help them feel and see ginseng plants.

The first day they arrived at the area of the mountains where they picked a dry place on which to build a shack and settled down for the night. As the leader of the group, Lao Wang could not fall asleep easily. In the vastness of the forest, where was the best place to look for ginseng that was hidden in the thick grass? He listened attentively to the singing of the birds. There is a nightingale known as a *Bangchui* (woolen club) Sparrow which the local people call ginseng *bangchui*. This bird is in a way a guide to the ginseng seekers. As a ginseng seed eater, its voice becomes hoarse after eating ginseng. If you hear hoarse chirping of a *Bangchui* Sparrow, take the opposite direction and you may find some ginseng.

It is by no means easy to find ginseng in the thick grass of the forests. People can wander for two or three weeks without seeing any shadow of it. Others go into the forests never to return home, lending force to the legend that the ginseng roots are guarded by tigers and snakes!

Because of their mysterious life, ginseng deeply believe in their dreams. It is considered a sign of good luck for somebody to dream of a white-bearded man with a laughing face or a group of dancing fairy maidens. Whoever the dreamer may be, he must be the first up in the morning to prepare breakfast. After breakfast, he must neither move nor wash the stove lest his good luck be carried off or washed away. When he picks up his path-beating stick and sets out, neither the leader of the group nor the members should ask him anything. Rather they must simply follow him to the place where the fairy maidens were dancing to find ginseng. Everyone is careful not to ask the dreamer to reveal the secret; otherwise, all will become bubbles. Of course this does not mean that everyone who finds a ginseng root has had an auspicious dream. And even if you do have good dreams, you may not be able to find any ginseng at all. This strong belief in dreams is primarily a clue to the difficulty in their search for ginseng.

When their search begins, the head of the team walks in the middle with the other members on both sides. They go forward in a row, each two members keeping a space between them no greater than the length of their sticks. They must ensure not to miss a root and call this "pressing the mountains." Another technique is "picking the mountains" where the members scatter all over the place to look for ginseng with their signal being the striking together of the path-beating sticks. Whatever way they take, both speaking and eating are strictly forbidden. It is said that once the ginseng child is scared, the ginseng will disappear. This is all nonsense of course. The real reason is that the searchers must not let anything interfere with their concentration.

Bangchui! Lao Wang at long last found a ginseng root. Following the traditional practice, he immediately planted his stick into the ground and fastened the red thread to the stem of the plant, spreading a piece of red cloth on the earth. It is believed that even if the ginseng child is capable of escaping through the earth, it will never get away once it is tied with the red thread. As a matter of fact, the red thread only marks the spot of the ginseng so that the excited gatherers will not stamp on it when they crowd around. As for the red cloth, it is mostly spread for the ginseng seeds that fall easily. Ginseng seeds are also a precious medicine for hastening parturition.

With the proper rites performed, Lao Wang shouted, "*Bangchui*!" Hearing the signal, his companions responded loudly in one voice, "*Kuaidang*, Sir!" In Chinese, *kuai* means quick while *dang* means smooth. This is the jargon of the forests. Whenever the lumberjacks or ginseng diggers and hunters meet in the forests, they exchange this expression to wish each other luck.

Seeing all the young men had come around, Lao Wang said, "Give me fire!" The lads immediately presented him with a cigarette and lit it for him. It is a rule to offer the ginseng discoverer cigarettes and fan him. By doing this, his grateful fellow team members on the one hand show their appreciation of what he has done and, on the other, calm him down so that in his excitement he will not damage any part of the ginseng. Should any bit of its skin or any one of its thin roots be carelessly cut, ginseng's value will greatly decrease.

After making sure there was no other ginseng around, Lao Wang finally began digging with his wooden chopper and deerhorn. Unlike other plants, whose roots go downward, ginseng plants lie horizontally with their tiny roots growing upward in the top soil. In this way they can absorb the nutrients of the dew and humus directly. So bit by bit, Lao Wang dug away the soil from the outside to the center, from bottom to top.

After less than two hours' careful work, the ginseng, without the slightest damage, was dug out, whereupon Lao Wang's lads brought over some wet moss and birch bark. They put it on the soft moss first, then wrapped it up with the air-proof birch bark so that the ginseng would be safe from the dry weather and remain intact.

Before they left, they peeled off a piece of bark of a nearby Korean pine and cut into the trunk four big marks as well as five small ones. This is called "leaving a good sign." Later when other ginseng diggers came they would know from the "good sign" that five people had once dug up a four-leafed ginseng plant here, so that they, too, stand the chance of finding something.

Later Lao Wang and his four friends dug up another eight ginseng plants—surely a bumper harvest! As a rule, whoever dug the ginseng must carry it back home. When they returned to the shack, Lao Wang said to the lads, "Let's have something sweet!" And they busied themselves making dumplings. Before their meal started, Lao Wang put a bowl with several dumplings in it before the mountain god to give thanks for what they had been given. Back in the shack, he said for all to hear: "The mountain god has had his share. Now it's our turn!" And everyone proceeded to enjoy his "sweet meal" specially prepared to celebrate the day's harvest.

Seeing that they did not have much food left, Lao Wang led his team out of the forests. Back home, the money they got for their ginseng was equally divided among all the members no matter how many plants any one person had dug. As traditionally practiced, the young men bought a pair of rubber shoes — a symbol of thanks — for Lao Wang. They call this reward "Sweeping Dew," for the head of the team always takes the lead in the forests, wetting his trousers and shoes before anyone else.

Hunters' Customs

The endless Changbai Mountains are also a world of wild animals, including "Northeast tigers," lynx, sika deer, musk deer, red deer, sables, bears, wild pigs, racoon dogs, and badgers. Except for the first six animals, which are protected by laws promulgated by the government, any other animals may be hunted.

In early winter when a heavy snow covered the grass and fallen leaves, the hunters got together to discuss and decide who was to be the head and which place that might teem with more animals should be their hunting ground. Then they set out with a few hunting dogs. Of course they carried with them hunting guns and bullets as well as axes, saws, food and cooking utensils. Leading the way, the dogs kept running and jumping ahead of them. Upon their arrival at the spot, the hunters, following the traditional practice, first of all set up a shack and a temple for the mountain god.

The next day they got up early to worship the mountain god and feed their dogs, then started hunting. At first they depended heavily on their dogs. When those in front barked neither nervously nor casually, the hunters immediately knew that they had come upon sleeping bears. When winter comes, each bear finds a hole of some kind in which it can hibernate. Nimble young bears usually climb into the holes of dead trees while clumsier grown ones must dig one out in the ground somewhere and hide themselves inside. With their sharp noses, the dogs can easily find the dens. Now, following the barking, the hunters noticed that the eight dogs had already surrounded a dead tree about six meters tall. The scared bear did not move at all, so those ax holders pressed forward and beat the dry tree while the shooters aimed at the mouth of the tree hole. Meanwhile, the clever dogs had stopped barking. When the frightened animal showed half its body outside the hole, the hunters took aim. No sooner had the shots rung out than the animal fell to the ground. Of course there are bears that will never come out from deep tree holes, in which cases the hunters cut down the trees and drive out the bears with their sticks.

When a bear is killed, the hunters first peel off its skin and get out the gallbladder, the juice of which is used in Chinese traditional medicine. When bears den up, they do not eat or drink anything, nor do they consume any of the gall that is needed in the digestion of foods. So gallbladders collected at this time are much bigger than usual. Once one of the hunters by the name of Li Shixian killed a huge bear of over half a ton, and he got more than seven hundred *yuan* for the gall alone. The paws of the bear are considered an especially fine table delicacy today, so the hunters are sure to take special care to remove them carefully. Finally, they reward the hard-working dogs with the intestines.

When snow accumulates to a depth of half a meter, their winter hunting ends, for both the dogs and the hunters find it difficult to move in the snow. They wait for the next good season for hunting — spring. In early spring the surface of the snow thaws in the daytime but freezes into thin ice at night. The wild pigs with heavy bodies but small trotters sink into the snow easily. Checked by the thick snow underneath, they cannot run as fast as usual. But the hunting dogs with their lighter bodies can run fast on the snow, never sinking into it. And what about the hunters themselves?

Someone, whoever it was, thought up the idea of putting on his feet "running circles," elliptic wicker rings one and a half *chi* (1 *chi* = 1.0936 ft.; half a meter) long and one *chi* wide with ropes crisscrossed inside. With the "running circles" on, the hunters will not sink into the snow since the space their feet contact is naturally enlarged. In this period, as far as hunting wild pigs is concerned, the hunter need not waste any bullets. By using swords alone, they can kill a large group one at a time. Even the dogs, relying on the force of their sharp teeth, can kill pigs easily. Nevertheless, acting in accordance with

114

local custom, the hunters will always release some of the animals. Otherwise, the animals would become extinct, would they not?

In early spring, the hunters usually go out before sunrise. After nine o'clock in the morning when the thin ice starts melting, they take off their "running circles" and return to their camps. To make it easier for the pulling of the felled animals they will stamp a path on the snow, which they call "beating paths."

Among the members of the hunting teams, specific ones are assigned to carry home their game and bring back necessary foods. When they have too much to carry home, they have to bury some in the snow, or crows will eat it up once they discover it.

As the tiger is the mountain god in the legend, every day the hunters worship it before they set out hunting. The heart, liver and the prime flesh of the first hunted animal are always offered to the mountain god after they are cooked. Only when worship is complete can the hunters themselves eat. Wherever they hunt, the hunters never kill tigers deliberately. If they are forced to kill one that is attacking them, they will regret that "a star has fallen" and contend that they had no other way out: "Its coming down from the mountains was all arranged by the Heavenly Emperor, it was not me...." Their worshipping tigers seems superstitious, but it has the secondary benefit of protecting the rare Northeast tigers.

When the hunters leave their headquarters, they never pull down the shack, even placing inside it their leftover matches, grains and salt for those coming later who may possibly lose their way in the forests.

Knowing well the animals' habits, the hunters seek prey by setting traps, iron clips and logs that fall down in heavy winds to hit the beasts. The way they freeze otters is one of the cleverest techniques of all. The hunters put one or two iron sheets near the holes of the frozen rivers which are haunts of the otters. Late at night, after eating some fish and frogs, the otters get onto the iron sheets to shake the water off their bodies and comb their hair unaware that the water they shake off will soon freeze them fast to the metal sheets!

CHAPTER IV

SHANDONG — Home Province of Confucius

CUSTOMS LEFT BY THE STATES OF QI AND LU

The Ancient Wheelbarrow

In mid-autumn, after traveling seven hundred kilometers southeast from Beijing, I arrived at Yishui County, Shandong Province. Lying in the hinterland of the Yimeng Mountains, Yishui belonged to the State of Lu in the period of the Warring States over two thousand years ago. Up till now, remains of the ancient Great Wall built of yellow soil and sand mixed with lime are still to be found at Muling Pass in the Yishan Mountains lying in the north of the county. This ancient wall about a hundred miles long, which was built by the State of Qi in the north, was once the border between Qi and Lu, which is why Shandong Province was later called the "Federation of Qi and Lu."

No sooner had I entered Yishui County than I saw wheelbarrows everywhere either carrying home corn, peanuts and *gaoliang* stalks from the fields or transporting to market fruits, vegetables, wood, etc. Made of planks, the vehicle is over four feet long and three wide. Its wheel, of course, is fixed in the middle with the upper half standing above the board, while the body is deliberately lowered for the sake of stability. Under each of the two shafts is a support which makes loading and unloading easier and enables the pusher to take breaks more conveniently. The pusher usually puts on his shoulders the cloth strap, that is tied to the two ends of the shafts so as to reduce the load his hands must bear.

Following the wheelbarrows into the busy produce market in the county's town, I noticed that nearly all the grains, meats, vegetables and fruits to be sold were put displayed on wheelbarrows rather than counters. To a stranger, it might have looked like an exhibit of the ancient push cart!

I seized the opportunity to chat with an old man selling celery as he took a break for a smoke. He pointed out that just as bicycles figure prominently in the lives of city people, here every family has a wheelbarrow. To make one, no one has to buy planks (there is plenty of wood in the mountains)—just the tire. What they do is ask a carpenter to come and work in their homes, where a wheelbarrow can usually be completed in a day's time. Be it a large flat road or a small mountain path, as long as a person can go through, the barrow will make it without difficulty. Of course going uphill is much harder than down and generally requires pulling.

"Though it looks small, the barrow can handle three or four hundred kilos without any trouble," the old man added proudly.

There are a number of folk tales and historical accounts in which the humble wheelbarrow's role as a friend to man is celebrated. One such concerns General Chen Yi's dependency on it in the liberation campaign in Shandong during the 1940s, for it was with the help of this very one-wheeled vehicle that the villagers kept the army supplied with food and ammunition. Yishui County alone could boast of half a million trips. Later, a legion of wheelbarrows crossed the Yangtze River together with the army, providing troops in the front lines with timely supplies. To acknowledge what they had contributed to the founding of New China, General Chen Yi once said, "Shandong's wheelbarrows have liberated half of China."

The Custom of "Planting Apricots Before the House and Peaches Behind"

To continue our visit, we drove to Niuchangzi Village the next morning. While passing by a mountain village we stopped to ask the way. A woman who was sunning peanuts on the threshing ground directed us to the right road first, then as she learned that we had come from Beijing she presented us with a large bag of peanuts through the window of our car. We had long heard that Shandong people were generous and friendly, and what we were experiencing surely bore that out.

In good time we arrived at Niuchangzi Village. Nestled in the mountains, its circumference being about fifteen square kilometers. The houses, about fifty in number, which were built on the mountainsides next to the road were all shaded by fruit trees. Guided by village official we arrived at the home of Zhu Wenren — our host family. As soon as we took our seats — low square stools — our host Zhu — a man of fifty odd, handed us cigarettes, made tea for us, and presented us plates of apples, pears, and fresh jujubes. Finally, the hostess brought out the taros, chestnuts and peanuts she had just cooked for us. Entertaining guests with dried or fresh fruits — their local products — was a traditional practice among the villagers of the Yimeng Mountains.

In Beijing, taros are scarce — usually imported from the South. When they are available, we stew them with meat. Here in this mountain area where loose soil is perfect for taro growing, it's a popular food. Peasants working in the fields fill up on them when hunger strikes.

An early mention in history of the taro occurred during the Qin Dynasty over two thousand years ago when it was still a wild plant and acquired the name *dunchi* because it resembled a sitting sparrow hawk. It comes up again in the context of first Qin Dynasty emperor's conquest of the State of Zhao (today's Hebei). He forced the slave owners out of their capital. One of these by the name of Zhuo, who had learned that the wild *dunchi* at the foot of the Minshan Mountains in Sichuan could make a staple food, asked for permission to settle there, and once there cultivated the wild plant which became today's edible taro.

Seeing that we had eaten our fill, the host showed us around his orchard where the persimmons hung in profusion like small golden lanterns and the pear trees seemed to be strung with tiny yellow bells. The haws were the most striking — a bounty of red agates. When our host told us that in the previous year he had picked more than three hundred kilos of haws from one particularly well-endowed tree, whose branches were now also bending to the ground with its burden of fruit, I observed, "This must be the 'king' of all haws."

"Not so. The real 'king' is in the neighboring village. I understand it bears about five hundred kilos every year."

Also known as "Mountain Red" locally, haws are sweet and sour. Children are special fans of them when they are strung into sweet gourds in the winter known as an appetite stimulator, haws are believed to reduce blood pressure and cholesterol, still more reasons for their popularity in the cities.

As the saying goes, "Those living on a mountain live off the mountain." The villagers of the Yimeng Mountains get most of their incomes from the large numbers of fruit trees they have planted all over the mountains, earning also, of course, from growing wheat, corn, rice, and sorghum with the help of the water they store up in the mountain streams as our host recited their folk rhyme with visible pride:

> March cherries and April apricots,
> "Red May" and "Fresh June" come in pairs;
> (Two species of peaches ripening at different times.)
> July walnuts, August pears,
> September persimmons fill the fair,
> In Red October haws are never rare.

Like the trees that bloom and bear fruit each year, the customs related to them survive from generation to generation. Some of their standard rules are: "Apricots must be planted in front of the house while peaches are planted behind" and "Elms in the front and pagoda trees at the back." Since elm seeds are believed to be "seeds of money," by planting elms in front of the house, the homeowner hopes that he will get rich some day. Since "apricot" and "happiness" have the same pronunciation in Chinese, the villagers believe that by planting apricots in front of their houses they have opened the door to happiness. As for planting peaches in the back, that is done because "peach" has the same pronunciation as "escape" in Chinese, so the homeowner fears that good luck will escape if peach trees are planted in the front.

Shandong Baked Pancakes and Yishui Mountain Scorpions

In the evening we were invited to dinner by the village official Zhu Wende. Entering his house, we caught sight of a table covered with a great variety of food. What interested me was that the chicken head lying on the dish of stewed chicken was pointing right at me. "It is always the head that counts. Offering the precious chicken head to guests is our custom here," explained our guide Lao Liu. "Only when you pick up the chicken head can the rest of us start eating." Hearing this, I immediately picked it up as kept nodding at the host to show my gratitude to him for all his hospitality.

A while later when the hostess brought up a cold dish, the guide shouted happily, "Oh, it is 'Yishui Mountain Scorpions'! What a rare dish!"

Neither my photographer companion Xiao Lu nor I understood what he said. We looked at the platter closely and found there nothing but fierce-looking scorpions. So how could that be called a famous or rare dish? Seeing our puzzlement, Lao Zhu explained the whole matter to us. There are many scorpions in the mountains of Yishui County. In the spring of every year, the local people go up into the mountains where they lift up stones and pick up scorpions they find with bamboo clips and put them into bottles. Back home they boil them with salt and then soak them in oil in an earthen jar, where they never go bad, and are kept for special guests. "Come on, try it!" urged Lao Zhu and popped two into his mouth with much ado to show us what we were missing.

Seeing the two of us taking no action at all, our guide joined the campaign. "This is a rare food found only in Yimeng," he enthused. "You can find them mentioned this way in cookbooks. And that's not all. It's said that regular eating of scorpions will prevent boils from developing and even have a curative effect on some cancers." Only then did we boldly take action, and indeed we had to admit to a unique flavor. The aftertaste reminded me of Lu Xun's (a great modern writer and thinker) words: "The first person who ate crabs is surely worth admiring and respecting, for he would not have dared were he not a brave man." It must have taken an equal amount of courage for the Yimeng villagers to bring scorpions to the table!

Once our drinking was done, our hostess served us the staple — Shandong baked pancake, or *jianbing* in Chinese. Though I had long heard of it, I had never tried one before. Following the lead of Lao Zhu, I opened the *jianbing* that had been folded into a rectangle, putting into it onions and pickled Chinese toon buds. No sooner had I bit into it than Lao Zhu asked, "How is it?"

"Not bad," I answered approvingly as I chewed. "The onions are fresh, the toon buds are tasty, and the pancake is very well made."

Jianbing is the traditional staple for all the villagers of southern Shandong Province. Listen to what they say about it: "We feel weak all over if we miss *jianbing* for one day."

As we talked I came to understand that their *jianbing* had at least three outstanding points: first, it is made from coarse grain in a delicate way; it is delicious, and it "sticks to the ribs." Actually, this mountain area produces mainly sweet potatoes, corn and other coarse grains. The villagers grind them all into a flour which is ultimately transformed into a pancake that is as thin as paper. Such cleverly cooked food is not only tasty but lasts a long time. The next point is that the pancake is easy to keep as it is thin and dry. One may be consumed three to five days after being made — and even as long as two to three weeks; — a great time saver since this way they do not have to cook every day. Finally, it is highly portable. As the villagers often work in the mountains two or even four kilometers away from home, they have to bring lunch with them, so they simply put onions, thick sauce, Chinese toon buds or other vegetables in the *jianbing*, fold it up, wrap it with a piece of gauze, and tie it to the waist or carry it on the shoulders. Slightly warmed by the body, the pancake remains soft and makes a perfect instant lunch. There is no formal record in history about *jianbing*, but in a collection of humor (*Qi Yan Lu*) written by Hou Bai of the Sui Dynasty, the solution to a riddle given to his ministers, when Emperor Qigaozu was entertaining them with a banquet, turned out to be *jianbing*.

From this we conclude that *jianbing* has a history of at least 1,400 years.

However, during our stay in Yishui County we also heard a very popular folk tale about *jianbing*: During the Warring States Period over two thousand years ago, the State of Qin attacked the State of Lu but failed to capture Lu's capital because of its high city walls. Hearing that Lu Ban, who was later cherished as the master of carpentry, had invented a kind of ladder specially used for the climbing of city walls, Qin, managed by devious means to acquire the services of Lu Ban. Mozi, a philosopher of Lu, became terribly worried when he learned of this. So one day he went to visit Lu Ban, bringing along some native *jianbing*. At sight of it Lu Ban could not wait a minute longer; he immediately grabbed one and proceeded to devour it. "I haven't had any *jianbing* for such a long time," he said blissfully. "Wonderful!"

When Lu Ban had finished, Mozi asked, "Do you want to have it often, or was that enough to last you?"

"Of course I'd like to have it often."

"No. I think you want no more than you've just had."

Lu Ban asked what he was driving at, and Mozi at last told him. "The ladders you are making for Qin will be used in their attack against Lu. Once your homeland is conquered, how can you have more *jianbing*?" Lu Ban understood his point. Without a word he collected his blueprints and returned home with Mozi.

We got up at daybreak the next morning in order to watch the housewife next door making *jianbing*. The moment she rolled across the hot iron pan (two feet in diameter) her dough kneaded from sweet potato starch and corn flour, a thin sheet was left on the utensil. She evened the sheet with a bamboo strap and waited for a second. Soon the edge stuck up, and a round sheet of *jianbing*, thin as paper, was made. Taking it up while it was still hot and soft, she folded it into a rectangle. Then it could either be served immediately at the table or stored for quite some time.

She was making *jianbing* and adding firewood all by herself, yet everything was in neat order. I could not help marveling

123

at her efficiency, but she made light of it. "There's nothing to it," she said, "I've been doing this ever since I was a child." And she picked up another sheet of dough. It is said that men from here in choosing wives never forget to ask about the future partners' skill in rolling *jianbing*.

Marriage Customs Differ From One Place to Another

Bidding farewell to Zhu Wende, we got on the road again. Soon we discovered a young man ahead of us pushing a young woman in a wheelbarrow. Wearing a fresh flower in her hair, the young man's passenger was wearing a red print blouse, a dark blue pair of trousers, and a pair of embroidered cotton shoes. "That's the traditional way Yimeng women dress themselves," said our guide. I quickened my steps to catch up with the pair.

Zhu Fasheng, twenty-three, was a thoughtful young man with heavy eyebrows and large eyes. His wife Zhang Xiufeng, also twenty-three, had just been fetched by her husband from her parents' home where she had gone for a two-day visit. Falling into conversation with the attractive couple, I learned they had been married for half a year. Would she mind giving an account of her wedding day? Not at all!

Her wedding day also found her seated in a wheelbarrow but that one was carpeted in red and had a beautifully decorated temporary roof. Led by a band that played continuously along the way, she was accompanied by several other wheelbarrows that carried her dowry of red-painted furniture, bedding, clothing and other household goods. Behind them were people from both sides of the family escorting her to her new home.

When she entered her new house, her sister-in-law took off the kerchief from her head with a dough rolling stick and reached up to hang it on the barn, thus symbolically praying for abundant harvests of all crops. Even though the bed was not high, to get onto it she had to mount a bench on which had been placed a plate of steamed cake, or *gao*, a homonym of another *gao* (high). The symbolism here was that the relatives and friends of the couple expected their social positions to become higher and higher, and their life to get better and better.

When she took off her cotton jacket on the bed, the jujubes, chestnuts, peanuts, and coins that had all been previously hidden inside fell out, spreading all over the bed covering. With all the Chinese homonyms possible with this downpour, well-wishers expressed their hope that the wife would give birth to a promising son at the earliest possible date and that they would become richer and richer. At this point all the onlookers crowded around and competed for the jujubes and peanuts, filling the bridal room with laughter and teasing. Only now could the bride as, a new member of the family, get down from the bed to propose toasts to her guests. Thus completing her account, Zhang Xiufeng drew out a handful of jujubes from her basket and put them in my hand. A nice moment.

The young wife's basket woven of slivers looked like a silver ingot, and that is just what it was called — *yuanzi*, which means silver ingot in Chinese. The ivory *yuanzi* had to be woven in cellars known as "mud houses." It is said that only the cellars are humid enough to prevent the slivers from breaking. Later when we went to visit Zhuge District, which is believed to be the hometown of the ancient Chinese strategist Zhuge Liang, we saw along the way many other women carrying *yuanzi*, each covered with red cloth.

"I'm sure that three days from now someone will get married here," said our guide. According to local custom, anyone who receives an invitation to a wedding should prepare pork, fish, chicken, sheet jelly, large steamed buns with red dots on the top and other gifts, then send them all in a *yuanzi* (or *yuanzi*s) to the bridegroom three days before the wedding. Naturally, these food gifts are welcome to the family of the bridegroom.

However, just as the saying goes: "Customs differ from village to village while practices differ from community to community," the customs observed within Zhuge District differ from village to village. Such different customs caused quite a misunderstanding when a young man from Dayetou Village married a girl from Shanggu Village. As the wedding drew near, it became an occasion for talk that nobody from the bride's village had sent over any gifts, a situation which continued right up until the Big Day itself, although on that day at least a dozen or so congratulators from Dayetou did show up. They were all well-dressed, but still came empty-handed. People of the host village began buzzing among themselves: "Have they come for the wedding feast, or did they really come for a funeral?" (Traditionally, when an old villager dies here, his friends and relatives will come to pay their respects, but they bring either nothing or at the most some "paper money" to be burned before the coffin as a fine wish for the dead.)

It turned out that the custom of sending gifts was hardly practiced in Dayetou. What they did instead was send the young couple on the wedding day a gift of cash called "Happy Money." They could not have anticipated that this different practice would cause such a misunderstanding!

"How far is Shanggu Village from Dayetou?" I asked our guide.

"No more than fifteen kilometers, although the winding mountain paths makes it seem longer," answered our guide.

"Mt. Tai's Shi Gandang"

While traveling in Shandong, I saw from time to time stone tablets inscribed "Mt. Tai's Shi Gandang" at the entrance to a village — sometimes at the corner of a house, sometimes on a wall. But why? What was it for? I soon learned that in the old days, due to their lack of scientific knowledge, people were governed by many taboos in choosing the site for a house. For example, it was their sincere belief that houses must never be built on the sites of temples, graveyards, ancient battlefields, by the gate of a town, at the beginning of a street, or on a spot directly facing the peak of a hill or mountain. Should they be unable to avoid building a house on one of these spots, they would have to lay there a stone with "Mt. Tai's Shi Gandang" carved on it. This stone was believed to be capable of keeping away all evils, turning bad luck into good fortune, protecting the inhabitants from all troubles.

The setting of the stone is believed to be related to the feudal emperors' *feng* and *chan* in Mt. Tai: building an altar and placing on it sacrifices to Heaven was called *feng* while cleaning

Liangfu Hills and making offerings to Earth was known as *chan*. It was perfect autumn weather and we did not miss the opportunity to climb Mt. Tai. (In China there are five mountains which were outposts of ancient China located at the four corners of the empire, with one in the middle. Mt. Tai was — and is — the eastern one of that group and the western one is Huashan in Shaanxi. And then there is South Hengshan in Hunan and North Hengshan in Shanxi, while the central one is Songshan in Henan.)

In my climb I was dazzled by the awesome peaks, steep cliffs, cascading waterfalls, busily running brooks, hardy green pines and lacy clouds. Unique to Mt. Tai are the inscriptions along all its paths. These stone inscriptions, over a thousand in number, are either primitive and simple, vigorous, or delicate, with the main styles of Chinese calligraphy represented: *kaishu* (regular script), *lishu* (official script), *caoshu* (cursive hand), *xingshu* (running hand), and *zhuanshu* (seal-character style). Many of these beautiful inscriptions were left by emperors of various dynasties when they were making their offerings to Heaven and Earth in the mountains. The real purpose of the emperors' religious practice was to show to the populace that their sovereignty was granted by Heaven so as to consolidate their power.

In 219 B.C. to show off his glorious success in unifying China and his concentrated power, Qinshihuang, first emperor of China, had roads opened all over Mt. Tai so that he could ride there in his carriage under escort of the royal guards when he was performing the grand ceremony of *feng* and *chan*. What he did was cherished as a great act for quite some time. Then Emperor Hanwu of the Han Dynasty not only ascended the mountains to make sacrifices to Heaven but also cleverly erected a characterless stone tablet at the very top of Mt. Tai, meaning his ability in managing civil and military affairs was too great to put into words. Participating in these grand ceremonies of *feng* and *chan* was considered the greatest possible honor that could come to them by the court officials. The historiographer Sima Tan, father of the great historian Sima Qian, for one reason or other never had an opportunity to accompany the emperor to Mt. Tai, and he was said to have been so distressed that he was still weeping over it on his deathbed.

Its age now established at 2.5 billion years, it was always known to go way back in time and was referred to as early as there are records as the "Grandfather of all the mountains in China." The ceremonies of *feng* and *chan* and the inscriptions of the various emperors turned it into "the Chief of the five Mts." Then it became "a pole in the east" that "supported the sky and held the sun," symbolizing national stability and social peace. Therefore, people began to erect stone tablets inscribed with "Mt. Tai's Shi Gandang" by their houses or at the entrances to their villages.

According to the folk legend, Shi Gandang was a brave and strong young man who lived on Mt. Tai and made his living by selling whatever firewood he could gather. One day, when this young man— an expert, at *gongfu* (Chinese boxing) — went to sell firewood in town, he happened to read a poster signed with the name Wang: whoever could subdue the devil who was tormenting Wang's family would be awarded half of his property; and if the victor was an unmarried man, he could marry his daughter with all his blessing.

It turned out that this devil was coming to Wang's house in a gust of wind every night and torturing his daughter until she was half dead. First Wang had asked Taoist priests for help, but their magic signs failed against the devil. So Wang put up his poster to find help where he could. Since Shi Gandang was always ready to right wrongs, he decided to take on this devil, and he hid himself inside Miss Wang's bedroom with a magic sword. When the devil showed up he shouted, "Mt. Tai's Shi Gandang is right here!" Whereupon the terrified devil beat an instant and hasty retreat. His deed accomplished, Shi claimed his bride and the young couple embarked on a life of bliss together.

But the hero was not left free to rest on his laurels, for the devil began to torture people in other villages. The harassed villagers, having heard of Shi's glorious success, naturally enough turned to him for help. However, no sooner did he

128

drive the devil out of one village than it started in on the next one. Finally, Shi's intelligent wife suggested, "Why not tell them to carve your name on stone tablets and put them by the entrances to their villages and on their walls? This might be enough to drive the devil away." Shi immediately passed on her suggestion, and all the villages set up stone tablets bearing the inscription "Mt. Tai's Shi Gandang."

Today, people no longer erect such stone tablets when building a new house. But Shi Gandang's spirit to challenge Nature and subdue devils has been a source of inspiration from generation to generation.

CUSTOMS OF FISHING VILLAGES

Cottages with Seaweed Roofs

Surging waves rebounded from the moles of the fishing port, creating snow-white spray. With pennants fluttering in the wind at the top the masts of the fishing boats anchored there looked like a small fleet in this harbor of Rongcheng County's Dayu Island known as "Raft Ring." With the rocky hills behind and the Yellow Sea before it, this harbor lies in the south of Shandong Peninsula, just two kilometers from Shidao Island, a well-known fishing port in the North.

More than two thousand years ago, the State of Qi, known as the "Great Proud State," was starting its booming industry of fishing and salt production along the coast of Shandong Peninsula which was under its jurisdiction. Nonetheless, Dayu Island was still but a reed marsh 170 years ago, its first settlers a group of hopeful migrants who planned to seek a living on the other side of the sea. While they waited for the next ferry, they went up into the hills to cut down some trees and make a raft from which to fish. But when they did go fishing, they happened to catch a lot so they changed their minds and decided to settle on the island instead. One day they caught a hairtail which was much bigger than a hairtail any of them had seen before. And that is how the island got its name, for *Daiyu* means *hairtail*. Because *dai* and *da* were so close in sound, people mispronounced *dai* as *da*, turning it into "Dayu Island." Twenty-seven years ago, the local people built a fishing harbor where their ancestors once fished and made rafts, and to show their lasting respect for these industrious forebears, they named it "Raft Ring."

The houses of the 1,800 or more families huddle close together on the seaside, their tall, pointing roofs of seaweed looking like ill-fitting tapered hats on children's heads. Like old clothes whose colors have faded from of frequent washing, the roofs have turned white or gray in the long years of hard weather. Scattered over the roofs were tufts of grass interspersed with small yellow or red flowers standing close by the TV antennae in the wind.

In the fishing villages of Hui'an County, Fujian Province along the southeast coast of China (See Chapter XIII), houses are built with rectangular slabs of granite from floor to roof. To resist typhoons that attack from May to October every year. But then why were the roofs of the islanders here built with seaweed? Could they withstand typhoons? Lao Song, the village official who received us, pointed at one thatched house and said humorously, "As far as age is concerned, it could be my grandfather. I'm sure it's much more than eighty years old. But you can see it's still in very good shape. I understand that some of these houses have been standing for over a hundred years without ever a need of repair.

The seaweed that grows over the shallow beaches is about one meter long and one centimeter wide with a smooth surface and tough fiber. After drying in the sun it is first tied into neat bunches, then laid closely on the frame of the roof. The passing of time only serves to toughen it, gradually turning it into a waterproof coating. Since the roof is also peaked and slanting, raindrops can never stay long, and both ends of the ridge are fastened so tightly that the roof is strong enough to resist typhoons. Besides, typhoons attacking this island are much milder than they are in Fujian, and there are not that many anyway.

Walking around the village, I saw that the western part of it was crowded with new brick houses. Then I was told that the building of a house with four rooms needed about five tons of seaweed, which is a growing rarity today. In addition, a thatched house's seaweed — with the building process it entails — make for much higher costs than for a brick house. So young people usually build brick houses instead. Old people, however, still prefer living in thatched houses, believing they are more comfortable — warmer in winter but cooler in summer.

An Old Fisherman's Family

After all, it was a fishing family! Entering Song Qisu's house, I saw that a corner of his yard was used as a coop for chickens and ducks that were fenced with a strap of worn fishnet. A used buoy cut into two halves became durable dippers. Our old hostess was sitting on the *kang* knitting away at her net.

On the *kang* were a row of "paper *dou*" (a unit of dry measure for grain = 1 decaliter) containing grains, dried shrimp and shelled shrimp. These containers were made of paper pulp, yellow soil, and a seaweed called *niumao cai*, or "ox hair weed." A mixture of these three components is first pasted over a jar, and then when it dries in the shade, they take it off and coat it with paper. Our dexterous hostess even decorated the paper vessels with papercuts, including flowers, birds and fishes, turning these homemade containers into folk art.

Learning of our visit, our old host had immediately returned to join us from the Center for the Aged. At sixty-five, Song Qisu was an outspoken man, still energetic despite his gray hair and rather deliberate manner. During his past forty years of fishing, he had worked side by side with his fishing comrades, sharing everything with them — sorrows as well as joys. Now he has retired like his old friends, but they still love to be together, and so the village has built a recreation center for them so that they can continue to share their lives.

We sat on the *kang*, talking about their family. Theirs was a traditionally big family with four sons. The eldest one was a fisherman on a modern fishing boat, the second worked at building houses in the village, while the third and the fourth served on a farm growing seaweed. They were all married, and their wives were either working in the fishnet factory or in the cannery. They all had fairly good incomes. All of them, except the second son and his wife, who lived by themselves at the west end of the village, lived in the same double compound. The aged host took pride in talking about his big family.

As it was getting late, he said to his wife, "It's time we started cooking. Let's treat our guests to what we fishing folks have." Then his wife and her daughters-in-law all busied themselves preparing the meal, some mincing fish meat for the stuffing of dumplings in the yard, others cooking in the kitchen. Our old host placed the low table in the middle of the *kang*, and to show his consideration, covered our mat seats with blankets and sheets.

Soon a rich meal of eight dishes and one soup was served. All the courses, including the stewed Spanish mackerel, braised fish balls, jellyfish, and shellfish soup, were products of the village. It was indeed a feast of sea food. Of these delicacies I liked the "stir-fried dried shrimps with cucumbers" most — so very tender and fresh. Dried shrimps, or *haimi*, are a kind of eagle-talon-shaped prawn. Such prawns sink into the seabed and bury themselves in sand during the daytime. The only time to catch them is at night when they come up to the surface to feed. One catch may weigh as much as one or two tons. Then as soon as they return home, the fishermen boil them in salty water. When their shells are stripped after they are dried, the shrimps become a nutritious delicacy of the sea.

The main course was dumplings with Spanish mackerel filling, much more tasty than those made with pork stuffing. Xiao Lu, the photographer accompanying us, said as he relished them: "Once you've had these, you cannot like any other dumplings."

Our host kept toasting us. As I watched him finishing one cup after another, I could not resist complimenting him on his capacity. He just laughed, "This is nothing at all," he told me. "Come to one of our Fishermen's Days during Grain Rain time and you'll see some *real* drinking!"

The Fishermen's Day

Grain Rain is a traditional holiday celebrated in the fishing villages in Shandong. To the villagers there it is nearly as important as Spring Festival. It takes days for the villagers to make preparations for the local festival, for which they slaughter many fowls and buy meat and liquor in quantity. The women also steam large date buns that symbolize peace and happiness. Fishermen returning from the sea pick the biggest and finest fish for this special occasion. If they catch a porgy, which carries the meaning of both "happiness" and "good luck" in Chinese, and they are able to share it with guests, they will believe that they have begun a new year of good luck and happiness.

On the day of Grain Rain every family burns joss sticks and sets off firecrackers. While their wives and children are enjoying themselves at home, the fishermen dressed in their holiday best usually bring along with them liquor and rich meats and gather either on the *kang* of their captain or at the fishing port or at the seashore. After the captain makes his offering — the first cup of liquor — to the Dragon King, everyone digs into their heavy slices of meat and begins to down large bowls of alcohol while playing finger guessing games. They will not stop drinking until they have become drunk. Only after night falls will the drunken fishermen lying over the fishnets and buoys on the seashore get up and begin their unsteady walk toward the central square of the village for the annual film.

Of the twenty-four divisions of the solar year in the traditional Chinese calendar, Grain Rain — or *Guyu* in Chinese — means: "Rains bring grains." This is a warm, rainy period when crops begin to grow. During these days, northerners plant melons and beans while busy southerners transplant rice seedlings. But how did Grain Rain become a major festival for the local fishermen? "This is the day when we wait for the coming of our annual big catches," our host told us.

As the fishing saying goes, "Grain Rain arrives and all the fishes come up alive." When Grain Rain is over, prawns, croakers, hairtails, herring, chub mackerel, butterfish and other fishes that have hidden from the cold winter in the seabed or in the South begin to return in search of food and to spawn in the Bohai Sea and the Yellow Sea. Large in size and many in number, the fish have to swim through this water, thus creating for the fishermen here a golden fishing season. And after the over joyed fishermen celebrate the Grain Rain Festival, they go fishing on the sea for over a month, not missing a day.

A ritual that inaugurates the Grain Rain Festival amused us. Beforehand the clever wives are required to make white rabbits with flour and water and steam them. Then on the festival day when the husbands come into the houses early in the morning, they suddenly thrust the rabbits to their breasts in an enactment of the old custom of "catching a rabbit and tying it to the waist." They then hand the white rabbits over to their husbands, who must carry them for their value as a good luck charm to assure not only happiness but safe voyages and abundant catches.

"But why do you have to drink till you are drunk?" I wondered.

"That's a traditional practice of the fishing village. It is said that only when you get drunk on Grain Rain will everything go well with you in the new year." Our aged host also told us that even as the fishermen lay drunk on the ground, they still had to drink up whatever was left in the bottles — either that or discard anything left over. Bringing liquor back home would ensure a bad year for them.

Unique Jar-shaped Fishnet

Early the next morning when I was walking on the beach I saw some fishermen carrying bamboo rods of five to six meters long with which they were going to make square frames. What were the frames for? I went over to ask them and was told that since autumn floods were coming they had to fix the frames for the jar-shaped net. Then when all was ready they would drive the stakes into the seabed and hang up their net for fishing.

Fishing with hanging nets is a special technique found only in Shidao Island. After driving the stakes into the seabed, they tie the two ropes from the stake to the two ends of the bottom rod of the frame, then fix buoys to the two ends of the upper rod. In this way, the frame is hung up in the sea. Fixed to the bamboo frame is a long square net, inside which lies a double-layered small net with opposing splinters hung up by another buoy. Fish that come with the currents and swim into it will find no way out. The fishermen only need to go and pull up the net for the catch once a day.

"Look, those are buoys." Directed by the fisherman's pointing finger, I saw many sealed jars covered with mooring ropes, which is how the name "jar-shaped fishnet" came into being.

In the old days it was by no means easy for the fishermen, who often had to row sampans against the winds and currents of the sea to a depth of ten meters to drive the one-meter stakes into the seabed until they went about three or four meters deep, and hang up the nets. Therefore, shortly before the arrival of the floods, the fishermen would organize stake-driving teams, each with eight fishing boats. They then would pool their money to buy a pig and slaughter it before the temple of the Dragon King. After they had made their sacrifice — the whole pig — to the Dragon King, the fishermen would also make three bows to the southwest.

Because the Shandong Peninsula is also a promontory, the inshore currents flow southwest with the rising tide and northeast with the ebbing tide. The reason the fishermen bowed to the southwest is that they did not want their long floating nets to be swept away in the surging waves and then become twisted around the ropes. Should this happen, they not only would fail to catch any fish but also would have to fix the nets again.

Returning from the temple, the fishermen would all dine together at the captain's home. The next day, eight boats that were loaded with nets, ropes, and bamboo frames came together to the spot where they would fix the nets. Two boats were tied to one another to form a driving vessel, which was naturally more buoyant and stable. When the fir pole with a stake fixed to it was pressed into the seabed through the open space between the boats, the young men proceeded to take turns hitting it with sledge hammers to the beat of their work song. You can realize how hard their work was when you consider that they had to fix 30 nets every day for nearly a month.

"Compared with the modern purse seines and trawl nets, such stake nets are primitive, for they passively wait for fish to go in. Sooner or later, they will all be replaced," said a fisherman. "However, since they are still effective, why not use them for a while longer!" Sentiment may have played a role here. We were told that when the prime fishing days came, swarms of floating buoys covering the sea could be seen from the top of the hills behind the village.

An Adventure on the Sea

After five days of anxious waiting, we at last had a clear day. Taking advantage of the favorable weather, the fishermen moved vegetables, foods, sweet water, firewood, and diesel oil drums onto their boats and set sail. Starting from the early 1960s, their sampans— about thirteen meters long and two or three wide— were installed with propellers powered by 20 h.p. marine diesel engines, thus ending the hard labor of rowing with sculls and setting sails.

At four o'clock in the afternoon, Lao Zhang, head of the inshore fishing team, led us to the fishing port. He spoke at the top of his voice to a fishing boat about to leave the port, "Captain Lan, bring these two reporters from Beijing with you. They have stood the test. Don't you worry about anything." Now I caught on that our half day of being tossed about was in fact a dry run— a kind of test— for our real voyage!

Captain Lan stretched out a large work-coarsened hand to help me first onto the bow and then point me to the aft deck. According to their fishing customs, the bow is the most important place on board and must not be occupied by anybody but the fisherman working there. Also, nobody is allowed to lie on the decks. And when sleeping in the cabins, no one should sleep with his face downward, for to do so would be viewed as courting the danger of capsizing.

However, these traditional rules seem to mean something

136

when you think about them carefully. If you lingered at the bow, you would surely get into the captain's or any wheelman's line of vision, making navigation much more difficult. Besides, since the narrow bow tends to toss about considerably, it is not as safe as the cabin. As for lying on the deck, doing that not only puts you in the way of the people working there, but puts you in danger of falling into the sea once you are sound asleep.

Our sampan began to sail toward the fishing spots. Looking at the vast blue sky, the endless green sea, and the sea gulls flying overhead, I felt excited and worried at the same time. So I asked the captain, "The weather will not change, will it?" Lao Lan — a heavy-set man in his late forties who radiated the confidence born of more than twenty years of fishing experience — said as he peered at the sky: "Don't you worry. We'll have at least a couple of beautiful days."

Fishermen on sea fear unexpected storms more than anything. In the old days when the weather suddenly changed and the roaring sea pushed ashore waves as high as hills, the old women of the fishing village would hurry with their grandchildren to the temple of the Dragon King to make prayers and burn joss sticks. The young wives, on the other hand, would go up into the hills behind the village to watch desperately for the return of their husbands. Fishermen's bodies could not even be found if they were lost at sea. If that should happen, the tradition was for the family to ask a carpenter to carve a wooden body, dress it in burial clothing and bury the coffin in the hills at the back of the village. They needed a grave to make offerings to every year.

In the past when they had no weather forecast, the fishermen made predictions based on the knowledge and lore passed on to them by the older generations. Early in the morning they would observe the sky and the clouds around them: "Three sides dark with one side bright, then wind will come from the bright side"; "Three sides bright with one side dark, then wind will come from the dark side." They also went to the seashore to listen to the waves — if the waves in the east were noisy, then there would be an east wind, which was expressed in the adage: "Noisy eastern waves means an eastern wind." They could also forecast the weather of the following spring's fishing season through the winter days. The local saying goes, "A foggy day in the nine nine-day periods (starting from winter solstice) means a hundred stormy days." For example, if the fourth day of the third nine-day period was a foggy one, the fishermen would make a mark on the wall: for the first hundred days, starting from this very day, they must not go fishing on the sea because there would be windstorms.

"Nowadays we have weather forecasts," said Lao Lan, looking toward the cabin where his transistor lay. "We can receive them from Beijing, Tianjin, Dalian, Jinan, or Yantai. Listening to the forecasts several times a day is certainly better than depending on our own experience."

Lao Lan told us that Dayu Island also had offshore fishing teams whose power boats with trawl nets and seines went so far out to see that a return trip would take about three weeks. But small boats like theirs could only fish inshore and had to return home once every three or five days. "Today we are going to catch some Spanish mackerel and we'll spend one night on the boat. Early tomorrow morning we'll come back." We could tell that he was trying to comfort us and cheer us up.

Before fish detectors were invented, fishing with seines mostly depended on "Fish Eyes" — veteran fishermen whose rich experience and sharp eyes enabled them to spot shoals on the sea. The "Fish Eye" would bring sufficient fresh water and foods before setting sail to last a while and seat himself in a box fixed at the top of the mast, watching as if his eyes beamed radar across the sea. If he discovered any darkening spot in the water, which meant there were schools of black carp, he would blow his whistle to signal his comrades to take action.

After the boat was anchored at dusk, the captain told Xiao Wang to light the lamp on the mast, a signal that would prevent ships sailing at night from bumping into her. Now they began to release their fishnet which was six to seven thousand meters long and about ten high, one end tied to the boat, the other carried by a buoy drifting from left to right. Spanish

138

mackerel that hid deep in the water in the daytime would swim up in search of food and get caught in the net.

When it was pitch dark, Xiao Wang went into the cabin to prepare supper, a simple meal. First he heated the steamed buns that they had brought from home, then fried two dishes of vegetables, and that was it.

As the boat kept tossing on the vast dark sea, I found myself growing increasing drowsy and headed for my bunk where the sound of waves beating against the sampan lulled me quickly to sleep. It was still dark when I woke up, but the captain and his men had already collected their fishnet, filling the fish cabin with a multitude of live mackerel.

Worshipping Turtles and Dolphins

The sun rose slowly, its dazzling rays reflecting in the clear sea. Suddenly I caught sight of a dim outline of an island ahead. "What island is it?" I asked the captain as I pointed to it. "Sushan Island," he said curtly, clearly displeased. A moment later the engineer whispered to me, "Out on the sea, no one is supposed to shout or point at anything." Oh, no! I had violated a taboo.

The fishermen here have so many taboos it's hard to avoid offending. Such expressions as "upside down" and "turn over" any word that might carry a connotation of capsizing — must never be spoken either on the boats or in the fishing village. That is why teachers at school who want to tell the pupils to turn over to the next page have to say "Tune to the next page" instead. Also, at the sight of mountains, islands, or big fish, one must never shout, still less point at them when he is on the sea.

I asked about the origin of these customs and they told me that fishermen going to sea often determined their courses, fishing spots and the positions of their boats with the help of the mountains and islands. In the course of time, they began to worship these objects, which meant that pointing at them casually became bad form.

This reminds me of a story which I heard when I was in the fishing village:

139

Long long ago there lived a young man in Dayu Island who was disrespectful to his parents. One day when he was at sea with some other fishermen, they suddenly noticed a big fish chasing them. Everybody was scared out of his wits. The captain began to burn joss sticks and say prayers, throwing into the sea buns and rice. But this did not work either. The big fish kept following them instead of eating the food. The captain suddenly thought of the unfilial young man: "Could this have been caused by the disrespectful lad who has violated the heavenly principles and must be punished by the big fish now?" He ordered the young man to kneel down before the fish and swear that he would be filial to his parents from now on. The lad did as he was told, and the big fish soon disappeared from the scene. And the errant son was as good as his word, obeying his parents and taking good care of them from that moment on.

Of course, that is only a legend, and the "big fish" in the fable was in fact a whale.

When I was a child living on the seaside in Guangdong, I often saw turtles sold in the fish market. It is said that Indonesian fishermen also use a "sucking fish" — a fish with a "dish" on its head that can suck up the shell when catching turtles. But the fishermen of Dayu Island call the turtle "My Lord," — worshipping the creature as if it were a god. And it goes without saying that catching turtles is forbidden. Once a turtle happened to swim into a fisherman's net and when the man pulled up his net and saw it, he bowed to it hastily saying, "My Lord, my Lord, how ever out did you get stuck here? Now please don't move and let me get you out." And he set the turtle free at once.

When fishermen fall overboard and face the danger of being eaten by sharks, dolphins very often come to their rescue, fighting off the sharks. Naturally such survivors view the brave dolphins as their saviors, for that's exactly what they are. The fishermen of one village in the African country of Mauritius even have a group of dolphins working as their assistants; each time they go fishing, the dolphins swim deep into the sea so as to flush out the hiding fish.

Fishermen in Dayu Island regard the clever dolphin as a

kind of deity. Once when they were seining inshore, they happened to snare a group of dolphins, which immediately began to struggle to get out of the net. "What a shame!" said one of the fishermen. "We never seine dolphins if we can help it!"

In the past, the fishermen had little knowledge about science. According to what was existing in the human world, they imagined another sea world: the Dragon King ruled the whole sea, issuing orders from the Dragon Palace; the four-legged turtle was the Prime Minister while the rapid dolphins soldiers patrolling the sea. Oysters wearing pearls were Dragon Princesses, and the fierce sharks despots....

The fishermen were still scratching their heads over that one, when one of these clever fish leaped high into the air and fell on the net, pressing it downward with its body. With the seine no longer holding them prisoner, the rest of them were able to jump out one by one. But those that had got out did not swim away immediately. All waited until the last one was free, and then they all left together at the same time. Marveling at the cleverness and spirit of unity they had just witnessed, the fishermen were both touched and relieved. "Now get on your way, Dragon soldiers," murmured one. "And stay far away from our seine from now on," added another.

Since marine animals are getting fewer and fewer today, such local customs as venerating turtles and dolphins are surely a great help in the effort to save them from extinction.

On our voyage home Captain Lan said, "Let's have a good meal today." And so Xiao Wang selected five or six big Spanish mackerel, with which we made dumplings, fried a big bowl of tasty fish slices and braised a dish of fish cubes. Before we started eating, the captain picked up a dumpling with his chopsticks and threw it into the sea.

"An offer to the Dragon King?" I asked.

"The sea offers us so much. Call it a small thank," he said.

CHAPTER V

HENAN — Center of the Central Kingdom

CUSTOMS IN NORTHERN HENAN

Yu (豫) — another name for Henan Province — is a pictographic Chinese character of a herdsman leading an elephant. In ancient times, the climate in Henan was mild and humid — good for elephant breeding. According to legend, some local people even domesticated elephants for plowing and transportation. Of the nine ancient Chinese prefectures, Yu was the one lying in the middle, and so it was also called *Zhongzhou*, or Central Prefecture.

Today's Henan is part of the area known as the cradle of Chinese civilization. Yinxu (Yin Dynasty Relics), which lies in the suburbs of Anyang in northern Henan, was once the capital of the country during the Shang Dynasty. Excavations here have turned up numerous inscriptions on bones or tortoise shells as well as bronzeware, all of which reflect a highly developed slave culture dating back three thousand years. The two visits we paid to Henan — one in the spring, the other in the autumn — both started from this historic spot.

Ceremonial Tiancang Festival Celebrations

Xun County lies seventy kilometers south of Anyang along the Wei River. Many of the songs in Confucius' *Book of Songs* originated with the people who lived on the two sides of this river. We were lucky in the timing of our arrival here — early spring — which gave us a chance to get in on a spring festival done the Tiancang way. Those folks knew how to celebrate!

Also known as "Granary-filling Day," the Tiancang Festival falls on the 20th of the first lunar month. On this important holiday, after breakfasting on millet gruel cooked with other coarse grains, these northern peasants either make rings of slag on the ground of the courtyard for use as granaries or set up storehouses with sorghum stalks. They then fill the storehouses with grains in a ritual which suggests that their granaries have been filled by heaven and that the farmers can anticipate abundant harvests of all food crops in the year to come.

Records show that the Tiancang Festival had its beginnings in the early years of the Northern Song Dynasty over a thousand years ago, but legend places it much further back. It seems that a battle erupted between rival clans, one headed by a chieftain named Gonggong, the other by one called Zhuanxu in northern Yu. When Gonggong was defeated, he struck out in his fury at Buzhou Mountain, an enormous pillar that held up the sky—whereupon torrential rains began pouring to the earth and floods were seen everywhere. Fortunately for the survival of the earth and the life it sustained, the goddess Nüwa mended the fissure in the sky on the 20th day of the first lunar month. This accounts for another name for the Tiancang Festival, "Sky-mending Day."

China has enough such legends to fill several libraries. But what in fact is that Niu Village and nine other villages indeed did suffer dreadful floods going way back in history. In those days the villages took turns organizing Tiancang Festival with the curtain raiser always being the offering of sacrifices to the Dragon King at the Dragon King Temple that stood at the river's edge. Today, thanks to a system of dikes, the river is under control, and the Dragon King Temple is no more. However, in keeping with tradition, the Tiancang Festival celebrations are each year held in the square in front of where the Dragon King Temple once stood.

On the day we were part of the crowd, all the bands, the banner holders and the gun salute teams were in place by noon representing the villages of Zhao, Hao, Jiang, Lei, Peng, Gao, Hou, Jiang and Guan. The teams to perform *wushu*, the lion dance, the boat act, stilt walking and donkey riding were on their marks; and the *caige* of every village was set up and ready

143

to go. The *caige* was actually a colorful pavilion about three to four meters high with two girls dressed up as classical opera characters tied at the top. Each one of these portable pavilions was borne from village to village by eight to sixteen carriers picked for their strength and endurance.

At today's gathering the "general" was a 50-year-old peasant who gave the order for the gun salute by waving a yellow flag. The thirty to forty thunderous blasts were accompanied by even more deafening drum rolls. Thus the teams of all the villages began their parade through the villages marching behind a flag big enough to require two bearers on which the words "Sacred Recreational Gathering" were emblazoned.

The entrance to each village was usually the stage where the troupe stopped to go through its paces. With so many people crowding around, how could I ever fight my way to a spot where I could see what they were doing? Luckily for me the village leaders took pity on me and pointed to a nearby rooftop. I lost no time in scrambling up.

From my balcony seat I watched the young men of the *wushu* team on the attack and retreat — here a feint with a stick, there a slash with a spear; when was physical attack so graceful, so controlled, so aggressive and nonthreatening, all at the same time? And then came the lion dance — each "beast" actually two men, one the head and forelegs of the king of the jungle, the other his royal hindlegs and quarters: all skilled acrobats. How else could two men move as one beast and in unison perform somersaults and handsprings and any number of other acrobatic feats so seamlessly! The "trainer" teased the lions with a ball of red cloth as custom demanded while both jumped to catch it. Finally their gleeful tormentor turned into a brave warrior and fought the lions to the ground where they lay expiring on cue so that their conqueror could sit in triumph on one of the beasts breathing his last.

Next came the big-headed babies — tall lads in masks amusing the crowd with the exaggerated gestures and antics of tots in split pants.

And over there were the boatmen, oars in hand, vigorously guiding their dryland vessel through imaginary waters

144

singing humorous sailing songs to the crowd's delight.

As soon as the performance was over, the troupe set off for the next village — the one dressed as a county governor from ancient times bobbing up and down atop a wooden pole carried by his friends close behind the flag bearers.

How long was the train? No real idea. But at sunset when the leading team in the front had entered the square of the last village, the final team — the team of Niu Village — had just entered the first village.

"How many people have come to watch the show?" I asked.

"Seventy to eighty thousand," answered Zhao Yongfu, a peasant of Zhao Village who carried a flag that identified him as an organizer of the day's activities. "If it hadn't rained yesterday, it would be a hundred thousand for sure."

The festival is a big event for villagers over a much wider radius than the original nine villages. They travel considerable distances to be a part of it — on foot, by bicycle, in carts, even driving tractors. Before entering the villages, according to their traditional practice, they buy one or two kilograms of dough fries and string them together with willow twigs to keep until they can give them to relatives as gifts. Two strings of such dough fries make an acceptable present hereabouts for a family you visit — so that on this day those who have a significant number of relatives and friends often have to hang dough fries everywhere they can find: in their central rooms, in their kitchens, from the eaves. If they have too many to eat up in a short time, they will have to dry them in the sun so that they can keep them much longer.

On the Big Day the performances continued well into the night. When all the dancing lions had completed their respectful bows to the god of fire — said to be capable of preventing any and all disasters caused by fire — the firecrackers hung on the tallest tree were lit and the string of ten thousand over forty meters long popped for forty minutes. Assured in this way were abundant harvests for every household and peace for every village.

145

Clumsy but Exquisite Clay Toys

On the 15th of the first lunar month and the 15th of the seventh month, when the peasants are not so busy with their farm work, the Grandma Temple Fair in Dapi Hill and Fuqiu Hill in the suburbs of the capital of Xun County commences. During its life of about two weeks, peasants living near enough to manage the trip swarm here to pray for blessings and to live it up.

The day I joined the swarm I found all manner of country toys — from wooden swords and spears to figurines and cloth tigers, anything and everything. I noticed that several old women were hovering near a stand which displayed colorfully painted clay toys — little red horses, lions with movable heads, cocks and hens that could actually cluck. Each bought a pair of lions and about three dozen "clay coo-coos" and left beaming with satisfaction.

The clay toys on display here were really cheap. Two lions cost no more than fifty cents. Placed on an old-fashioned Chinese tablet in the central room, they not only looked as grand as anyone could want but the resident also had acquired a guard who would drive out all evils! And at the same time they could be used as candlesticks.

The thumb-sized birds, which were also whistles and each cost only one cent, made marvelous gifts for small children, and it was expected of adults to bring home toys. They were considered a good omen — a symbol of good luck and happiness. In the past when there was no highway here, fairgoers had to return home by boat. On the way they often heard children singing by the riverside:

> Give me a clay coo-coo, Granny —
> Back home you'll have a grandbaby.

The old women who had come for the primary purpose of praying for grandchildren got a special lift from hearing such blessings sung. They would pick out a few clay birds from their baskets and toss them to the riverbank.

When I talked with several of these clay toy vendors I

found that every one of them was from Yangqi Village — quite a record. Later when I visited this small village, a cadre of the Cultural Center of the county named Zhang Xihe, who was an authority on this folk art form — among many others — kept me company. He told me how it had grown up in Xun County.

Yang Qi was the leader of a peasant uprising toward the end of the Sui Dynasty some 1,300 years ago. He led his men in a fight with imperial forces that lasted three full days and nights, ending in his seizure of the imperial government's granaries where he stationed troops to maintain his claim. When they were burying their dead, they remembered the traditional practice of burying with them pottery figurines and other artifacts of daily life to use in the next world. How to produce all these things from the battlefield? Noting that there was an abundance of cohesive yellow mud on the riverbanks, artisan soldiers proceeded to dig it up and use it to make clay figurines which were then buried with the fallen. Thus began the history of molding clay figurines in Yangqi Village.

Remembering that the ancient people rarely buried the dead with birds, I asked what special use their clay birds had.

"Well, what the rebels made was conches, not birds," said Zhang Xihe. It turned out that conches were used as bugles in the ancient armies. The different calls of the conches told the soldiers when to get up and gather together, when to line up for exercise, when to assemble for a meeting, when to blow out their lamps and go to sleep. This is why the artisans made so many clay conches and buried them in the tombs with their comrades-in-arms. But later, when clay conches became toys, because they were difficult to make and unappealing to children, they were gradually replaced by birds. However, vestiges of the ancient conch are still found in the clay birds here — in their small heads, large bodies and short tails. When you blow through the tiny holes in their tails, there is a kind of "coo-coo" sound emitted much like that of conches. Hence the name by which they've come to be known.

Nearly all the seven hundred households in Yangqi Village are engaged in the making of clay toys. The home of

147

71-year-old Wang Tingliang, one of the village masters, is a veritable museum of clay sculpture. The old-fashioned square table in the central room was covered with recently done lambs and calves. A long table against a wall displayed colorfully painted figurines of historical personages such as military commanders as well as characters from the great classic, *A Journey to the West*, and life-like lions and tigers. In one corner were baskets filled with little birds ready for the market and piled high on the sill of the huge window in the front were dozens upon dozens of clay replicas of small carp.

As the time for the temple fair approaches, everyone in Yangqi Village has to work around the clock for several weeks. First they must dig up the yellow mud from outside the village, dry it in the sun, grind it into powder — sieving out unwanted material such as pebbles or leaves, adding cotton cloth, paper pulp and water and pounding the mixture until it is smooth. Only then are they ready to begin molding the toys.

When they cook their meals, they place on the slabstone as many toys as are ready and that will fit. Then when mealtime is over and while the clay is still hot, they give them a coat of black or brown rosin. This primer is homemade — a mixture of soot or red brick powder which has become molten rosin — and then when it freezes up after cooling down, it is ready for use. When the primer dries, they paint on various designs in white, scarlet and green, among other colors, turning them into finished products instantly. Then they lose no time in carrying them to market for sale.

I picked up a little red horse and in looking it over noted that its long neck and raised head were together at least three times as long as its trunk or legs.

"Though it's not well-proportioned," explained Wang Tingliang, "the large head and long neck reveal the spirit and strength of a horse. That's the kind of horse we folks like here." The country clay sculptors indeed do have their own notions about what is beautiful and artistic. Through exaggeration and through distortion, they create primitive and rather clumsy images that are lovely in part because of these factors.

The younger clay sculptors of Xun County, while inheriting the simple but lively style of Yangqi Village, have been making new achievements. One representative is Zhang Xihe, who has made more than a hundred monkeys, some sitting, some standing, some running, some jumping. Their facial expressions differ from one another also — some are laughing, some crying; some appear scared, some furious — and their postures are in keeping with the looks on their faces. Among all these lively creatures is a father monkey who, having discovered an enemy, stands with arms akimbo, eyes wide and fierce as if he's ready to do battle. In sharp contrast is the mother monkey, who holds her baby tenderly in her arms listening attentively to her youngster's whispery cooing.

Flagstone Houses on the Cliffs

In autumn we visited Lin County in the Taihang Mountains region in Northern Henan, our jeep chugging along on the winding mountain highway. Lying on one side was the bottomless ravine and on the other sheer cliffs dotted with pink, yellow or lavender chrysanthemums. Like the brush of a master painter, autumn had turned the distant forest golden and crimson.

With a screech our jeep stopped in front of a small hydropower station and our guide Lao Chen pointed at the cliff overhead. "There's a Daniudao Village up there," he said.

I was at a loss when I looked up and saw nothing but overhanging rocks. "Where's the village?" I wondered.

"You'll see it when we get to the top of the cliff," he assured me.

Taking the stone path, we climbed up step by step. Half an hour later when we had nearly reached the top, I finally heard sounds of life — cocks crowing, dogs barking, and other noises from the threshing grounds. At this moment lines by Du Mu, poet of the Tang Dynasty, came back to me:

On the cliffs hiding in white clouds,
You find many a dwelling house.

Later I found out that many of the villages in the Taihang Mountains were built on sheer cliffs. The Shibanyan District, where we now were, consisted of twenty-four villages, twenty of which stood on the flat tops of cliffs on the slopes of the mountains. The villages that stand on the tops of cliffs look for all the word like the heads of human beings, or more accurately the brains, pronounced *nao* (脑) in Chinese. Therefore, the local people replace the first half of this human *nao* (脑) with another radical meaning "earth" (垴), turning these "heads" into "earthen heads." The names of the villages reflect their shapes and locations.

It was the busy time of the autumn harvest. All the men and women of the nineteen households that made up the village were bringing in their crops or sowing winter wheat in the mountain fields. A young man was unloading from his back a large bundle of millet on the threshing ground built in the shape of a crescent moon against the natural curve of the mountain. The sturdy peasant women were removing soybean pods by beating them with chained sticks. An old woman was winnowing out the pods left in her red beans with a shallow bamboo vessel. The only ones around who seemed exempted from harvest duty seemed to be two little girls we saw merrily skipping rope.

Hidden in the green woods were the slabstone houses that made up this village. The roofs were of natural stone slabs over an inch thick. Shibanyan District is well-known for its large thin flags which can easily be cut off from the huge rocks that lie one on top of the other.

Nearly all the local men work as stonemasons in their spare time, acquiring their building materials by first driving drill rods into the grain of a previously chosen rock on all four sides. When the rods have gone in far enough, they insert long iron bars from all sides and slowly pry up the stone until the thin side is perpendicular in a slab about ten feet long and three wide. As a house is constructed, the builders first set up the stone walls, then frame up the roof with beams and purlins and cover it tightly with yellow twigs and mud. Finally, they hand up the heavy slabs to the seven or eight young men standing on the roof. The moment the flags are in place over the entire roof, a new stone house is complete.

150

"You use slabstones as tiles, but aren't they much heavier than regular tiles?" I asked.

"Not really," smiled our host. "Tiles absorb water, stone does not. So on a rainy day the flags are even lighter than tiles." I was told that stone houses were not only firm but durable. Since the flagstone does not absorb moisture, the wooden frame beneath does not decay, which is normally caused by wetness. Generally speaking, the stone house can easily stand for two centuries. In addition, because flat space is hard to find in this mountain hamlet, such flat stone roofs also serve as ideal areas for sunning grain and other crops. Looking down a slope in any harvest season on the roofs where corn and hemp are being sunned and pumpkins are piled and if you squint so as to make your view more impressionistic, you can imagine that you're looking at a host of painters' palettes or a patchwork quilt spread over the ground.

A Unique Dining Ground

That night we stayed at the home of a family of six: the grandma, her son, daughter-in-law, one grandson, two granddaughters. They had once lived in a house consisting of five rooms facing south, but a few years back they had built another of three rooms. Added to the sides of the house were two more rooms — on the east side a storeroom, on the west side a kitchen. Joined together in this way it became a *siheyuan* (quadrangle) — a very spacious and comfortable house.

At dusk our host Chen Hulin, forty, returned from the fields to welcome us to his home. A ruddy-complexioned man who looked as solid and reliable as the mountains, he brought with him piles of apples, pears and haws. "They are all produced by ourselves," he said with quiet pride. "Do help yourselves." A moment later his wife came in with a bowl of steaming ears of corn. "In this mountain village we have little to offer," he said simply, without apology. "But these were picked just before they were steamed, so if you value freshness you have it."

These had been appetizers. Now our hostess ladled for each one to be fed a big bowl of millet gruel cooked with fresh kidney beans. Then came a pile of *laobing* (a kind of pancake) and an additional bowl of potato shreds. All this together counted as a special treat for honored guests. These thrifty villagers, who work hard from dawn to dusk every day, offer to the city people whatever they have produced — haws, chestnuts, persimmons and apples — while they keep to their simple diet, eating coarse food themselves.

We "tourists" found it amusing that whenever meal time came around, the local people would bring a bowl of "soup" with a steamed bun and come to the village "dining ground"— a place where the villagers gather to eat. They come here every day all year round except in fierce, windy, rainy or snowy weather. Most of the families here have no tables at all. That evening, because of our presence, Chen made an exception to the usual rule and set a table in the courtyard, placing a little circle of small stools around, turning the cauldron cover woven of sorghum stalks upside down and putting it over the stools to make a table.

"What is so great about eating in the dining ground?" I asked.

"Well, it's the traditional practice here," answered Chen. "I think it comes from the fact that there are so few people in this mountain village and we don't work together in the fields, so we get lonely and want to see each other and we take this opportunity."

The next morning as breakfast time approached for the villagers, my photographer sidekick and I took ourselves to the dining ground, bowls in hand. There we saw old and young, men and women, leaning against the large Chinese scholartree, squatting on the stoops before their doors, sitting on the stone benches by the road. As they devoured their salted vegetables and steamed buns, they chatted about household and village affairs amid much joking and chuckling and even whoops of laughter. Clearly, a very ordinary meal had become a banquet.

A woman of about sixty who saw us eating our breakfast of noodles mixed with greens came over and asked, "How come you have no soup?" and without waiting for an answer she went home and fetched us bowls of millet gruel mixed with pumpkin pulp. "Come on, try our pumpkin soup," she insisted.

At the dining ground it was easy to see who was eating what. I was told that in the past when someone who was in straitened circumstances had nothing but porridge to eat, fellow villagers would break their buns into halves and give their down-and-out neighbor the half inconspicuously. Some would simply ask such a person to go and ladle from their pots at home. It was just this sort of neighborly behavior that made it possible for the villagers in this remote place to survive one famine after another.

This tradition of helping each other they inherited from their ancestors, the founders of the village. Over a hundred years ago, three families that had been driven up here by a natural disaster made a pact to stick together in their fight for survival. A forest full of wild life surrounded them, so first they drove out the beasts that were threatening them and then they built houses, opened up farmland and planted crops. Though their surnames were all different, they agreed that their children would all use one family name and be treated as members of one family, expecting that in this way they would treat each other as brothers and sisters. Their habit of meeting each day on the dining ground helps them maintain this solidarity from generation to generation.

Persimmons and Persimmon Flour

Covering the slopes behind the village were persimmon trees red as bonfires, their drooping branches heavy with fruits that looked like strings of miniature lanterns. Even more nutritious than apples, pears or peaches, persimmons are the basis for a mellow red wine, a fragrant and super sweet sugar, and a delicately flavored vinegar — quality products all.

One of the villagers who saw us munching persimmons under the tree gave us a shout. "Come with me," he called. "I have much sweeter persimmons at home!" We fell into step behind him and before long came upon several lush persimmon trees dense with black and red fruit. We learned that this type of persimmon first changed from green to red,

153

then from red to black, and was commonly called a "black persimmon." Our new friend picked for us a number of soft ripe fruits and thrust them into our open palms. Even though they did not look as lovely as the red ones, they were indeed exceptionally sweet. "You are right," I congratulated him. "These are the sweetest I've ever tasted!"

"You show your good judgment," he smiled smugly. "You won't find ripe fruit like that in the city!" He told us that persimmons normally had to be picked before they were ripe all the way through. After that they were either transported to town for sale or dried after being peeled. In 1972, archeologists excavated persimmon seeds and dry persimmons from a Western Han tomb at Mawangdui, Changsha, Hunan Province— proof that the planting of the trees and the drying of the fruit dates back at least 2,100 years in China.

The local people also make "hung persimmons." They accomplish this by first cutting off the fruit together with the twigs, making a small cut on each one, and then hanging them on the walls or from tree branches— exposing them to the sun and wind. When the water inside them has evaporated, the persimmons become exceptionally sweet and tasty. When visiting relatives and friends during festivals, villagers often present them a few bunches as gifts.

Remembering that people in Beijing had the habit of eating dried or frozen persimmons during the Spring Festival because the word *persimmon* is a homophone for the expression "all's well" in Chinese, I asked, "Do people here eat persimmons during the Spring Festival?"

"Oh, we have too many of them," he said. "Nobody here really likes them. What we do like, though, is parched persimmon flour."

Parched persimmon flour is also known as parched flour, which may also be mistaken for fried noodles in Chinese. You first fill ripe persimmons with millet bran, sun them till they are dry, and then bake them till they are crisp. In the cold dry winter you grind them into flour which you seal in jars. Since it does not go bad for at least ten— sometimes even twenty— years, it is usually kept for famine times. Our host's moth-

154

er was still keeping a jar that had been parched ten years before. When we tasted it, we found it somewhat coarse, but it was still sweet. We learned that with the most basic necessities of the villagers guaranteed by the free economic policies, it is no longer necessary for the local people to make persimmon flour.

VILLAGES ALONG THE YELLOW RIVER

Eight hundred thousand years ago, people in the Yellow River Valley had already begun to create China's ancient civilization. But this second longest river in China, in addition to giving birth to a great culture, was also the author of untold suffering. Named for its turbid yellow water, the river's dikes have burst more than 1,500 times in the past 2,000 years, and the course of its flow has changed 26 times. Inevitably, the impact of such a powerful force is revealed in the customs of the people who live along its banks.

"We Call Them House Beds"

The houses of Outan, a village of fifty households lying on the Yellow River some twenty kilometers northeast of the famous ancient capital Kaifeng, are different from houses anywhere else. Certainly we had never seen their like. They are built on foundations of earth two meters high and surrounded by a mini forest of tall, leafy trees. "We call them house beds," our host Li Changhe told us. He explained that because the village lay on the banks of the Yellow River, it often suffered from floods. At some point in the past, the villagers began to build these high, firmly packed foundations for protection. The trees check the sand blown up from the river banks and provide a place to wait out floods if it comes to that. In addition they often intercept floating objects, preventing them from dashing against the houses.

During the rainy seasons, every summer and autumn; the rainwater carries sand and soil from the loess plateau into the Yellow River, lending credence to the local saying: "One ton of Yellow River water contains six hundred kilos of sand." When it flows through the plains of Henan Province, because this section becomes wider, the currents slow down. Every year about 1,200 million tons of mud and sand flow into the sea while another 400 million sink into the riverbed. The result is that the riverbed grows higher and higher, becoming part of the aboveground river and producing that rarity of the world — a river whose bed is higher than the land. Compared with the span just two kilometers north of the village, that part which flows by Outan is more than a meter lower than that of the river. Depending on the embankment of five meters wide and three meters high, the indomitable villagers have been living out their lives of risk from generation to generation. Behind the village about five kilometers lies the mammoth dike that protects Kaifeng City and any number of towns and villages along its length.

In the days before the dike was built, the river bank was often flooded, Li Changhe recalled. Now sixty-four, he spoke of those days with lingering fear. "What we dreaded most was the bursting of the embankment," he said soberly. "Those waves came rushing at you like ferocious tigers and wolves ready to devour everyone and everything in sight." The flood waters swept away crops and submerged their village. Those who could not escape in time climbed trees or scrambled onto roofs. By day they shouted and beat gongs and by night lit torches hoping to attract the attention of passing boats or rafts that could float them to safety. Here and there in the swirling yellow waters persons hung on for dear life to logs, bundles of sorghum, haystacks, corpses of boars or dogs, anything at all that offered a reprieve from the Yellow River's deadly depths. Still the more floods the neighbors of the Yellow River suffered the more ways they worked out to cope with them.

There are four high water seasons in the Yellow River's year: "peach flood" in the spring's warmest time, "summer flood" in mid-summer, "autumn flood" and "ice flood" in early spring when it first begins to thaw. In the old days when there was no weather or flood forecast, villagers would take turns keeping watch during flood seasons to detect the first signs of rising water. When foam appeared on the surface, it usually meant a torrent was on its way. Then the villagers would dispatch their elderly family members and the children —together with their grain— to the homes of relatives living on higher ground. Traditionally, Outan people seek marriages with persons from villages that are safe from floods so that they will have a refuge when their home village is flooded.

Once the elderly and the youngsters were out of harm's way, the women busied themselves steaming buns and packing up clothes and other household items while the men tied planks to trees for the emergencies that may lie around the corner. In addition, they hung from the trees and beams of the houses strings of dry radishes and sweet potatoes for neighbors who left their homes for tree perches or climbed roof retreats and for those who returned home from a respite on higher ground. There is no stigma in helping oneself to anyone's hanging vegetables. That's what they're there for.

Asked to describe a typical flood day from his memory, Lao Li got into the spirit of it. "*Clang! Clang!*" he intoned. "Flood's coming!" Hearing the warning, every household immediately took down their doors and tied them together as rafts. Then picking up their belongings, food supply and cooking utensils, they pushed off without a backward look.

"And you just left your houses wide open?"

"Why not?" he shrugged. "Nothing really valuable was left inside."

Nonetheless, a flood could easily sweep away everything they had, so the villagers did not buy furniture. Usually they simply wrapped up their clothes and other belongings and hung them on the walls. Well-to-do families tended to have more belongings and so they filled up their doors with bricks as they left.

Most of the Outan inhabitants used to live in simple thatched cottages. Except for the four corner pillars which were made of regular clay bricks, their walls were all constructed of mud bricks. A flood could easily turn the bricks into soup, of course, but as long as the pillars and the roof remained firm, it was easy for the owner to build new walls.

157

Since the founding of the People's Republic of China, thanks to the constant harnessing of the Yellow River, the local peasants have suffered fewer and fewer floods. As they become better off economically, more and more are building brick houses instead of mud ones. At the moment our host was living in a brick house of three rooms and was in the process of building another house in front of his courtyard for his son who was about to get married. Whether clay or mud bricks are used, however, the villagers stick with their traditional method in building houses: they do not dig trenches for the foundation of the walls but rather carry sufficient soil to the site to ram a bed of one or two meters on which to set the house.

Our visit coincided with the autumn harvest, and all the villagers on the Yellow River bank were hard at work. As Lao Li and I plucked peanuts on the threshing ground, he told me that people farming here had to get to know the temperament of the river. Because it dries up in the winter and spring, an abundant harvest of the spring wheat is normally guaranteed. But because summer and autumn are flood times, it can be risky to grow autumn-harvested crops. It is safer to grow sorghum and corn since they can slow down the flow of a heavy flood and thus help to protect the embankment. Small floods won't submerge the crops but simply silt up a layer of mud which becomes a kind of fertilizer for the next spring wheat.

On the threshing ground were large boat-like baskets. An old woman picked up a sheaf of sesames and tapped it against one of the baskets, causing a shower of seeds into its depths. Another granny and her granddaughter were shelling corn into another basket. When I asked our host what the baskets were made of, I learned that they were woven from willow twigs, which being waterproof made the baskets indispensable to the local people. Ordinarily they served as containers, but in case of a heavy flood one could become a small lifeboat in which a child might sit or sleep.

The threshing area was on high ground — so high that the carts pulled by donkeys scaled it only with difficulty.

"Why did you build the threshing ground way up

158

here?'' I asked my elderly host.

"This is not just a threshing ground. It's our refuge in times of flood. If it's not high enough, it will be of no use," he explained.

The villagers on the Yellow River bank pack new earth onto this platform every winter and spring when they are free from farm work. Ordinarily, when it changes from a threshing ground to a refuge, the villagers gather here, carrying their beds, grains and cooking utensils with them.

For the 240 people of Outan Village, the present three-meter-high platform covering a space of 2,600 square meters is not big enough. They are planning to enlarge it and build a new village on it so that they will be free from floods forever.

Ancient Methods of Flood Control

Leaving Outan Village, we came again to the bank of the Yellow River, a northward trek of two kilometers. Here we found the autumn floods at their climax. The yellow turbulence pounding against the embankment was terrifying to see.

To the west were sixty to seventy people working to shore up the dike. With handcarts they were loading stones onto wicker bundles on the river bank. Accompanying us was Lao Pang, who was in charge of the flood control project of Kaifeng's Office for Harnessing the Yellow River. He told us that six days before, several sections of the first embankment had been breached.

When news of the emergency reached Kaifeng's headquarters, workers were immediately dispatched to bring the breaches under control. Towns and villages along the river sent out transportation teams, medical teams, and squads specially trained to cope with all facets of flood emergencies. With thick wires they tied together masses of willow twigs with stones wrapped inside, turning them into "willow-stone pillows" five to six meters in length and one in diameter which were then hung across the breaches to fend off rushing waters. Their quick actions saved the dike. Now the flood control construction team reinforced the "pillows" with still more stones to strengthen them further.

159

"When the dike exists, our home exists" has been a slogan of the people living along the Yellow River from generation to generation, who have traditionally considered it their sacred duty to join in efforts at flood control, including mending breaches in the dikes. The moment the general commander gives the order, thousands and thousands of people will at once rush to the spot from all directions with bundles of willow twigs. On July 17, 1958, when an exceptionally threatening flood peak was lashing the embankment of the river, two million soldiers and civilians commanded by Premier Zhou Enlai in person worked together to build on the large dike a smaller one six hundred kilometers long and one meter high within twenty-four hours.

This simple method of mending breaches with such cheap materials as "willow-stone pillows" goes way back in China's history. It is a matter of record that in 109 B.C. when Emperor Hanwu came to inspect the mending of the Yellow River breaches, he ordered the ministers and generals to come with him to help the local people carry wood and straw to fill them up. In the Song Dynasty, however, people used bundles of sorghum stalks, reeds, and tree branches known as *sao* in Chinese with which to mend breaches and build dikes and dams.

This ancient method of coping with floods along the Yellow River is still in use today. When surging waves lash the embankment, people hang out one or two rows of wicker bundles which will reduce the water's force. Should it rise to the top of the dike, flood fighters first lay a row of the bundles along the edge of the embankment, fix them tight with stakes, and then pile up packed earth behind them. If despite all this, a breach occurs, flood fighters will add "willow-stone pillows" to stem the tide.

How ever did these simple materials acquire such magic power?

As we have seen, the bed of the Yellow River is as deep as that of any river anywhere and the water itself is thick with sand and earth. Pilings will not hold in such soup. The simple "pillows," on the other hand, in the course of helping fend off the waves, gather mud and sand from the water in the spaces

160

between the twigs, which become filled up before long. Thus an aggressive force is turned into a means of defense.

Standing on the river bank, I was overwhelmed with feelings of respect for the inhabitants living on both sides of the Yellow River who had built these thousand-*li* dikes with their sweat and wit. Then I suddenly thought of the old saying: "An ant hole may collapse a thousand-*li* dike." So I asked Lao Pang, "Are there any ant holes in the dikes?"

"Oh, sure," he answered. "But the workers keep close watch on them every day." Lao Pang went on to explain that ant holes, mouse holes, badger caves, rotten tree roots, cracks caused by freezing ice and snow — all are apt to cause a disastrous collapse. That's why the dike-keepers frequently drill what they call exploratory holes in the dikes with iron rods. If they drive into a hollow space, they know there is a hole underneath, in which case they simply pour in slurry through a funnel, filling it up instantly.

The villages bordering the Yellow River long ago evolved a set of rules for protecting the river which are passed on from generation to generation. For example, nobody is allowed to take any of the willow twigs, earth, stone and other material from the dikes that have been put there for use in emergencies. Cutting down protective trees and bushes is likewise forbidden. Nor can wells be drilled or tombs built on or near the dikes.

An Anchor as Propeller

A village in Gong County, Nanhedu is the spot where the Yellow River joins its tributary, the Yiluo River. In sharp contrast to its parent, the Yiluo is clean and clear. This particular section, which is wide and deep, has been a ferry crossing ever since ancient times. At present, two ferries make four round trips every day.

The wait seemed forever, but finally the boat came — a big wooden tub that could carry about two hundred passengers. When everybody was seated, the boatmen began to pole the vessel toward the middle of the river. Realizing that this tossing boat was heading toward choppy waters made me nervous.

Soon enough the bowman, who kept testing the depth of

161

the water with a pole, gave a signal to his mates, who then put aside their wooden poles and moved toward the bow. It turned out that near the middle of the river, the riverbed became too deep to reach. At that point one of the crew picked up the anchor and threw it into the water. My heart sank with it: what had happened? Why would they want to anchor the boat in the middle of the river?

I was still wondering this when I suddenly felt the boat being pulled by some mysterious force. The man at the stern immediately turned his rudder, and the boat moved ahead sideways to the opposite shore. When it stopped, the boatmen immediately pulled up the anchor and dropped it again within moments. They repeated this operation six times by count until we had cleared the middle of the river, when they went back to using their poles.

Usually, of course, when you drop anchor, you do it to stop the boat and hold it still. Here they moved forward in the water as a consequence of dropping the anchor. I found it puzzling. Only when I asked an old boatman did I understand.

Because of the depth of the water and the strength of the currents, the poles would not work, Boatman He explained. So someone invented this method of propelling the boat. Here is how it works: when the boat sailing with the currents receives the reacting force of the anchor biting at the mud of the riverbed, it is suddenly pulled back. Making the best use of this force, the man at the rudder shifts it to temper the rushing water, thus making the vessel sail sideways. You might compare the anchor to the center of a circle and the anchor's rope to a radius string. With the force borrowed from the currents when turning the rudder, the boat sails slowly sideways to the opposite shore as if it were drawing arcs.

The course and level of the Yellow River are subject to sudden change. Its maximum flow in flood seasons may hit twenty-two thousand cubic meters per second while in dry seasons its flow may be two hundred only. Meanwhile, its muddy water makes it hard for anyone to tell which part is shallow and which is deep, so boats may easily become stranded. To avoid accidents, the boatmen, knowing the Yellow River very well,

have learned to tell the depth of the water by noting the directions of the wind and the changes in the color of the water itself:
the water of a deep section turns red in an east wind, in a west
wind it becomes gray. On a peaceful day without winds you
should sail only on water that appears clean.

Houses with Well-like Yards

Seen from afar, Dongcun Village, fifteen kilometers south
of the capital of Gong County, was but a loess hill consisting of
two slopes with a gully in between and no houses in sight. So
when our guide told us that there were 1,200 households over
there, I simply did not believe it: where in the world were they?

Only when I entered the village did I discover a network
of caves different from those in Northern Shaanxi where they
were dug into hillsides. Here caves were dug into the sides of a
well-like square sunken yard. The sorghum stalks lying in bundles in the yards and the several trees rising from each yard hid
the houses.

Cave dwellings are traditional among the inhabitants of
the Loess Plateau. They go back to ancient times. Today there
are still forty million people living in cave dwellings inherited
from their dead elders. Thanks to the fine-grained, firmly
packed loess, some caves still stand in good condition that go
back over a thousand years. Nanyaowan in Gong County is the
hometown of Du Fu, one of the great poets of the Tang Dynasty. When I visited his residence, I found the cave in which he
was born still standing and in fairly good shape at the foot of
the Bijia (Brushholder) Hills despite 1,200 years of weathering.

Caves in Dongcun Village that are dug after a square pit
is sunk are called "pit caves" locally. People from other
places call them "caves with well-like yards," for the yards
do indeed look like wells. In Xipoding, Li Deyao and his third
brother share a cave house of this type. The yard is over ten
meters long and wide and eight deep with three caves dug on
each of the four sides. Excluding the arched cave door in the
southeast corner leading up to the ground, there are altogether
11 caves. The central cave facing south, which lies on the northern side, is called "Big Cave," a place occupied by the eighty-

four-year-old granny who has children of three generations living in these cave dwellings. The "Big Cave" is also used as everyone's kitchen. The other caves are used as bedrooms, storerooms or extra rooms of one sort or another by the two families of her sons.

Li Deyao's eldest son offered to show us around his cave. Inside I found a room three meters wide and seven long in which I saw a table, a wardrobe, chairs and suitcases.

"I don't see a bed," I said—whereupon with a flourish our host pulled aside a long curtain and revealed a small bedroom. Such small arched caves within caves built of bricks are called "niche caves" by the local people. Big families with few caves build many other kinds of niches as well: a "cup niche" for keeping cups and other kinds of dishes; an "oil-and-salt niche"; a "knife niche" for keeping chopping boards as well as knives. There are niches for storing grains and for sewing machines. These tidy recesses in various sizes become part of a unique and charming interior design.

An advantage of cave dwellings is that they are warm in winter and cool in summer. On a scorching summer day when you drip perspiration you need only go into a cave to find air-conditioning. On summer nights it is essential to sleep under warm covers. Yet on freezing winter days cave dwellers are comfortable in their homes without the help of stoves.

Of course cave dwellings also have their shortcomings. The air does not circulate well, so you may feel short of breath if you stay inside too long. In the summer you often have to sun your quilts since it gets to be very humid indoors. Also, it begins to get dark inside early in the afternoon and the doorway leading up to the ground is on a steep slope, which can make it awkward for elderly people whose legs aren't as nimble as they once were.

"We cave dwellers fear heavy, long-lasting rains more than anything else," our host told us. Although low fences or sometimes trenches enclose the yard up on the ground, one purpose of which is to prevent playing children from slipping into the deep yard, raindrops still fall into the open yard. To meet the problem this presents, the cave dwellers all dig what they call a "draining pit" in the yard. In this way the water first flows into the pit and then drains into the earth gradually. But during a long and heavy rain the pit may be filled up and the water flows into the caves, sometimes even provoking a cave collapse.

In the past the poor peasants always felt it was cheaper to dig a cave, costly only in terms of time and manpower, than to build a brick house, which required not only bricks and tiles but also wood. Then in recent years, as they began to gain in prosperity, they felt able to afford more expensive housing. But other factors came into play in the switch to brick. Traditional cave dwellings occupy much more land for one thing, and today for the money it takes to dig the well-like yard alone, a builder can nearly cover the expenses of a brick house. Thus, brick houses are increasingly common and the two new brick-making factories in the village are finding it hard to keep up with the demand. Still, for many the old ways retain their appeal. When Li Deyao's brothers built their brick house of twelve rooms, for example, they stuck to the familiar design of the cave-dwelling house.

CHAPTER VI

JIANGSU — A Land of Rice and Fish

CUSTOMS OF SUZHOU — A REGION OF RIVERS AND LAKES

The Sweet Regional Dialect

Walking along the streets of Suzhou, I stopped from time to time to listen to the local women talking in their dialect. Although I could not make out what they were saying, I found the sounds as sweet as music. Their voices were soft and gentle — and there was a definite rhythm in the clear melodic line.

The Suzhou dialect is a subdivision of the Wu dialect used in Shanghai, southern Jiangsu, and most parts of Zhejiang Province. Wu is one of the seven major dialects in China with about eighty million speakers. It is said to have been used in the lower valley of the Yangtze River during the Six Dynasties (222-589), which was then spread to Japan, with which Sun Quan had established diplomatic relations on behalf of the Kingdom of Wu. As a result, it was popularly used among the Japanese monks, so that today its pronunciation still exists as one of the three major divisions of Japanese.

"The dialect is the first thing to learn, even though you should be informed of the customs immediately upon your arrival at a new place," the Chinese saying goes. So I made an effort to remember the Wu dialect word by word by matching them with standard Chinese phonetic letters.

With the increasing of communication between the North and the South in the past decades, some words and expressions have become nationally accepted. For example, *bin* which means "stream," *kaixin* —"happy," *guanghuo* —"angry," *dayang*— "close stores," and *youzhong* — "courageous" have long been used across China. However, expressions like *niantou* (hobby), *miantang* (water for washing one's face), *rijiao* (life, livelihood), *zhangzhang* (pay somebody a visit), and *jijihuahua* (many) must never be interpreted literally; otherwise, one will only appear ridiculous.

According to Professor Weng Shouyuan of Suzhou University, the Wu dialect dates way back. During the Spring and Autumn Period over 2,500 years ago, Taibo and Zhongyong, sons of Zhou Taiwang, Chief of the Zhou Tribe, led his people from the Central Plains to the south of the Yangtze River. Uniting with the local inhabitants, they set up the Kingdom of Wu, which consisted of today's Zhejiang, the greater part of Jiangsu, and some areas of Anhui. Thereafter, the Wu dialect came into popular use.

Different from the national *putonghua* (common dialect), the Wu dialect inherits many of the ancient voiced consonants, reading "pi" as "bi," "qiu" as "ju." *Putonghua* has four tones— "high-and-level," "rising," "falling-rising" and "falling," whereas the Wu dialect usually has eight, dividing each of the four into two. Nevertheless, the Shanghai dialect, which tends to simplify itself year by year, has only five tones while the Suzhou dialect has seven. The grammar of the Wu dialect is quite similar to that of *putonghua*, yet sentences with an inverted word order are often heard in the former. For instance, people in Beijing usually ask, "Suzhou *kuai dao le ma*?" (Are we about to arrive at Suzhou?) but the local citizens say "Suzhou *dao kuai* zai?" instead.

The creative people of Zhejiang have developed many vivid local expressions out of their daily activities. During their short breaks from farming in the fields, the peasants usually *chiyan*— smoke a pipe or two to refresh themselves— so *chiyan* has become a substitute for "rest." *Chuke* means making up and dressing elaborately, for before a woman leaves home to visit somebody (*chuke*), she usually takes great care with her makeup and dresses in her holiday best. As one has to put thread through the eye of the needle, or *yinxian* as it is called locally, before sewing, *yinxian* accordingly stands for "needle." A stage set up hastily collapses easily, or *tatai*, which is expanded to express the meaning of "loss of face" or "making a fool of oneself." As regards *zuorenjia*, it not only means "saving," whereas also carries the connotation of running a family in an economical way.

The Wu dialect consists of the Shanghai, Suzhou, Wuxi, Hangzhou, Shaoxing, Ningbo and Wenzhou dialects, which differ one from another. Though the saying "I'd rather listen to Suzhou folks quarrel than hear a speech of the Ningbo people" seems to flatter the former by belittling the latter, it surely reveals the elegance of the Suzhou dialect.

Beautiful Dresses of the Local Women

Luzhi, a small town in Wu County, lies thirty kilometers east of Suzhou. On the stone banks of the stream running through the town stand row upon row of residential houses — their white walls, yellow banisters, and evenly laid blue tiles a study in contrasts.

Two countrywomen carrying bamboo baskets walked in an alley paved with slabstones, each wearing an embroidered white blue cotton kerchief sewn with white silk ribbon wound round the hair coils at the back of their heads. They wore identical blue aprons as well, the belts of which emphasized their slim waists. I watched admiringly as the handsome pair stepped onto an arched stone bridge and finally disappeared into the far end of the alley.

I learned that women here chose their colors according to their ages. At the age of thirteen, girls begin to dress themselves showily with their bright head-kerchiefs and figure-flattering aprons. But after marriage, they all wear blue dresses, striving instead for elegance and a sedate appearance. Older women, however, wear dark clothes — the belief being that a somber look is more reflective of experience and dignity. White cotton that does not hide stains is naturally not welcomed by the countrywomen, who must work in the fields all day long. Of course, the woman who can transplant rice seedlings in a white dress without soiling it will be hailed as the "Queen of Rice-seedling Transplanting."

The clothes they wear are usually self-made, girls gather in their spare time in somebody's house or in some convenient place to learn from one another skills in tailoring clothes or to embroider on their aprons spring peaches, summer lotus flowers, autumn chrysanthemums, winter plums; they also embroider magpies, mandarin ducks (standing for loyal lovers) and carp, all of which symbolize happiness. On her wedding day when she appears in the beautiful wedding dress she has usually made herself, she will be greeted with tributes to her "clever fingers."

In the evening, while chatting with Lao Wang of the Administrative Office of Cultural Relics, who knew the local customs very well, we talked about the countrywomen's dresses, which were said to owe something to Xi Shi, a patriotic girl living over 2,400 years ago. Xi Shi was a common girl of the Kingdom of Yue in the Spring and Autumn Period when her country was defeated by the Kingdom of Wu. Gou Jian, King of Yue, had for years been undergoing self-imposed hardships for the sake of strengthening his resolve to avenge the defeat at the hands of Kingdom of Wu. One day, his minister Fan Li overheard Xi Shi, who was washing clothes by the river, talking passionately with other country girls about avenging their country so as to wipe out the memory of their humiliating defeat. Deeply touched by their words, he at once engineered a trap, arranging for Xi Shi to be sent as a concubine to King Fuchai of the Kingdom of Wu. If the plot worked, the enemy King would indulge himself in drinking and sex, neglect his state affairs, distance himself from his ministers, expel loyal critics, and finally send his troops out of the kingdom. Everything happened as plotted, affording, the Kingdom of Yue the opportunity to defeat its enemy, whereupon Fuchai committed suicide.

But the specific point I wish to make here concerns the topic of women's clothing. The story goes that one day when Xi Shi accompanied King Fuchai to Taihu Lake to enjoy the lotus-flowers, she caught sight of a lovely woman picking lotus seeds from a little boat whose beauty was set off by a lotus leaf on her head and flowers around her waist. The woman looked so beautiful that upon her return to the palace, Xi Shi dressed herself in the same way but with a lotus leaf and flowers made of silk. Before long, the "Blue Lotus Kerchief" and "Lotus-flower Apron" spread from the palace to all women in the Kingdom of Wu. Ever since then, from generation to generation, this ornamental dress has been handed down from mother to daughter and mother-in-law to daughter-in-law in the region of Wu.

These river women choose their clothes not only for the purpose of beautifying themselves, but also for the sake of their actual daily life and work. Since they always start their work before daybreak when it is apt to be cold and windy, they certainly feel warmer with a kerchief wrapped round their heads. And it produces a neat appearance to wear fitted blouses with narrow cuffs. The fact that the opening is placed on the right also protects them from the pricking of grains during the harvest seasons.

What about the apron? It is even more useful. When they wash rice, vegetables and clothes in the river at dawn or in the evening, the apron protects them from cold winds, preventing attacks of rheumatism. And thanks to the apron, their clothes do not get soiled easily when they do their cooking and cleaning, transplant rice seedlings, plant arrowheads, and harvest water chestnuts. Besides, since a woman working in the fields far away from home sometimes must relieve herself where there is no privacy, she simply unties the apron — which is long and wide — and covers the part of herself that would otherwise be exposed. Yes, surely a most versatile apron!

Mosquito Curtains Dressed with Fishnet

Early in the morning we went to Taobin Village on the boat that also served as the local government's mobile film theater for the villagers of this town.

Over the network of waterways, which seemed to have the same hue as the sky, lay several villages which we could not see too well from the middle of the river. When we went ashore, we found that the houses had all been built with their

170

backs to the water. At a *tatou* of the river, a woman was washing away the earth from her arrowheads in a bamboo basket while in a nearby bamboo grove, chicks searched for food and red-crested white geese chased and honked at one another, their necks craning.

Following our guide, we went to visit Lu Linyuan's family. Lu worked in a shop while his daughter had a job in factory run by the village. His wife Hu Meilang was weaving straw bags with a girl of the neighborhood when we arrived. Rice is their staple crop, and rice straw is not only used as a kind of cooking fuel, but also in the making of bags that are usually sold to outsiders.

The hospitable hostess showed us around her house. Apart from the three principal rooms occupied by the three members of their family, the rooms included in addition a kitchen and one for sundries such as farm tools and straw. The spacious central room lies in the middle with a bedroom on the left and one on the right — one for the parents, one for their daughter. Compared with the bright central room and kitchen, the bedrooms are very dark indeed because of their small windows. I later learned that it is their traditional practice to build "houses with bright kitchens and dark chambers," the reasoning being that a bright kitchen enables the hostess to see things more clearly when she does the cooking at dawn while the dark bedrooms invite sleep and allow the peasants to feel safer about hiding their money and valuables there. But it seems clear that the lack of sunlight and poorer air circulation in these rooms are handicaps, and I have no doubt but that this traditional design will gradually change over time.

In the South, every family owns mosquito nets because there the weeds and sewage always breed mosquitoes. But above the opening in the mosquito net of our host's old-fashioned bed carved with flower patterns there hung an attractive fishnet of over three feet long and one wide. I just could not believe my own eyes, "Is it for decoration?" I wondered.

"No, that's there to drive out evils," smiled our hostess, who then went on to explain that traditionally the local villagers believed that ghosts feared holes, and since fishnets were masses of holes, one hung on the bed could scare off any and all evils, including the most formidable ghost.

The belief that ghosts and devils could visit troubles on the living people was but a product of a primitive time when humans were unable to explain death and dreams. Then sorcerers and priests spread the belief that a person changed into an immortal spirit after death, a ghost who traveled through the sky and returned to earth on occasion. They also believed that it was evil ghosts that caused natural disasters, diseases and other human woes. Thus, in order to avoid misfortunes, they worked out ways to frighten away hostile ghosts. Living in this place so rich in rice and fish, the villagers knew well that fish and shrimp could not flee a net once caught and so they figured that the hole-fearing ghosts would be caught in the same way—a belief that survives from ancient times until today.

Thanks to the spread of a knowledge of science through education, fewer and fewer people believe in the power of the fishnet. It is only over the beds of the elders that you still find hung as in the old days. Today most families instead of a mosquito net hang up a curtain embroidered with fine wishes such as "The Dragon and Phoenix Bring Good Luck," or "A Life of Perfect Conjugal Bliss."

To prepare lunch for us, the hostess ladled some rice out of the small granary built at one corner of her bedroom. The one-meter-high granary with a diameter of over two feet, which was woven of thick straw ropes, we found in no place other than Jiangsu. The two granaries in this house contained about eight hundred kilograms of rice, enough to feed this family of three for one year. An alert spotted cat was lying on the cover of one granary, guarding against mice that might come to eat the grain.

"Keeping the rice covered all day long, won't insects grow inside?" I asked.

"This granary is very well ventilated," explained the hostess. "As long as you ladle out the rice from the top and avoid stirring it up, it won't go bad even after two years."

In ancient China, the order of priorities in construction was: first ancestral temples, second warehouses, and third residences. Today, granaries still play an important part in the villagers' life. Peasants throughout China build with whatever material is at hand storerooms adapted to different sorts of weather. With sorghum stalks northeastern villagers build their "Corn Towers" that point to the sky. Since they allow air to circulate, the grain remains fresh for a long time. The people in the north of Shaanxi Province, however, build their mice-proof granaries of slabstones, while in my home village people put up small house-like "Rice Barns" with logs and planks fetched from the mountains. People in Sichuan, a province rich in bamboos, on the other hand, store grains in granaries woven of bamboos, whereas in Gansu's Minqin County, three sides of which are surrounded by the desert, some people simply dig holes in the sandy soil and bury their sacks of grain in this dry earth. Of course, Taobin produces mainly rice, so it is only natural that they should weave granaries of straw ropes.

The Ceremony of Setting the Central Beam of a New House

Sailing from the town early in the morning, we saw three new houses being built within a short distance of about two kilometers. In recent years, the peasants have been getting increasingly better off, and their top priority is housing. Every village in Luzhi sees more than two dozen new houses go up each year. "So many people are building houses — must be a lucky day," observed the guide.

The setting of the large central beam on the ridges of the walls marks the coming into being of a new house and calls for a celebration. For this event people in various places not only choose "propitious dates," but also hold grand ceremonies. In the mountain villages in Changyang County, Hubei Province, people sing the "Song for the Setting of the Central Beam" when they lift up the main beam in the morning sun:

> The first step up starts your everlasting happiness ...
> The sixth step up your domestic animals are thriving ...
> The ninth step up brings you a long long life to live.

People in the Loess Plateau of Shaanxi Province, as we have seen (see Chapter I) lay a slabstone as the central beam right in the middle of the top of the arched stone cave.

As traditionally practiced here, the setting of the central beams takes place either at dawn or at nightfall. When we were sailing back to town at sunset that day, we saw the villagers still busy at the work sites. Shen Baohua, owner of the new house — a tall man of about thirty — welcomed us with a quick handshake and excused himself to hurry back to his boat where he had been mixing the mortar. The local people who build houses on the river banks not only move bricks and stones by boats but also mix the mortar on the concrete vessels that carry the sand and lime. Since water is within easy reach, they are spared the hard work of carrying it. The villagers — a good four score in number — were rushing about purposefully, some carrying bricks, some moving mortar from the boats, others building up the walls. The local masons are highly-skilled at building up very firm hollow walls.

Suddenly I noticed a millstone being inserted in the wall just below the window. When I asked the guide about it, he explained that it had been put there "to keep out devils." As the local people put it, a house facing the water runs the danger of "being rushed at" by surging waves. A millstone in the wall becomes a talisman to turn danger into good luck.

At nightfall, the ceremony of the setting of the central beam commenced. Two elderly women placed in the central room of the new house an incense burner table on which they arranged a carp, a pig head, "Booming Cake," and "Prosperous Buns" together with two stalks of sugarcane. These offerings were made to assure a happy new life for the owner of the new house. With the lucky words "Booming" and "Prosperous" they expressed the hope that the dwellers in the new residence would lead a life filled with comfort and the taste of sugarcane. After the offering, they hung on the wall of the central room the household articles they had brought along: a sickle, a ruler, a mirror and the arm of a steelyard which were together tied around a sieve. The local saying goes, "A ghost fears being measured," which means that those beautiful women who are actually incarnations of ghosts change into their original shapes once they are measured with a

174

ruler. The mirror can expose devils to light. As with fishnets, the sieve's many holes give it the extraordinary power of frightening devils away. The sharpness of sickle and scissors give them the power to cast a chill over devils and ghosts too. With so many helpful weapons, the family tries to improve its chances to live peacefully.

At the popping of firecrackers, the villagers lifted up the central beam dressed with colored silk with the words "The Setting of the Central Beam Sees Good Luck" written on it. When the beam was properly set on the walls, the carpenter, a wine pot in hand, started to spray wine onto the beam as he sang:

> With the pot that's silver white,
> I spray wine on the beam for peace;
> Everyone hails this day with delight,
> You will enjoy more wealth and bliss.

Soon the carpenter came down from the ridge of the wall to carry back up on his head a plate containing nickle coins, "Prosperous" steamed buns, "Booming Cake" and "Immortal's Peaches" made of wheat flour. Mounting the ladder, he sang:

> I climb the ladder made of gold,
> Sesames bloom node upon node;
> With bullion our host will flood each road,
> Happy will be his folks, young or old.

To respond to the carpenter, the host and hostess immediately spread a carpet of red brocade on the floor of the central room. Then the carpenter continued:

> A gust of wind, a cheerful face,
> Congratulations to the host:
> You spread the brocade and then embrace
> Silver and gold which your house boasts.

175

While singing, he threw the "Immortal's Peaches" onto the red brocade, which is known as "receiving treasures" locally.

Finally, the carpenter threw the coins to the crowd that had been waiting on his plate for the ceremony of "receiving grains," the coins, "Booming Cake" and "Prosperous Buns." At the same time he went on with his singing:

> Now I throw grains to everyone,
> Soon guests will go home with good cheer;
> Our host will be blessed for what he has done,
> And his name will re-echo for all to hear.

It is said that after the ceremony of "throwing grains," the family that owns the new house will become more and more prosperous with each passing day while neighbors who have seized something on this occasion will have better luck in the days to come. Thus, the ceremony of the setting of the central beam ended in an atmosphere of joy. After the ceremony, the host invited all the villagers, who had for days been helping him with the building of the house without pay, to a "Central-Beam-Setting Dinner."

But why do people hold such grand ceremonies for the setting of the central beam? Because it holds the most important position on the roof, bearing the heaviest load among all the beams, since it connects all the purlins. Obviously, the setting of the main beam determines the stability of the house and the well-being of the descendants. That is why the host held the traditional ceremony. And he did so for two other important reasons: to stimulate the carpenters and the villagers to work hard until the principal beam was properly set and celebrating at the same time the coming into being of the new house.

CUSTOMS OF TAIHU LAKE AREA

Suzhou's Embroidery and the Legend About Its Origin

People who have read the classical Chinese novel *The Water Margins* know that Shi Jin, one of the Liangshan heroes, is nicknamed "Nine-Tattooed Dragon" because of the nine dragons tattooed on his arms and chest. To my surprise, during my visit to Suzhou, home of embroidery, I learned that this craft owes its origins to tattooing.

The legend goes that long long ago the low-lying land to the south of the Yangtze River was often flooded. The dragons hiding in the water were the cause of many of these floods and other sorts of storms which resulted in boats capsizing and drownings, and so they came to be called flood dragons. When the local inhabitants learned that animals of the same species did not eat each other, they began to seek freedom from the flood dragons, by painting dragon heads and nailing dragon eyes on the bows of their boats to convince these creatures that they were of the same family. At the same time, they cut off their long hair and tattooed designs of dragons on their bodies in an effort to keep from being eaten if they should fall into the water. In fact, this is the origin of the ancient practice of "cutting the hair and tattooing the body" recorded in Chinese classics.

In the beginning of the Zhou Dynasty over three thousand years ago, Zhou Taiwang's two elder sons Taibo and Zhongyong, in order to leave the way open for their younger brother to succeed to the throne, left home for the faraway region to the south of the river. With the advanced techniques they had brought from the Central Plains they dug rivers and canals which directed the floods into Taihu Lake. Having no more water in which to hide themselves, the flood dragons gradually disappeared, and the grateful local inhabitants rewarded their benefactor by making him monarch of the Kingdom of Wu.

"Do in Rome as the Romans do." After they moved to the new land, Taibo and his brother endured the agony that accompanied the process of having flood dragons tattooed on their bodies. But now, even though the land had been rid of flood dragons, the practice of tattooing remained as popular as ever seemed so ingrained that there would never be a way to eliminate it. After Taibo died, as Zhongyong was one day consulting some elders about it, his granddaughter Nügong overheard everything while at her sewing. All of a sudden, an idea struck her: "If we sewed designs of flood dragons on the clothes, couldn't they replace the tattoos?" she asked herself. And she shared her idea with her grandfather and the elders, who immediately pronounced it brilliant.

So Nügong locked herself up and went right to work. After seven days and nights, she finished her first coat embroidered with flood dragons. Zhongyong wore it in public at once, winning the praise of everybody who saw it. After that the common women all imitated what she had done— first embroidering dragons, then flowers, birds, fishes and other things, with the quality of their work becoming ever more detailed, realistic and splendid. In order to commemorate the initiator, all embroidery, sewing, spinning and weaving done by women have been called *nügong* ever since ancient times.

According to classical books, however, embroidery actually came down to us from the Zhou Dynasty. During that period, after the autumn harvest every year, the king ordered government officials to wear formal embroidered garments when making sacrifices to Heaven and Earth during their praying for bountiful harvests. And during the Spring and Autumn Period and the years of the Warring States, the states that were fighting each other all had the surnames of their generals embroidered on their army flags so as to encourage the men to continue charging forward.

The earliest embroidery that has ever been found up until now may be that of the Chu Tombs excavated in Changsha, Hunan Province. The designs of dragons and phoenixes were neatly and vividly embroidered, demonstrating the consummate art of the Chinese of over two thousand years ago. China's embroidery is mainly produced in Jiangsu, Hunan, Guangdong, and Sichuan.

Known as the "Home of Embroidery," Suzhou makes products for daily use such as clothing, quilt covers, pillowcases, lampshades, as well as ornamental works that are all smooth of surface and brightly colored with remarkably neat and even stitches which show no signs of the needle. *Kimonos* made here, which are much in demand in Japan, can take a first-class embroiderer one to two or even three to four years to finish. Characteristic subjects for a woman's *kimono* include phoenixes, cranes, and pine trees.

Over one-third of the thirty thousand people of Guangfu, an old town of Wu County, are embroiderers. There, we got a chance to visit Madam Zhang in the suburban Hushan Village. While the other family members were out working, she embroidered at home with her neighbors, looking after her grandchild at the same time. From time to time she also had to shout away chickens that had stolen into the yard to peck at the rice she was sunning on the ground.

A pink quilt cover was hung over an embroidery frame in her central room. Peering through her glasses corrected for far-sightedness, she was stitching with green thread the leaves of a peony in full bloom. Over the flower a singing golden phoenix flew toward her companion.

"Ma'am, you've embroidered living phoenixes," I told her.

"Well, well, I'm getting on in years, and my eyes are poor now. My *nügong* is not as good as the girls'."

Madam Zhang told me that girls here started to learn embroidery at the age of eleven or twelve. In old China, girls of the poor families had to sell their works in order to help support their families. Girls of the rich, according to local custom, also had to learn to embroider. Through embroidery, they not only kept occupied but schooled themselves to become the sort of patient, careful, gentle young women daughters of the rich were expected to be and in the meantime embroidered love tokens such as pouches and cases for writing brushes which they could present to their future husbands. They also embroidered their own wedding dresses as well as quilts, blankets and pillowcases, which became a part of their dowries. Such works were known as "Boudoir Embroidery." I was also told that any girl who could not embroider might never be wanted by any man at all.

Traditionally, when a local girl is married, she brings with her an elaborate embroidery frame as part of her dowry, which symbolizes good luck and wealth for the whole family of her bridegroom.

Fascinating Cradles and Carrying Belts

The baby in the cradle burst out crying all of a sudden. I am not sure whether it was startled by my voice or my camera flash. I thought sure that Madam Zhang would have to stop embroidering to coax the baby into sleep again, but she continued her work without so much as raising her head. Instead she rocked the cradle with her foot and the baby gradually quieted down.

Seeing the baby was asleep again, I tiptoed over to study the cradle. Fixed to its bottom, of course, were the wooden rockers that produced the back and forth motion that lulled the infant back to sleep so readily.

In recent years, while collecting folk customs across the country, I have seen quite a few different types of devices for babies to sit or lie in, which are always made of materials produced locally. In Anchang Town, Shaoxing City in Zhejiang Province, people make "sitting carts" out of bamboo. Babies also can stand inside this wheelless cart and, with their arms supported by the upper ring, take their first steps. In Luzhi, Suzhou, villagers cooper a kind of round "standing barrel" with a large bottom and a small mouth, which is also known as a "stool barrel" or "stool nest" in other places. Inside the "standing barrel" babies can stand and sit freely. On the boats of the fishermen of the Zhoushan Islands, however, cane cradles are enclosed in wooden frames so as to reduce the rolling motion of the sea and prevent accidents.

In northeast China, peasants hang their boat-shaped cradles on the roof beams, which was even regarded once by people of other places as one of the "strange things" there.

In the southern villages of Shaanxi Province there is a unique sitting barrel which looks like a flower pot that has been used ever since ancient times. To make it more comfortable, two holes are placed in on the wall of the barrel through which babies can stretch out their legs. In addition, a hole on the wall of the barrel and another bigger one on the sitting board are strategically placed for easy elimination.

In Sichuan, a province rich in bamboo, parents carry their babies strapped to their backs in a bamboo basket which look like a round armchair when they go outdoors. In this way, the baby feels cozy while the carrier saves energy. On a rainy day, a parent can still climb mountains and hills safely with one hand holding an umbrella and the other a walking stick.

My own Guangdong hometown lies in a mountain area covered with bamboo, but the villagers never carry babies in baskets. If there are no elderly people who can look after the child, the mother usually wakes up the baby early in the morning and carries it on her back with a "carrying belt" — a cloth strap of over ten feet long and one wide. Women with babies on their backs do all their regular work — cooking and washing, carrying water, herding cattle, gathering firewood in the mountains. I spent my infancy on my mother's back myself, and when I reflect on this, I feel a surge of gratitude to my seventy-year-old mother who still lives in my hometown far away from me.

Customs of the People of Taihu Lake

After traveling six kilometers eastward from Guangfu Town, we arrived at the Taihu District, a community of nearly ten thousand people. Out of this number, six thousand dwell on boats like their ancestors did.

It happened to be May, a month when fish were spawning and fishing was forbidden. There was a forest of masts by the lakeside, since the fishing boats were all at anchor. Making the best use of this month, the fishermen either build new boats, repair old ones or knit fishnets. The legend goes that the ancestors of the citizens of this community were the navy men commanded by Yue Fei, admiral of the Southern Song Dynasty. While they were drilling on Taihu Lake, the wily prime minister Qin Hui falsely accused the admiral of treachery and had him killed. Hearing the shocking news, the navy men mutinied, declaring that they would no longer risk death for a stupid ruler and his murderous officials. Since they had no houses or land, they used their war boats as dwelling places and turned to fishing for a living. Today's fifty or so villages around Taihu

181

Lake developed from these ancestors.

Strolling by the lakeside, I caught sight of a splendidly decorated fishing boat. Amid the popping of firecrackers, it slowly pulled into shore and cast anchor. It turned out that, in accordance with the new economic policies, the villages had been selling at reduced prices the boats owned by the collective to individual fishermen. The buyers then held grand celebrations much as if they were launching new ones.

Invited by owner Jiang Jiayu, we went aboard for a look. Four skeins of colored silk ribbons — called "auspicious happy nails" were nailed on the bows. Before the launching of a new boat, the owner hides one of the "nails" so that the carpenter will have to come to him and say, "My dear host, there is a 'happy nail' missing," whereupon the host gleefully brings it out. The local people believe that an owner who has such a blessing of good luck will become prosperous and acquire more boats as well.

The horizontal wooden cabin on deck, the largest and brightest of all the cabins, was where the Jiangs ate, chatted, received visitors, and officiated over the celebration. Stuck on the door of the cabin was a large word in red— "HAPPINESS." Eight plates of food were laid out for visitors, including steamed red rice cooked of red beans and glutinous rice, popped rice lumps, "Bullion Cake," "Booming Cake" and a "Basin of Treasures."

The "Basin" was a pyramid of ten different kinds of colorful food: carp, pomegranates, onions, bamboo shoots, etc.— all sculpted from glutinous rice flour by the young hostess herself, all the foods represented being homonyms in Chinese for good wishes.

After bidding farewell to Jiang Jiayu, we came to another fishing boat twenty-four meters long and four wide with seven masts. Except for the old people and the children who had to go away to school, all the members of Jiang Pinyuan's family, more than a dozen in number, lived aboard year round. The hospitable host proudly showed us around his domain. Of the thirteen cabins eight were storerooms for nets, tools, fresh fish, foods, sundries and such, while the other five were rooms. Left-hand side space of the tenth cabin had been turned into a bridal room for the host's son who had been married the previous year: its floor was fixed as a bed, along which they placed the wardrobes and suitcases, forming a partition for the bridal room.

Next to this cabin was the kitchen, or "fire cabin," as it was called by the fishermen. The stove was a pottery vat plastered with thick mud with a protective wooden frame around its top. Fire was every fisherman's deadly enemy. Although an earthen stand had been built under the mouth of the stove, anyone who cooked always asked somebody to watch for the outbreak of fire. At the same time, to be on the safe side, the fishermen had carved on the lintel of the door the names: Jade Emperor, Jade Mother, Tathagata, and Avalokitesvara__ all the gods whose blessings could help protect them. In the old days, young wives who had been married for less than a month were considered to have "fiery legs," and were forbidden to visit people on other boats. Violators would be driven away by elders, after which firecrackers would be set off so as to prevent disastrous fires.

At the two ends of the boat were seven or eight pots of miniature landscapes with onions and evergreens growing inside which the fishing family cherished as special treasures. During holiday seasons they also placed little red pennants in the pots to add to the festive atmosphere. The host told us that in busy fishing seasons they would have to work around the clock for two to three weeks without being able to go ashore. During such times the few pots of evergreens were the only things that could bring a ray of brightness to their monotonous days. And when they ate up all their vegetables aboard, they could pick a few green onions from the pots as a condiment to add to their fried fish.

In the years when there were no weather forecasts and they had no communication apparatus, the fishermen had to predict the weather based on their experience, and they exchanged signals by waving torches. In their vulnerability to danger and dependence on the generosity of nature, and of course in these ignorance, they were especially prone to superstition. In the past, before casting the first net in a new season, they would throw into the net a handful of broad beans together with the ashes from the "Treasury Basin" — a stove placed on the bow. Good catches were supposed to result.

Villagers in Jiangsu are in the habit of laying chopsticks on their bowls to announce that they have eaten enough, but this is strictly forbidden in the Taihu area, for the fishermen there consider it an invitation to being stranded. In the tenth lunar month every year the fishermen go to the Temple of King Yu, the first king of the Xia Dynasty (21 c. B.C.-16 c. B.C.), the first dynasty of China, in the Pingtai Hills on Huxin Island to offer sacrifices to Dayu (King Yu). According to the legend, this ancient conqueror of the waters once came to Taihu Lake and subdued the evil dragon, locked it up in the dragon cave at the bottom of the lake, and pressed against the entrance a heavy iron pot so that the monster could never again start storms that would strand fishing boats. Thus it was that Dayu brought peace and happiness to the people of Taihu Lake.

In addition, urinating at the bow is forbidden, for if you offend the god of water, how can you expect to catch any fish? Besides, certain words or expressions such as "wreck," which implies capsizing and "catching fire," which can destroy any boat are never used among these fishermen.

It is usual for villagers to slaughter chickens and prepare special dinners for the rare visitor. Yet the fishermen on Taihu Lake consider the killing of chickens bad luck. Looking into why, I learned that in the old days when these boat dwellers fell ill without being able to get a doctor to come or go to a hospital, they would kill a chicken and offer it to Buddhist idols, praying for quick recovery. As time went on, the slaughtering of chickens came to be associated with illness and got added to their list of taboos.

With regard to children's education, the fishermen also had their own way of dealing: twelve boats that had school-age children together hired a teacher. In the first month the teacher and all the pupils stayed on one boat; the second month, another boat; the third month, a third boat. For each month of the year the school moved.

About twenty years ago the people's government built

184

new villages for the fishermen. From then on, old people could live out their lives free from the torturous pitching that accompanied life aboard the boats; those who are ill can go to see doctors in the local hospital; and children have their own schools to go to. However, still true to their traditions, young and middle-aged men and women still cannot tear themselves away from their houseboats.

Customs of the Town of Pottery

At sunset we arrived at Dingshu Town of Yixing County situated on the south bank of Taihu Lake. Walking around the old town bathed in the sunset glow, I seemed to be lost in a world of pottery. Almost all the houses were enclosed in walls built of pottery jars filled with earth. Many families had flowerbeds in the middle of their yards with such jars arranged in the shape of plum blossoms. Households facing streets displayed by their doors earthen articles for sale, such as *zisha* (purple-cinnabar) teapots, flowerpots and fishbowls, as well as lovely steeds, fawns, and elephants. What was the town gift shop was simply a museum of earthenware.

Yixing has long been known as "China's Pottery Metropolis." It used to be said that "every household makes earthen vases, and the whole county is covered with kilns." Today, 20,000 workers have been organized into twenty-six factories which turn out 6,500 types of products with an annual output of 70,000,000 pieces.

Zisha teapots, a treasure among the local products, are baked of a mixture of violet, cinnabar, and Tuanshan clays in the shapes of melons, pinetree trunks, and ancient pots with loop handles. With classical poems, landscapes, flowers, plants, fish and the like carved on the pots by artists, who usually also add their name seals, the earthen articles are also works of art combining sculpture, calligraphy, painting and epigraphy all in one.

Zisha pots are said to have one unique strong point: they are well ventilated because they are not glazed. Tea infused in them comes out with its original natural color. In the hot summer infused tea can stay in them for a long time without going sour. Pots that have been used for some years accumulate a thick layer of tea stain over the air holes inside. Hot water going through such pots will have a refreshing taste of tea even if you do not put in any tea leaves. No wonder they are called "magic pots."

Popular stories about the *zisha* pots are told all over Yixing County. One concerns the dissatisfaction a rich family came to feel with the new house they were building, particularly with the brick walls that had just been completed, so that they insisted on pulling down them for rebuilding. Then when the pulling down was done, they found a teapot inside the hollow wall and remembered it as the very pot containing tea for the bricklayer. When it had been handed to him, he had carelessly put it down on the wall, so that it had ended up encased inside. Lifting the lid and sniffing, they found the tea infused seven days ago still fragrant and the taste refreshing. This story was repeated many times, adding to the fame of *zisha* teapots.

Zisha pots also play an important role in the marriages of the local people. When a boy and a girl decide to get married, it is customary for the young man to bring to the girl's parents a first-class *zisha* pot when he makes his proposal. If they accept the pot, that means they accept his proposal.

In this town of ceramics we saw *Juntao* glazed pottery everywhere. That day we attended the wedding ceremony of a young couple, two workers in a ceramics factory. Their sitting room was furnished with a pottery dining table, a tea table and stools; displayed in the cupboard were figurines made by their own relatives, friends and colleagues, such as running horses and tigers, vases and beautiful women. In the bridal room we noticed that their clothes tree and the stands for the desk clock and lamp were all ceramic products as well.

I've been told that in Japan items of *Juntao* glazed pottery are called "Japanese receptacles." There, receptacles for house heating, bathtubs, monks' food containers, and even coffins for elders of Buddha monasteries are all *Juntao* glazed pottery products. It was Jin Shihuan ceramist of the late Ming Dynasty, who introduced Juntao ceramics to Japan. And for this he has been and still is honored as the Japanese father of ceramics.

186

It was surely an aesthetically satisfying experience to watch the ceramists creating patterns on their earthenware. A woman worker picked a little handful of clay from the colored lumps beside her, and as if she were drawing in the outlines for a traditional Chinese painting, she drew on the vat with her fingers, adding something at one place and pressing in a stroke at another. In a twinkling, a fine horse emerged running on the surface of the vat. We were amazed how quickly and skillfully she fingerprinted in the perfect bristles and tail during her acts of smoothing. After it was glazed and baked, it became another old-fashioned *Juntao* article, bright and colorful. Interestingly, the longer such pottery is weathered, the brighter its sky-like glaze becomes.

Facing a two-meter-high vase with a diameter of one full meter, I asked Bao, a ceramist accompanying us, "How ever do you manage to bake such huge things?"

"It's easy with modern ovens," he said. "In the past, everything, big and small alike, was baked in the Dragon Kilns." Their long arched kilns were so named, of course, because they looked like representations of giant dragons. The one we saw was eighty meters long and two wide; its lower part was two meters high and its upper part three. Along its two sides were "dragon eyes," one a meter in length, through which kindling is first placed. When laying the earthen pieces in the kiln, the workers put the smaller ones in the lower part and bigger ones in the upper. They first pile them up in orderly fashion and then move them onto stone stands. After closing the kiln, they put in firewood through the "dragon eyes," and start the baking. As the fire goes from the lower to the upper part, it bakes the earthen articles in order, saving not only wood but also time.

Five days later when the pottery is properly baked, to the pottery out of the hot kiln, the men have to put on felt hats, heavy cotton-padded coats, thick gloves and protective shoes made of bamboo husks. The soles of the shoes must also be soaked with water to keep them from catching on fire. The workers must be extremely cautious— anybody who bumps against the walls of the kiln will be severely burned instantly.

187

After emptying the kiln, they move in raw articles at once. If they wait until it cools, they will waste firewood. Still more serious, if they bake the earthenware in a cold kiln with intense fires, more products will come out with cracks inside.

In the past what the kilnmen did could be viewed as making a living on fire, with the number of good products that would eventually come out of the kiln always remaining unknown to them. Consequently, they began to place their hopes in the god of fire, the god of kilns, and Tao Zhugong, creator of ceramics.

Tao Zhugong, generally known as Fan Li, was originally a minister of the Kingdom of Yue 2,400 years ago known for helping King Gou Jian defeat King Fuchai of the Kingdom of Wu. Learning that the successful king planned to demote him in the days to come, he went into voluntary exile, ferrying across Taihu Lake with the beauty Xi Shi to settle down in Yixing. Seeing that the clay there could be turned into pottery, he taught the local people how to dig it up, and mold it, build kilns, and bake pottery. In the beginning, their products either came out distorted or partially baked. Quite a number even cracked or broke apart.

One day, Fan Li observed Xi Shi cooking: she laid three stones under the pot and her rice was easily and thoroughly cooked. Imitating her, he put the clay products on stone stands. In this way they were evenly baked, and the number of distorted and partially burned articles decreased gradually. Later he also watched her controlling the fire before her rice was removed from the stove: she drew out the strong fire suddenly, keeping inside a mild fire. In this way all the rice was well done without getting burned. Through this Fan Li learned the techniques of baking pottery with intense fires interrupted with slow fires. Thus, fewer and fewer products cracked inside the kilns.

In memory of Fan Li who created the new method of fire control, the local people built temples and statues in his honor, worshipping him as "Tao Zhugong." On his birthday every year, the seventh of the fourth lunar month, kilnmen everywhere light candles and burn incense, conveying their heartfelt thanks to the creator who fathered today's prosperous ceramic industry.

CHAPTER VII

ZHEJIANG — Home of Many Famed Men of Letters

CUSTOMS OF ZHEJIANG — LU XUN'S HOME PROVINCE

It was March in a spring as pleasing as that which Du Mu, poet of the Tang Dynasty, described:

Orioles warble the country sky showers with—
Bar flags flutter across a meadow of flowers.

In my relentless search for new folk customs or variations on the themes that kept unfolding, I came to Keqiao Town, Shaoxing County, Zhejiang Province. Rising with the lark, I looked out from the hotel over a vista of green wheat seedlings and golden vegetable flowers crisscrossed by a net of rivers.

Black Awning Boats Rowed with Feet

Two swift little boats like willow leaves suddenly appeared at the turning of a river branch. With their black awnings, the boats reminded me of identical craft from Shaoxing — Lu Xun's hometown, which Lu Xun (1881-1936, the great modern writer) introduced in his works. Although we had decided to take a scheduled motorboat to Hutang Village that day, we changed our plans and hired one of these small boats instead.

The boatman Feng Laifu was a burly man of medium height and ruddy complexion who appeared to be in his forties though we knew him to be over fifty. One has to be very careful when boarding such a boat, stepping into it with one foot from which the shoe has been removed, and right away turn around to take off the other one. Only without shoes are you welcome to sit in the boat covered with straw and cotton-padded mattresses.

Over three meters long and no more than one wide, the boat refused to stop rocking after I got on, which startled me. But the boatman fastened it tightly to the bank so as to keep it steady, and I soon relaxed. Small as it is, the vessel normally carries two to three passengers, though it can take six in a pinch. When we were seated, it became much more stable. With six sections, the awning is made up of two layers of bamboo strips with bamboo leaves in between. Since it can be lifted away as easily as it can be spread out, the awning adapts to all kinds of weather. When it rains during the journey, the boatman plants a large, long-handled umbrella at the end of the bamboo roof directly in front of himself, which provides shelter without blocking his line of vision. Meanwhile the passengers sitting under the awning can enjoy the sound of rain hitting the bamboo and the splashing from the bow.

What surprised me was the peculiar way the boat was rowed. Looking through the bamboo strips, I saw the boatman rowing with his feet, which alternated at pushing the oars, forcefully driving the vessel forward. The hand paddle, strangely, was clamped under his arm — for use only as a rudder controlling the direction of this "foot-rowed boat," as it is referred to locally.

Finding the whole thing so strange, I could not resist asking the boatman, "Is this really an effective way to row boat?"

"Oh, yes," he said firmly. It turned out that this fellow had started rowing with his feet at the age of twelve, and he had long been able to use them with as much dexterity as he did his hands. In fact, by sitting with the "bench board" firmly behind his back at the end of the boat, he not only felt completely comfortable, but could push the paddles as hard as he wanted to. Perhaps it was because he wanted to show us how skillful he was that he rowed so fast and lifted his oars so high. At such speed, he covered as much as ten kilometers per hour.

The boat was so small and short that one had to sit straight up; no room for lounging at all. Yet sitting so close to the water was a very pleasant experience: I could caress the water just by stretching out a hand, and by opening the awning I could enjoy every bit of scenery along the way. Occasionally I saw boatmen towing boats along the shore and got a close look at the villages and fields that had seemed to be spread over the net of clear rivers from my hotel lookout point.

We passed Yuzi, our boatman's home village. Feng told me that more than three hundred people from his village rowed passengers from place to place around Keqiao Town year round. Most of the time they live on the boats. In the evening, returning craft anchor all over the river branches. Sitting at the end of the boat with smoke curling up into the sky, the carmen begin to wash the rice and vegetables and cut up the fish. Then they move their stoves up close and start to cook. Early in the night, after arranging the awning over the boat carefully, they get into this "cabin," — which is big enough for no more than one person to stretch out — for the night. Only in the busy seasons will they go home to help with the farming, such as the times for harvesting wheat, collecting rapeseeds, or transplanting rice seedlings. Once back home, they may also repair boats that need it.

Finally, we arrived at Hutang, a village of about two hundred families. Most of them go in for farming, fishing, brewing alcohol and raising ducks. Every family has a *tatou*, a flight of stone stairs, in front or in the back of their house. It is the home harbor of the villagers, where the women wash rice, vegetables and clothes.

A small boat bathed in the rays of the setting sun was pulled over, and jumping ashore were two little girls, their arms full of azaleas to give their grandmother who had come to meet them. The guide explained that they were returning from a visit to the graves, or a "tomb sweeping."

Most of the graves belonging to the local villagers lie in the faraway mountains. Their tomb-sweeping trip to the mountains on Qingming Day (the Pure Brightness Festival, the day marking the 5th solar term) usually takes one full day. In the old days when wealthy, influential families went to pay respects to their dead relatives at the tombs, they not only had a special boat for male visitors and another for female ones, but also had a special cooking boat to prepare lunch for them. For the rich girls, slaves of the feudal codes which forbade them to leave their well-guarded houses for any other reason, Qingming was the happiest day of the year. As the old folk saying goes, "A catkin in a girl's hair on Qingming Day keeps her beauty from fading away," so traditionally girls dressed themselves with catkins from willows, which symbolized everlasting youth and beauty. Young men, on the other hand, took their pleasure in meeting beautiful girls on the boats. And that is exactly what the following folk rhyme means:

> The first (lunar) month sees lamps hanging high;
> On the following, kites fly in the sky,
> And you meet women lovelier than flowers,
> In the third month on the river.

All the families in this region of rivers own boats. A new wooden boat normally costs no more than three hundred *yuan*, but if they borrow a mold and make one with cement themselves, they need to spend only fifty or sixty *yuan* — much less than what urban dwellers pay for a bicycle! They use boats wherever they go — to the fields for the day's work, to carry crops home from the fields or vegetables to town for sale, when fishing, tending ducks, gathering chestnuts. Of course they will not be without their boats when they go to visit friends and relatives, take in a film or play in any of the villages nearby, attend the birthday celebrations of elderly people, carry coffins for burial.

When a bridegroom's family goes to accompany the bride from the same village to her new home, even if their houses are within a stone's throw of one another, several large boats are still used: one for her trunks, suitcases, clothing, wooden basins and other dowry items; one for the busy band that never stops piping and drumming; another for those who come to meet the bride. And there are still two more — one carrying those who escort the bride to her new family, the other transporting the congratulators. But the star of the fleet, of course, is the sedan boat. Although sedan chairs are no longer used, the bride who, according to local custom, must carry a pair of handwarmers to symbolize the act of burning incense and wishing happiness to the bridegroom's family, will still be carried onto the boat by four young men after she seats herself on a bamboo chair. Then, directed by an elder who holds high a "Descendant Lantern," the boats set sail for the bridegroom's house. Traditionally, the marriage ceremonies are held in the evening. So throughout the Spring Festival season, when most of the weddings take place, the river branches ring with loud music and blaze with burning torches until after midnight.

Unique Customs of a County of Bridges

The Anchang River goes right through the center of Anchang, so that boats are its primary means of transportation. Besides ferries, there are boats privately owned by each of the factories, stores and organizations. If a factory is to be built at some distance from the river, the first thing they will do is cut the river through to the new factory's entrance.

The more rivers you have, of course, the more bridges you build. Looking into the distance from the Anchang Bridge, I saw three bridges on the river's upper reaches, and another three on its lower reaches: a high arched bridge in the shape of a crescent moon, a long steel and concrete bridge, and a flat bridge of slabstones.

Bridges go way back in human history, of course. Over six thousand years ago primitive clans living in Banpo near Xi'an dug trenches around their dwelling places about six meters deep and wide to keep away wild animals. And when they went in or out of their villages, they walked on single-log bridges or stair bridges of stones stacked one upon the other. We know from "picture-bricks" of the Eastern Han Dynasty (25-220) that arched bridges spanned rivers 1,700 years ago, and research tells us that the development of the arched bridge was spurred by its use in city gates and brick tombs. Because of

194

its beauty and practicality, the design spread all over China and to Japan and other countries. The Glasses Bridge in Nagasaki, which was designed by Ru Ding, a Chinese Buddhist monk of the Ming Dynasty, has withstood many floods and is cherished as one of the national treasures of Japan.

There are forty bridges in Anchang, and about eighty times as many of various sizes in Shaoxing — an entire county of bridges. But during the thirty days or so when I was there, I never saw a wooden bridge. I was told that in the Tang Dynasty most bridges were built of wood but because of the frequent rains, they decayed rapidly which is why they came to be replaced by stone structures in the Song Dynasty.

The bridges were mostly named according to the functions they were expected to perform. The local inhabitants called pedestrian bridges "Safety Bridges" or "Healthful Bridges," expressing typical hopes for the well-being of their users. They named those joining stores or workshops "Profit Bridges" and "Golden Bridges," to court booming business. Those close to the temples were called "Beneficence Bridges" and "Incense Bridges" expressing the expectation of swarms of pilgrims every day. As for those taking the surnames of prominent families, they even have become the names of some of the local villages and towns.

Walking around the small town, I discovered that some of the old bridges were flanked by a pair of stone lions squatting at either end — a well-known custom of all manner of designers in China — not only of bridges. On the Lugou (Marco Polo) Bridge in Beijing the stone lions in different sizes are simply too many to count. Indeed, the lion image is everywhere to be found in China probably because the beast came to be associated with the power to drive away all evils.

In the past, superstitious citizens thought there was a god of bridges. During festival seasons, old women who brought incense, candles and fake paper money to honor the dead would kneel down before the bridges to pray for the firmness of these important structures and for the safety of those who walked or rode on them and the boats that sailed under them. A woman who was about to give birth would pass over three bridges with-

195

out stopping, carrying a few pounds of noodles in her hands in the hope that both she and her child would thus be insured safety and a long life in good health. Rich families that rowed coffins to the graveyard would carry along a kind of altar of pine boughs, bamboo, and paper flowers as a blessing for the dead near whatever bridges their boats would pass under.

Today, these old superstitious customs are no longer observed. But yet, on National Day, the Spring Festival, the Lantern Festival and other important holidays, people still decorate the grand bridges which connect major streets with pine, cypress branches, colored pennants and festive lamps. And after a snowy night, some citizens especially responsible will of their own accord get up very early to sweep off the snow on the bridges and spread over them rice husks and ashes to prevent pedestrians from slipping.

It is superfluous to talk about the importance of bridges in the county of bridges. But what is worth mentioning concerns the new concrete one in the west of Anchang: its balustrades were built into two long rows of benches. It was the first time I had ever come across such a feature, and I had to praise the thoughtfulness of a designer who would make it possible for people to take breaks on his bridge!

"It's far more than 'breaks'," said the guide. "On summer nights, with the breezes coming from the river, the bridges become ideal places to while away the hot hours. After a day's busy work, you can sit with your back against the balustrade as you swap stories with your friends and watch the scattered lights of the fishing boats. Now, that's really living!"

Dawn Bustle at Anchang

The activity by the river started before daybreak. The peasants of the suburbs, whose boats with vegetables ready for market had left home in the dark, were now arriving at the town wearing black felt hats with round curling rims — warm hats good in bad weather but also excellent containers for items like chestnuts and, I learned, fine cushions for peasants needing a rest from field work. Moreover, I was told, a gentle pat relieved it of its dust covering and it stayed clean as a whistle!

196

Getting to town, the peasants first went to the teahouses for breakfast. There they learned from each other about prices of vegetables as well as happenings in the town. At daybreak they scattered to set up their stalls in the streets as the inhabitants of the town began to appear to fill their bamboo baskets. All of a sudden I caught sight of a group of women crowding to the riverside, pointing from left to right. Coming nearer, I saw what they had seen — two boats selling vegetables rowing toward them as their shouts went up: "I want a bundle of rapes!" "A lotus root here!" Buying things from boats used to be a typical morning event in this town, with peasants hawking their meats and vegetables along the rivers by beating at the sides of the boats as they rowed and at the same time fried bean curd. But in recent years, as the economic policies for the rural areas have increasingly encouraged private initiative and as the markets in the towns and the countryside have become ever more prosperous, sellers with various stands instead crowd along the streets all over the town, taking the place of the boats on the rivers.

The fish market, consisting of a row of about two dozen fish filled wooden basins, buckets and baskets, was the busiest place of the town. The fish, including big carp, crucians and eels which were breathing with open mouths in the water, reminded me of the delicious fried carp I had the night before.

This is one of China's famous regions for rice and fish. The peasants here, when free from their farm work, often row their boats out to catch fish and shrimp from the rivers with spears, rods, and different kinds of nets. The way they catch eels with "Eel Tubes" should count as the cleverest of all.

In the evening the fishermen throw about seventy bamboo tubes strung together into the river. The meter-long tubes, baited with wheat and sorghum, are sunk into places that eels frequent at night in their search for food. Taking the bamboo tubes with food floating inside for their own dwelling holes (After three years' soaking in the river, the tubes carry no bamboo smell at all.) the eels swim right into them. After eating their fill, they will linger inside for a rest. At daybreak the fishermen, who have spent the night on the boat, will pull up the tubes and pour out the eels for sale in the town early in the morning.

At the east end of the fish market a group of women chopping field snails with small axes tried to attract customers with the natural sound of their chopping ("toot, toot, toot") instead of the usual shouting. "Chop snails while drinking yellow rice wine; robbers can never take away these things of mine" goes the local folk rhyme, which actually means: Get a plate of cooked field snails with their ends chopped off and enjoy their delicious meat with a bottle of the fine local Shaoxing wine. The point is that if you drink in the way Li Bai did, you will find such pleasure in it that you will not leave it and flee for your life even when you see robbers coming to attack you.

Here I would like to say a word about this remarkable local wine. Brewed from glutinous rice. Shaoxing wine is yellow in color, fragrant in scent and sweet in taste. Local lore has it that the frequent drinking of it effectively dispels cold- and wetness-evil, makes one strong and healthy, and prolongs one's life. In the old days, when a child was born, either boy or girl, the family would brew several jars of this yellow wine and keep them in the cellar. The liquor would not be consumed until the child had grown up: if a boy was going to take an important examination or would be married, they would bring out the aged wine, calling it "Red Doctor," to wish him the best of luck and success; in the case of a girl, the parents would bring out the "Daughter Wine" with decorative flower patterns carved on the jars as part of her dowry. It was thus only to be drunk when they married her off.

Upon their return from the market, the housewives washed the vegetables and cut open the bellies of the fish, then hung them in bamboo baskets on a beam where the air circulation was especially good. All this was done to make the cooking of lunch easier. Finishing this, they would carry a basin of soiled clothes to the *tatou* where they would wash them either with a brush or beat them with a stick. It goes without saying that dawn is the busiest time of the day for the women of this region.

198

The breaking up the early morning market brought out a couple with a boy of five or six all dressed in their Sunday best. I saw them in a grocery store buying dried longans, litchis, and cakes. Knowing that they were preparing a gift package, the owner of the store became particularly attentive: he not only wrapped the items in gilt paper but also put over them a red piece of gift wrapping. After they had left, I asked the shopkeeper what it was all about and learned that they were paying a visit to the woman's parents. According to the local custom, married daughters should return to their parents' homes on or around the third day of the third lunar month, bringing gifts of a chicken, two fish, several bottles of wine, and two packages of dried longans and litchis, which are meant to help the parents keep fit and strong.

Later watching on this warm sunny spring morning the boat with the beautiful young wife, the child gleefully holding his hand in the water while the young husband rowed at the stern disappear into the distance, I felt a warm current of joy myself at this reenactment, in what appeared to be idyllic terms, of a living tradition.

Feasts Held in Celebration of One-Month-Old Babies

It was believed to be an auspicious day, and in Jiangtou Village, because twenty-eight-year-old Mao Dexing's son happened to be exactly one month old, his whole family was holding a "hair cut feast."

It was still early in the morning when the boy's maternal grandmother and other relatives arrived with gift boxes containing baby clothes, shoes and socks, longevity locks, tiny bracelets, combs, curly knives with handles, mirrors and other silver articles as well as chickens, geese, fish, pork, cake, candies, jujubes, oranges, longans and other things. The silver articles for the baby all were supposed to have special properties: the round mirror could detect demons, the curly knife could drive away devils, the longevity lock could prevent the baby from being taken away by any evil monster so that he would live to be a hundred or even older. In the past, because medical care in the country was poor, newborn babies were often threat-

199

ened by death in the early days. That is why people kept the custom of dressing them with jewels or ornaments: to ward off bad luck and evils.

The haircut ceremony took place in front of the central room of the house lit with red candles placed high up enough to give a bright light. Two old-fashioned square tables with incense smoke curling up from them were piled high with all kinds of food and gifts before which sat the granduncle holding the baby. Finally, amid the popping of firecrackers, the ceremony began. The barber started by smearing a mouthful of well-chewed tea leaves over the baby's head, the belief being that this inflammation-resistant tea would make sure that the baby would be free from scabies after the haircut and would grow an abundant head of hair.

Of course, it does not mean that all the baby's hair is cut off. A little square of "Wisdom Hair" must be kept right above the forehead with a tuft of "Anchoring Hair" behind. Boatmen in this area who want to stop their boats need only plant a bamboo pole into the river through the stern hole. This pole is known as the "anchoring pole." By keeping a tuft of "Anchoring Hair," then, they expect the child to grow healthily and steadily like an anchored boat. With regard to the eyebrows, they must be completely shaved off so that heavy dark ones will grow in to give him a manly look.

When the haircut was done, the young mother at once dressed the baby with warm clothes, including a cap on his head. Then she appointed a male cousin of the baby around the age of ten to carry him into the kitchen. The boy did not bring him back until the baby had lain on the stack of firewood and straw for a moment. What was all that about? Well, it is believed that after his cousin had done this, the baby would not mind being carried by anybody at all, for "elder cousin" and "everybody" in Chinese happen to be homonyms. And if the baby did not mind who it was that wanted to hold him in his arms, then the mother could spare much more time for other work. As for being laid on the stack of straw, this would help in sure that the child would be as easygoing as dogs and cats, and like these animals be strong and healthy but not subject to diseases. As a matter of fact, some parents even named their little ones "Doggy" and "Kitty."

Besides such names as "Doggy" and "Kitty," parents used to name their children in the following traditional ways:

Some children got their names from their weight at birth—for example, "Eight *Jin*" (four kilograms) and "Nine *Jin*." However, when the babies were being weighed, people often liked to add books and abacuses for the purpose of raising their weights, expecting them thereby to grow to be learned and good at business.

Other babies were named according to the actual ages of their grandparents. For instance, if the grandfather was sixty-one in the year the baby was born, then he or she might be named "Sixty-one." If their grandparents had passed away already, the babies might take the ages of their own parents. (I understand that people in Japan share this custom in naming babies. For example, Yamamoto Fifty-six was so named because in the year of his birth his father was fifty-six.)

Lucky children who happened to come to the world in the Dog's, the Ox's, the Tiger's, the Rabbit's and the Dragon's Years of the twelve-animal-year cycle that represents the twelve Earthly Branches, however, might be named after the animals: "Oxy," "Dragon," etc. By contrast, names of animals considered by many to be disgusting, such as snakes and mice, were never given to children.

Another type of parents would invite fortune-tellers to work out the "five elements"— metal, wood, water, fire and earth for the babies. If a baby lacked any of the five elements, he would be named after it. In addition, some parents who feared that their babies might die young might even take them to the temples along with incense, candles and offerings and ask the Buddhist monks to name the children for them. Some, for the sake of their babies' health, would even name them "Zhang Heshang" (Monk Zhang) and "Li Heshang" (Monk Li) themselves.

Today, educated young parents are doing away with most of the old customs. Some ask the elders to name their children; others by looking through dictionaries find names that seem to

201

set their bearers on an ambitions or worthy course in life. Mao Dexing, for example, named his haircut-receiving son Jianyu ("Piercing the Universe"), expecting him to explore the universe in the future.

As for girls, they are often named after flowers, plants, according to the different seasons, or a season of flowers. A girl born in December may be named "Meixian" (Plum [Fairy] Maiden), while one born in June "Hegu" (Lotus Girl), and one in August "Guixiang" (Laurel Fragrance).... Of course, all parents delight in watching their daughters grow in lordliness so that they are compared to flowers.

The loud noises of the visitors outside the central room and deafening popping of the firecrackers together sent the baby into continuous loud crying since he had already been frightened during the haircut and being laid on the straw. "That's all right," said Mao Dexing. "It's only natural the first time." The friends and relatives were similarly determined to put the best face on things. If the baby had not cried, they would have chorused: "The child is so bold; he'll grow up to be a general for sure." But since this particular baby just would not stop crying, they praised him for his alertness and sharp ears. Imagine a baby crying so loudly at the first popping of the firecrackers! Surely a great future awaits such a fast-reacting boy!

After the ceremony, they moved all the foods into the kitchen in preparation for the feast. The infant's grandparents were busy delivering to all the neighbors sweet cake, "Happiness *mantou*," and fruit, thus offering everybody a share in their happiness. Nonetheless, I saw the grandmother surreptitiously draw out a vigorous live carp the moment the firecrackers were lighted. But what was she doing? Oh, she is going to send the live fish back to the river, explained the guide. "Everyone wants his child to grow up to be somebody. It is said that if you set a live carp free in the river, your child will pass all examinations and become a 'Number One Scholar' just like the carp jumping over the Dragon Gate!"

By the way, in the past when one-month-old girls had their hair cut and their eyebrows shaved off, it was done in perfunctory fashion. No ceremony like a "haircut feast" was ever held for them. But now there is a movement to eliminate the old idea of preferring boys to girls. And since the national policy of family planning is being carried out, which means that the average couple can have only one child, be that child a boy or a girl, it is a darling in the parents' eyes all the same. Consequently, in recent years haircut ceremonies for baby girls are becoming increasingly common, with parents hoping against hope that baby daughter will grow up to be a Number One Scholar!

CUSTOMS OF THE HOME OF SILK

"Wheat is green while barley is gold; silkworms growing in every household." Just as this local children's song describes, early May saw barley ripening and a busy season of silkworm breeding. Then, starting from Hangzhou, the capital of Zhejiang Province, we traveled eastward along the Qiantang River to reach Haining County, the home of silk. On the way we saw more and more mulberry fields. The new leaves hanging on the luxuriant trees were already as large as one's palm.

The Beautiful Goddess of Silkworms
Being in the home of silk, you would naturally talk about it. Lao Dong, our guide, who knew well the history of Haining and its customs, told us a touching tale about the Goddess of Silkworms, a story known to all the local people.

Once upon a time, there was a family of two members— father and daughter— who depended upon each other for survival. They owned a white horse who was very robust and energetic since the daughter fed him with mulberry leaves every day. One evening the father did not return home from his day's work as scheduled, and the daughter looked for him everywhere but in vain. In desperation she murmured: "To Heaven now I swear: he who helps me find my father, I will willingly accept as my husband." Strangely, the white horse kept nodding at her as she spoke, going around her three times. After giving out a long neigh, he ran into the distance.

After combing the mountains, the horse finally found his owner, ill and last, and carried him home. Thereafter, whenever

203

the girl was sleeping, the horse would stand by her door. No matter how hard the father tried to drive him away, he simply would not leave her. The suspicious owner questioned his daughter again and again until she finally told him of her promise to Heaven. Now furious, the father exclaimed: "It's the duty of a horse to find its lost owner— how can a horse ever marry a girl!" To indicate his protest, the horse kept neighing, snorting and kicking the earth, refusing to eat or drink anything. Finally the angry owner stretched his bow and shot an arrow into the horse's brain. Immediately, he skinned the animal and sunned the hide in front of his house. When his daughter returned home and saw what had happened, she nearly cried her heart out as she recalled what the horse had done and what she had sworn. Then as her tears fell onto the horsehide, it enveloped her and she flew into the sky. Soon after, people began to see snow-white silk cocoons hanging over the mulberries.

"Look," said Lao Dong, "isn't the silkworm's head like that of a horse? It is the incarnation of the girl and the white horse. People here all call it 'Horse-Head Girl.' Since the girl missed her father so much but could not speak a word, she spun through her mouth the silk of affection, and that is the original reason why silkworms spun cocoons."

In the past, whenever they had a good harvest of silkworms, the breeders would set tables with burning incense and offerings in the central rooms of their houses to convey their thanks to the Goddess of Silkworms. The portrait of the Goddess carved on the woodboards was one with a horsehide draping from her shoulders, having become one entity for eternity. However, there was an extra in the forehead of the goddess eye placed there by the silkworm raisers, who could not bear to see the arrow wound that would otherwise have been there.

It is interesting that the legend about the "Horse-Head Girl" also spread to Japan as silkworm breeding was introduced there from China in the third century. What is different is that after she settled in Japan, she became a beautiful Japanese girl on horseback dressed in a *kimono*.

Classical books record that China owes its first silkworm

breeding, silk reeling and weaving to Leizu, Huangdi's wife. According to legend, Huangdi, chief of the tribe alliance of the Yellow River valley over five thousand years ago, invented the boat, the cart, palaces, the compass wheel, and ordered Cangjie to create characters and Linglun to make musical instruments. For all these reasons, he has long been respected as the founder of China's civilization. His wife Leizu was not only industrious but also highly intelligent. Once she discovered some silkworms spinning cocoons on a tree. To her surprise, the cocoons survived a long winter. Then it occurred to her that since they had been able to survive cold winds and snow, they should be good material for winter clothes. So she had them made into clothes, which turned out to be warm and soft, much superior to furs and clothing made of hemp. The next year, she collected the wild silkworms and raised them indoors where, as she had expected, they spun many cocoons. Later, she taught others to breed silkworms. To commemorate this legendary mother of silkworm breeding, the people built temples and carved statues of Leizu, worshipping her as yet another Goddess of Silkworms.

The Yellow River valley is thought of then as ancient cradle of Chinese silkworm raising. Among the cultural relics of the New Stone Age ruins in Banpo, Xi'an, there is a pottery bowl six thousand years old which still carries a gauze print. In Xiyin Village, Xiaxian County, Shanxi Province, archaeologists also found a silkworm cocoon of the same age which was seen to have a knife cut.

Among the objects excavated in 1958 from the New Stone Age ruins at Qianshanyang, Wuxing County, Zhejiang Province were remains of carbonated silk, fine herringbone silk belts and silk thread. As scientifically determined, they were buried some 4,700 years ago.

Back in the Shang Dynasty over three thousand years ago, silkworm breeding was already an important industry. From the inscriptions carved on bones we know that the imperial court not only had a special agricultural official supervise silkworm production, but also had the old custom of praying to the Goddess of Silkworms for abundant harvests of cocoons with a sacrifice of three cows or six sheep.

Driving out Mice with Pictures of Cats

Finally we arrived at Yunlong, a village of some eight hundred households, and one of Haining's centers of silk production. In addition to breeding silkworms and growing rice and hemp, the villagers also engage in reeling raw silk and silk weaving.

No sooner had we entered the village than we caught sight of people washing bamboo poles by the river that were to be used in the building of silkworm shelves and trays for use in the raising of silkworms. The rectangular trays of about three feet long and two wide were woven of bamboo strips which had to be thoroughly cleaned, then dried in the sun and sterilized in medicinal liquid. Other villagers were busy soaking silkworm nets in jars filled with the medicinal liquid, then spreading them in the blazing sun to dry. These nets that are woven of thick straw ropes are laid over the trays, which being dry and well ventilated, they prevent mulberry leaves from going rotten and silkworms from catching diseases caused by dampness. Such nets also make it easy for the breeders to clear away the excrement of the silkworms; all they need do is lift them up and sweep it away.

The following evening we saw a large crowd of villagers gathering outside the local government office where we stayed. They were waiting for Zhang Lin'gen, the expert breeder of the village, who had gone to the county's hatchery to fetch them silkworm eggs. When he finally returned, all the villagers crowded around him to get what they had ordered. A page of silkworm eggs, seven inches long and three wide, contained over 23,000 eggs. Carefully wrapping them up in a piece of red paper, they carried them home in their mulberry baskets.

In the old days, the breeders bought eggs from special peddlers who went from village to village. In the daytime, breeders put the eggs under their pillows, while at night they would have them kept warm by women who usually put them close to their breasts.

Since the newly hatched silkworms are dark green, the

local people call the process "hatching greens." The primitive way of accomplishing this, is, of course, far from reliable. Today the county's hatchery, whose humidity, temperature and light are all precisely controlled, hatches for them much healthier silkworms with a higher survival rate. They pick up their silkworms in the evening simply because if they get them in the daytime, the well-hatched eggs might break when exposed to light, whereupon all the little worms will run away. As for the use of red paper, that is because it repels lamplight.

Walking through mulberry trees and paddy fields dotted with ponds where frogs croaked in that moonlit night, we arrived for our visit to Zhang Jixing's family. Unlike those in Shaoxing County located in the south of the Qiantang River, the houses of the sericulturists here were two-storied and spacious. The six members in Zhang's family lived in a house with sixteen rooms, the second floor of which contained bedrooms separately occupied by the couple, the three children and Zhang's mother, while its free ones were used as storerooms. The first floor, however, consisted of the kitchen, rooms for breeding newly hatched silkworms and for sundries, while the two central rooms facing the entrance were for grown-up silkworms during the busy seasons of breeding. Our capable host, a man about fifty, whose primary job was in the local textile factory, was growing as a contractor seven *fen* (1 *fen* = 66.666 square meters) of mulberries for the village in his spare time.

With special permission from our host, we took advantage of this chance to look around the rooms where young silkworms were being raised. Against the wall was a bamboo shelf for them. Burning stoves with chimneys were set at the south and east corners. Since it was still quite cool with the temperature rising and falling irregularly, they must keep the stoves going to regulate the indoor temperature. Through the carefully spread plastic sheets we saw on the shelf over fifty rectangular trays, a bamboo utensil for raising newly hatched silkworms, a kitchen knife, and a chopping board for cutting up mulberry leaves, as well as goose feathers for brushing young silkworms. All the objects used in these rooms must be sterilized carefully. After arranging everything in perfect order, they waited to "gather silkworms."

"Gathering silkworms" is an important step in their breeding. In this traditional ceremony is described in detail. Mao Dun's novel *Spring Silkworms*, however, nowadays the sericulturists employ scientific methods instead of the primitive traditional ways. We noticed the hostess spread a damp-proof piece of paper on top of the bamboo utensil, over which she placed the hatched eggs, finally covering it with a thin net. After spreading the pieces of mulberry and peach leaves, she covered the utensil with a tray to shelter it from the light.

Early the next morning, they removed the tray. As the "black ants" (so named because that is what they look like) were exposed to the light, they broke the eggshells and all came out at the same time. Drawn by the fragrance of the peach leaves, the young worms crawled up to the net and began to eat the mulberry leaves.

"In the past," Lao Zhang explained, "people would paste a cat on the silkworm tray before the laying of silkworm eggs." The so-called cat was only a picture on a woodblock. A fatal enemy to the silkworms, the hostile mice would take the opportunity in the dead of night when the watchers dozed off to sneak onto the shelves and eat the sericulturists' little darling. This is why the sericulturists not only raised cats but pasted pictures of them on surfaces to scare the mice away — a practice the origin of which remains a mystery.

A picture of a cat alone, of course, is not that threatening to the mouse. In recent years, a new ruse has been added to the sericulturist's bag of tricks: tape recordings of meowing set to play in the middle of the night. I was told that they do the job quite well.

From the hatching of eggs to the spinning of cocoons, the silkworm has to go through four inactive states and shed its skin four times. During these twenty-five days the silkworm raisers have to look after the silkworms as attentively as if they were their children: they must regularly feed them with mulberry leaves, keep a fire to regulate the temperature of the rooms, spread medicine to prevent diseases, and clear away the excrement.

After the last inactive state, the now sizable silkworm keeps eating mulberry leaves day and night, growing even more rapidly. At this time, the 23,000 silkworms from the page of silkworm eggs have to be moved onto fifty rectangular trays. When the fully grown silkworm's mouth grows pointed and it stops eating, that means it is about to spin silk. Now the sericulturists spread out the hemp stalk screens with umbrella-shaped straw bundles over them, scattering the silkworms all over the screens so that they can crawl up the bundles to spin cocoons. The villagers begin to pick out the cocoons the moment the silkworms change into pupae, putting the cocoons into large bamboo baskets with ventilated straw bundles in the middle and sell them to the purchasing centers immediately. The cocoons then have to be baked in the ovens in order to prevent the pupae from changing into moths, which will ruin the cocoons.

As far as silkworm raising is concerned, there are five crops every year in Haining — spring, summer, early-autumn, mid-autumn, and late autumn silkworms, with the spring yielding the most with the finest quality. The local saying goes, "In the first half of the year you count on sericulture, in the second half you count on farming; a good harvest of cocoons lasts a year, a fine harvest of rice feeds you two half-years." After the spring sericulture, the silkworm raisers are often emaciated as a result of overwork, but their delight at the sight of the snow-white cocoons shows on their faces.

After each good cocoon harvest, every family celebrates by having rich dinners with fish, meat, chicken and wine. During these days, the country paths are usually crowded with visitors carrying *zongzi* (glutinous rice wrapped with bamboo or reed leaves in the shape of a pyramid). They present their "Cocoon Flower *Zongzi*" to their friends or relatives as cordial greetings or inquiries about their latest cocoon harvest.

"Cocoon Flower Girls" Who Wear Cocoon Flowers

The term "cocoon flower" does not refer to an actual flower but is used as a substitute for "cocoon harvest" in sericulture. Traditionally, the local silkworm raisers like to weigh the silkworms after the fourth inactive state is over. If they get six *jin* (1 *jin* = 0.5 kilogram) from one *jin* of big silkworms, they call this "a six-*fen* cocoon flower"; if they get eight *jin*, then it is "an eight-*fen* cocoon flower."

With the passing of time, as a symbol of abundant harvests and good luck, the term has not only been used widely in sericultural activities and the annual festivals and holidays, but has also brought about the women's practice of dressing with "cocoon flowers."

Female sericulturists have come to be called locally "cocoon flower girls." Early in the morning of the Spring Festival, as traditionally practiced, "cocoon flower girls" sweep the silkworm rooms from the outside to the inside. The superstition holds that in this way they sweep in more "cocoon flowers," abundant harvests, in other words.

When the villagers greet each other during the Spring Festival, after exchanging wishes such as for a bonanza, they will add "and a twenty-four-*fen* cocoon flower!" Even though a cocoon harvest of twelve *fen* is already very rare, they still follow the form of wishing for a number actually beyond anyone's reach.

The eighth of the second lunar month is the day when Haining holds its annual "temple fair" in the capital town. Sericulturists from all over the county gather at the bustling fair, buying new silkworm trays, bamboo articles and other items that are needed in later raising. This grand gathering is named "Squeezing Cocoon Flowers."

On Qingming Day (April 5), "cocoon flower girls" all wear "cocoon flowers." They make little flowers with color paper and silk ribbons, or simply cut a cocoon into four petals and dye it, or pick a golden vegetable flower and wear it in their hair. On this day, they go in groups to the Lingyin Temple at the West Lake in Hangzhou. After worshipping the Buddhas with burning incense there, they usually buy a cocoon flower made of silk to place at the edge of the silkworm tray at home, a custom known locally as "begging for cocoon flowers." They believe that the flower from the sacred Buddhist temple will keep the silkworm nurseries safe from evils and bring about a good harvest of cocoons. In the evening, the hostess prepares a reunion dinner with numerous delicacies and a pot of warm wine for all the family. As everybody drinks a cup of "cocoon flower wine," the whole family in effect pledges that they will work as one to insure an abundance of healthy silkworms.

After the harvest of cocoons, the leading sericulturist families even invite troupes to put on "cocoon flower operas," or shadow plays, to entertain all their relatives as well as the other villagers. It is said that the tissue paper used as the stage curtain of the shadow play—the "cocoon flower paper,"— becomes in and of itself a harbinger of good fortune because of the occasion of its use. Therefore, the organizer keeps it as a treasure after the show. The next year, he spreads it over the silkworm trays, believing that it will bring about a better harvest of cocoons.

Closely Tied to Silk from Birth to Death

It was early on a spring morning that I saw two pretty young women with bamboo baskets tied to their waists picking mulberry leaves. Since silk comes from mulberry leaves, the sericulturists who pick them regard them as if they were gold. According to the sizes of the silkworms and the amount they consume, the raisers can calculate quite easily how many basketfuls of leaves are needed and whether they should pick new leaves or old ones; they even know how many leaves they should pick from each branch of every tree. For the fully grown silkworms they do not pick leaves only, but even scissor off whole branches. The snipped-off places, however, will put forth new branches with luxuriant leaves for the summer silkworms in a month's time.

One of the women carried a new basket which was so beautiful that it caught our attention immediately. The head of the village who accompanied us, Mr. Lu said with a smile, "Zhaodi, you brought this beautiful basket from home last year when you were married, did you not?"

And the wife grinned back with a nod.

In this sericultural region, brides not only bring to their new homes such things as silk clothes and silk-padded quilts, but also two mulberry seedlings, silkworm eggs, bamboo trays for newly hatched silkworms and baskets for mulberry leaves. Using *shuang* (double) as a substitute for *sang* (mulberry), people wish the bride and the bridegroom wedded bliss and a prosperous life, expecting that the bride will contribute significantly to the rapid development of her new family's sericulture rapidly.

Their unique marriage customs reminded me of a tale from *Stories of the West Region in the Tang Dynasty* written by the famous Buddhist monk Xuan Zang. In those days, Qusadan (today's Xinjiang) had neither mulberries nor silkworms. In order to acquire these resources, the prince proposed marriage to a princess of the neighboring country to the east. Joining her bridegroom, the clever princess hid mulberry seeds and silkworm eggs in her hats, managing to make it through all the passes undetected. After that, silk became a flourishing industry in the region.

To the brides of the sericultural villages, the most important thing for them to do in the first year is to raise the silkworms well. If they fail to do so, they will be considered a harbinger of bad luck instead of a "cocoon flower woman."

Mr. Lu told me that beginning from the day they were born when they were clad with soft silk clothes the people here were one way or another closely linked to silk, the community's primary mechanism for survival. On the first birthday of a baby, the parents clothe him in mulberry green silk, hoping that when he grows up, he will be competent at raising silkworms. On the birthdays of the elders, their respectful juniors not only provide them with silk clothes and shoes, but also make balls of red silk which they hang in the central rooms where the celebrations are held. While in Beijing people whose birthdays are celebrated are treated to long noodles, the local villagers, with endless silk, wish the old people a life as long as the silk thread.

When an old person dies, the members of his family immediately cover his face with silk floss. His sons, daughters, sons-in-law, and daughters-in-law go around the coffin in succession holding a lit candle, passing it to the next in line. The last one blows out the candle and the family saves it, lighting this "cocoon flower candle" in the silkworm nursery to make things there easy and smooth. When the remains are finally removed to the coffin, there is a ceremony called "tearing the cocoon flower," in which they tear up a silk-padded quilt and cover the body with the silk floss, layer after layer. The thicker the body is covered, the grander the ceremony is, which in turn means that they have torn a "24-*fen* cocoon flower."

Taboos in the Silkworm Nursery

Beginning with the first day of spring silkworm raising, a chill falls over the village. Men and women, old and young, all stop visiting each other; children no longer shout at the top of their lungs; men do not work with bare backs no matter how hot it is. In the old society, this was also the time for those in heavy debt to relax: creditors who came to press for payment had to withdraw at the sight of a door dressed with a peach branch or a magic figure from the temple or a piece of red paper saying: "This Month of Silkworm Raising Sees Good Manners."

With regard to the silkworm nursery, there are many more taboos. That afternoon, Zhang Zixiang, an experienced silkworm raiser of over sixty, told me more than ten without much thinking:

First, strangers are forbidden to enter the nursery;
Second, no pounding or digging of earth is allowed nearby;
Third, no knocking at doors or beating at silkworm trays;
Fourth, no weeping is permitted inside;
Fifth, dirty language is prohibited;
Sixth, alcohol, vinegar and pepper are not allowed to be brought in;
Seventh, there must be no splashing of hot soup over ashes;
Eighth, no burning of furs or hairs;
Ninth, no exposure to the sun or facing the west;
Tenth, the temperature must not be high one minute and cold another.

213

Of course there are more, such as the prohibition of women who have just given birth or are having menstrual periods and of people in mourning; and no mulberry leaves brought from other places can be eaten by silkworms until their evils have been beaten out (three times) with a mulberry lash. These all are obvious superstitions. However, the purpose of all these taboos is to avoid noise and air pollution so as to enable the silkworms to grow up healthily in a clean environment. Somebody once made the experiment of blowing several mouthfuls of smoke at the silkworms, and the little creatures soon began to toss from left to right, vomiting a sort of yellow water. From this we see that the taboos in the silkworm nursery are but unwritten laws for silkworm breeding!

Staring at Zhang's nursery, I longed to go inside and take a few shots of his silkworms, but when I reflected on all the taboos he had just recited, I could not but keep silent. At last I plucked up my courage and asked him if I could go in and have a look.

"Please do," he said without hesitation and held up the enclosing plastic film to signal me to step in.

When I asked him later why he had decided to break the taboos he explained it this way: "People used to worry that strangers might bring bad luck to the silkworm rooms, it's true, but obviously that's simply superstition. Of course, if you have a lot of people going in and out, the temperature inside is going to be affected, which could have a harmful effect on the fragile silkworms. You also have to watch out for strangers bringing in infectious diseases." He added with joke! "I decided to take a chance on you."

When I asked about silkworm diseases, Zhang spoke out of his long years of experience. There are two common diseases, he told me: "white belly disease" and muscardine. When the silkworms catch the first, they only eat, but do not spin silk, and finally die of festering. In the past when this disease was discovered, they sprayed some salty water over the mulberry leaves, which being anti bacterial and counteractive to inflammation helped to control the spread of the disease. Muscardine is much more terrifying, for it spreads very rapidly. Sometimes even though you see that cocoons are already in sight, a number of silkworms with muscardine can ruin everything in two or three days' time. In the past, once the sericulturists discovered a stiff white silkworm — a sure sign of muscardine — they would swallow it down immediately. Looking back from today, we can see that through swallowing it instead of throwing it out, they prevented the disease from spreading to other households. And by the way, it is harmless for humans to swallow muscardine-affected silkworms, which in fact provide an ingredient used in Chinese traditional medicine prescriptions for treating headache, sore throat, convulsions, and scrofula.

"To tell you the truth, in the past, nobody would ever be so daring as to say the word 'muscardine' out loud while raising spring silkworms!" admitted Zhang Zixiang. "But nowadays, we spread anti-muscardine powder right after the young worms come out of their shells, so it doesn't really matter whether I say the word or not."

Yes, superstition may linger but quite shorn of its power to strike terror to the heart — certainly of the enlightened sericulturist, which clearly Zhang was.

CHAPTER VIII

SICHUAN — The Land of Heaven

CHENGDU'S TEAHOUSES, HOT SNACKS, ETC.

"Oh, how dangerous!
Shu's roads so rough and cliffs so high,
They're harder to climb than the sky!"

With these vivid lines Li Bai, celebrated poet of the Tang Dynasty, described the rough mountain paths and walkways made from wooden planks laid over rocks. Shu is the short form for Sichuan Province, which lies in the southwest of China. Two to three thousand years ago there lived a tribe known as Shu in this area. During the period of the Three Kingdoms (220-280), Liu Bei founded his State of Shu (221-263) here. So Shu and Sichuan are interchangeable names for the same province.

Last winter, after traveling over two thousand kilometers southwestward from Beijing, I arrived in Chengdu, the capital of Sichuan Province. During my train ride, I kept thinking of how arduous it must have been for the ancients to climb over all these high mountains around us. When passing Qinling Peak, the train went through one tunnel after another. Statistics show that the railway between Baoji in Xi'an and Chengdu, though only 669 kilometers long, has 335 tunnels and 998 bridges.

Entering the plains of Chengdu, I found that the piercing northern wind and swirling yellow dust were both kept out by Qinling Peak. Winter here was as warm as spring. This warm weather coupled with an abundance of rainfall meant that plants remained green throughout the year. Over the vast fertile land lay an irrigation network of streams and ditches, serving the young wheat and bean seedlings, the vegetables and other green plants. Such golden fruit hung all over the orange trees. No wonder the ancients compared this beautiful land to their imaginary heaven, naming it *Tianfuzhiguo*, or "Land of Abundance."

Old-styled Teahouses

Early in the morning drizzle cyclists were a steady stream in the streets of Chengdu, many of them carrying babies on their backs, a practice strictly forbidden in Beijing. Of course such permissiveness here might be based on the special abilities of the local people.

Most of Chengdu's produce markets were located in the old residential quarters with narrow busy streets. I entered the flow of people, passing one by one the numerous vegetable, meat, fish, egg and daily necessity stalls, and the snack stands. A man of about thirty was shouting at the top of his lungs in rhythmic Sichuanese:

Come right up for
Super spiced duck to
Bring you good luck!

Leaving the busy market, I caught sight of a teahouse on a crossroad. As the old saying goes, "China's teahouses rank first in the world—Chengdu's teahouses rank first in China." Chengdu's teahouses are well-known not only because of their large number but also because they play a special role in the citizens' lives, providing both a social outlet and entertainment.

I went straight into a two-roomed teahouse. Its tables, some of which were set up outside on the sidewalk, were fully occupied. Five or six retired workers were relaxing in comfortable bamboo chairs under a large tree chatting and drinking in leisurely fashion despite the drizzle. From time to time, they lifted their cups, sipping fragrant jasmine tea through the narrow opening between the cup and its cover that stopped the leaves from flowing out.

The waiter known as "Dr. Tea" hereabouts was a thin, sharp-eyed fellow in his forties, a white apron tied round his waist, who somehow managed to provide prompt, courteous and efficient service to all comers, never mind their number. What was his secret? Speed! Speed and dexterity — and of course there were those quick eyes of his that never failed to note a new customer. He'd be there in a flash, all smiles, his left hand holding a tea set and his right a teapot called a "Black Hen" by the local people. He'd set the table as he greeted his customers with a line of patter, taking seconds to set the cup in its saucer, pour the water and put back the cover. And thus he darted among the tables like a character in a movie being shown in accelerated motion. I watched him raise the pot of hot water, pouring into the customers' cups from behind their backs or over their heads, when the cup was nearly full he suddenly stopped by lifting his right hand. In this way, which is known as "Snowflake Covering," not a single drop ever fell from his pot. How skilful he was!

The tea set itself consists of three elegant ancient-styled articles: a small tray (or saucer), a cup, and a cover. In the middle of the tray there is a round dent which is properly designed for the ringed foot of the cup. Since the tray supports the cup as if it were a boat, traditionally it has been called a "teaboat" by the local people.

Here is a legend about the "teaboat." During the Jianzhong years of the Tang Dynasty (684), the daughter of Cui Ning (envoy to Xichuan) was fond of drinking tea, but because she was afraid of holding the hot cup, she had her cup put in a dish. Then because it could easily fall off the dish, she had it fixed to the middle of the dish with wax. Her father loved her idea so much that he had carpenters make wooden trays with lacquer rings in the middle as a variation, and once he began to use the novel tea sets in entertaining his guests, others followed his lead one after another. Later, to replace the raised lacquer ring, clever craftsmen added a ringed foot to the tea cup and dug a dent in the center of the tray. Ever since then, a tea set of three articles has been used without much change.

The cover has many uses, including keeping the tea hot and regulating the dissolving speed of the tea leaves by keeping a proper amount of steam inside. Impatient drinkers can have strong tea immediately simply by turning the tea leaves over and over again with the cover. Sipping through the opening between the cup and its cover is surely a pleasure for the drinker, for thus the tea leaves cannot easily get into his mouth.

However, few teahouse customers really go there to quench their thirst. A group of elderly people, each of whom paid only about twenty cents in the first place, can spend their whole day here chatting from morning till night. The bird fanciers among them even hang their cages on the branches of trees, with their birds inside singing all day long. When their old friends praise the birds for their beautiful singing, the old folks grin in smug satisfaction. At present, the apartment for the average citizen in Chengdu is not spacious, so that when the rare visitor comes along, most people will suggest going out to a teahouse where they can sit over a cup as long as they please, cracking melon seeds as they chat.

One morning we invited some of the elderly people to introduce to us their local customs. Our talk, appropriately enough, took place in a teahouse, in this case an elegant one. In the corner sat two middle-aged men whispering to each other gesturing vigorously. It was quite apparent that they were talking business— bargaining over the terms of a deal.

In the old days, the teahouse was a place where people from all trades and organizations in Chengdu gathered to exchange business information, negotiate deals, look over samples, and strike bargains. In brief, every trade had its own teahouse which served as its "business center." Even the unemployed coolies and teachers had to look to the special teahouses that offered jobs openings for laborers and teachers. Only through these teahouses could they find work.

After the founding of New China, all such "centers" to an end, but in recent years, as China opens itself to foreigners and practices free economic policies at home, people are returning to the teahouses to exchange market information and hold business talks.

The seats, about eighty or ninety in number, of one spacious teahouse located deep in a lane were usually taken up early in the afternoon. Customers came no later than three o'clock to listen to the storyteller telling *The Romance of the Song Dynasty* as they drank tea. Aged nearly fifty, the square-jawed storyteller played different roles as the story unfolded. One moment he fanned himself gently with a paper fan and spoke gracefully, at another he struck the table and rose to his feet, a knight on horseback with his fan becoming a sword smiting a deadly foe. Among the audience was an old customer who was so enthralled that he did not realize he had forgotten to light his cigarette until his fingers felt the flame of his match.

Of course entertainments differ from one teahouse to another: elsewhere were comic crosstalks, Sichuan dulcimer, as well as Sichuan operas, like those put on by amateurs in the nearby Tea Yard of the Builders' Club. There, a well-equipped band and tuneful singing won the enthusiastic applause of the audience. One of the old opera fans told me, "You only pay thirty cents (slightly higher when there was opera singing or storytelling) for a comfortable seat, wonderful service and pleasant entertainment at this teahouse."

In recent years, teahouses inside the theaters and parks have been redecorated. These attractive cafes with folding tables and chairs as well as modern music attract boys and girls dressed in the latest fashions, becoming an ideal setting for young people to meet their friends or sweethearts.

But not only do teahouses in Chengdu serve as reception rooms, clubs and centers for various exchanges, but also as informal courts where civil disputes are mediated.

Here is a typical scene where the teahouse is being used in this fashion. The contending parties are led in by the mediator and take their seats. "Dr. Tea" counts the number of cups but never asks them to pay in advance. After each side has narrated his side of the dispute, the mediator decides who is right and who is wrong, whereupon the wrong side must pay for the tea.

Strangely enough, the hostile disputers' anger begins to dissipate the moment they sit down over tea perhaps because they feel too embarrassed to argue in the presence of other tea drinkers. Then after listening to the reasoning of the mediator, someone well respected in the community, they make up. The winner, of course, can have no complaint. But even for the lose it can be counted well worth it to cover the small costs for the tea, since the elimination of rancor brings with it a new lease on life. And that is actually the real meaning of the local saying: "The four-legged table talks you out and walks off."

Sichuan's Interesting Local Expressions

Before coming to Chengdu, I was warned by one of my colleagues never to use strange local expressions like *chuizi* (hammer in Sichuan). He himself had been sent to work in the countryside in Sichuan in the early 1960s. As he was tidying up his room just after his arrival and decided to ask his elderly neighbor for the loan of a hammer, he nearly got into serious trouble, for in Sichuan *chuizi* is a very dirty word. One is well advised to substitute the word *langtou* instead.

Following the precept to do in Rome as the Romans do, I made a point in Chengdu of observing its customs. However, sometimes I still took things for granted and often caused misunderstandings as a result. One day that busy "Dr. Tea" happened to have a few minutes to spare, so he came over to chat with me. "Your camera is very *bashi* [firm]," he observed.

"Yes," I agreed. "Last year I dropped it on the ground and it didn't need a bit of repairing."

But Cui Xianchang, who was accompanying me, laughed. "What this gentleman means is that your camera is very good," he informed me. Only then did I learn that *bashi* was often used to express the meaning "good." For instance, you might say, "The fish I got today is truly *bashi*," or "That dinner was certainly *bashi*." Yet I had taken it to mean "firm."

Cui Xianchang was an editor on *Longmenzhen*, a popular regional magazine dealing with local culture, history, and folk

221

customs. In this context, it is well to understand that the term *longmenzhen* also means "chatting" and "storytelling."

There are two ways of explaining the origin of this expression. The first is that when General Xue Rengui of the early Tang Dynasty was on a punitive strike to the east, he deployed his troops in a *longmenzhen* — a very changeable battle formation. People of later generations thus began to call any telling of complicated, interesting stories *bai* (deploy) *longmenzhen*. The other version has it that to keep all evils off their houses the ancient country folks in Sichuan painted the doors (*menzi*) of their yards with colorful dragons (*long*). During the slack seasons then, the farmers would sit around the *longmenzi*, listening to the old folks tell stories. Thus, relating to this traditional practice, the local people refer to both idle conversation and storytelling as *bai longmenzhen*.

Being one of the seven major Chinese dialects, Sichuan belongs to the northern ones. Some of its tones and pronunciation of words differ from those of the Beijing dialect, but generally they can be mutually understood. Nonetheless, the meaning of some standard characters has changed in local speech and must not be interpreted without real understanding. For example, *anyi* (easy and comfortable) carries the meaning of "good" while *dundu* (honest and sincere) means "well-built" instead.

Having stayed in Chengdu for a couple of days, I found that most local citizens had the gift of gab and were able to use very vivid language as well. But why?

"Probably this is because Sichuan is a culturally developed and prosperous province, and its citizens seem to have been born optimistic and argumentative," Lao Cui conjectured, adding that the Sichuanese had to have their bit of humor every day. People who work together, people in the same family, relatives, friends, neighbors — everyone it seems likes to joke with one another.

As a lover of aphorisms, Lao Cui collected notebooks of proverbs and two-part allegorical sayings. No wonder his conversation was sprinkled with them. One day he accompanied me on an interviewing visit. The subject said modestly, "I have

222

nothing worth telling you at all. I'm afraid. This is a case of 'a mosquito biting at a Buddha — picking the wrong person.'"

"I know you are the right person, and have plenty to tell," said Lao Cui. "So come on now, let's hear it. You can't let our reporter leave, having come from Beijing to do no more than 'spread lime on the road — waste all the way.'"

Another time we wanted to get a taxi to the countryside, but the driver refused us with all sorts of excuses. Then Lao Cui said, "Forget it. That's someone who 'holds a walking stick while wearing nailed shoes — too prudent.' On a rainy day the roads are muddy; he'll never drive us there anyway." In Sichuan, the frequent rainfalls make the roads very slippery, so to help them make it through, people wear sharp nailed shoes and hold a stick when going outdoors. The source of the two-part allegorical saying.

Some expressions in dialect had their origins in Sichuan opera. One example is *chanlingzi*, or "shake the plum." Originally, when the male pheasant courted the female it would shake its feathers. Later, on the stage of Sichuan opera whenever a warrior appeared he would shake the plumes inserted in his helmet to signal his status as hero. Therefore, from the shaking of plumes on the stage, people began to call those who wanted to be in the limelight *chanlingzi*.

In Sichuan *chijiu* — drinking wine or other liquor — also has its special meaning. Traditionally, when a couple gets married there, the bridegroom must entertain his guests with a wedding feast served with alcoholic drinks. Gradually, the expression *chijiu* became a substitute for "getting married."

Pungent Foods in Sichuan

I was worried about Sichuan's hot foods even before I came. As expected, what I had at my first meal in Chengdu was a particularly pungent pork hash. I had to stick out my tongue to cool it in the cold air. The next day I found a snack bar nearby and ordered two bowls of *shuijiao* (dumplings with soup). When the waiter brought me my order I didn't know what to do with it: both bowls were covered with a thick layer of red chili oil!

223

That people in Sichuan love chilis is said to have something to do with their damp rainy climate. Being pungent, chilis warm one's body up and have the medicinal effect of eliminating the "wetness-evil" (Chinese traditional medicine term) from the system. That is why people in the wet regions, such as Yunnan, Guizhou, Hunan, and Jiangxi, like to eliminate "cold-evil" and "wetness-evil" with chilli and peppers. In the old days the wretched poor who lacked clothes to wear kept themselves warm by chewing chilli with salt, since before long this hot stuff would make them sweat all over. Some doctors of traditional Chinese medicine have said that due to their frequent eating of hot foods, the Sichuanese sense of taste is not so good because their tongue coating is usually thicker than that of the inhabitants of other places. Consequently, they will lose their appetite once their food is not cooked with chilli — they simply find it tasteless.

Obviously I could not get a refund on those two bowls of dumplings before me, so I feel I at least had to try them. I found the red oil not so bad after all: there was even a sweet fragrance in its hotness.

"Sichuan food," "Shandong food," "Jiangsu food," and "Guangdong food" together are counted the four major types of Chinese cuisine. In these provinces, the most ordinary snack bars produce delicious food out of bits and pieces of meat and vegetables.

At my first hearing of the term "Husband-and-Wife Lung Slices," I just could not make anything out of it. When I entered the eating house which featured this oddly named dish, I found it to be a bar selling bits and pieces of beef. The beef slices from ox heads were slices so thin they looked almost transparent. Dressed with a gravy mixed with garlic, onions and celery, they had a wonderfully fresh and savory flavor.

But why "Husband-and-Wife Lung Slices"? Asking an elderly customer at my table I learned that in the years when the two pioneers Guo Chaohua and his wife were establishing themselves, they cut into thin slices ox head meat, hearts, tongues and stomachs and stewed them in one pot, which they called *Huipian* (choice slices). With a trolley the couple hawked their stews in the streets. But as *hui* (choice) and *fei* (lung) sounded like homonyms in Chinese, some naughty fellow wrote on a piece of cardboard "Husband-and-Wife Lung Slices" and hung it over their trolley. And that is how the name came into use. "Though it's far from an elegant name," said the old fellow, "in those days whenever their cart passed by, it would fill the air with pleasing smelling. Indeed, 'The cart was going along one side of the road, but its delicious meat smell tempted everyone in the street.'"

Though some eating houses in Beijing also serve Sichuan "*Dandan* Noodles," or "Shouldered Noodles," the true flavor of this Sichuan food is still found in Chengdu. It is said that the first maker of these noodles was a peddler: he carried a load with a shoulder pole with noodles and condiments on one side and the stove and pot on the other. When he had a customer, he stopped and cooked the noodles for him right on the spot.

Spending sixty *fen* that day, I enjoyed four kinds of noodles, each with a different flavor. Among them was a bowl of sweet and sour "*Dandan* Noodles" covered with "red oil," another was "burning noodles" with green garlic, bean sprouts, peanuts, sesame, and sesame oil added. Because of the quantity of sesame oil, the noodles would start burning once lighted. So that is how the dish got its name.

"Rather Eat Without Meat Than Live Without Bamboo"

At present, there are about 1,200 types of bamboo in the world, and China's species and output both rank first in the world. In Chengdu's Wangjianglou Park alone there are over a hundred kinds. From the distant past right up to the present moment, Chinese scholars have written about bamboo. Probably out of his affection for the bamboo of his hometown — Meishan County, Sichuan Province — Su Dongpo, a great writer of the Song Dynasty, detailed the uses of bamboo in the daily life of the time: "We eat bamboo shoots, cover roofs with bamboo, carry things in baskets of bamboo, turn bamboo into firewood, make clothing from bamboo, write on paper made of bamboo, and wear bamboo shoes...." He's

225

also the author of the line: "Rather eat without meat than live without bamboo." Sichuan is not only the major producer of bamboo in China but consumer as well.

Nowadays, having come to be regarded as a folk art, summer bamboo shirts that are woven of tiny bamboo tubes strung together are no longer worn but only exhibited in museums of arts and crafts. Bamboo shoes, however, are still found in many places. During my visit I saw a group of mountain villagers selling bamboo shoes called *Mawozi* at a country fair in Hongya County, and one seller explained how they were made. Tender pieces of bamboo are first baked over a fire until they become soft, then raked with iron teeth into sizeable strips which will finally be woven into shoes. Strong and durable, dry and well ventilated, *Mawozi* are ideal for mountain climbers since they are both comfortable and grip well.

Situated by the Yangtze River are Jiang'an and Changning counties whose bamboo forests are known as a Sea of Bamboo. Mountain villagers of Changning make bamboo tiles by splitting bowl-shaped bamboo segments, knocking out the joints and layering them with one half face up and the other face down. A strong building material, bamboo can not only be made into frames and cages, but, when filled with pebbles can even be used as piers of bridges. As for other articles woven for daily use, they are simply too many to count.

One day when I visited my friend Lao Guo, I had the opportunity of studying a bamboo house. The walls of such cottages which are pleasantly cool on the hottest days of summer, are constructed of a woven bamboo fence fixed to the frame of the house and then covered with mud on both sides. Actually, the bamboo purlins alone are strong enough to withstand the pressure of the straw roof.

In the central room where we were received, the chairs, the tea table, the dining table, and the flower stand in the corner were all made of bamboo. When the hospitable hostess served us oranges, she also put the fruit on an elegantly woven tray. In our host's study and bedroom, his bookshelf, his pen container and writing brush stand were also bamboo products. Lao Guo then showed me a little bamboo basket. "In the hot summer I often pick a few flowers and put them into this little basket," he said, "then hang it over my bed. It isn't long before the sweet smell of flowers sends me off to sleep."

When the hostess was cooking for us, I followed her into her kitchen. Her utensils, including the baskets with which she carried firewood, the broom, the containers for rice and vegetables and the steamer were all made of bamboo. The pyramid pot cover consisting of dry husks strung together was remarkably easy to lift. "Sichuan people can do without anything but bamboo," said Lao Guo. "A baby grows up in a bamboo cradle and in a basket carried by the mother. A bride sits on a bamboo sedan chair on her wedding day. Even when a person dies, his coffin is laid on a bamboo 'burial sedan chair' when it is carried off to be buried. Anyway, we cannot do without bamboo from the day we are born till the day we die."

Chongqing County, known as Shuzhou in ancient times, is located forty kilometers west of Chengdu. As we drove westward, I noticed that all the houses in the green open country were surrounded by tall bamboo plants swaying in the breeze. In the shade of the bamboo lay buffalo chewing their cuds, their eyes half closed.

Led by our guide, we came to visit Le Shujun in the Daoming Township. Stepping into his house, we saw the host in the yard scraping the green cover off bamboo stalks, which he then split into strips for sunning on the roof. Once they became their honey-colored, they would never change again. His two sisters and their mother sat weaving at the entrance, causing fine bamboo strips to turn quickly into lovely round baskets.

A few years ago Le Shujun had built this house, planting bamboo around it as soon as it was completed. The enclosing bamboo fence keeps the blazing sun off the house in summer and fierce winds in the winter, naturally making it much more comfortable to live in. Nonetheless, the local saying, "Growing bamboo is better than bringing up a child," somehow does seem to go a bit far. But Le Shujun defended it, pointing out that it is taken twenty years to bring up a child, but in the case of bamboo only two or three years are

227

needed. One year after the planting, the fast propagating bamboos begin to provide you bamboo shoots, and in the third year they are old enough to be cut, with whose strips you can weave various articles.

Out of the 4,000 families or more in this district 3,200 go for bamboo weaving in their spare time. The second day of our visit happened to be Daoming's market day. As the villagers around gathered at the fair with all sorts of woven articles, the small town immediately became a beautiful world of bamboo products.

TRADITIONAL WAYS OF FISHING, PAPERMAKING, AND DIGGING BAMBOO SHOOTS

Fishing with Lazy Rods and Cooking with Boiling Pots

Heading from Chengdu for Bingling Village in Hongya County, we drove 180 kilometers southwestward, our goal a sacred place of Buddhism located at the northern foot of the Emei Mountains. Our car ran slowly on the mountain highway winding among the peaks. Seeming to float on a sea of clouds were these green mountains with their leafy trees, tall bamboos, frequent brooks, and footbridges hanging across valleys.

When we had almost reached Bingling, I suddenly saw through the window of the car curved bamboo poles dipping into the river. "What are those?" I asked our guide Lao Gao.

"Fishing rods," he told me.

"But how come nobody looks after them?"

"Because no one is needed. That's why they came to be called 'Lazy Fishing Rod'."

My curiosity aroused, I asked the guide to show me just what was involved in this unique way of fishing right after our arrival at the village. I soon found out that the fishermen first built up stone piles in the shallow parts of a river or stream and then planted their fishing rods there. Hanging from the top of each rod was a water-resistant string made of fine bamboo strips to the end of which was tied to a bamboo loop which was in turn tied to a moss-covered stone. Thus the weight caused the pole to be bent into a bow. How could they catch fish with such a simple device? To show me the "trap," our guide went into the river to bring up the line. The real secret of the "trap" turned out to be seven or eight iron hooks fixed to a length of the string, one end of which was tied to the bamboo loop. Then fishhooks were hung beside bamboo strips which were wound around the mossy rock. So the mossy rock was really the "trap."

At night, *ya fish* (named after their birthplace, the Ya River) go out to feed. Living in the rivers and lakes of the highlands, this small fish mainly lives on moss. Probably because of the difficulty in biting the moss off the rocks, the fish first swims against the current, opens its mouth wide, then swim rapidly with the current right at the rock to take each big bite. It is when the fish rushes at the rock with its mouth open that it may swallow one of the hooks, or otherwise get hooked. As it struggles backward, it loosens the bamboo loop fixed to the strips tied around the stone. Thus the hooked fish can only struggle in the river, and the next day the fisherman just comes to pick off the fish and refasten the string to the strips around the stone.

"The 'Lazy Rod' is a marvelous device since it doesn't need any bait or anybody to look after it," I said. But what would you do if the fish decided not to rush at the stone?"

"They do have ways out," admitted the guide. "To deal with those that escape getting hooked in the trap, they get them with 'Turning Hooks.'" The so-called Turning Hooks are actually two fishhooks fixed to a string. First they are thrown into the river, and then as the fisherman winds up the string as fast as he can, fish that bump into them simply can't escape. Skillful fishermen can hook some fish nearly every time they throw the string into the river.

As we entered the dining hall for lunch at noon the following day, I saw a cook cutting out bones from *ya fish* they had slit. I called out: "Hey, wait a minute! Let me have a look first." He just smiled. "Take it easy," he advised. "We still have plenty of live ones in the vat." I went over to see for myself and noted that each one of those fish with dark green mouth and back, silver belly, long fins and closely placed teeth really did have hook cuts in its body.

In the central room our host Lao He, who had invited us to a *ya fish* chafing dish meal (*huoguo* in Chinese), built up a hot fire in the stove and put on a pot. I've been told that North China already had copper *huoguo* 1,400 years ago. In the Tang Dynasty this cooking method became very popular and began to spread to China's neighboring countries. People in Beijing eat instant-boiled mutton with *huoguo* mostly in winter, but in Sichuan they have *huoguo* food all the year around. And though Chongqing is known to be one of the hottest cities in China, people there still love to sit around the boiling *huoguo*, enjoying crisp tripe as they fan themselves continuously and keep mopping their brows. It's worth it to them to enjoy this "hairy tripe" chafing dish with its unique Sichuan flavor.

It was a cold winter day as we sat around the hot stove. When the soup was well blended with the ingredients boiling in the pot, we dipped in the boned fish chunks piece by piece. The fish chunks were ever so tender and delicately flavored and the soup was ever so strong and spicy. So together with the fresh bean curd, celery, green garlic and cabbage, we had ourselves a perfect Sichuan meal.

Digging Bamboo Shoots in the Mountains

That day, in order to take a few shots of the beautiful scenery of Bingling, we climbed up into the mountains. Suddenly we realized that behind us two mountaineers were gaining on us. On their shoulders were home-made shotguns and tied to their waists were ox horns filled with gunpowder and iron sand. Each was equipped with a curved knife. Both men, are learned, were from Liutiao Village: Liu Shijin, about fifty, a tall, thin man, and his companion, surnamed Li, also tall but burlier and much younger— say twenty-six. Since they were both working in the mountains that day, they decided to dig some bamboo shoots and do a little wild game hunting.

They were dressed in a very special way. Their caps were made of oak bark with a pointed peak and a flat back. Lao Liu told us that with this convenient cap one felt safe when pushing his head into the bamboo groves for shoots. Draping from their shoulders were palm rain capes woven from palm leaves. The cape was light and smooth and did not get hooked on tree branches — and since it swelled when wet, it was waterproof. Their shoes were woven of strings processed from bamboo. With the eight iron teeth fixed under each sole, such shoes kept their wearer from slipping and were thus ideal for mountain climbing. The men wore no socks; their feet were wrapped in palm fibers instead. The reason turned out to be that in the dense forests of the high mountains it was often rainy and foggy, and once the socks got wet they became very uncomfortable. Palm fibers, however, were not only warm but also dry and comfortable because they were water-resistant.

In my own hometown, a mountain village in Guangdong (See Chapter XIV) there is bamboo everywhere. I can still remember clearly how exciting it was when I as a boy followed my father and elder brothers up into the mountains where they went to dig for bamboo shoots. But I discovered that in this mountain area there were many taboos surrounding this activity.

In April every year when spring bamboo shoots begin to break through the earth, Liu Shijin and the other twenty villagers pack up their bedclothes and their bowls, pots, ladles and basins with enough food for three weeks and head for the high mountains. When they pass by a huge stone, they suddenly stop to burn joss sticks before it, praying for protection against dangers — believing that particular this huge stone is the mountain god that dominates all the forests in the vicinity. It is unknown when this superstitious activity really started.

It is never easy to dig bamboo shoots in the rainy season. Though they have worshipped the mountain god, accidents such as falls, sword or ax cuts, and snake bites still occur frequently. For that reason, the diggers fear most of all the word "hang" and will never hang up their caps, curved knives, or rain capes lest they themselves fall and get hurt, having invited it by hanging up things. In Jilin of the Northeast, ginseng diggers and hunters in the Changbai Mountains greet one another with the word *Kuaidang* (at high speed and with luck) when they meet to wish each other good luck in digging ginseng or hunting. But to the local villagers the word *Kuaidang* must be avoided at all costs, haste being so often associated with accidents. In addition, since the words *xi* (wash) and *si* (die) in Sichuanese have the same pronunciation, the word *xi* must to be avoided. If you wish to ask somebody whether he has washed his face, you must either make a gesture or say instead, "Have you *mo guang* (cleaned) your face?"

Each member of the temporary team starts his work according to the job assignments. After breakfast, the young men force their way into the bamboo groves to cut the shoots breaking through the earth with their curved choppers. They first pare the shoots, then put them into their gunny sacks. The elders work as "Master Bakers" — boiling or baking the shoots. The quality of the dried shoots largely depends upon the master's experience in controlling the temperature of the fire.

We noticed that the cook was beginning to prepare lunch. All he did was to dig open the bonfire and put upside down on the burning charcoal a basin of kneaded corn flour. Then he covered the basin with more charcoal. Before long the tempting smell of baked corn cake was floating in the air of the bamboo groves. Once it was done, the cake was first cut into pieces, then made into sandwiches with cured meat as the filling. To get rid of the charcoal ashes, one had to slap the cake three times and then blow on it three times. And that's how the mountaineers came to call it "Three-slap-three-blow Ashy Cake."

When the cook called the villagers together for lunch, he shouted, "Come and fill your backs now!" If he said, "Come and have lunch now," he would be roundly cursed, since, as traditionally practiced, they use the term "have lunch" only when they make offerings to lonely ghosts (those with no friends and relatives alive to offer them sacrifices).

Twenty days later, when the season for digging bamboo shoots is over, the villagers return home from the mountains with their dried shoots. In the past, when they all believed that the bamboo shoots were equally given to them by the mountain god to share, everybody got an equal amount regardless of the

232

effort he had put forth. But in recent years as the influence of economic reform has spread to the mountain villages, they also have adopted the policy of "More work more pay and, less work less pay," thus ending this time-honored practice.

The Buffalo's Day

On our way back to the capital town of Hongya County from Bingling Village I saw two old men and a group of children herding buffalo by the river. The smart "king of kids" who saw me taking out my camera immediately mounted an animal and begged me to take his picture. In no time, it seemed that as many children as there were buffalo had scrambled onto the animals' backs, each pleading for the camera's eye.

The buffalo grazing there were long-legged and powerfully built with fully rounded bellies and lustrous, obviously healthy hair. Hongya buffalo are said to be well-known far and wide for their well-proportioned bodies, strong pulling power, ability to stand both cold and heat and for being adaptable to all manner of places and conditions. Before the spring plowing season every year, farmers from the southern provinces come here to buy buffalo— the Hongya Buffalo Market being one of the six major cattle markets in China.

According to the elderly herdsman— yet another Mr. Liu— Hongya produces good buffalo because it is a wet and warm place and has an evergreen grass cover all year round. It has a lot to do also with the local peasants' rich experience in raising buffalo. Hear herdsman Liu on the subject: "The buffalo is a treasure to us peasants. We couldn't plow without him and we need his dung for fertilizer. And, you know, when you sell him, if you should need or want to, you can realize quite a decent sum, too." Stroking his animal tenderly, he added, "The buffalo cannot speak, and he cannot tell you when he is hot and when he is cold. We have to take care of him the same way as would a child." For example, in the cold of winter Liu adds thick layers of straw so as to give a warm pen to his buffalo. If it is a snowy day, he must cover the beast with a straw mat or a quilt. When it is particularly

233

cold, he must shorten the hours of grazing and feed the buffalo salty rice porridge in the morning and again at night.

The peasants never let their animals graze near the ditches, for they can get into serious trouble if they swallow leeches with the water. Should this happen, the buffalo will lose his hair, and his nose will stop sweating. Observing these symptoms, an experienced peasant can guess that the beast has leeches in his stomach and he will mix some eggs with water and pour it into the animal's mouth. The moment the leeches smell the strong odor of eggs, they open their sucker-like mouths. Meanwhile, after the egg treatment, the owner feeds the animal honey, which the leech will receive in his open mouth and will cause him to be discharged in the buffalo's dung.

Legend goes that the first day of the tenth lunar month is the birthday of the King of Cattle, originally one of the gods in the Heavenly Palace. In their plowing times, the farmers had no buffaloes to help them with the plowing, so their harvests were poor. The populace suffered from hunger and took their grievances to the Heavenly Palace. When the Jade Emperor heard of their sufferings, he sent Cattle Buddha to transmit his decree to the people on earth: "Have one meal every three days; then there will be enough to eat." The King of Cattle came to the world and helped the peasants with their plowing, but he often felt hungry and listless, even though he allowed himself one meal a day. He came to feel sorry for the people on earth who had so much less, and he took it upon himself to change the heavenly decree, telling the people on earth to have three meals a day rather than one every three. The Jade Emperor became furious when he learned of all this and expelled him from the Palace, driving him down to the earth. Cattle Buddha reacted by saying, "May Your Majesty turn me into a buffalo so that I can plow for the common people." To this the Jade Emperor agreed, and from then on plowing was done by buffalo instead of people.

Research has shown that the present buffalo was tamed from its wild ancestor over eight thousand years ago. Buffalo in China, in particular, replaced people at the plow back in the

Spring and Autumn Period. The King of Cattle in the legend actually refers to the first ancient man who invented the plowing techniques, and the tale itself praises highly the selflessness of the hardworking buffalo who has contributed so much labor to mankind.

On Buffalo's Day peasants in Sichuan not only let their buffalo rest for a day, but also give them all kinds of special treatment. Peasants in Chongqing County in Chengdu, for example, make for their buffalo large dumplings with glutinous rice filled with pork, bean curd, celery, and chives. People of the Qiang nationality who live in the highlands of west Sichuan, on the other hand, get up early in the morning to polish the buffalos' horns with vegetable oil until they become bright and shiny. Then they tie some red silk around their horns and feed them with large basins of noodles, wishing for the beasts a life as long as the long noodles.

Hongya County, which is well-known for its production of buffalo, is busier than anywhere else. The peasants place in the shrine that lies in the center of the central room a tablet of the King of Cattle together with the Bodhisattva and tablets of their ancestors. In some places they even carve a little wooden buffalo — an idol of the King of Cattle — and place it in the shrine. On Buffalo's Day, the peasants all make offerings to the King of Cattle by burning joss sticks, praying for ever more vigorous buffalo.

The morning of Buffalo's Day sees every peasant household steam glutinous rice which they then pound into a mass known as *ciba*. The owner first wraps up two large *ciba* with palm leaves and hangs them on the horns of the animal. This done, they lead the buffalo to the lake to let him drink some water, but, more important, to let him see the two *ciba* hanging on his horns through the reflection in the water. After that, the owner opens the *ciba* and feeds it to the animal. It is believed that a buffalo that has eaten *ciba* will work still harder for his owner in the following year than in the year just past. Then to find out whose buffalo has grown to be the handsomest, the owners all lead their animals into the open in front of the village temple in a kind of procession, the villagers call "the Buffalo Race."

Nightfall brings the Day to its climax. When the tall torch planted before the temple ("Heavenly Lamp" used by the common people on earth when they worship the King of Cattle that had come down to the earth as a buffalo) is lighted, several groups of "Buffalo Lamps" begin their performances. "Buffalo Lamps" is a simple local folk dance. The villagers first paint two large eyes on a manure basket, inserting two burning sticks as horns, one on the left and the other on the right, then sew two pieces of palm fiber on the two sides as ears. When the "buffalo head" is created, they sew to it a gunny sack to make the body and sew a bundle of palm leaves torn into hairs to the body as the tail. Four young men take part in the performance. One plays the head while another hiding inside the bag keeps waving the palm-leaf tail. Cooperating harmoniously, they imitate the buffalo's actions in grazing, drinking water, jumping, and lying on the ground when ruminating. The third one acts as a buffalo boy, jumping from left to right in front of the animal. One moment he is leading his animal to the grassland, in the next he is cutting grass and feeding his buffalo with it, and in the third moment he is sitting on his buffalo playing the flute. Though that is a lively and charming buffalo boy, the clown behind the buffalo will count as the most interesting of all. One minute he is fanning the buffalo, but in another he is blowing at its rump with his blowpipe. His humor and mischievous performance usually keeps the villagers convulsed with laughter from beginning to end.

As a traditional folk dance, "Buffalo Lamps" has become a part of the repertory performed at the Lantern Festival — the fifteenth of the first lunar month. From the 1950s on, before its spring plowing each year, Hongya County holds a "Buffalo Race." When the winner leads his buffalo, wearing a large red flower, around the competition field, the audience goes wild. One would think the buffalo had won an Olympic medal. The award is no more than a sickle and a basket, but what it implies is clear: cut more grass and raise ever better buffalo.

236

A Visit to a Village Papermaking House

We got up very early to visit Shijiao Village in Jiajiang County, a village famous for producing traditional Chinese painting paper. Dawn was still breaking when we arrived there. Soon after we entered the village, we saw an old villager of about sixty adding firewood to the stove that was boiling raw material. The upper half of the steaming boiler was made of planks about two meters in diameter and in height.

When I asked about the process of papermaking, the old villager pointed at the two rectangular ponds nearby and said: "In August every year you cut down the tender bamboo shoots that have grown in the same year, chop them into pieces of about two feet long, split them up and smash them, then soak them in the lime ponds for half a month. After that you get them out and wash them with clean water, then put them into the boiler and boil them for about a week. When the contents are boiled into pulp, a group of young men standing on high stools pound the pulp with a pestle. They work rhythmically as they sing their work song led by the one who is turning over the pulp. Their forceful, but paced, work song not only directs the rise and fall of the pestle, but also reduces the hard work of pounding the paper pulp."

Walking up along the stream, we saw steep cliffs stretching up to the sky and huge stones lying across the gullies; no wonder people call this eight- or nine-kilometer-long valley "Messy Rock Valley." However, it is these very mountains that turn out tender bamboo shoots with thin, supple fibers and offer cliffs that flow with clear spring water—both of which are the essential materials for the making of the water-absorbent and ink-retaining paper that are traditional Chinese painting paper. Almost every family of the villages (over a dozen) along the valley go in for papermaking.

Passing a col, we saw ahead of us a small village that hides in the bamboo groves lying on the mountain slope. Facing the stream was a papermaking house consisting of ponds for soaking bamboo, steamers, a pestling room and a dredging room. In the quiet mountains it looked simple but elegantly beautiful.

237

The busy papermaking house started its work early in the morning. In the stream a barefoot girl standing in the bamboo "washing bag" was stamping the processed contents as she kept turning them over and over again. A group of young men beside her were pouring water through a filtering cloth into the "washing bag" to wash away the alkali of the material. Others were pestling in the pestling room the processed contents into paste. Still others were stirring the paper pulp in the rectangular vats with bamboo rakes.

In the complicated procedure of papermaking, dredging paper is the most important step of all. With the help of a leveled bamboo screen of over four feet long in their hands, two papermakers gently dredged up a thin layer of paper paste, then shook it back and forth for a little while to get rid of the water drops. As they carefully turned the screen over, a standard sheet of Chinese painting paper was left on the table.

Leaving the papermaking house, we went up the steps leading to the dwelling place of owner Lao Shi. Simply a world of paper, both sides of the walls of the bamboo house were covered with paper hung up to dry, and so were the bamboo poles planted on the enclosing fence. Lying on the long desk in the central room were piles of paper waiting to be cut; properly cut paper can be sold downtown at any time.

An attractive sheet of red paper was pasted in the middle of the wall of the central room. On it were the words "Seats for the Gods of Sky and Earth, Monarch, Kin, and Teachers"; written on the right above it was "Seat for Our Ancient Master Cai Lun."

"You worship Cai Lun as a god?"

"Oh, yes," answered our host. "If a papermaker does not worship Master Cai Lun, he will surely be gossiped about: can one who forgets the inventor of paper make good paper?"

Cai Lun (?-121) was the inventor of paper in the Eastern Han Dynasty. Before him, the ancients had to carve characters that recorded various events on tortoise shells and bones of animals, or cast them on bronzeware. Later progress was made and bamboo and wood sheets were used instead. Nevertheless, the large, heavy bundles of writing sheets were still very inconvenient. Even though the development of silk spinning and weaving had made it possible for humans to paint and write on silk bolts, silk was too costly to enable the spread of education. Consequently, when Cai Lun succeeded in making cheap but convenient paper from bark, bits and pieces of jute, rags and useless fishnet, he was immediately commended and granted a title by the emperor and honored by all the people. Ever since then, as the master of papermaking he has been revered in the trade throughout China.

As the home of paper, Jiajiang County not only has built a shrine for Cai Lun with his statue in it, but also holds "parties in memory of Marquis Cai Lun (he was granted as Marquis in 114 by Emperor An)" in the eighth lunar month every year. During this season, because their old materials are used up and the new bamboo is not yet well soaked, the papermakers on forced holiday slaughter pigs and sheep with which they worship Cai Lun and visit friends and relatives. They also put on performances, taking full advantage of this time off.

An Ancient Town in a Boat's Shape

Luocheng, an ancient town built at the top of a mountain in Jianwei County, was designed in a unique way. Unlike the common straight streets, its central main street is wide in the middle and narrow at both ends. The stores on both sides that crowd upon one another and the roofs of the five-foot-wide verandas are all old wooden structures, whose materials were tenoned into each other. Seen from high above, this old town which is surrounded by green fields looks like a boat sailing on a vast sea.

It happened to be the market day. So the nearby villagers who had come to the market crowded along the two long verandas, looking as if they were trading in the hold of a ship. The long verandas, or "cool halls" as they are known locally, make a perfect market — cool in summer, keeping off not only the wet rains but also the hot sun.

Among the most attractive objects should be counted the ancient-styled stage with an arched doorway over it standing in the

239

center of the main street. During holiday seasons while Sichuan operas are acted on the stage, the street becomes an ideal place for *wushu* (martial arts) teams, *qilin* (Chinese unicorn) and dragon dancing teams. The verandas on the two sides naturally become the sets: those from the town itself bring along bamboo chairs and stools while those from the country simply turn their bamboo baskets upside down to make temporary seats. Everybody seems quite satisfied. No wonder some people say that compared with Spanish hotel theaters and medieval European city squares where performances are often given, Luocheng Theater is not inferior in any way.

Some years ago, Australia's city of Melbourne decided to build an ancient-styled resort for tourists, but its plan was aborted because of a lack of novel designs. Later, after they visited Luocheng— "Boat at the Top of a Mountain,"— an agreement was immediately reached: a new town in the shape of a boat would be built in emulation of Luocheng.

Luocheng was built during the later years of the Ming Dynasty over three hundred years ago. With regard to the purpose of this special design, there are two ways of explaining it, the first of which is that as a trading center where goods were exchanged, businessmen from all corners of the country would want to know that they could expect stability— in other words, that its citizens led a harmonious life. Therefore, the building of this boat-like town implied that the people there would strive as one for its prosperity and live together in peace. The second opinion goes that since the mountain top was a dry place lacking water, by building the town in the design of a boat, they would be calling upon providence to bring water to float the boat. However, this long ago wish was not fulfilled until the 1970s when a reservoir was built at the foot of the mountains, which at the same time marked the end of the days when they had to use water carried by trucks in dry seasons.

SLIPPERY POLES, HANGING-COFFIN BURIAL AND DRAGON DANCES

"Slippery Poles" — Simple Sedans

The long-distance bus was about to start when a small, wiry man of over sixty came up hurriedly carrying a frail old woman on his back. With the help of the passengers, he managed to scramble on and get himself and his older charge settled onto the bus. It turned out that the man had taken his 80-year-old blind mother, who had lost the use of her legs, to see doctors in the town hospital.

When we stopped for a break on the way, the old woman said she needed to relieve herself, and her dutiful son who carried her off gently. The filial behavior of this man — himself no longer young — moved the passengers deeply. "Surely a good son," they kept repeating approvingly. Even the driver restrained his impatience to get on his way, stretching his head out the window to say reassuringly, "Take your time, we're waiting for you!" Staring out the window as the son struggled back to the bus on the muddy road, I found my eyes filling with tears.

When I heard that the pair were to get off at a small town ahead of us, I began to worry about them because it was getting late and the roads were very slippery. With his disabled mother on his back, how could this poor fellow get home? I had reckoned without his kindly neighbors. Two young men with a pair of "slippery poles" were waiting for them when we got to the bus station. Carrying his old mother off the bus, the son laid her down on a "soft bed" covered with cotton bedding and put a quilt over her. When the two young men, one walking in the front and the other at the back, lifted the poles and proceeded on the narrow mountain path, I said to myself with a sigh of relief: "Wonderful slippery poles!"

The "slippery poles" consist of a soft bed of bamboo stalks strung together in a row which is tied to two bamboo poles, each more than three meters in length. The front and rear ends are fixed to a short bar, from which the bed is suspended. A pole is hung in the front for the feet to rest on, and

241

a pillow is fixed at the back. In this way, the "cooling sedan" looks much like a deck chair.

The first sedan was called a "shoulder cart" in ancient times. It is said to have developed from the cart, so that it can be viewed as a cart with its wheels removed. At first it was used only by emperors and elderly or feeble ministers who would otherwise have to walk or travel by a cart. Sitting on a sedan doubtless was much more comfortable than taking the usual rocking carriage pulled by a draft animal. Ban gu, a celebrated writer of the Han Dynasty, mentioned this ancient means of transportation in one of his works. During the Southern and Northern Dynasties aristocrats loved to ride in a sedan chair: some even sat in one when they commanded troops or went hunting. The well-known aristocrat Shi Hu, Emperor of the later State of Zhao, was one who went hunting in a sedan carried by twenty men. One can imagine the grand show of it all!

In the Tang Dynasty the Royal Court promulgated that no officials, except those who were ill, should ride on horses. Consequently, sedans became rarer and rarer. But during the Song Dynasty they came to be widely used again. In the painting, "Crossing the River on Qingming Day" by Zhang Zeduan of the Song Dynasty, now in the Palace Museum collection in Beijing, many sedans are clearly seen.

As for the slippery poles, they came into being only about seven decades ago. In the beginning of this century the Revolution of 1911 led by Dr. Sun Yat-sen overthrew the Qing Dynasty, but then Yuan Shikai came to power and made himself Emperor. The patriotic General Cai E could not allow this and organized troops in defense of the republic, waging battles against Yuan in Yunnan and Sichuan provinces. During the war there were not enough stretchers for the wounded, so people cut bamboo and made stretchers from the stalks. Because these were all made of the bamboo they called slippery poles, the name extended to them.

Before long, the local sedan-bearers found that slippery poles were much easier to carry than sedans. Users also found them more comfortable and cooler than closed sedans and had the further advantage of allowing them to enjoy the scenery all along the way. Ultimately, slippery poles replaced the conventional sedans, coming into popular use throughout the mountain areas in southern Sichuan Province.

Carrying slippery poles, however, is a hard job. It is particularly difficult for the bearer at the back who, because his view is blocked, has to be told of objects on the road by his comrade ahead. With the passing of time, a special type of cant has developed among the bearers. For example, when they meet some one walking on the road, the front one will sing, "There is a cloud in the sky" and the other will answer with, "Someone's on the earth nearby."

If he sees a dog lying on the road, the leading bearer sings, "A tuft of black hair lies on the ground," and his partner replies, "You must not tread on it but walk around."

When a group of buffaloes come toward them, the first one chants, "Cattle speak no words," and the other answers, "Make way for them first."

Before taking a turn, they exchange with each other: "Slow down — there is a turn ahead to take; the back be stable though the front may shake."

When passing a footbridge, they warn each other, "Two stones form a seam; step on the bridge but not the hole in between."

If they have to cross somewhere covered with water, they inform each other with "The sky is so bright; there's water in sight."

These cant phrases not only regulate the steps of the bearers and prevent accidents, but also reduce the difficulty and loneliness along the way as they are all like rhythmic short songs. No wonder some people call them "Slippery-poles Poems."

After the founding of the People's Republic of China, railways and highways were built across Sichuan, making transportation available and convenient for all the citizens, so the primitive slippery poles have gradually disappeared. Nowadays, only those in the remote mountain villages who have to carry somebody to the hospital resort to them. If this type of the carrying is needed, the villagers first cut some bamboos and tie them to

243

a bamboo chair or a soft bed—the making of which takes about ten minutes only. In Changning County's "Sea of Bamboos" we happened to meet several bride-receiving processions equipped with slippery poles. Carrying brides with newly decorated slippery poles shaded by colored canvas is one of the traditional practices in the mountain areas of southern Sichuan.

Commemorative White Kerchiefs

After supper I took a walk along the street. The fruit stands on both sides of the street were piled up with lustrous local oranges. This is an ideal place for orange growing, for its climate is mild, its air humid, and its red sandy soil easy for water to permeate. I hear that over four hundred species of oranges are found in Sichuan, so that there are some varieties ripening all year round.

Every one of the twelve orange sellers, I counter—but not the five younger peasants—was wearing a blue apron and a white kerchief on his head. Finding their way of dressing intriguing, I asked a middle-aged seller about it. I learned as he told me that the white kerchief not only kept off cold winds but had other uses: "If you leave home without a bag, this kerchief may make a perfect wrapper should you happen to need one. When you do heavy work in the fields, you can take it off your head and tie it around the waist, which strengthens the body and protects the back. When you are selling something, it becomes a purse as well—you can put your money into the winding head-kerchief."

Knowing that people usually used red objects in cases of happy events but white things on unhappy occasions, I was wondering if it was against the traditional practice for the locals to wear a white kerchief.

"Right you are," agreed the farmer. "We have been told by our elders that with the white kerchiefs we Sichuanese are mourning for Kongming."

Zhuge Kongming was a famous politician and strategist in the period of the Three Kingdoms. After Liu Bei named him his military counselor, Kongming became a devoted supporter of Liu, helping him establish the Kingdom of Shu Han, or

244

today's Sichuan. As counselor, Kongming made great contributions to the prosperity of the kingdom and the peaceful life of the local people, so when he died they went into deep mourning.

But how did the white mourning clothes change into today's white head-kerchief? It turned out that, according to the local custom, they had to be in mourning for three years. But to the peasants, it was inconvenient for them to wear long mourning dresses when they climbed the mountains or worked in the fields. So one day somebody wrapped up the mourning cloth around his head instead so that he could move about more easily, attracting the notice of his neighbors. Mourning for Kongming in comfort made a lot of sense, the custom spread rapidly, and ever since then the white kerchief has been popularly used. •

But not everyone in Sichuan wears a white kerchief. When we visited Maowen County that day, which lies 160 kilometers north of Chengdu, we saw men and women of the Qiang nationality living in the mountain areas wearing black head-kerchiefs instead. The story goes that Kongming once dispatched troops to drive away the people of the Qiang nationality, and so they consistently refused to wear mourning for him.

Whether the story is true or not we were not able to verify, but it would not be surprising if Kongming really did attempt to drive away the Qiang people in order to open up the frontier land. However, as a politician Kongming knew well the importance of national unity. He not only laid down the policy to "unite with the western armies and comfort the southern neighbors," but did his best to put it into practice. Up till now stories about Kongming's brilliant deeds continue to circulate among the people of the different nationalities in the southwest.

One of the stories concerns *mantou* (steamed buns). Here is the legend about the origin of this common food:

When Kongming led his army southward, on seven different occasions he captured and released Meng Huo, the head of the Nanman Tribe (Southern Ethnic Tribe). Finally when his victorious troops wanted to ferry across the Lushui River on their trip home, they were stopped by violent waves. The local people told them that only by sacrificing to the river forty-nine heads of the Nanman people would they be able to cross peacefully, to which Kongming retorted, "How can you kill people who have committed no offence?" But a bright idea had struck him, and he sent for the cooks. He told them to make enough dough to knead forty-nine human heads and stuff each one with a filling of mutton and beef and throw them into the river. The ruse worked. The turbulence subsided and the troops were able to cross the water without incident. And from that day to this, steamed buns have been daily fare for the common people. Deeply moved by Kongming's humanity, Meng Huo at last surrendered unconditionally to the Kingdom of Shu Han.

Strange "Cemetery in the Sky"

In Xingwen County in the southern mountain area of Sichuan Province there lie large stone forests and many marvelous caves full of stalactites and stalagmites which attract tourists from all over the country and the world. The day when I was touring these stone forests, directed by the tourist guide, I, too, could see the nature sculptures of squirrels, mischievous monkeys, camels, lions, pagodas, warriors, and even an affectionate couple that would not bear to part from one another. There were small neat square holes looking as though they had been put there by human hands above a cave called *Yuguan* (Jade Crown).

"These can't be the Creator's work, am I right?"

"You are right," answered the guide. "These were left by the Bo people, ancestors of the locals, put there for the hanging of coffins."

I had never seen a coffin hung on a cliff before. So when I heard that there were still about fifty of them hung on the steep cliffs by the Dengjia River of Suma Gulf in Gong County, just forty-eight kilometers from the tourist spot I had to see them.

Arriving at the Dengjia River, I really did see coffins hanging horizontally on the cliffs — some laid in caves dug on the rocks, some put on the two or three logs inserted into the square mortises on the rocks, some piled on top of others. The

246

coffins were carved out of whole logs from tough and corrosion-resistant wood and positioned in places facing the sun that were free from windstorms as well as human beings and wild animals. Consequently, many of them still stay there safe and sound even though they have experienced about five hundred years of all kinds of weather. Scholars call them examples of "hanging-coffin burial," but the locals prefer to speak of "cliff hangings."

The coffins were normally hung forty to fifty meters above the ground, though some were hung thirty meters higher than the average. It is said that the Bo people were buried on different cliffs according to different clans. The longest and largest coffins hung on the top usually belonged to chiefs or clan founders — their size and position intending to show their elevated position in life and their legacy to later generations. The piled coffins often contained the remains of a couple or of a family.

Staring at the "cemetery in the sky," I could not help but ask, how the Bo people had managed to hang up the coffins.

"I'm sorry to have to tell you that this remains a mystery right up to today," answered the guide.

Later I learned that some years ago, after protracted study, a group of researchers from different parts of China developed three different theories on the subject. The first one goes that this was once a thick forest with tall trees; that the ancient locals cut down trees with which they built high stands against the cliffs. Then, after they mortised holes on the rocks and drove in the supporting logs, they lifted up the coffins step by step. This theory could account for the lower ones that lie close to one other. The second group of scholars, however, conjectured that stonemasons with ropes tied around their waists slid down from the top of the mountains to mortise the holes and plant the logs on the cliffs. The coffins were then released down onto the supporting logs. The top ones, those of the chiefs and founders, could have been hung up this way. The last theory projects that a plankway was built for the carrying of the coffins. Few people place much credence in this notion since no mark of any plankway has ever been found.

247

The special living environments, cultural backgrounds and customs of the different Chinese nationalities have determined their different modes of burial. Among the Han people deep burial of the dead in coffins is popularly practiced. People of the Tibetan nationality practice celestial burial with the dead dismembered and left exposed to birds of prey. The Han people feel relieved when the coffins are buried deep in the ground while the Tibetans feel honored to have their remains eaten by birds. The Pumi people, on the other hand, practice cremation, keeping the ashes in caskets in a special cave identified for that purpose. Dais, and Qiangs also practice water burial, throwing into rivers bodies of dead children and victims of sudden death. As for hanging-coffin burial, it is not only found in Sichuan, but also in some mountain areas of Hubei, Hunan, Guangdong, Guangxi, Yunnan, Guizhou, Jiangxi, Fujian, Taiwan and other places. It is favored by the ancient minorities of the South, including the Bo, the Ba, the Pu, the Liao, the Yi, and the Yue nationalities.

But why did so many hang their dead high on the cliffs? Local folklore has it that in the days when Kongming and his troops were trying to conquer the southern territories, they met with the stubborn resistance of the Bo people. Therefore, the wily general devised a plot. He first spread a rumor that because the Bo people lacked quintessence and their clan could not prosper. Only by burying their dead on the cliffs so as to enable them to absorb the quintessence of the sun and the moon could they have a flourishing population with truly intelligent and vigorous descendants. Taking this rumor for truth, the Bo families began to dig up their ancestral coffins and mortise holes on the cliffs and plant logs. But while they were busying themselves removing the tombs of their ancestors, Kongming's troops were seizing their villages without opposition.

Of course, that is merely a folktale. As a study of history shows, Kongming never led his army here or ever tried to conquer this place. My own personal belief is that this custom developed out of the totem worship of the Bo people. Since they looked on eagles as their first ancestors, by burying their dead high on the cliffs, they made it possible for them to return to their source.

The Bo nationality is one of the ancient nationalities of China. Going through all kinds of difficulties, they turned the wild hilly land of the Southwest into cultivated fields. Their name *Bo*, in Chinese " 僰 " means thorns and "披棘" man, so putting together *Bo* is an honor to people who had managed to open up new land in the face of enormous hardships. Some years ago, archeologists studied ten coffins taken from the cliffs and discovered all the adults bearing evidence of the knocking out of upper side teeth. That is one of the Bo people's customs— "knocking out teeth marriage." It is said that the Bo people all knocked the upper side teeth before marriage. Bridegrooms did so to show their bravery and heroism while brides did so to prevent bringing misfortune to their husbands. The artifacts of daily life buried with the dead, such as embroidered clothes, daggers with sheaths, bone carvings, carved bamboo tubes, and chinaware— as well as the cliff frescoes of boxing, horse racing, dancing, shuttlecock kicking, swordplay, birds, animals, and flowers around the coffins— all demonstrate that the culture and art of the Bo nationality were highly developed.

However, the Bo people disappeared over four hundred years ago. The superstitious have blamed their custom of hanging-coffin burial, since the coffins touched neither heaven nor earth but were exposed to the sun and rains, thus destroying the quintessence of the ancestors. However, history records that in the middle of the 16th century the Bo people rebelled against the local officials who were oppressing them, and their own chief overstepped his power and declared himself King. The Emperor of the Ming Dynasty sent an army of 140,000 to put down the rebellion, and when they were totally defeated, the Bo people either fled their homes to settle in other places or stayed on to be absorbed by other peoples, their names and customs changed. Since the Bo people were nowhere to be found thereafter, their traditional burial of hanging coffins became a historical remainder of their existence.

Dragon Dances in the "Home of Dragons"

In an old temple in Anju Town, Tongliang County, over

249

twenty folk artisans were busy making dragon lanterns: some were shaping the bodies with bamboo strips and white silk, others were drawing scales with writing brushes, while still others were sitting gracefully in the sheds embroidering bright, colorful patterns on dragon costumes.

"Spring Festival is coming and many places want dragons from us. We've been working day and night to keep up with the demand," said Lao Fu, a man of about fifty who was painting a dragon head.

Truly, Tongliang could well be called the home of dragons: fossils of dinosaurs have been excavated here, dragon dancing is its popular traditional activity, and its making of painted dragons is famous throughout the country. When Beijing was celebrating the 35th anniversary of the founding of the People's Republic of China, nine colorful giant dragons made in Tongliang danced in Tiananmen Square.

The Spring Festival's dragon dance in Tongliang is stellar event. Accompanied by rhythmic drumbeating and gong clanging, a team of "dragon lanterns" shows up. The dragon stops in front of the residents' houses, the stores and office buildings to nod at the owners, wishing them good luck and success throughout the coming year. Then it proceeds to jump up and down and from left to right and right to left. As traditionally practiced, the host welcomes it by getting off firecrackers and presents it with some sort of gift as a thank you. In the old days, two red packets with money wrapped inside had to be presented to the dancers. Nowadays, though things have been simplified, cigarettes and candies still have to be offered.

Dragon dances are seen in most parts of China, but few places have such a great variety as Tongliang does.

A group of children with "straw dragons" and "vegetable dragons" were running and jumping happily toward us. The "straw dragons," as the name suggests, were made of straw bundles with bamboo handles inserted in them. Especially interesting was the "vegetable dragon." The children had brought huge cabbages from home, inserted a bamboo stick into each of them, and then strung them together,

250

thus creating a dragon. If they played with it in the evening they would also stick burning candles into the cabbages. Watching the children performing their "Two Dragons Play with One Pearl," "Soaring into the Sky," "Turning Over" and other acrobatics as the adults did, you had to chuckle at their charmingly awkward imitation.

On the Lantern Festival, the 15th of the 1st lunar month, a "dragon-lantern" party was held. After nightfall, the various teams of "dragon lanterns" were seen dancing through the streets decorated with bright holiday lamps much as if they were real dragons swimming in a river of lights. Dragons whose several sections were lighted with candles inside were called "Fiery Dragons" while those dressed in dragon coats in various colors were named "Color Dragons." Among the different dragons, about two dozen in number, the "Bench Dragon" was the smallest. A bench was first sawed into three sections which were linked with iron rings; a head was fixed on one end and a tail on the other. Behold the dragon! The longest and most magnificent was the "Vermes Dragon" which consisted of 24 sections, measuring about twenty meters.

The dragon dance originated out of the peasants' traditional habit of praying for rain during the Han Dynasty. At that time, people believed that dragons could create clouds and cause a rainfall. Therefore, they would hold dragon dances and send up prayers whenever rain was needed. They also had the rule of using blue dragons in spring, red ones in summer, white ones in autumn, and black ones in winter. Ever since then such activities have been held in China every year.

In Tongliang there is an amusing legend about the origin of "dragon-lantern" dances. It seems that one day the Dragon King felt a violent pain in his back, so he turned himself into an old man so as to see a doctor on land. Feeling the Dragon King's pulse, the doctor became puzzled. "Are you really a human being?" he wanted to know. The Dragon King admitted the truth, and the doctor asked him to revert to his original form, whereupon he seized a centipede out of the drag-

251

on's back. Once the doctor had drawn out the poison and treated the wound, the Dragon King fully recovered. To thank his healer, the Dragon King revealed a heavenly secret to him: "After you return home, make a dragon after me and dance with it. You'll be rewarded by a year of fine weather and a bumper harvest."

As a matter of fact, of course, there is no such being as a dragon on earth. A totem of the Han nationality, the dragon originally consisted of a snake's body and a man's head. In Chinese mythology the Hans' first father Fuxi and first mother Nüwa, Huangdi — creator of Chinese civilization, originator or inventor of the compass wheel, clothing, houses, palaces, the boat and the cart; and Gun, father of Yu, the conqueror of waters — all had human faces and snakes' (dragons') bodies. Or perhaps they changed into dragons after death. Later, when uniting with or absorbing other clans and nationalities, the Hans borrowed certain aspects or details of their totems. Consequently, the dragon totem evolved over time to its present form with a head like that of a camel, horns like antlers, eyes like those of a shrimp, ears like those of a buffalo, its neck like that of a snake, its belly like that of a clam, its scales like those of a carp, its talons like those of an eagle, and paws like those of a tiger. Thus, "the dragon with nine 'likes'" has long been the model for folk artisans who make, paint, or embroider dragons. Over time the dragon became ever more versatile: it could change its size freely, give out light or become dim, fly up into the sky, dive into the sea, create clouds, start rains.

What really shocked me was that when the "dragon lantern" party reached its climax, they burned up all the dragons. The celebrators set fire to them by throwing firecrackers or shooting fireworks at them. Some even poured out molten iron from furnaces to let the flying sparks set the dragons aflame. At this moment, in order to keep from catching fire themselves, the dancers danced even more vigorously. Thus the annual "dragon lantern" party came to a thrilling climax with the flames of the burning dragons shooting into the sky.

But why burn the dragons? There are two possible an-

252

swers to this question. One goes that only by sending the dragons up to heaven, can they be assured of fine enough weather to produce a year of abundant harvests. Another reason might be that by burning the dragons, they burn away all the ill luck and diseases existing in them. The pearl in the mouth of the dragon, in particular, is believed to be particularly miraculous. Childless couples will beg somebody to pluck it out before the dragon is burned and pass it to them during the happy noise of drums and gongs. Since "send a pearl" and "send a child" are homonyms in Chinese, the couple can thus expect a baby the next year.

Of course, to the bold young men bare to the waist, the burning of dragons is a great opportunity for them to show off. If any of the unmarried young men really happens to win the love of a girl on this occasion, then the local saying "You dance into good luck at dragon dances" is verified.

CHAPTER IX

YUNNAN— Home to Over Twenty Ethnic Minorities

CARAVANS, MAGPIE BLOUSES AND THE TORCH FESTIVAL

Caravans

One winter's day when I was visiting mountain villages in Fumin County, Yunnan Province, which lies on the southwest frontier, I happened upon a caravan of horses carrying goods to market. Driver Jin, a man of about sixty, whose decades at his work had left him with a powerful physique, walked to the rear. On that particular day his train was carrying potatoes and radishes to the market in Zhebei Town— my destination and that of several other horse drivers of his village. I fell into step with him and learned about his work as we walked along.

A place of high mountains and deep ravines, Fumin is forty kilometers away from Kunming and lies on the Yunnan-Guizhou Plateau. There used to be no highways in the mountains, so that the salt, brown sugar, medicine and furs which retailers purchased from Sichuan Province were all carried to Northern Yunnan on horseback, as were other products from Sichuan— cloths, dyes and items for daily use. Going the other way were charcoal, rice and rapeseeds produced by the local peasants for sale in town.

Normally, a horse driver is responsible for four horses, each of which carries about sixty kilograms. As they make their way, they join other horse drivers, making up together what are known as "horse gangs" in Chinese.

In the old days, caravans of the headmen (called *tusi* in Chinese) of the national minorities, of large trading companies, and of the families of officials, might include as many as twenty drivers with sixty to seventy animals. In front was a husky mule whose bridle was dressed up with red tassels and round mirrors and hung with two sizeable bells. Next came a gelding with twelve small copper bells hung from its bridle around its chest. A young donkey, who brayed from time to time, its head raised, brought up the rear. The braying was believed to guarantee the caravan a peaceful journey by frightening off wild beasts and evil spirits. At night when the horse drivers stayed at an inn, the donkey brayed once every two hours, serving as a clock for them.

Also in the old society, bandits in the mountains often robbed caravans at out-of-the-way places. Even though the government employed strong men and organized them into "merchant-protecting teams," the horse drivers could not feel secure. Some of these teams went so far as to disguise themselves as bandits and rob the caravans themselves, which certainly made it hard to tell friends from enemies. That is why sizeable caravans were usually armed. When they were about to enter places known for holdups, they would fire several warning shots into the air. Some teams also inserted into the bridle of the front horse tree branches as a sign of warning or hung up flags featuring the names of prestigious headquarters. Seeing caravans belonging to powerful people, the bandits would often retreat and go into hiding. But at the sight of smaller groups with no more than two or three drivers, the lookouts would immediately send out their signal: "The ox is eating wheat now!" — and the bandits in the trees would jump out.

Another worry of the horse drivers was the health of their animals. They kept careful watch on the horses at all times. When a horse did not want to move, was tired of eating fodder, and had dry lips and a pale coating on the tongue, they would know that it had caught cold and was running a fever. When a horse lay belly up on the ground tossing from side to side with its hoofs contracted, it could be deduced that it was suffering from spasms in the small intestines. If a horse suffered from constipation, had a bulging belly and kept looking backward toward its behind, it was safe to assume it had intestinal stasis from overeating.

Since the caravans had no veterinarians to care for the animals, the horse drivers gradually accumulated a set of simple "home cures." For example, in case of a high fever, they would first tie up the horse, then pry open its mouth and lift up its tongue to give the underside of it some acupuncture treatments, then sprinkle the tongue with inflammation-allaying salt. Thus the horse would begin to recover gradually. They treated horses suffering from spasms with water from bamboo water pipes and treated those ill with intestinal stasis by feeding them sesame oil to lubricate their intestines.

Some caravans brought along a monkey who worked as a "watchman" and "horse doctor." On the way, the monkey would sit on the back of the first horse, looking searchingly into the distance ahead. If it discovered any danger, it would give squeaking warnings at once. When they got to an inn for the night, the monkey would jump into the inn first to sniff at the stables and the mangers. If any ill horse had stayed there at all recently, the monkey could tell by the strange odor that remained and would squeak a warning to the drivers, telling them to keep the horses away from possible infection. Through the use of its nose, the monkey could also find out which horse had just caught cold or had fallen ill from overlong traveling and would let the drivers know right away. All this is why horse drivers called the monkey a "horse disease preventer," to translate literally. It is believed that Sun Wukong (Monkey King) in the classical Chinese novel, *Pilgrimage (Journey) to the West*, once had the title "Bi Mawen" (homophone of "horse-disease preventer" in Chinese) conferred upon him by the Jade Emperor in the Heavenly Palace.

When the caravans were going through the flatlands of the mountain areas, the horse drivers would feel reassured. The smoke curling up from the houses nearby, the green crops and the sight of the women working in the fields would be comfortingly familiar. But they had to feel homesick, too, and miss their wives and children back home. And so they would sing songs like the following:

> Pomegranate blossoms become redder and redder,
> Never marry your daughter to a horse driver—
> He eats as if he were a hungry wolf, my dear,

And he returns home only once or twice a year.

Or:

> Don't drive your horse through foreign lands
>   (those of national minorities):
> There you'll face dangers and sorrows;
> Grasslands will be your green blankets,
> And rocks your embroidered pillows.

After the founding of the People's Republic, highways were opened up to the towns and villages in the mountain areas. Consequently, long-distance caravans, the once principal means of transportation, began to disappear. But in recent years, those living in mountain villages without highways nearby have been stimulated by the development of commodity production to start raising horses again to earn money transporting goods or people short distances. Bandits have long disappeared in New China. Today two people who can help each other load or unload the goods are enough of a transportation team for safe travel. Large caravans are not needed.

We were still talking away when I suddenly caught sight of Zhebei Town and realized that we had already covered more than four kilometers of the mountain road.

A Horse Inn

It was Zhebei's market day. On both sides of the asphalt road that ran through town and in the small stone lanes, peasants of the nearby villages displayed what they had to sell, turning this little town of 210 households into a bustling place.

Led by our guide, I arrived at the home of Liu Yunxiang. It was an old house that he lived in — a one-time horse inn — situated along a small lane. Indented on the worn stone steps that led to the arched doorway you could still see hoofprints from those old days. On the second floor of the spacious two-storeyed building were rooms for guests and bedrooms for the family running today's inn. Downstairs, the central room was a small lounge for lodgers, a comfortable place

257

where they could sit and visit with one another. In the west was the kitchen and a storeroom for pack-racks and the lodgers' goods. In the east was a stable large enough for seventy horses. Zhebei was a place caravans had to go through; it was a one-day trip both to go north to Luquan and south to Kunming from here. No wonder there were once as many as seven inns in Zhebei.

Since Liu Yunxiang was off doing woodwork downtown, his wife received us on his behalf. No sooner had we taken our seats than she offered us water pipes, inviting us to smoke. Our guide accepted but I declined, and as he drew on the gurgling pipe I measured it with my eyes. It was fashioned of bamboo, typical of the pipes smoked by the peasants of the Southwest: about eighty centimeters long with a diameter of maybe eight centimeters. A small bamboo tube of about twelve centimeters held the bowl at a slant near the tube's bottom. The water poured into it must not be higher than the top of the bowl. I've heard that smoke going through the water is cool and pleasing and some of its nicotine can be filtered out. It occurred to me that the modern cigarette filter tip probably originated from a water pipe much like this one. Large pipes like this were found in all the local households. Some people carry them when they go to work in the mountains or in the fields.

Our diminutive hostess was clearly an intelligent, capable woman. She told us that in the past when a caravan from Sichuan got to the inn at sunset, the whole family would immediately set to work helping the "Mage Tou" (headman) and his men unload the packs, arranging rooms for them, chopping grass and carrying water for the horses. And the landlady would at once start cooking for them. As a rule, the inn would take responsibility for guarding the horses and goods through the night. If the lodgers lost anything during their stay at the inn, or say their cured meat was eaten by a cat, the inn had to pay them according to the actual price of whatever the loss might be. At four o'clock in the morning when it was pleasantly cool, comfortable for traveling, the caravans set off again.

What interested me was that inns did not charge for the horse drivers' lodging — they only got fifty *fen* for each animal head, called a "forage fee." However, when they came on the 28th or 29th of the last lunar month every year, they did not have to pay anything at all as long as the headmen told the owner of the inn that it was their last trip of the year. Hearing this, the owner would also give them a treat known as "Cleaning Day Dinner." In the first month of the next year, tradition directed that the first caravan should present to the owner of the inn a package of rice cake and set off a string of firecrackers at the entrance to wish the inn a prosperous year. Again, as a rule, the inn would not ask for any forage fee, which was named "Opening Day Money."

Caravans of the Tibetan nationality from Aba, Sichuan Province, camped out rather than stay at inns, bringing with them their own food and equipment for sleeping outside. When it got dark, wherever they were, they would find some flat land outside the village and stay there for the night. They first drove sticks into the ground to tie up their horses, then went into the village to buy some forage for them. After that the horse drivers would make a bonfire and hang up their pots in preparation for supper. With butter, tea and salt they prepared "milk tea," then mixed highland barley flour with just the right amount of water and kneaded it into a cake known as *zanba*. Those who brought beef or mutton would cut it with their waist knives and eat it with *zanba*. After they had finished eating they wrapped themselves up in their long loose robes and settled themselves around the bonfire for the night.

Our hostess was cooking for us now. In Beijing cooks prepare rice in a small pot over a slow fire, whereas this cook first washed the rice in an open vessel woven of bamboo strips, poured it into a large pot and boiled it for a while, then got it up from the water and steamed it. The cover of the pot looked just like a bamboo hat to me and reminded me of some verse, a portion of which goes:

> Yunnan has eighteen funny things:
> Bamboo hats used as pot covers,
> Eggs for sale hung up in strings,
> Above each shoe's heel a cloth strap swings.

Old women shinny up trees faster than monkeys—
Climbers that appear propelled by wings.

The reason that outsiders find "the eighteen things" strange is that they simply don't know much about the life and customs of the Yunnan people and especially about geography's role in all that. The point is that the local climate is mild and humid—quite like spring all year round—which enables trees to grow in all seasons. That is why women here often climb trees to pick fruit and eventually become as nimble and skillful at it as monkeys. As for the "cloth strap" above the heel of a shoe, it is in fact no more nor less than a shoehorn, while the wrapping of eggs with strings twisted of straw before selling them in the market shows their special skills in wrapping things. With regard to the "bamboo hat" that is woven of the local material available everywhere, the moment our hostess uncovered the steamer the whole point of it was clear, for inside were potatoes, cured meat and sausages. A flat cover couldn't cover up all those dishes and bowls.

Cured meat is an indispensable item of every peasant household in Yunnan, Sichuan, Guizhou and many other places. In the last lunar month—a dry month when the Spring Festival is drawing near and when their pigs have fully grown—the villagers slaughter their pigs one after another. According to the local practice, they treat their neighbors to a dinner prepared with some of the meat. As for the rest, it's seasoned with Chinese prickly ash, soy sauce and sugar and salted up. Then after ten days' salting, they hang it in their ventilated sheds where it gradually becomes cured meat. When visitors come, the host cuts off some of this golden transparent meat and steams it to offer his guests. With its sharp flavor, it goes especially well with wine.

In the middle of our dining table was a small bowl containing salty water mixed with sesame oil, chilis and other flavorings— "dipping water." When the people here cook cabbage, bean curd and most other dishes, they do not add oil or salt, leaving it up to the diners to season by "dipping."

My hospitable hostess kept urging me to eat again and

again as she raised her chopsticks. "But I haven't stopped eating," I protested.

My guide lowered his head and whispered, "You mustn't use the word 'eat.' You should say, 'I'm helping my-self' instead." Seeing my bewilderment, he went on to explain, "'Eat' is considered a vulgar word here. It is used only when you talk about starving people who fight over food and devour it like hungry animals."

According to the local practice, when you have finished eating, you should raise your chopsticks and say, "Take your time" to the host and the other diners in order to tell them that you have had enough and that you want them to go on en-joying themselves in a leisurely fashion. With this you put the chopsticks on the left side of your bowl. If you put them to the right, that means you have not eaten enough yet and the host will at once fill another full bowl of rice for you.

In the old days horse drivers staying at inns had many more taboos at the dining table. They never moved the rice steamer and bowls on the table; otherwise, as they believed, their carts would turn over at some point on their way. Spoons must not be left inside the soup bowl; otherwise, their packs car-ried on horseback would fall into the mountain streams. Cara-vans carrying salt were also cautious about "touching water," lest their cargo fall into rivers and get wet.

When a caravan was about to get on its way, nobody was allowed to lean against the door with his hands holding the doorframe or squat on the threshold. Since "wooden door" and "fortune's door" are homophones in Chinese, such activity could result in their door leading to good fortune being blocked. And if their "fortune's door" was blocked, then not only would they fail to get rich, but they might run into robbers on the way. If any horse driver broke this rule, the headman would immediately order, "Unload the packs. We'll start out some other day." And the rule breaker must pay for the additional forage needed because of the delay. Indirectly, these rules and practices demonstrate that the trips made by the caravans were always full of danger and hardships.

The History of the Magpie Blouse

Among all the provinces in China Yunnan has the greatest number of nationalities — twenty-four in all, including the Han, Yi, Dai, Bai, Tibetan, Naxi and Miao. Jinning County in particular, which lies to the south of Dianchi Lake, is not only inhabited by Hans but also by the Yi, Hui, Hani and Lisu nationalities. As we Chinese say so often: "Customs differ from region to region and practices vary from place to place." But during my visits to the neighboring Yi and Han villages, I found that because of the mixing up of different nationalities, many of them actually did share the same customs and practices.

Wakuang Village (a place rich in iron ore and thus named after it in Chinese) in the Baofeng Flatlands is one inhabited by Hans. There I was received by village head Luo Meiying dressed in the typical costume of the local countrywomen; her head covered with a black scarf, she wore a close-fitting white blouse under a lace-trimmed black vest, blue trousers and embroidered shoes and apron. Noting my scrutiny, Luo pointed out the similarity between her outfit and the magpie with its black head and body and white wings.

The magpie is a bird of good omen in Chinese mythology. In the fairy tale about the cowherd and his lover, the "girl weaver," it was a group of magpies that formed a bridge across the Milky Way in heaven which enabled the lovers to meet on the 7th of the 7th lunar month. Later, when magpies came to rest or sing in the trees in front of somebody's house, some people would congratulate the owner of the house, saying that this was an auspicious sign. By and by there came to be the saying, "A magpie brings good news."

As we talked I learned that it had been Luo Meiying, a Yi woman from a neighboring village of that nationality, who had introduced the magpie blouse to Wakuang Village. On her wedding day more than ten years before, when her husband went to her village on horseback to bring her to her new home, as was done traditionally, she wore a black scarf instead of a print kerchief and blue vest. "In this way I became a magpie that brought good news to the Han village," she explained.

Young men living in the Baofeng Flatlands consider it a

great blessing to marry a Yi girl from one of the mountain villages, calling these beautiful girls "half *Guanyin*" (Buddhist goddess of mercy) whom they adore for their kindness, industry, honesty and tenderness. While cutting firewood, going to the market, celebrating folk holidays and enjoying recreational activities such as "Singing Tunes," "Drinking Mountain Wine," and "Kicking Leisure," the young people of the two nationalities often make friends and end up falling in love.

On our way to the Yi village, Tianba, we were lucky enough to see a joyful scene of "Kicking Leisure" with our own eyes. According to the convention here, girls can only "kick leisure" with boys from other villages, never with those of their own. When boys of the Han nationality receive invitations from the Yi girls, they will go to the appointed place and light a bonfire while they are waiting for the girls, who will offer them cigarettes when they arrive in exchange for the picnic of sweets, cured meat and wine the boys have brought to share with them. Later, slightly tipsy, they form a circle for enthusiastic singing and dancing. When one group gets tired, they take a break on the grass where they drank more wine and cured meat and another group goes on dancing, kicking their feet after a shout of "*Hehei*!" Between their shouts and singing, they express their feelings and matches are made. When a girl ties an embroidered wallet to the waist of a boy, it represents her promise to marry him.

However, if the boys of a certain village break an appointment and thus hurt the feelings of the Yi girls, the girls will retaliate by cutting down brambles and spreading them all over the appointed place, thus bringing an end to their relationships with these particular boys.

Finally we reached Tianba, a charming village with green pines and firs covering the mountain slopes behind it, a community of 150 households lying along the two sides of an ever-running stream. In the old days the houses here were rammed up with earth, with a watchdog on every roof looking out for armed men from other villages who might come to attack. But during recent decades the Yi and Han nationalities have been on the friendliest terms with many marriages between them.

Noting that the sloping tile roofs of the Hans living in the flatlands are not only rainproof but also very solid, the Yi people have gradually adopted their design. We saw how closely the Yi houses resembled those we had seen in Wakuang Village when we went to visit the family of a Yi woman cadre, Guo Xiaolan. Entering the courtyard, we were confronted by a two-storeyed house consisting of three principal rooms: two bedrooms and a living room. On either side were a kitchen and a storeroom. A yard that was for drawing light and draining rain water was right in the middle of the house — again just like the Han houses in Wakuang Village.

It was winter, a season when the villagers had little farming to do. Several young people of the amateur opera troupe were rehearsing a *huadeng* (lantern) opera. Originally, *huadeng* opera was light folk opera of the Han nationality popular mainly in Yunnan and neighboring provinces. Three to five actors and actresses, bringing along their simple paraphernalia, usually toured the villages in the Spring Festival and Lantern Festival seasons. I would never have expected Han opera to take such firm root in a Yi village, but clearly it had. Hearing the pure voice and clear articulation of Fang Qinying, Lao Li, head of the Cultural Center of Jinning County who had been accompanying us, was delighted. "We'll invite you to give one of your performances in the county town this coming Spring Festival," he declared. "You will come, won't you?"

The Torch Festival, and Obsequial Drum Dance

Upon our return to Baofeng, we learned that many people there had gone to Housuo Village to attend the obsequial drum dance of Yin Caiyun, an old woman who had just died. We hurried off in the dark of night so that we could also attend the funeral.

The central room of the house had been turned into a hall of mourning with "flower hills" and colorful balls made of paper hanging from the ceiling. In front of the coffin burned two red candles and at its sides were branches of pine and cypress. In accordance with local practice, all the mourners — relatives, friends and neighbors of the family of the deceased as well as folks of the neighboring villages— burned joss sticks and lighted candles in front of the coffin, bowing their last respects to the remains. They then presented to the Yin family glutinous rice cakes, sugar, wine and other gifts, after which they kept vigil around the coffin. When the members of Yin Caiyun's family began to cry beside the bier, eight men and women with drums tied around their waists followed a man who was holding a dragon head into the courtyard where they proceeded to beat their drums and dance. They kicked and turned, dancing round and round and shuttling back and forth by turns. Their steps were vigorous, and it was apparent that feelings were running high. After a while they switched from dancing to slow walking, singing the mourning song;

> The dutiful sons who are dressed in white
> Kowtow to the coffin by candlelight.
> Every family has sons and daughters;
> It's a duty to bury dead elders.

Funerals are normally considered sad occasions. But in some localities, of which this is one, when a person dies at a ripe age— normally over sixty— his family and the villagers regard it in a different light, indeed as a happy event. Most often, in the case of a Han's funeral, the relatives and friends of the family pay their last respects and just send gifts to the family of the deceased with condolences. The family reciprocates with a banquet, and that is it. Here knowing that by getting the whole village together through a drum dance, the Yi mourners not only paid their last respects to the deceased and their condolences to the bereaved family, but also turned the funeral into a notable event, the local Hans adopted the Yi custom.

After we had headed back to Baofeng and left Housuo Village far behind us, the mourning song could still be heard:

> There are few thousand-year-old trees in the mountains;
> Rarely can you find hundred-year-old persons.
> Here we all dance on and on and keep beating
>   our drums

When our aged folk return to the west heavens.

I was told that the mourners would take turns singing and dancing through the night and that the next morning when they carried the coffin to the mountains for burial, they would stop to dance around it once every 100 meters until they reached their destination.

On our way back to Baofeng, we walked along the moonlit road chatting about the mixing up of customs of the Han and Yi nationalities. Our guide described the local Torch Festival, which falls on the 24th of the 6th lunar month each year. It used to be a festival for the people of the Yi, Bai and Naxi nationalities only, but nowadays the Hans living in Baofeng and the Shangsuan flatlands also celebrate it the way the Yis' do. On this day they slaughter chickens and buy meat, preparing rich dinners to share with guests. At night they light a bonfire in front of their houses, and then everybody marches through the fields holding a torch high in the air. Finally they gather in the village square for the singing and dancing.

As to the origin of the Torch Festival, people of different nationalities in different places have different legends about it. According to the local tale, in midsummer when the paddies are about to ear up, the fields are full of insects. When they march through with burning torches, they can lure moths to fly into the fire. Thus they guarantee a good harvest of their crops by killing the harmful insects. And so the villagers have come to regard the torch as a symbol of rice ears, referring to it as a "torch ear." As a result, they carry bigger and bigger torches each year.

On the night of the Torch Festival, when the fire soars up to its highest point, old ladies cut up parts of old clothes and hairs of relatives as well as the colored silk strips tied around the young ones' wrists at the last Dragon Boat Festival and throw them into the fire. "Burn it all up. Burn up all the diseases and disasters and quarrels of this year," the old women will murmur, hoping thus to dispel all evils and insure the arrival of good fortune.

Inhabitants living in the flatlands of Shangsuan also have

the traditional practice of "scrambling for a torch son." Families with boys born after the last Torch Festival enjoy themselves by marching through the paddy fields with tall torches. At sight of this, childless couples will crowd around to fight for their torches, believing that carrying a torch associated with the birth of a son will improve their own chances of having a son themselves in the next year.

Perhaps it is because the Han and Yi nationalities have many intermarriages that the Hans in Baofeng and Shangsuan celebrate the Torch Festival on the 24th of the 6th lunar month while the Tianba and other Yi villages celebrate theirs one day later. Naturally this makes it easy for relatives to visit one another. When a husband accompanies his wife to her parents' home in a Yi village for the Torch Festival, traditionally he should present to each of his parents-in-law a new suit, a new pair of shoes and a new hat.

GUIZHOU— Home of China's No. 1 Liquor *Maotai*

CUSTOMS IN THE DISTILLERIES

Maotai, first among Chinese spirits, takes its name from the town in which it is produced, which is located in Renhuai County, Guizhou Province. I flew there last winter seeking lore about this famous drink.

At dusk I arrived in Maotai Town, a small river valley town surrounded by mountains. A warm breeze filled the air with the fragrance of the mellow drink. In China it's called a wine, but since it's not made from pressed grapes, it's actually a kind of liquor. Anyway when that fragrance hit my nostrils, the following lines came to mind:

> Wine in the breeze makes all drowse nearby—
> The fragrance in the rain floats far and high.

I soon found that besides the Maotai Distillery there were about two dozen more of various sizes in the town.

That evening when the director of the Maotai Distillery brought out some *Maotai* at dinner, I said, "You needn't bother— I'm already drunk from breathing in the aroma here!"

We had come at just the right time. The saying urges "make wines in the cold days and extract oils when it's hot." Yes, it was a good time for making wine— or liquor for that matter, which, we must repeat, is what *Maotai* actually is. All the thirteen hundred or more workers of the six workshops of the Maotai Distillery were working without pause.

In the workshop I visited I found the cellars sealed with

yellow mud, heaps of fermented crushed grain, and steaming distilleries sending forth their incomparable perfume.

Four workers were removing the steamy raw materi- al — sorghum and wheat. After digging out the first- distilled stuff, they spread it over the ground to cool, adding more crushed sorghum and spraying water over all. Then they re- turned it for more steaming. Again they dug it out and put it on the ground for cooling. Finally they mixed it with wheat leaven and processed the mixture at high temperatures, following which it was stored in the cellars for a month of fermentation.

The process is called "making the paste," ground sorghum being the paste, and is repeated over and over. During a nine- month period they add raw materials twice, ferment it all eight times and distill out the spirits seven times. Spirits at different stages are kept in different jars and stored in the cellars for three years. As the years pass, the unwanted and bitter tastes disappear and the spirits become increasingly pure and mellow. Finally experts with cultivated senses of taste mix the spirits of different fragrances together and send samples to an overseeing committee for further evaluation. When all these ex- perts decide the blend is up to standard, it is moved back to the cellars for further aging. Half a year later it is again put to the test. Only when the final approval is given can the liquor be bottled for sale.

Our guide Lao Wang told us that the distilleries had started their processing on the 9th of the 9th lunar month known as the Double Ninth and also the Double *Yang* Festival. Because the Chinese concept of *yang* is associated with bright- ness, such qualities as strength and assertiveness and the time of this festival is considered ideal for the distilling of spirits. Howev- er, the fact is that it is a season that is neither cold nor hot and is cool enough to work inside the workshops. Sorghum has just been harvested and the local sorghum, with its big, soft, thin- husked grains, produces the best *Maotai*. In addition, by the Double Ninth Festival, the Chishui River, usually muddy throughout the summer, has become clean and clear, providing water well suited for distilling.

But despite all these auspicious circumstances, distilling is still a complicated process, and any carelessness along the line can easily spoil the product. Accordingly, special customs and superstitions have grown up in the distilleries. For example, women who bring meals to their men are not allowed to enter the distilleries lest the smell of food turn the spirits sour. The superstition runs so deep that even the word sour must not be uttered inside any distillery. No one wants to take any chances since a year's labor hangs in the balance.

One of those stories that is handed down by word of mouth shows the influence of this fear.

In ancient times a scholar who was asked to write a couplet for the owner of a winery came up with the following:

Wines made here are all as sweet as the vinegar is sour.
Pigs raised here are all as fat as the mice are all dead.

Naturally the scholar had meant to wish the owner good luck in his making of wines and vinegar and in his raising of pigs. But in reality the owner was a hard taskmaster who was strongly disliked by his workers. The wine master who received the couplet to read to the men thus added and subtracted a bit to get even:

Wines made here are all as sweet as the vinegar—
all sour
Pigs raised here are all as fat as the mice— all dead.

And so the abused workers had the satisfaction of puncturing the self-importance of their boss with a hearty laugh at his expense.

In the old society, when the first wine of the year was made, the owner of the winery would burn joss sticks and light candles at the place where the scroll carrying the words "The Holy Seat of Our Foremaster Du Kang" was posted. Then he would present to the god of wine a roasted cock and some pork, praying for a good year of wine making. His prayer made, he would let his workers enjoy the food offerings.

270

In addition, in the time of the first lunar month, the wineries and distilleries and brewhouses held an annual get-together which provided all the workers a chance to dine as a group and watch operas, thus fostering good relations between owners and workers and between the wine and spirits-making houses themselves.

Du Kang, generally known as Shao Kang in history, was king of the Xia Dynasty over 3,000 years ago. According to legend, after Xia was destroyed, Shao Kang fled to Youyushi, where he became the keeper of kitchen and warehouse. One day as he was sitting idly at the entrance to the storage cave smarting from a reprimand he had just received for allowing some of the stored food to spoil, he saw a ram fall dead on the ground after drinking from a small stream running out of the cave. He went to fetch the fallen animal, intending to slaughter it for its meat. But the moment he raised his knife the little creature revived and ran off. What then was in this stream that could cause an animal to lose consciousness. He had to find out. When he tasted it he found it deliciously sweet, but it also made him feel strangely light-headed, even dizzy. He continued to drink until he, too, fell unconscious to the ground. When he regained his senses sometime later, he seemed to be stronger than before. Realizing that the secret to all these reactions were to be found in the sweet liquid he and the ram had drunk, he determined to study it until he could find a way to duplicate it. And thus it was that the art of wine making was born and that Shao Kang became known as the foremaster of wine making and the god of wine. The ancients even took his name as a substitute for the noun "wine."

However, archeologists have unearthed from the Longshan remains that are over four thousand years old wine pots, small flagons, wine cups of various sizes and designs, and other vessels used in wine making or drinking. The obvious conclusion was that China's wine making far predated the Xia Dynasty.

No Wine, No Etiquette

At nightfall we visited Mao Guangcai, a retired winemaker of seventy-two still aglow with health and vigor, who continues to work as a consultant to a local winery.

As we entered the living room, Mrs. Mao urged us to warm ourselves at their "Beijing stove." Typically of Guizhou, the plate of this stove made in Beijing had been enlarged until it was big enough to be used as a small round table in the winter time on which drinks and food could be served. Mrs. Mao produced a bottle of *Maotai* and a dish of fried peanuts and Mr. Mao filled cups for us. In most places that we visited we would first be offered cigarettes, then tea. But here *Maotai* was king. No household is without its supply and no guest escapes. Showing the respect I knew was expected of me, I received the cup with both hands and drained it without pausing. "There you go!" cried Mr. Mao, delighted. "Just like a member of our own family!" And he filled my cup once more to the brim. Even this had a name — a "double-cup drink" —traditional for hosts to offer visitors to wish them good luck and safety throughout their travels.

The local custom of entertaining visitors with wine or spirits has its origins in a folk tale, which goes like this:

One dark and freezing winter night in Maotai Town a young girl dressed in rags was seen shivering in the cold outside their hut by a poor old man and his wife. The old man asked his wife to invite the young girl in to warm herself by the stove. As she hovered there, he heated some food for her and offered her the only cup of spirits he had in the house.

That night the country girl appeared in a dream of the old man as a beautiful fairy maiden. Smiling as she came toward him holding a cup in her hand, she stopped to spread its content around the poplar tree in front of his house. The next day the old man dug a well under the tree and came upon crystal clear water underground. Using this pure water he distilled the first *Maotai* spirits. The picture of the fairy maiden who is holding a cup decorates today's bottles of *Maotai* which are found where spirits are sold around the world. The two red ribbons that are tied around the bottle's neck are said to be the two floating belts fastened around her waist.

"No wine, no etiquette" is a popular saying in Maotai. Consider the weddings in this area. When the bride-price is presented, leading the procession is someone carrying a wooden tray with two bottles of *Maotai* on it. On the wedding night before the bride and bridegroom can retire they must finish off a cup of spirits together. Three days after their marriage, when accompanying his wife to the home of her parents, the young husband must present two bottles of *Maotai* to his father-in-law. In addition, where applicable, the couple is expected to send a bottle to the matchmaker as a way of saying "thank you" for introducing them to each other.

During festival seasons, the local people consume more liquor than usual. At the Spring Festival, the first day of the first lunar month, they treat the most casual of visitors to a cup of the liquor. And at the Qingming (Pure Brightness) Festival they pour *Maotai* into the rice to be offered to their buried ancestors.

Maotai plays a role also in the Dragon Boat Festival, the fifth day of the fifth lunar month, when the inhabitants of the town crowd along the two sides of the Chishui River to watch the races. Before the oarsmen take their places in the boats, the townspeople present bowls of *Maotai* to them to boost their courage. Their skill and strength as oarsmen is not the only test they face. They must also scramble in the water for a duck and a red balloon — the prizes of the champion team — and then run up the bank as fast as they can to seize the silk banner. When the exhausted oarsmen go ashore, be they winners or losers, those on the sidelines crowd around to offer each bold participant a cup of *Maotai*. "This will help restore your strength," they are told.

A Glimpse of the Marketplace

Maotai is a town with nearly ten thousand citizens, over thirty percent of whom are involved in making the spirits that have given the town its name. The rest of the working population are engaged in buying and selling commodities, in manufacturing, transportation, handicrafts and professions such as teaching, medicine and ancillary services.

The marketplace lies primarily on a large street facing the river bank. Most of the small shops facing the river are known as "hanging cottages." Taking advantage of the slope of the river bank, the local people first drive several logs into the bank and then frame them up with horizontal logs. Next they connect the horizontal logs and the slope with other logs on which they cover with planks to make a floor. Finally, they wall it all up with wooden boards or bamboo poles and then roof it over. Thus a cottage, half of which is situated on the slope while the other half hangs above the water, is completed. Building houses in this way, they not only save the trouble of leveling the hilly land but also protect themselves against floods, surely a practical structure for the people of Guizhou, a place that never has three clear days in a row or a square meter of level land.

One of the four best-known towns in northern Guizhou, Maotai still follows the old tradition of having a market every day. Unlike other cities in the area, however, its market opens noon. We saw the drama unfold during our visit as we watched peasants from the other side of the river carry to market cabbages, radishes, celery and other such vegetables on their backs. Then came those from distant mountain villages bearing oranges, potatoes, sugar cane, and other mountain produce. As they trooped in, they turned the streets into a bustling carnival.

Most of the small shops that crowd together along the streets sell articles for daily use and most follow the same design — the front for merchandise, the living quarters behind. Many of them were only recently established and are run either by a couple or by a mother and daughter team. The shops are all small — some really tiny — yet the window, which doubles as counter, makes it very easy for customers to spot the things they want to buy. All they have to do is look through the window and point to what they want. They don't have to go inside at all. To villagers with baskets on their backs eager to get back home, it couldn't be more convenient.

But not all the customers are in a rush to get back home or to embark on a journey that can stretch to ten miles. So no matter how small a shop is, the owner reserves one corner for a Beijing stove and a few stools or benches. Here the mountain villagers can put down their heavy loads and gather in groups around the stove for a drink— usually a few cups of spirits served with a plate of peanuts—and gossip. After their social time is over, they stock up on such items, for their families as soap, candy, shoes and socks and start the trek home.

Lao Jiang, a man of fifty odd, runs one of these small shops with his wife and two daughters. When I asked him about the amount of his investment and income, he shrugged as his eyes rolled heavenward. "Our total capital is about one thousand *yuan*," he said. "You can't make a fortune out of an investment like that. We just barely make it."

Through my conversations with Lao Jiang and others like him I learned that shopowners used to believe firmly in the god of wealth, and that he and other supernatural beings and forces could be harnessed on their behalf. Taboos were many. It was important to stay on the right side of the gods and goddesses who could spell the difference between prosperity and penury. When a new store opened, it was elaborately decorated both inside and out with couplets like these pasted everywhere:

Handsome profits flow in from all parts of the land—
Business extends to all corners of the earth.

Or:

Large chests of gold walk in every day—
Foreign treasures show up every hour.

Couplets were complemented by fine scrolls with bold calligraphy declaring such sentiments as "A Good Start Brings Fortunes" or "All's Well That Begins Well." Accompanied by a trumpeting band, the popping of firecrackers and the coming and going of the people, a store opening ceremony was a major event to the local people and customers from the mountain villages—a minifestival of sorts.

Once the gilded sign of the shop was put up, the owner's chief concern was how to make the maximum profit possible. In the case of a peasant the popular saying went: "A year's harvests depend on a good start in spring" — whereas in the case of a businessman superstition had it that "A day's profits de-

275

pend on a good beginning in the morning.'' If the first customer of the day left happily after making a purchase, then the
shop would do good business all day. The first customer being
a woman was another auspicious sign, since women were the
keepers of the family budget. However, if the first customer was
a man who looked at the merchandise with indifference or dis-
dain and left without buying anything, a bad selling day
stretched ahead. Some stores went so far as to fire off a string
of firecrackers in such cases to head off the bad luck that an
owner could expect in the wake of a male first customer.

The last day of the last lunar month was the busiest for
all the shops since that was the last chance the shop owners
had to collect on money owed them. Some people to whom
they had extended credit went into hiding to escape the
shop owners. But nonetheless, the moment the clock struck
twelve midnight, tradition dictated that debts were forgiven.

In the eyes of the shop owners, the old abacus was the
sign of a booming business, and of course this ancient device is
still the way of totaling bills and making change all over China.
In these bygone terms, the shop owners would wrap up their abacuses with red paper as they closed for the Spring Festival and
write on the top, ''Big profits come out of small
investment.'' Then when they reopened on the fifth day of the
first lunar month and the owners uncovered the abacuses, they
snapped the beads loudly as they murmured to themselves: ''A
seed sown in the earth will yield one thousand
grains.'' Naturally they hoped to redouble their profits in the
new year.

In those days posters were put up all over such stores
wherever there was a surface that could accommodate one or
more which bore mottoes such as ''Superior products at low
prices'' ''Honest with all customers — old and young
alike.'' In actuality, however, shopkeepers in the old society
were more interested in fleecing customers than giving them bargains and dealing honestly with them. They were known to
weigh goods inaccurately, giving short measure to customers,
and for selling substandard merchandise as quality goods. Sometimes, to strike a bargain, the buyer and the seller both hid

their hands inside the sleeves, talking through their professional dactylology like "pendulum-seven," "fork-eight," and "trigger-nine." Today, nearly all these old ways and practices have disappeared from the business circles.

Trackers Who Worshipped Mice

The Chishui River, over 480 kilometers long, which begins in the Wumeng Mountains in Yunnan, makes a turn to the west of Maotai Town before it flows northward into the Yangtze River. Early in the morning, I saw boys living on the bank carrying water from the river while girls in high boots stood in the water washing clothes and vegetables.

Three hundred years ago this town bore the same name it does today "Maotai Village" for the wild grass used for thatching grew everywhere (the original meaning of *Maotai* is cogongrass platform). Later, when the Chishui River was opened for transportation, two-thirds of the salt consumed by the people of Guizhou Province was shipped through the village, which became a center for both land and water transport serving northern Guizhou. From that point on, boats and rafts came and went continually, moving not only salt but also cloth, grains, timber, raw lacquer, furs and wines.

In March 1935, when the Chinese Workers' and Peasants' Red Army were on the Long March under the command of Mao Zedong, the troops crossed the Chishui River back and forth four times, breaking through the enemy's encirclement after casting off its pursuing troops and continuing to march northward. Maotai was the very spot where the Red Army crossed the river. There the soldiers tied wooden boats together with thick ropes and wires to form a bridge while the villagers took off their wooden doors and helped to set up three additional floating bridges in no time to expedite their passage. Today Today an engraving on a monument standing next to the large ficus tree tied to which the floating bridges records this event.

As I watched the early morning work detail of the young people on the river bank I heard the cry of a work song *"Hei-Yo-Hai"* and saw two boats start their slow journey up

277

the river pulled by three young men straining against "pulling girdles" hanging in a harness from their shoulders. Sometimes these "trackers," all of whom wore straw shoes, walked on the bank by the water; sometimes they climbed onto the cliffs and walked along the meandering footpath, still leaning forward to pull along their heavy burden. Their faces had been turned a ruddy brown by the combination of the blazing sun and the river winds.

Later when the men were carrying sand for construction ashore in baskets balanced on their shoulders, I had a chat with Lao Zhao, the "front man," as he stood, pole in hand, in the bow of his boat. This old fellow had been working on the river for thirty years and had a lot to say about the shoals and rapid currents the boats had to negotiate as they passed through the mountains and valleys. He said that they often had to track their boats upstream.

Generally speaking, there are three to a dozen trackers on each boat, depending on the size of the vessel. When they are about to confront rapid currents, the helmsman ties the towing rope around his seat known as "the general's stump" and puts the rope through the iron ring fixed on the mast from where it extends to the trackers. The ring can slide up and down, going up when the trackers walk on the cliffs and down when they walk along the bank close to the water. When the rope is securely tied, the men fix their girdles to the ropes, put the girdles on and go ashore to track their boat forward.

The man leading the tracking team is called the *biangao*, usually a tall, strong man with many years of experience. The second man, the *erbian*, looks back from time to time to note the helmsman's signalling gestures and direction, conveying them at intervals to the *biangao*. The *erbian* also leads in the singing of their work song, thus regulating the movements of all the trackers. Should the towing rope be caught on a tree or a jutting rock, he is the one who will take off his girdle and go to fix it.

Boat tracking requires that no boat set sail alone; there must be at least two. In this way trackers can cooperate—tracking one boat through the rapids and shoals

278

and then coming back for the other one. As the boats are moving along, and a boat is seen coming from the opposite direction, the one going upstream must stop by the bank and make way for the other. Such encounters are fraught with danger. Often a boat going upstream will berth their vessel when they know a boat is on its way downstream in order to avoid a possible collision.

Trackers may be dragged into the water if any of the following dangers occur: running into unexpected rapids or fierce winds, the helmsman's failure to bring the boat under control, insufficient force in the towing. The boat can be swept toward the center of the river by strong rapids with its bow pointing to the opposite bank. When this happens, called *dazhang* by the boatmen, the trackers must at once pull off their girdles, shake off the towing rope and take a few quick steps backward. Only in this way can they avoid being dragged into the river.

Because of this particular danger, trackers in the old days were governed by more taboos than other boatmen. For example, no one was allowed to wash his face aboard since a wet head or face was taken as an omen of drowning. Before a new boat was launched, and when it was about to make its first sail, the helmsman would slaughter a cock and stick feathers coated with its blood into the bow, the handle of the helm, the masts, and both sides of the vessel, appealing for safety to "Bodhisattva, the River Guard" and the god of boats.

The local boatmen even deified the mice hiding in the cabins, calling them "boat-keeper," and paying them homage. It was considered an omen spelling imminent disaster if a mouse ran onto the bank or fell into the river. Should this happen, the helmsman called for a stop at once. Only after a few days had elapsed and they had burned joss sticks, lighted candles and made offerings such as chickens to "Bodhisattva, the River Guard" and the god of boats would they resume their sail.

After the founding of the People's Republic of China, the Chishui's waterway was dredged and machines with capstans were installed at places with rapids and shoals to help in the towing of boats. Some boats today are also equipped with motors and propellers. Consequently, towing is seldom seen anymore. And since sailing is becoming safer and safer, the boatmen's customs based on superstitions are rapidly disappearing.

CHAPTER XI

HUNAN — Birthplace of the Dragon Boat Festival

DRAGON BOAT FESTIVAL CELEBRATION ON THE MILUO RIVER

> On the fifth day of the fifth month—
> The Dragon Boat Festival—
> Mugworts planted at the door
> Refresh all rooms and the hall.
> We eat *zongzi*
> With cane sugar;
> We're so happy:
> Dragon boats appear
> On the river.

Just as this children's song says, on the fifth day of the fifth lunar month, which is the date of the Dragon Boat Festival, people throughout China, especially those in the countryside in the South, all plant at their door mugworts with cattails hanging on them, eat *zongzi* (pyramid-shaped dumplings made of glutinous rice, usually wrapped in bamboo or reed leaves), and enjoy watching dragon boat races on the rivers.

As the legend goes, these traditional activities developed out of the funeral of Qu Yuan, a patriotic poet who died over 2,200 years ago. The Dragon Boat Festival of this year fell on June 4, the day before we arrived at Miluo County, Hunan Province where the poet drowned himself in the river after traveling 1,500 kilometers from Beijing.

281

A Visit to Quzici Village

The peasants along the Miluo River were not very busy in early summer as they had just threshed their wheat and intertilled the early paddy fields twice. On our way to Quzici Village from the county's capital, we saw from time to time young men carrying their young wives on the backs of their bikes as they went to pay their seasonal visits to the wives' parents. The young women held were cloth umbrellas over their husbands to keep them from getting sunburned. Various gifts were hung on the handlebars together with two palm-leaf fans. It is a rule that married daughters who return with their husbands to visit their parents during the Dragon Boat Festival bring them *zongzi*, stuffed buns, pork, dry cuttlefish and bottled liquor as well as fans, which will be needed by the elders because it gets hotter and hotter with each passing day after the Festival.

" Rat-a-tat-clang — '' we heard the beating of drums and clang of gongs ahead. As our car brought us near, we saw a group of village boys having fun rowing a dragon boat on the river. They had sneaked onto the boat while the adults were having lunch at home, crowding aboard before it came to a full stop by the riverside. Two late-comers had even jumped into the river in order to get onto the boat before it shoved off.

Soon we arrived at Quzici Village where we were met by our guide Ren Shenwang, who took us to visit Zhou Taigan's family. A tall thin man of forty-six. Zhou was not only a capable man in general but well known as an excellent swimmer and a skillful boatman. On the following day he would participate in the annual dragon boat race as the helmsman of the " Black Dragon Boat'' of Quzici Village. We were welcomed to a comfortably spacious two-year-old brick house of ten room which Zhou shared with seven others, including his wife, two daughters, two sons, one daughter-in-law and a month-old grandson.

Hardly had we sat ourselves down than our considerate hostess, seeing that our foreheads were glistening with perspiration and our clothing was soaked through, offered each of us a bowl of cold tea to quench our thirst. Immediately, she boiled some water and made us a pot of hot tea to which she added ginger powder and salt. Before she presented it to us, she put in a handful of fried soybeans and sesame seeds.

"This is salty ginger tea with soybeans and sesame seeds" our guide explained unnecessarily, adding that the tea leaves could be eaten as well. He then demonstrated the proper way to drink— first shaking the tea bowl repeatedly between sips. Finally he threw back his head and poured into his mouth all the soybeans, sesame seeds and tea leaves, chewing with great relish. We were told that this special compound tea greatly benefitted one's health since tea leaves could quench thirst and moisten the lungs, ginger warm the stomach, while the salt could replace the saline sweated out of the body. The soybeans and sesame seeds, on the other hand, could count as a sort of light meal. During their breaks from transplanting rice seedlings, the peasants always have some of this compound tea.

We were still enjoying the tea when the hostess brought us "sweet egg tea," which was made of diluted eggs and sugar. It was sweet and fresh. People here have their own ways of drinking tea. During the Spring Festival, when offering sweet egg tea to visitors, they also add into it jujubes, dry persimmons and tangerine shreds, which together express their best wishes for good luck and success to their guests.

A Day for Worshipping the Dragon Becomes a Day to Commemorate Qu Yuan

Quzici Village was named after the Quzi Temple on the Yusi Hills lying to the east of the village. Qu Yuan was a senior official and a poet in the State of Chu 2,200 years ago. But due to the slander of the treacherous court officials, his fatuous king not only rejected his suggested policies for reform at home and allying with the State of Qi against Qin, but also exiled him. During his fifteen years of exile, he wrote many remarkable poems in which he expressed his great concern for the fate of his state and people. In A.D. 278, the army of the State of Qin occupied the capital of Chu. On the fifth day of the fifth lunar month that year when Qu Yuan who was living by the Miluo River learned the heartbreaking news, he jumped into the river with a heavy stone in his arms, thus remaining a loyal citizen of his state to his last breath.

On hearing the grievous news, people from miles around rushed to the spot by boat in a futile effort to rescue him. To prevent the fish and shrimp from devouring his body, they threw *zongzi* into the river. That, according to folklore, is the origin of dragon boat racing and the eating of *zongzi* at the time of the Dragon Boat Festival.

As a matter of fact, however, these customs had been practiced in China long before the birth of Qu Yuan. The famous modern scholar Wen Yiduo has proved through his research that the precursor of the Dragon Boat Festival was "Dragon's Day," on which people of the states of Wu and Yue living south of the Yangtze River worshipped the dragon. Following the ancients of the Huaxia Clan, they worshipped the totem of the dragon, calling themselves children of the dragon. With their hair cut and their bodies tattooed, they dressed up like dragons and sought a look of nobility. On that day they would row dugout canoes painted with dragons and throw into the river foods stuffed in bamboo tubes or wrapped in tree leaves to worship these mythical aquatic beings. Finally they would celebrate by holding a canoe race.

By the later years of the Spring and Autumn Period (770-476 B.C.), as society progressed, the people of the State of Yue broke away from totemism, claiming that the racing of dragon boats had originated from the glorious activity of their king Gou Jian, who had endured hardships and personal humiliation for the sake of reviving his state. They claimed that on the fifth day of the fifth lunar month, under the pretext of a dragon boat competition, he had maneuvered his navy in such a way as to wreak revenge on Fu Chai, King of the State of Wu, for destroying Yue.

Qu Yuan's lofty moral character and his remarkable poems impressed later generations deeply. So the story that in order to save Qu Yuan, people of the State of Chu rowing dragon boats threw *zongzi* into the river, spread all over the land. In the Song Dynasty (960-1279) the royal government of China designated the fifth day of the fifth lunar month as "Dragon Boat Day," telling people to commemorate

Qu Yuan. The citizens were also asked to wear small scented bags which symbolized the poet's moral integrity that should be remembered and appreciated from generation to generation.

Decorating the Doors with Mugworts and Cattails

"Get up, sir," our host woke me up from my dream when it was still dark. "We must go to cut mugworts now." Quite right! Before going to bed we had made an appointment to go together to cut mugworts in the fields early in the morning!

Cutting dewy mugworts just before dawn at Dragon Boat Festival time is a traditional practice observed everywhere. The hillsides behind the village were covered with mugworts about five feet tall, and a few cuttings were sufficient for the special occasion. Then they went to cut flags by the lakeside in front of the village. Finally they got some creeping plants from the woods. As the sun rose high in the sky they all returned home with their mugworts.

When they reached home, Lao Zhou planted some mugworts on the two sides of the door, hanging cattails on them. Then he decorated the door frame with the creeping plants. In no time, the entrance became garlanded in green and the house filled with the fragrance of the mugworts.

"Why plant the mugworts and hang the flags?" I asked Lao Zhou.

"Look here," Lao Zhou answered as he picked a mugwort. "Isn't it like the whip in the classical operas? This is a horse. The straight flags look like magic bronze swords while the creepers are like an iron chain that can lock up ghosts." In other words, symbolically the hero who conquered ghosts in the legend now guarded the door on his horse with his magic sword and iron chain. Seeing the hero, no devils would dare to enter the house to make trouble. So, "Mugworts planted at the door on the Dragon Boat Festival" in fact carries the planters' hopes for happiness and peace.

In ancient times, the fifth lunar month was considered an "evil month," and the fifth the most unlucky day of the month. Babies born on this day were sometimes even deserted by their parents. The reason the ancients hated this month so much was because it got progressively hotter after the fifth month, which caused plagues across the land. Besides, it was the season for mosquitoes to propagate; and the "five poisons" — the snake, scorpion, centipede, gecko and spider — all began to threaten the peace of human beings.

Facing these threats, women pinned up pictures of these "five poisons" with needles stuck on the bodies of the harmful beings, believing they could thus wipe them out. People at the same time discovered the magic effect of the mugworts. Dried mugworts rolled into bars could cure many diseases when lighted. Mugworts collected on the Dragon Boat Day that were washed and dried in the sun could cure diarrhea and gynecological conditions when they were made into soup. The strong odor of this plant could also drive mosquitoes and flies out of the house. That is why people planted mugworts next to their doors: to keep away evils and harmful insects.

From *Eventful Years of the State of Chu* written by Zong Lin of the Liang Dynasty (502-557) we learn that 1,300 years ago people wove mugworts into the shape of a man and hung it on the door. During the Ming Dynasty, however, mugworts were made into tigers that guarded the house. Then later people thought if Zhong Kui had a horse to ride, he would catch devils more easily — and that is how the mugwort whip became a symbol of the steed.

The roots of the flags growing near the water are a medici-nal herb that relieves pain and invigorates the spleen. Wine flavored with the fragrant flags is refreshing — a drink much appreciated by the ancients. Ouyang Xiu (1007-1072), a literary man of the Song Dynasty said of it in one of his poems: "Flag wine guarantees the king a long long life."

Bathing children with mugwort water on the Dragon Boat Festival is a popular practice in China. I remember what my mother did on this particular day in my home province of Guangdong when I was a little boy. She would put in the yard a wooden basin of water with mugworts, flags, balsam, and magnolias in it and then late in the morning when it was warmed by the sun, she would have me jump in. As she poured the scented water over my body she prayed: "May this herbal water wash away all diseases and keep you safe and sound."

I've been told that those living along the Songhua River in the Northeast have the habit of washing themselves with mugworts in the river, believing that they can thus remain free of disease and even ill luck. Of course, this is obviously an exaggeration, but some traditional Chinese doctors do say that water boiled with mugworts really can alleviate skin diseases.

When the mugworts were planted and the flags hung, our host brought up a basin of water mixed with smashed garlics, whiskey and orpiment (yellow flower also called "live forever") and began to sprinkle it all over the central room, bedrooms, kitchen and stable.

In the past, orpiment wine was something they always prepared for the reunion dinner of the family. Everybody would have a few sips for the sake of the holiday. The elders, however, would put one or two drops of this wine on the ears and noses of the young ones. Sometimes they wrote with a writing brush the Chinese character *wang* (王), or "king" instead, believing that orpiment wine had the effect of preventing plagues and thus the children would enjoy a long and peaceful life.

Nowadays, with the spread of medical knowledge the villagers no longer put orpiment in wine, for they know now that orpiment is poisonous and can cause vomiting, diarrhea and stupor. "Here I spread my orpiment wine; there insects all go far away," joked the host as he sprinkled the liquor. After vaporizing, orpiment can indeed kill some germs and drive certain insects out of the house. Accordingly, we conclude that decorating the doors with mugworts and flags and spreading orpiment wine on the floor during the Dragon Boat Festival are a healthy habit which prevents diseases that thrive in the summer.

Eating *Zongzi*

During the Dragon Boat Festival, traditionally people start their lunch by eating *zongzi*. As the hostess brought a tray, the house filled with the fresh scent of reed leaves and we all helped ourselves. After untying the strings and peeling off the reed leaves, we began to eat the contents with sugar. I found it particularly tasty, perhaps because I had helped with the wrapping myself. I ate eight of them one after another.

Eating *zongzi* at the time of the Dragon Boat Festival is a common activity in China, although the ingredients and flavors differ from one place to another. The local *zongzi* are soaked glutinous rice wrapped in reed leaves in the shape of a pyramid which are cooked in alkaline water and eaten when hot. These are very different from the date *zongzi* typical of Beijing which are eaten only after being cooled in cold water.

Lu Huang, the cameraman who was traveling with me, was doing some painting in Jiaxing County, Zhejiang Province four years before our visit here and told me that the ham *zongzi* there were rich but not greasy. Their glutinous rice was first mixed with soybean sauce, then with small ham cubes with sugar added, wine and salt; each two slices of lean ham were folded in with a fat slice in between so that the right amount of lard could permeate every grain of the rice.

Zongzi made in my home province of Guangdong consist of fine ingredients and have their own unique flavors. An assorted one whose ingredients are chicken and duck cubes, roasted pork, egg yolk, dried mushrooms and green bean mash, weighs as much as half a kilogram and has to be wrapped in a lotus leaf rather than reed leaves.

According to legend, the earliest *zongzi* consisted of a bamboo tube with rice cooked in it and was called *tong zong*. They were not wrapped in leaves until the Han Dynasty. There is also a folk tale about this change. One day in the early years of the Eastern Han Dynasty, a man by the name of Ou Hui from Changsha was taking a walk along the Miluo River before the Dragon Boat Festival when he suddenly caught sight of a man with scented grass covering his body who was wearing a cloud crown and a long sword. After telling Ou Hui that he was Qu Yuan, the stranger said, "It's good that you worship me, but all your offerings are eaten up by the creatures of the deep every year. You should wrap your rice with chinaberry leaves in the shape of a pyramid and tie it with colored silk threads so that the aquatic animals won't dare to eat it again."

Ou Hui told the other villagers what had happened. Thereafter, *zongzi* were wrapped in the shape of pyramids in chinaberry or reed leaves.

During the Tang and the Song dynasties there were many kinds of *zongzi*. As the book *Historical Events* records, there were pyramidic *zongzi*, rhombic *zongzi*, cone-shaped *zongzi*, tube-shaped *zongzi*, *chengchui* (sliding weight of a steelyard) *zongzi*, and so on— all of which were named after their shapes. Their ingredients not only included dates and sugar, but also pine nuts, chestnuts, walnuts, musk and the like. In the Ming Dynasty, there was a kind of mugwort *zongzi*, the rice of which was soaked with mugwort leaves; the royal court of the Qing Dynasty invented cheese *zongzi*, the rice of which was soaked with cheese for a night before the wrapping. Both the mugwort *zongzi* and the cheese *zongzi* were well-known in those days.

Of course *zongzi* was not the only food for the Festival. After a morning's busy work in the kitchen, the hostess and her two daughters prepared a very rich dinner, including stewed bamboo shoots, fungus soup with pork, fried eel meat, and sauteed amaranth. Since the edible red amaranth is in fact a common plant that the villagers can eat every day, it actually should not have been given a place on the festival dining table. Since it is believed that whoever has it on this particular day will have no stomach-ache, everybody eats at least a little at that time.

The Offering of the Dragon Head

We were still eating when somebody shouted, "Let's go and offer the dragon head now!" As a rule, before the dragon boat race started, the oarsmen went to Quzi Temple to worship Qu Yuan with the dragon head, a rite called "offering the dragon head." We put down our bowls and chopsticks and hurried off to the temple.

Accompanied by the continuous popping of firecrackers, a team of oarsmen dressed in white from head to foot and led by the No. 1 oarsman carrying the dragon head were marching into the temple with their boat flag and oars, beating drums and gongs all the way. They were men of the White Dragon Boat belonging to the neighboring village. Placing the dragon head on the altar, they proceeded to kowtow before the idol of Qu Yuan. The ceremony did not end until an official tied a red ribbon on the dragon head and ran toward the river with it; then after jumping into the river and bathing with it he finally placed it at the head of the boat. The villagers believed that after worshipping Qu Yuan and bathing the dragon head, their dragon boat race would be a successful one. Then, one by one, the "Crimson Dragon," the "Black Dragon" and the "Golden Dragon" boats came to offer their dragon heads.

I measured with my eyes the "Black Dragon" Boat of Quzici Village: it was about twenty meters long and one and a half wide. The wooden dragon head with its big round eyes and drooping whiskers stretched high above the water; the end of the boat decorated with long pieces of bamboo resembled the beautiful tail of a phoenix. Meant to ride through all waves and winds, the helm controlled by our host Lao Zhou was designed in the shape of the heavy saber of Guan Yu, a famous warrior featured in *The Romance of the Three Kingdoms*. The boat, including the oars and helm, had scales painted on it, and in the distance it did indeed call to mind the dragon described in the legend.

In the past all the fir used in the making of the dragon boats was stolen from somewhere. It was believed that only those made of stolen fir could go fast and those made of legally purchased wood didn't stand a chance of winning the race. Strangely, owners of firs did not mind at all when their trees were stolen for this use. "Let the thieves cut as many as they want" was their attitude. They were in fact honored to contribute their tallest trees to the making of the village's dragon boat.

Nowadays they do not steal wood anymore. The dragon boat of Quzici Village was built four years ago. The day it was launched, the village was alive with festivity and crowded with the relatives and friends of villagers who had come just for this occasion. The launching ceremony was held on the spot where the boat had been constructed. Deafening sounds of drums and gongs came from the boat. On the two sides of the new boat decorated with colorful flags stood the smart oarsmen dressed in blue with their oars in hands. In front of the boat was an altar from which smoke of burning joss sticks was curling up. On the table was a tray of offerings, including wine, *zongzi*, and pastries.

The ceremony at last began after the setting off firecrackers. The master builder of the boat lifted the tray and sang the traditional prayer:

> The new dragon boat is a swallow:
> Like a swift wind it comes,
> Like an arrow it goes;
> With a successful start
> It will beat all its foes.

With this he kowtowed to the sky, the earth and the dragon head, sprinkling three cups of spirits from the tray, one toward the sky, one over the earth, and another toward the dragon head. Finally when he threw up into the sky all the offerings, which the shouting children all tried to grab for themselves, the oarsmen carried the boat onto the Miluo River marching to the rhythm of a work song.

From then on, on the first day of the fifth lunar month every year, the oarsmen carry the boat out of the storage shed, paint it with tung oil and practice rowing on the river. When the boat passes the neighboring villages, the villagers there will set off firecrackers to welcome the coming of the dragon boat. The oarsmen must row toward them as fast as they can to express their thanks to them and tie the red ribbon given to them by these neighbors around the dragon head. This is called *guahong*, or "catching red," — a way the ancient villagers expressed their thanks to the fishermen who had found Qu Yuan's body. Clearly, their purpose in practicing this old custom is to promote good relations between the villages and the districts.

Dragon Boat Racing

Along the two sides of the peaceful clear Miluo River were crowds and crowds of villagers who had come to watch the dragon boat race. Each two boats formed one team. With the firing of the signal, the boats started off like flying arrows, the sound of their drums and gongs all but causing deafness among the watchers.

The oarsmen of the "Black Dragon Boat" belonging to Quzici Village, directed by the helmsman, rowed forward quickly in rhythm. The forty-two men on the boat, including thirty-eight oarsmen, the speed commander, the drummer, the gong striker and the helmsman, had been selected at a village-wide meeting. They were all strong men who were good swimmers; they always cooperated with one another and acted as the commander directed. The No. 1 and No. 2 oarsmen sitting in the first row at the front were the best of them all. The day before their race I watched them exercising on the river. On one occasion their boat almost bumped into the dike because it was pulling in too fast, but these two jumped into the river just in time to protect it with their own bodies.

The oarsmen were giving their all. Now, the "Black Dragon" pulled past the "Crimson Dragon," as the spectators cheered it on. A group of young men even ran after the "Black Dragon" to urge it forward. And ultimately the "Black Dragon" did indeed win first place. As a visitor to its home village, I was pulling for it and even found myself swelling with pride. I kept waving my hands to show my admiration and respect for Lao Zhou, who as the helmsman had led his team in winning the championship for three years in succession now. Feeling grateful to him, the oarsmen and the other villagers had thrown him into the air. Today he would have to be thrown into the air again!

aaaaa "Rather lose a year's crops than lose a yearly race" is a popular local saying from which one can see how much the dragon boat race means to the villagers. It is said that winning the race brings to the village not only great honor but also abundant harvests and year-long happiness.

Today, as a popular sport, dragon boat racing is seen on lakes and rivers throughout China. But because every place has its own customs, the ways the race is conducted differ from place to place.

Dragon boats in Guangdong are particularly beautiful, decorated as they are with colorful flags and sheltered with huge umbrellas. In some places the boats are normally buried in the earth in order to protect it from the scorching sun; they are dug up just a few days before the race to the lighting of joss sticks and the making of offerings.

In Mianyang, Hubei Province, the fifteenth day of the fifth lunar month is called the "Big Dragon Boat Festival," a day for dragon boat racing. On this day, with dragon heads put in place at their fronts, little fishing boats all turn into dragon boats. It makes for a glorious scene — the sight of one or two hundred dragon boats competing on one lake!

Some regions of rivers or lakes in Guangdong have dragon boats that give performances only. On the boats they play music, set off firecrackers, beat drums and strike gongs. Following the example of the dragon boat of Qu Yuan's hometown Zigui in Hubei Province, the oarsmen, pretending to be Qu Yuan's sister, keep calling out "Dear brother — do come back!" This certainly sets it apart from observances elsewhere.

People of the Miao nationality living along the Qingshui River in Guizhou Province, however, have a four-day-long dragon boat festival. The dragon boat consists of three canoes with a big one in the middle. In contrast to those of the Han people, their dragon boats do not take part in a race but merely carry the owners from one village to another or to the homes of their friends and relatives. Wherever their boats go, they are always warmly received by the local villagers, who will offer the oarsmen wine and hang on the dragon heads their offerings — chickens, ducks, pigs and sheep. In return, the oarsmen deliver their food — glutinous rice cooked with meat and vegetables — to the women and children along the way. Traditionally belief has it that whoever eats something from the dragon boats will be safe from misadventures and have good luck throughout the year.

In Guangxi, the Zhuang Nationality Autonomous Region, dragon boats are divided into two kinds — men's boats and women's boats. Besides those rowed with the oarsmen's hands, there are those rowed with the feet. The winning of a race here is not determined by the speed of the boat only, but also by its design and decoration. That is why boats in this region are particularly beautiful.

Thanks to the cultural exchanges between China and other countries in ancient times, the custom of dragon boat racing long ago spread to Japan, Korea, Vietnam, and other Southeast Asian countries. And in recent years oarsmen from American and European countries have been attracted in ever swelling members to this entertaining and challenging activity.

CHAPTER XII

HUBEI — Center of Ancient *Chu* Culture

CLOGS, WAYS OF FISHING AND REAPING LOTUS

Uncommon Clogs

I remember that in the classical novel *The Romance of the Three Kingdoms* Zhou Yu, a general of the Kingdom of Eastern Wu in a single night of the Chibi Campaign burned up all the water and field camps, including the fighting boats of the hundred thousand troops of the Kingdom of Wei. The defeated Cao Cao took the muddy Huarong Path, and thanks to the merciful General Guan Yu of the Kingdom of Western Shu who allowed him to escape from his sword, he managed to return to Jingzhou by walking on the straw his soldiers had laid out for him.

Now we had an opportunity ourselves to walk on the muddy roads of Magang Township, Huchang District, Mianyang County. It was a low-lying area, and as it had been raining for three days, the roads could not have been muddier. Even though we had put on the rubber shoes our guide Lao Liu had borrowed for us, walking was still difficult and tedious.

Passing by Magang Town, we heard steps behind obviously getting down and closer, and finally two girls caught up with us. I took a look at their feet and noted that their rubber shoes were inside still another pair of sizable shoes whose soles were spiked with large iron teeth. They walked on the muddy road steadily, one carrying a bottle of oil, the other a bowl of thick soybean paste.

"What kind of shoes are those?" I asked our guide.

"Clogs," he told me.

"Clogs?" I asked myself. "What sort of clogs could they be?" I knew that in my home province of Guangdong, the sole of the clog consisted of one piece of tung wood with teeth cut beneath and a one-inch wide rubber belt nailed on the front in the shape of a bamboo awning. I found them very comfortable to wear after bathing. But never had I seen wooden sandals like those I saw here.

When the girl with the oil bottle in her hand reached home, she took off her wooden sandals and entered the house in her rubber shoes only. How strange! There was not even one stain of mud on her shoes or clothes. It turned out that with the thick spiked soles and the large vamps at the front, no mud could reach the rubber shoes. To prevent mud that might travel to the trouser legs from the heels of the sandals, the soles were deliberately made very short. So I came to know that it was wooden sandals like these that kept all the houses clean in this muddy little town.

A story in which clogs figure that took place in the State of Jin 2,600 years ago is a touching one: Suffering from the result of court fighting, Jin Wengong lived as an exile for nineteen years. Then when he returned to power as king in 636 B.C., he rewarded all his subjects who had shared his hard lot but forgot the devoted Jie Zitui. Having no interest in fame or wealth anyway but being hurt at the slight, Jie carried his old mother on his back to start a new life in the Mianshan Mountains as a hermit. When Jin Wengong learned of this, he went to the mountain to beg Jie to return to the court, but his messages were ignored. In order to drive Jie down from the mountains, Jin set fire to them. Three days later, the charred bodies of Jie and his mother were found under a big willow tree. The sad king had the willow cut down to be made into clogs, and from then on he would look at his clogs every day and say, "How sad, *zuxia* (under foot)." So it is believed that the term *zuxia*, carrying the present meaning of "my friend," thus came into use.

History books and poems record many other anecdotes about clogs. In A.D. 383, on hearing the exciting news that his

80,000 soldiers had defeated the one million men of Qin's troops, the prime minister of the State of Eastern Jin ran into his house so fast that he broke the teeth of his clogs at the doorsill. Drawing a lesson from this, his grandnephew Xie Lingyun, a landscape poet, had a special pair of clogs made for mountain climbing: when he scaled the mountains he would take off the front teeth and when coming down, he would remove the back teeth. Such clogs were called "Xiegong clogs." During the Song Dynasty, painted clogs became an item in the dowries of brides.

Clogs had been something every family in the South could not do without until thirty years ago. I remember that during my childhood on my way home from school, I often stopped by the clog shop to watch the craftsman there making clogs. To change the parts that needed to be, now and then he would deftly throw the clog base up and catch it just in time — much as if he were a magician. His apprentices were hard at work, too — some planing the clogs with their special planers, others painting them. The results were waterproof, durable, beautiful. Men wore black ones, children red. Women, on the other hand, wore very colorful ones painted by old artists who were sure to come up with a traditional product.

In recent decades, clogs have been replaced by cheap but beautiful plastic sandals. Nonetheless, in Japan clogs are still as popular as ever. A Japanese I know has told me that the shapes of their clogs change according to the seasons and environment: ones with long teeth are used on country roads, but ones with leather vamps are used in winter snows.

"Oh, I see." I was somehow delighted to hear that. "Mianyang's clogs and those of the Japanese are not much different then."

No Way Out Without a Boat

Leaving the town, we found ourselves standing before a branch of the river. "We have to take a boat now," said Yin, the head of Magang Township who accompanied us, and went to borrow a boat from a villager living by the roadside. Before long he returned with a bamboo pole. Planting the pole in the river, he jumped onto the boat like a bird. He was carrying us to Nanzui Village for a visit. I praised his skillful rowing and he just smiled. "It won't do if you can't row a boat here," he said. "When we go to carry out our work in the villages, sometimes there is no way to go except by boat."

Hubei Province, with *hu* meaning "lake" and *bei* "north," was so named because it lay to the north of Dongting Lake. It was once a misty marsh in ancient times and did not become a plain until the water of the Yangtze River washed it into a flat area of over 30,000 square kilometers. Hubei, known as "Lake Province," is a province crisscrossed by rivers and with more than a thousand lakes. The capital town of Mianyang County lies in the west of Wuhan, the capital of Hubei, with a distance of a hundred kilometers. Many of the villages here are located on lakes, with simple small harbors built for boats a recurring feature.

As the saying goes, "Those living on a mountain live off the mountain, those living near the water live off the water." In the old days, the villagers all lived off the lakes, using boats in whatever activities they had, such as fishing, picking lotus seeds, raising ducks, going to town or to the market, calling on friends and relatives, sending children to school, and receiving brides. After the founding of New China, and work of irrigation canals was dug, turning this area into "a place where you will find no way out without a boat."

Sitting on the river bank I saw green grass and hanging willows on the dikes and herdsmen dressed in rain capes and straw hats all mirrored in the river— a scene of charming beauty. The soft sound of the running water and the meeting of the bamboo pole and the water seemed to add even more quietness to the still evening fields. Lost in reverie, I was so startled when another boat suddenly came up before us that I almost jumped into the water, but Yin veered westward just in time to avoid a collision.

"Do you have any rules for the boatmen here?" I asked him.

"Yes, we do. But they aren't as strict as those for the large rivers," he answered as he continued his rowing.

"When two boats meet, the light one should make way for the heavy one. If there is any boat spreading a fishnet nearby, we try to keep away from it in order not to damage its net."

I had heard that fishermen had many taboos. For instance, they avoided words like *fan* (capsize) and *chen* (sinking, also a surname in Chinese), so that when they had to summon somebody by the name of *Chen*, they would split the character into two parts and address him as "Mr. *Er Dong*." Therefore I asked him, "Do the fishermen here have any taboos?"

"Every family here has two to three boats, or at least one. The villagers have to use them many times a day when they go to work in the fields, so that our boats are just like bikes in the cities. Besides, the rivers and lakes are all very calm and safe. So taboos just haven't developed here."

Indeed, at lunch the next day when we were eating the upper half of a crucian, the host turned it over. In Fujian, you must never do that, for turning over any sea animal is tantamount to inviting the capsizing of a boat.

As far as the making of a boat is concerned, the local villagers have many traditional rules to observe. Their fishing boats vary in size with their lengths starting at 14.5 *chi* (one meter equals three *chi*), and continuing 20.5, 24.5, etc. The final figure must always be a "5." That is called "A boat must never go without a '5' (five)." It is said that solid boats must always be made according to the measurements set by the legendary master carpenter Lu Ban.

The first day is called "laying out the materials": the master carpenter first lays the firs on the ground one by one, deciding where they are to be used. As a rule, the owner prepares a rich dinner for the carpenter, hoping that honoring him in this way will help to persuade him to be saving in his use of timber.

The last step is to saw open the biggest and longest fir and fix the two thick boards on both sides. This is just as important as the setting of the central beam of a new house. On this day, neighbors, relatives and the carpenters nearby all come for the occasion with gifts and firecrackers. As soon as the boards are fixed they set off the firecrackers. Finally the owner of the new boat prepares a feast for the carpenters and his visitors in celebration of the completion of the boat.

In front of us was a middle-aged woman slowly rowing toward us a boat piled with water plants. The river was thick with plants, which the villagers would clip with two bamboo poles, twist them, and throw them onto the boat. The next day they would spread the plants in the fields, for they made first-class fertilizer. Though the muddy roads made walking difficult, the branches of the rivers connecting all the villages of this area did provide easy transportation.

Cottages That Withstand Floods

Night had fallen by the time we got to Nanzui Village and it was pouring. Had it not been for the help of our host Fu Erjin, who came to meet us just in time, I would not have been able to make it ashore.

Perhaps because of the rarity of visitors here, our hostess, finished clearing up after supper, lost no time in starting over to prepare food for us. There were five people in their family — the couple and their three children, two boys and one girl — living in a five-room brick house. Aged thirty-four, the host was a muscular man of medium height with a sunburned face. He had harvested five tons of rice from his ten *mu* of farmland the previous year. And with the extra income he got from his jute, rapeseeds, lotus, fish, pigs and chickens, his family led quite a comfortable life.

Nanzui Village, or "South Mouth Village," was so named because it extended into the lake like the mouth of a fish — its twenty or so houses placed close together in a neat row, like a company of soldiers. Built on a spot only one meter above the lake, Nanzui Village used to suffer from frequent floods which could easily be caused by just a few days of heavy rain. A local expression refers to "nine floods out of ten years." The spates and the ebbings of the Yangtze River and Hanshui River frequently swallowed up this small village. It was lucky that they came on slowly enough so that villagers would have time to take off their wooden doors and erect a tall shed on which they could put their household articles. Then they would pack up enough clothing and food to last out the emergency, get into their boats and either head for the homes of their friends or relatives or spend their days fishing on the rivers. Some even had to make a temporary living by singing ditties or performing as acrobats, for there was no way they could return home until the floods had receded.

"What would you do if the houses collapsed in the floods?" I asked.

"In the past, the substantial house we had built could be swept away in one flood," Fu told me. "Then we put up simpler sheds with poles, sorghum stalks, and reeds. But it was still a lot of work to rebuild them once they were swept away. Later somebody figured that the water passages in arched bridges could be duplicated when we built houses. With holes in the walk, the houses could stand firm in floods."

Looking around, I discovered no doors other than the large entrance to the house and the usual doors of the individual rooms. Our host knew that his words had puzzled me, so he pointed at the foot of a wall, "Look there. That is a water passage."

Following the direction of his finger, I could see how their so-called water passages were constructed. During the building of the house, when the walls were about one meter high, they laid a one-meter long plank in each wall to support the bricks over it while they laid moveable bricks underneath. Some other houses were built with arched doors, which were firmer though less material was needed. When oncoming floods force them to leave their houses, they just kick away the moveable bricks from under all the water door, and move them aside before getting into their boats. In this way, even if the whole house is bathed in water, it will remain safe and sound, for by letting in the water, the water doors reduce the outside pressure, and in the meantime the house is firmly held together by the well-connected wooden structure of the roof. When the floods recede, the returnees only need fill up the holes again with the same bricks.

"I see. In other words, you share your house with the fish," I joked.

"Right you are! You never can tell how many times the Dragon King has used your house as part of his palace. Yet the houses are still in good condition," he parried.

As we were taking a walk the next day we noticed that many of the families had painted under the eaves illustrations of stories from *The Romance of the Three Kingdoms*.

It turned out that this was a region that the three kingdoms— Wei, Shu, and Wu—were fighting for over 1,700 years ago. Seventy kilometers southeast of the village lie the ancient battlefields of the Chibi Campaign. Jiangling City, 100 kilometers to the west, is the ancient Jingzhou which Guan Yu lost due to negligence. Because of this heritage, the local villagers are fond of the characters of the novel. In addition, it is said that they also worship the heroes of the three kingdoms deified by later people, praying to them to guard their houses against evils and devils.

Fishermen's Ways of Fishing and Their Customs

One of the songs from *Red Guards of Hong Lake*, a popular opera of the 1960s, describes the scenery here:

> Hong Lake water: waves there, beating waves—
> My hometown lies there, lies on its bank;
> Morning boats go to spread fishnets there;
> Nightfall sees them back stacked with fish.

I was hoping to go boating on the lake, and as luck would have it, our host said after breakfast as he looked at the sky, "It's finally cleared up. How about an outing on the lake?" Before long he was rowing us around the lake.

I noticed a young man fishing in front of us in a boat the likes of which I had never seen. It consisted of two basin-like small boats (1.5 meters long and 0.5 meters wide) tied together by two wooden poles laid above them. He was picking out the fish from his net as he pulled it up. When he went home, I was told, he simply carried the two mini boats with the poles on his shoulders, a load of only about thirty-five kilograms. I learned that these were called cormorant boats after the bird that dives into the water to catch fish. Now these boats are also used to carry fishnets when the villagers go fishing.

The river was becoming wider and wider, and more and more fishing boats came into sight as the clear waves turned golden in the rising sun. The fishermen were fishing either by spreading a round net over the water or by throwing a lampshade-shaped gunny trap at the darting fish. Our host's father was a master at using the fish trap. With a glance at the fish swimming in the river, he would know what kind they were, male or female, and how much they weighed. The fish would find no way to escape the moment he threw his trap.

There are many ways of fishing in this region. As far as fishnets are concerned, they have more than twenty types. The "hold net" is one of them. They first spread a net of hundreds or even thousands of kilometers into the river, then wind their winches from time to time to hold up the net so that they can pick out the fish that have been snared.

Another is the "confusing trap." Here they plant poles in the river which they encircle with netting. Because the net twists from beginning to end, fish bumping into it feel frightened as if they were lost in a confusing trap, which is how the net got its name. At the end of the "confusing trap" is a bag-like double net. Since its long mouth is large outside but narrow inside, fish can only go in but not get out.

Fishing on the lake differs from other daily activities, and the villagers have many rules and scruples that govern its practice. Before we set off, our host warned me: "When you meet anyone fishing, never say, 'Casting your net, eh?' He not only will refuse to greet you, but will also think you are cursing him. That's because casting a net does not mean catching anything. On the other hand, if you say, 'You're fishing, eh?' he will take it as a generous wish and feel pleased."

"All fish are children of the Dragon King; they are for anybody to catch." This saying has long expressed an unwritten law under whose protection the fishermen believe they can fish wherever they like. However, the fishing villages are careful to observe the custom of avoiding fishing during the spring and summer seasons when fish are spawning. This, of course, is in their own interests.

When several fishing boats that use gunny traps discover a fish, it is the first discoverer who has the right to throw his trap first. Only if he fails to catch it are others free to try. Anyone who violates the rule will be looked down on by his colleagues, and even if he catches the fish, he will not be able to keep it but must return it to the first discoverer.

The fishermen are known for their friendliness and loyalty to each other. Whenever they meet on the lake, whether they know each other or not, they treat each other like their own kin. At night when they finish their day's work, they will tie their boats together and eat and drink to their hearts' content on one boat. Choruses of fishing songs are often a part of such get-togethers. Should any one of them have failed to catch any fish or have had difficulties at home, the rest of them will offer him money or give him some of the fish they have caught.

We asked a fisherman to stop and sell us some fish. When he lifted the cover of his cabin we saw live fish jumping up and down in the cabin filled with water. Without the water plants in it, the fish might jump out and back into the lake. The fisherman, a man of fifty-odd, told us there were many ways to keep the fish alive. If the cabin was too small to hold all his catch, he would put some into a net bag, secure its neck and tie it to the end of the boat, placing the bag into the water. Others string the fish through their mouths and tie them to a bamboo pole, letting the boat drag the floating pole with the live fish back home.

Village Rules for Digging Lotus Roots and Picking Lotus Seeds

From our boat I saw in the distance endless green lotuses along the lakeside. How I wished we could go nearer to them. "Okey, let's go up and have a look," said our guide. "At the same time we can dig some lotus buds. I guarantee you'll like them."

I was the first one to jump ashore the moment the boat was stopped. The new lotuses in early summer were especially lovely. Some put one in mind of slender young girls as they trembled gently in the breeze. Others had floating round leaves

304

with drops of water rolling back and forth on them with the gentle waves. Little lotuses that had just come up put forth two pointed leaves, exquisitely fragile. And the blossoms simply dazzling. How big was this ocean of lotuses? You could not tell— for looking into the far distance, you could see a belt of lotuses around the lakeside.

Two days before while passing by the suburbs of Mianyang's capital town, we saw peasants with their trouser legs rolled up weeding, and spreading manure in the fields where lotuses grew. Every family had lotus ponds— some large, some small— in front of or behind the house. The growing of lotuses dates back to ancient times. In 1972 two lotus seeds were excavated together with a jar of charred grains from the New Stone Age remains of Dahe Village, Zhengzhou, Henan Province. Scientists determined their burial as five thousand years ago.

All the lotuses here are wild plants, and nobody knows in which dynasty the lotuses began to grow along the lakeside. They have been dug and picked every year, but they keep growing year after year. At some point in the past the spots of lotuses were divided among the villages, and now each village has built a watchtower by the lakeside and sends people to watch the lotus beds in turns.

When the lotus seeds are ripe in early autumn, the villagers together choose a day for the picking. At dawn this day, the village slaughters a pig bought with money that has been collected and prepares a meal for all the villagers. Right after eating, all the families set off in their boats, heading for the lotuses. All the boats spread out in a horizontal line with the men rowing and the women picking whatever seeds are within reach. The old people, however, first dig up the cover above the seeds with a double-tooth bamboo fork, then knock the seeds into the cabin.

Rowing in the pleasant autumn weather a boat as light as a leaf through the green leaves and red flowers to harvest nature's free offering produces a special happiness. In the Han Dynasty, women sang this folk song while picking lotus seeds:

We southerners pick lotus seeds,
Lotus leaves cover all our fields;
Between the leaves fish swim with delight:
Now they swim in the left,
Now they swim in the right.

Later writers and poets wrote more poems and songs in praise
of lotus seed picking. Tang Dynasty poet Li Bai wrote:

Girls picking lotus seeds rowed singing back
At the sight of strange faces about;
With a shy smile they hid in the flowers
And refused from them on to come out.

Every Spring Festival and Lantern Festival features folk boat-
dancing everywhere in Hubei Province. They tie bamboo straps
in the shape of the boat used on the lotus lake, decorating
them with colorful ribbons and tying them around the waists of
the women— lotus seed pickers followed by oarsmen. They sing
as they dance, vividly re-creating on the stage what has happened on the lake.

At sunset, the villagers gather around the watchtower and
put their lotus seeds together. Then they divide the seeds into
equal shares. Back home, all the family members, men and
women, old and young, participate in the processing of the
seeds. With their shells on, the lotus seeds are called "shell
seeds"; these can be stored for a long time. (Lotus seeds unearthed from the marshes of Paozi Village of Dalian in the
Northeast, though buried during the Tang Dynasty some 1,200
years ago, still yielded blossoms, when they were planted.)
Seeds whose shells are broken are called "meat seeds" while
those whose bitter buds are picked out are called "hollow
seeds."

Rich in protein, starch, and various vitamins, lotus seeds are
well-known for their nutritional value. Lotus-seed soup stewed
with crystal sugar has the medicinal effect of expelling summerheat. The lotus seed is believed to nourish the heart, build up
one's vital energy, cure blood deficiency, disperse blood stasis,

benefit the stomach, calm the mind, and, through strengthening the kidney, restore their astringent function. Li Shizhen, the great herbalist of the Ming Dynasty, wrote in his *Compendium of Materia Medica* that frequent eating of lotus seeds "may prevent all diseases."

When the lake dries up in early winter with the lotus roots having attained their full growth, the villagers around the lake begin to dig them up. Yet they do not treat this work with the seriousness they do the picking of lotus seeds. According to the village rule, whoever has the time can dig them and keep whatever he has dug. But digging lotus roots is no easy job. You can spend half a day digging nearly a meter deep into the mud before finding anything. The experienced elder peasants, however, have their ways. They go to places that have not entirely dried up and identify spots covered with thick lotus leaves in summer. When they find small old leaves bearing dark red webs on the back, they immediately know that there are large roots underneath. Then with their feet they try to feel them as they begin their digging. "Now, lotus roots!" goes the cry. The upper ones can be pulled up by hands. For the deeper ones, diggers first determine the direction in which the roots have grown, then tread on one end. In this way the roots will soon come up by themselves. The villagers call this "treading on lotus roots."

Lotus roots usually remain fresh only for four or five days. Broken ones with the holes filled with muddy water will not last more than two or three days. Because of this, the peasants send them to the market in town as soon as they are dug up. However, the villagers do have some simple, practical ways to store the lotus roots. They coat the undamaged whole roots with wet mud, which offers nutrients the roots need to survive. Then the local people either bury them in sand or put them in the kitchen and cover them with straw. In this way they can be preserved for two months. Then with their knowledge of the way lotus strains are preserved, the villagers simply bury the roots in the paddy fields that are free throughout the winter. Thus the roots will stay healthy until the next year when spring farming starts.

After hours of hard work, our host Fu Erjin managed to dig a small handful of young lotus roots, as thin as thumbs. The tender roots looked like white jade when the mud was washed off. He passed one to me, urging, "Try it. That's something you can never find in the cities no matter how much you are willing to pay for it." It was my first time to sample such rare roots, and indeed I found them fresh, crisp, and sweet, just to my liking. Interestingly enough, small though the young roots were, their fibers also stayed joined when they were snapped. This characteristic explains why lotus roots have come to be a metaphor for an unbreakable emotional attachment. (See the Chinese proverb "The lotus root snaps but its fibers stay joined.")

A Typical Local Food — "Mianyang's Three Steams"

When it was nearly noon, our host urged us to return to the boat so that we could get back, "My wife is waiting for our fish at home. She needs them in her 'Three Steams.'"

"Three Steams" is a typical food in Mianyang. Our hostess first cleaned the food steamer, one *chi* (1 *chi* = 1.0936 feet) in diameter and two *chi* in height, then placed from the bottom to the top rice, potatoes mixed with seasonings, cabbages, fresh fish and pork, and finally covered it all up tightly. The steaming took about half an hour. Then she picked out the meat and vegetables and placed them on the table separately. This dish is called "Three Steams," simply because the rice, vegetables and meat are steamed in a single steamer.

At first sight, I did not think too much of this pile of fish and pork, for with the rice grains stuck to them, they were far from attractive. But after I tasted everything, I was full of praise. The pork was rich but not greasy— the lard dripping into the fish, making it wonderfully delicious. Then because of the mixed juices of the fish and meat, the cabbages and potatoes were more tasty than they could possibly have been cooked in any other way. Throughout the dinner, our host kept urging me to eat and drink more, and I found no problem in obliging him. When the hostess finally brought to us the flavorful rice, I had already eaten so much that I could barely down two mouthfuls of it.

Our guide was delighted that I had enjoyed the food so much, informing us proudly, "As a course of Hubei Province, 'Mianyang's Three Steams' is discussed at length in the *Book of Famous Chinese Foods* published in Beijing."

I asked him about the history of "Three Steams," and he told me it had originated among the boatmen. Later, because cooking rice, meat and vegetables in one steamer was easy and also saved firewood, this way of cooking became popular throughout the villages around the lakes, where firewood was not easy to find.

Mianyang is surely a place rich in fish and grains. Among the twelve courses prepared by our hostess, three were fish: steamed carp, fried crucian, and a soup of bream. My host picked a crucian head and put it into my bowl, "We have a bit of doggerel about eating fish here: 'Crucian's head, carp's mouth, bream's belly, and silver carp's tail.' All these are the finest parts. Now try this."

Truly, the longer I nibbled on the crucian head, the more delicious I found it to be. As for the tender crisp mouth of the carp, the greasy fat belly meat of the bream, and the fine meat of the silver carp's tail, only "old hands" at fish eating can fully appreciate their marvels.

WEDDING AND FUNERAL CEREMONIES OF THE MOUNTAIN VILLAGERS IN WEST HUBEI

Basket Carriers on the Mountain Paths

A small path stretched into the mountains as if it were a colored ribbon winding through the rocky slopes. Looking up at the lofty peaks, sometimes we saw only a sliver of light peeking through from the blue sky. Below us was a stream where three men were rafting fir logs held in iron hooks.

After traveling two hundred kilometers westward from Mianyang, we had reached Yichang City where over thirty thousand builders were building the Gezhouba Hydropower Station across the Yangtze River — the biggest of its kind in China up till now. Different from Mianyang, Yichang is a part of the lofty Daba and Wushan Mountains, referred to as the "Mountain Area in West Hubei." From here we took a liner sailing upstream on the Yangtze. Passing the Xiling Gorge, one of the three magnificent gorges of the River, we soon found ourselves in Zigui County, the hometown of the ancient Chinese poet Qu Yuan.

Now we were walking on the stone path leading to Lepingli — the birthplace of Qu Yuan. Even though every step on the uneven mountainous path was arduous, the reward in picturesque views along the way made it worth the effort. Two men carrying baskets on their backs walked slowly ahead of us, and caught up with them after a few quickened steps. Seeing us strangers walking so hastily, they made way for us by stopping on one side of the road. I was rather touched by their kindness, especially in view of their heavy burdens and the sweat that glistened on their faces and soaked through their clothing. "It's so kind of you," I said, "but you really needn't. Why not walk together? We can chat as we walk along."

The tall thin middle-aged man was carrying a sack of grain which was clearly not nearly so heavy as, the fifty-kilo sack of chemical fertilizer borne by the sunburned young man. Their bamboo baskets with bigger tops than bottoms over two feet high, looked like loudspeakers. With two bamboo belts, the basket was hung from the shoulders.

"Do you feel tired carrying that heavy bag of fertilizer on your back?" I asked the young man.

"Not really. I'm quite used to it." The young man told us that because the roads on the mountains were narrow and uneven, the villagers there always carried baskets whenever they went to the fields or to the market, visited friends and relatives, or went up to the mountains to cut grass. It was much easier to carry things on their backs than hold them in their arms. Besides, then their hands were free to grasp tree branches to avoid slipping or hold an umbrella in the sun and rain.

Leaving the peak behind us, we soon passed the col. In front of us lay a cave tucked away at the foot of the cliff. Sheltered from the sun and the rains, the cave had long been a refuge for pedestrians. The two mountaineers stopped with their baskets against the cliff, and with a T-shaped wooden stick supporting the baskets from the bottom, they took a needed rest. The stick, over two feet long and one foot wide, is something of heavy loads over long distances cannot do without. With this third "leg," they can feel much safer walking on the mountain paths, for whenever they feel tired, they can let the stick take over for a while.

Coming toward us were two women, the leading one of whom was a pretty young mother carrying a basket which held a kind of circle chair standing upright. Her baby, its head falling to one side, was sleeping soundly as she walked with slow even steps. The basket on the back of the girl behind her, however, had a small mouth with a large bottom, looking much like a huge ivory vase.

Since bamboo trees grow around all the mountain villagers' houses, the local inhabitants can conveniently cut them down and have bamboo weavers make baskets for them. When the weaving is done, elder housewives place around the new basket two rings made of red cloth, praying for safety for its carriers. Girls, on the other hand, ask the craftsmen to weave beautiful designs into the baskets. Girls are fond of going to town with such baskets on their backs so that they can bear them proudly on their backs when they go to town.

The baskets carried by the two men were plainly designed for heavy loads; woven of large bamboo strips they were exceptionally strong. In the town of Zigui County we saw people carry in such baskets about 150 kilograms of cloth bolts, sugar sacks and oil. More surprising still was how they carried clumsy cigarette boxes. The carrier had two helpers one on the left side, the other on the right. They first put one box over the basket, then another two over the first one with one on the left and the other on the right. In this way they built the boxes into a pagoda. Finally the carrier tied them with a rope handed to him from the top and safely carried seven boxes into the shop.

Intelligent Oxen in Qu Yuan's Birthplace

Crossing the mountains, we caught sight of something

completely different: in the open valley smoke was curling up from the chimneys of the villagers' cottages. In the fields of rice seedlings, newly transplanted frogs were croaking from all corners. Several girls were washing clothes by the stream. When we saw the three Chinese characters "Lepingli" carved on the wall of a tower by the entrance to the village, we knew that we had arrived at Qu Yuan's birthplace. It was in this very mountain village that the first great Chinese poet was born in the year 340 B.C.

A young man was plowing a field from which grain had just been harvested. In other places, peasants tie ropes through the noses of their buffalos, which they pull to signal the animals to take their turns. What amused us was that no ropes were tied through the noses of the oxen here. With their owners' shouting "Now up" or "Now down," the oxen turned punctually.

"That's the intelligent ox found only in Lepingli," joked our guide Xiao Li. "Any ox bought from outside will become intelligent here in just seven days and then its rope may be untied. But when it's sold to another place, it will change right after the seventh day and have to be tied with a rope through its nose again." So, according to what he said, this beautiful place not only has produced a great poet but also turns oxen into intelligent beings.

Here is a very popular local folk tale about the brainy oxen: One day Qu Yuan was going to Yingdu (capital of the State of Chu at that time, capital town of today's Jiangling County) with his page boy, but the latter slipped to the ground and broke the rope that tied his luggage to the shoulder pole, spreading every which way his bamboo slips with their memorials to the throne and his poems. The villagers plowing in the fields came to help, but since they could not find any ropes nearby, they untied the ones that were tied through the noses of the oxen. They then tied up Qu Yuan's books, but Qu Yuan was worried that now they might not be able to control their animals. But the farmers reassured him, saying "Everything will be all right, just get on your way." And believe it or not, the oxen turned docilely whenever their owners shouted "Now up," "Now down." After that, no more

312

ropes were tied through the noses of the oxen in Lepingli.

In reality, however, the fact that the oxen are docile is due to the owners' patient taming. But as they do with other stories spread all over Lepingli, with this tale the villagers express their love and respect for Qu Yuan.

A Bride Teased on Her Way to Her New Home

At noon on our second day in Lepingli, our ears were assailed by the heavy beatings of drums and gongs accompanied by the popping of firecrackers. Had anybody in the village got married? My host told me that it was the Tans from Shangang Village who had come down from the mountains to receive the bride.

I had never seen such a troop receive a bride before. They were all strong men who carried in the baskets on their backs large wooden basins, desks, suitcases and even wardrobes. The slow-moving long line of red-painted furniture was reflected in the green paddy fields, creating a unique country picture.

In Beijing, when young people get married, it is usually the men who buy the furniture. But in this place, girls are married out with furniture. That day the bride's side needed ten people to carry her dowry items, so that she brought was counted as "a ten-carrier dowry."

After unloading their baskets on the sticks by the stream, the carriers went over to the other side to carry across the bride, the bridesmaid and the other female guests. I lost no time in stealing a look at the trousseaux in the large wooden basin, discovering to my surprise that it was like a stall ready to set up business, with everything from thermos flasks, tea sets, washbowls and candy containers to brushes, oil lamps, umbrellas and radios. Since the occasion was a wedding, all the items came in pairs.

The daily necessities included here were naturally meant to carry good wishes from the bride's new family: the oil lamp dressed with red paper symbolized brightness and happiness for the young couple; the wooden basin was for their future baby.... The bride's mother said, "My daughter has been such a great help to me since she was small. Now that she is getting

313

married, I want to do everything I can for her."

The bridegroom's house stood on the Xishan Mountains, a white-washed new house. Though it was vaguely visible, there was still a distance of about five kilometers. The carriers had to be very careful when climbing the zigzag mountain path, for any slipping or breaking of dowry items would be considered an evil omen for the young couple. The high mountains were steep and the weather was hot at noon, so the carriers had to stop to take their breaths every two or three minutes.

I was waiting for them half way up the mountains. A good long time has passed, but I still saw nobody coming up. Returning to find out why, through the woods I saw the carriers teasing the bride in the paddy fields! "I'm tired, light a cigarette for me please." Said another: "I'm hungry, give me some cake to eat." Still others begged for candies and drinking water.

At first the twenty-one-year-old Xiang Wenfeng hid shyly behind the bridesmaid. But the carriers were not to be deterred. "If you don't give me a cigarette and let me rest," threatened one, "you won't be home before dark and you'll miss your own wedding ceremony."

"Right," chimed in another. "I'm so hungry I may fall and break your furniture. If you don't give me some cake now, you'll be sorry if I really do fall down."

Their campaign was beginning to get to the bridesmaid if not the bride. There was whispering between them and it appeared that the bridesmaid won out, for the bride distributed candies and cigarettes to the carriers one by one. Now the atmosphere was lightened and everyone in the wedding party caught the spirit. It turned out that teasing of the bride was part of a time-honored technique to rid her of shyness so as to prepare her for the coming festivities.

The inhabitants of Shangang Village were all gathered in groups outside their village eagerly awaiting the bride's arrival, but they were left only with the sounds of drums and gongs hour after hour. Finally, the long-expected bride and her company showed up. Immediately, the bridegroom Tan Fuqiang (aged twenty-three), his face aglow with excitement, set off his

314

firecrackers at the door to herald their arrival at his house.

Traditionally, carriers with suitcases and wardrobes walk in the front the reason being that all the bedding is housed inside. The mother-in-law who is responsible for receiving the bride at once takes the bedding into the bridal room to make the bed for the young couple. After she unfolds the quilts she covers them with dates, peanuts and oranges, thus expressing the wishes that the couple have a baby as soon as possible and that their life be as sweet as the oranges.

The wedding ceremony was held in the central room next to the bridal room. This new family had a spacious house of over 50 square meters, consisting of three rooms: a central room, a bedroom, and a kitchen. In the years to come, when their children would be grown, they could simply add a top storey and have another three rooms easily.

The central room was a din of loud voices and louder music. A large red character *xi* (happiness) decorated with fine embroidery was pasted in the middle of the wall, having been put up by the bridegroom's uncle the day before as he sang a traditional local song: "Mounting the first step, you will be known throughout the world;... Mounting the eighth step, in the eighth lunar month you will have grains bursting your barns...." As he descended, each step was similarly accompanied by fine words: "The first step down gives you everlasting happiness.... The ninth step down brings you piles and piles of gold dollars; with the tenth step down your family flourishes year by year." Each time his uncle finished a line, the bridegroom standing by had to make a hand bow to him to show his gratitude for the fine wishes.

In the past, brides and bridegrooms kowtowed to the heavens, to the earth, to their parents and to each other. But nowadays they make bows instead to their guests, their parents and to each other. As for any sharing on the part of the young couple concerning their days of dating—which would prove that their marriage had been based on free choice—this they were too shy to do. But no sooner had the master of ceremonies announced, ''Fire the crackers and play the music—now the bridegroom and the bride enter their bridal chamber'' than

315

shouts of "Hurry up! Hurry up!" were heard from all corners. And the young couple began elbowing their way toward the bridal room, each trying to be the first to enter it — much different from the more common practice where the bridegroom shows the bride into the bridal chambers in leisurely fashion.

"What is this custom?" I asked the guide in a low voice.

"Here whoever enters the bridal room first is counted the more capable one."

So that is it! When I saw the bride managing to run in front, I could not resist asking the guide, "Who was the first to enter the chamber when you were married?"

"Of course it was she!" he admitted. "And she is more capable than I. Besides, I work outside and she's the one who runs the family." From what he said I realized that in encouraging this competition the message that comes through is one of urging the young couple toward individual self-mastery.

Obsequies Dance— Dancing for the Dead Around the Clock

We headed for Ziqiu in Changyang County lying in the south of the Yangtze River to learn about these villagers' customs. Upon our arrival we heard villagers telling each other, "Last night Tian Zhengui's family fired three shots." (Gunpowder is first stuffed into an iron tube and then lighted, making reports so loud they can be heard at a considerable distance.) "His mother has left us."

"Oh, let's go and join the dance!"

According to the customs here, whenever an old person dies, the young people of the family are supposed to fire shots outside their house to inform their neighbors. When they get the news, the villagers will come to express their condolences by dancing and singing. That is what they call an "obsequies dance."

After supper, led by our guide Lao Liu, we got on the narrow, steep mountain path leading to the Tians'. In the distance we caught sight of a bonfire on the threshing ground, from which came loud drumming. It was, of course, the Tian home.

Entering their house, we found the central room aglow with glorious lights. Right in front of the main entrance lay an open coffin, whose cover— on which stood a bowl of rice up-side down— had been placed on the square table before it. An oil lamp burning around the clock there was said to be capable of lightening the way through which the dead would travel to the west. In deep mourning holding obsequies sticks, the dead mother's children had been busy for a whole day and night: moving the remains into the coffin, decorating the mourning room and receiving visitors. Whenever a relative or friend brought them some elegiac couplets (usually fine wishes for the dead), they had to receive them by firing firecrackers, then kneel down to the dead to pay their respects. They would all dance through the night, and the coffin would be buried early the next morning.

With flashlights or torches the villagers came one after an-other. After they bowed to the remains and consoled the sad children of the dead mother, they began to dance in front of the coffin to the beating of the drum. Two by two they waved their hands in the air and shook their hips from left to right, vibrating from head to foot, all robust and unrestrained dancers. A few minutes of such vigorous dancing saw them perspiring freely and gasping for breath.

On the west side of the coffin was the drum with a leather face, the only instrument accompanying the dancers. Its beater Tian Qifeng was a white-haired man of 83 whose hearing and eyesight retained the sharpness of youth. This energetic old man was a well-known "mourning dancing leader" (one who leads in the mourning singing), open-hearted and unrestrained. With a coat draped over his bare shoulders he beat the drum as he sang:

> The loud mourning drum strikes my ears,
> And out I set with my bright torch;
> I face all hardships without fears.
> Defying the long tough mountain way
> With deep rivers perilous to cross,
> I frighten fierce animals away.

317

This leader of the mourning chorus was very quick-witted; songs simply tumbled out of his mouth. He not only told in song historical stories like those from *The Romance of the Three Kingdoms*, but also interesting events and love tales. Whenever he finished one section, the dancers would repeat the last line after him: "I face all hardships without fears" and "I frighten fierce animals away."

On this special occasion, one could not help thinking of the Chinese idiom *xiali* (or *haoli*) mourning folk songs. That is why many important people, including Song Yu, poet of the State of Chu, and Chairman Mao Zedong, used this idiom when they wanted an art form to communicate to masses of people.

When the "mourning leader" was taking a break from his singing, I questioned him about the dancing. He told me that mourning dancing was also called "mourning drum-beating." Anybody—even an enemy of the dead's family—who hears the mourning shots, regardless of distance and current relationships, should come to express his condolences. That is what the saying, "When a person dies all hatred ends," really means. The more mourners they have, the prouder the members of the dead's family feel. "Should a family be on bad terms with other villagers and have too few mourners when one of its members dies, then they may have to go to the villagers' houses to invite them in person."

"Why do you take the funerals so seriously?"

"The old people have worked hard all their lives, and how can we handle their funerals carelessly when they die? But it is not easy to find helping hands around you because this is a sparsely populated mountain area and we're scattered all over the place. Sixteen people—two groups working in turn—are needed in the carrying of the coffin alone; then we need others to dig the pit. That's why we have one rule here: 'Anybody's death saddens all; come and help beat out the mourning call.' When someone dies, every family sees it as their own affair and comes to help."

"But it's a grievous thing when someone dies, why do you sing and dance?"

"When a person over age sixty dies, that's a natural death. It's an honor for the dead and his family, and it's also looked on as a happily sad thing." (In China marriages and childbirths are regarded as red [happy] events while the death of an old person is a white [sad] event.) So the villagers who never stop singing when transplanting rice seedlings, weeding grass, collecting firewood and picking tea gather before the coffin to dance and sing around the clock. On the one hand, they mourn for the dead; on the other, they reduce the grief of the family of the dead, creating a lively atmosphere out of the sad funeral. In the old days, people believed that such dancing and singing could even rid the sins of the dead, enabling his soul to travel up to the "Western Heavens." Some dying old people were said to have asked their family members and neighbors to dance for them before their deaths. Naturally, this is all superstition, and young people today do not believe such things.

Today's mourning dancing was called "mourning songs" in ancient China and is believed to have originated from "Basin Songs" by Zhuang Zi, a philosopher of the Warring States over two thousand years ago. When Zhuang Zi's wife died, Hui Zi came to express his condolences, but he saw Zhuang Zi sitting on the ground with his legs stretched out singing mourning songs to the beats of the basin he was striking. In today's Jingzhou, about two hundred kilometers east of Changyang, the custom of singing mourning songs accompanied by beats on basins is still practiced. However, the custom of keeping vigil and singing mourning songs can be traced back to the primitive society. The ancient folk song advises:

> Cut a bamboo, form a bow—
> Make a pellet, kill a foe.

It is believed that by cutting a bamboo and forming a bow from it with a string and by shooting a few small clods at any animals that might have come to eat the remains, the ancients in a way expressed their undying affection for the dead.

In recent years, certain critics have proved that mourning

319

dancing is also related to the life of ancient soldiers. Over three thousand years ago when the Ba people, led by Zhou Wuwang, were conquering the tyrannous ruler of the Shang Dynasty (c.17th-c.11th B.C.), they were already in the habit of singing and dancing. Before they set out, the soldiers would sing their majestic songs, dancing in pairs as if they were grappling with the enemy at close quarters. They danced for entertainment and to keep up the spirit of the army. When the war was over, they danced in the same way to bring back the scenes of the battles, mourning for their dead comrades.

Day broke and the villagers stopped dancing. Together they nailed shut the coffin cover and wrapped the whole coffin in bamboo strips. At last, accompanied by the loud popping of firecrackers and rhythmical drumbeating they carried it to the pit for burying.

CHAPTER XIII

FUJIAN— Point of Departure of the Silk Road on the Sea

A PROVINCE OF FLOWERS

"Baihua" Village

During my ten-day visit to Fujian, a province of flowers lying along the southeastern coast, I saw more plants and blossoms than I had in the previous entire decade in the North. But what impressed me most of all was the enormous variety on display in Baihua Village in the suburbs of Zhangzhou City. As the name "Baihua" (Hundred Flowers) is meant to suggest, they were everywhere to be seen: on the flat roofs, on the arches over gateways, on the walls of courtyards, anywhere you looked. The pots in which they were invariably planted became invisible except to close scrutiny. In the yards of the houses too there were flower beds enclosed by cactuses featuring camellias and orchids and other exotic blossoms; and there were flowering plum, peach and crab apple trees artistically placed. A recitation of all varieties of flowers and trees that adorned yards would read like a nursery catalogue since there are more than three thousand different kinds of flowers and plants grown in this one small village.

A pair of old banyans with large crowns and numerous weeping aerial roots stood in front of the temple in the center of the village, looking like two venerable sages guarding the sacred place. Most of the trees inside or outside the village were fruit trees, many of them lychees and longans, whose small, pale yellow blossoms attracted large numbers of bees and filled the air with a heady fragrance.

321

Welcoming the Spring Festival with Narcissuses

We stayed at Zhu Wenshu's house in the southern part of the village. Unlike Northerners, who usually invite visitors onto their warm *kang*, this host showed us into the central room where we sat in armchairs. Since Fujian is a province with a rainy climate and muddy roads, people normally clean the mud and dirt off their shoes by wiping them before entering the house on the palm rugs placed outside the doors. And so we did.

The central room was clean and bright. On the table was a pot of tall narcissuses on the stems of which were wrapped rings of red paper. Welcoming the Spring Festival with narcissuses is an old practice in Fujian and Guangdong.

It is said that narcissuses are an incarnation of the immortals in the water and have magic powers that can exorcise evil spirits, dispel bad luck and bring good luck to human beings. Generally speaking, the bulbs send forth blossoms after they have been soaked in water for about thirty days. That is why when the first day of the last lunar month comes every year, people begin to put the bulbs into shallow flower pots filled with water over a base of pebbles and place them around the house. The growers control the timing of the blossoms by regulating the temperature of the water and the amount of sunlight the plants absorb. Seeming to know what is expected of them, the narcissuses usually put out fragrant blossoms with white petals and yellow pistils one after another on Spring Festival Eve when each family is having its reunion dinner or on Spring Festival Day when the firecrackers are being set off. And if the narcissuses do not blossom on the Festival due to unexpected changes in the weather, it will be considered bad luck.

Overseas Chinese also show special love for these flowers that announce the arrival of spring. When they receive narcissus bulbs from China, they carefully strip off the protective mud outside, put them in red cloth bags, and place them in the shrines between the memorial tablets in their living rooms.

During this festive season the local villagers are at pains to remember their hardworking buffalo. They offer them glutinous rice wine and dress their horns with narcissuses in full bloom. By extending greetings to their animals in this way, the people believe they will be more likely to continue serving them well.

The narcissus is actually an herb that belongs to the family of short-tube lycoris known as "graceful garlic" in ancient times. Because it looks fresh as it begins to grow when placed in water, it is commonly called "water fresh" in Chinese. And since "fresh" and "immortal" are homophones in Chinese, the name *shuixian*— or "Water Immortal" — has been used ever since ancient times. Over a thousand years ago, narcissuses that loved warm and wet winters with little frost and snow were popularly grown in the provinces of the Yangtze River's southern basin. Later, because of changes in the water, soil, climate and other natural phenomena, narcissuses were only able to grow in a few places: Zhangzhou in Fujian Province, Taiwan, and Chongming Island at the mouth of the Yangtze River. Among these places Zhangzhou produces the best species.

Although China had never particularly excelled at flower arranging as a home art, before the arrival of the Spring Festival, florists in Fujian always weave a variety of flowers into flower baskets. Clever hands also weave designs of beings such as dragons, phoenixes and deer that are symbols of good luck and place them in the baskets in the living room where they are to help assure an abundant harvest of all flowers. Traditionally, women insert chrysanthemums, a symbol of longevity, onto yeasty, spongy rice cakes that have risen to be as high as hills, and these are then put in the living room or on the kitchen range.

China began to grow chrysanthemums three thousand years ago. Perhaps assisted by their quality of purity, chrysanthemums blossom in spite of the cold frost, earning them renown as the "nobility among flowers" by Chinese poets of all the dynasties. Moreover, they have been proved effective in Chinese traditional medicine against various ailments, especially those involving the liver. They are even used as a vegetable in any number of dishes. Indeed, some two thousand years ago the patriotic poet Qu Yuan wrote of having "fallen petals of chrysanthemums for supper." Tao Yuanming, poet of the Jin Dynasty, wrote of having chrysanthemums with wine. And ever since the Tang and Han dynasties, the Chinese have been in the habit of drinking chrysanthemum wine and eating chrysanthemum cakes on the Double Ninth Festival (the 9th of the 9th lunar month). All this demonstrates that inserting chrysanthemums onto steamed cakes certainly does them no harm.

No Flowers, No Etiquette

While in Zhangzhou, from time to time I heard the saying "No flowers, no etiquette." And what I saw and heard really proved that it was no exaggeration.

Traditionally, women in Fujian have the habit of wearing fresh flowers. Throughout our traveling there we saw women with flowers in their hair carrying baskets of flowers obviously as gifts to friends and relatives. Even elderly women had flowers inserted in their hair coils at the backs of their heads as they attended the fair in town.

One afternoon during our stay when I was roaming around the village I heard the rat-a-tat of firecrackers going off nearby. Following the sound, I discovered that some villagers were celebrating the setting of the central beam of a new house. The house was not yet completed, but pots of cactuses were in place and a fence of them was planted around the house. I asked one of the villagers what it was for, and he told me that the large numbers of thorns on the cactuses were believed to be effective in scaring off evil spirits or devils that might sneak in and establish residence in the new house!

An enthusiastic gardener told me, "We flower growers are tied to flowers from birth to death." He explained that as soon as a baby is born into a family, the grandfather will go to the flower bed and pick a pomegranate, cut it open, lay it in a dish, and put it before the ancestral tablets. It is a traditional practice here for people to announce the good news of a new baby to their ancestors through the pomegranate which "has numerous seeds in one ovary sharing the same membrane."

In the case of a wedding, they also have the custom of

seeing off or greeting the bride with flowers. The day before a girl is married, her close friends pluck for her twelve kinds of flowers and tie them into a big bouquet. On her wedding day, the shy bride covers half her face with the flowers, thus adding an extra touch of grace and mystery. But why twelve kinds of flowers? I would guess that with this number they wish for the new couple's conjugal bliss throughout the twelve months of the year.

Flowers presented to brides differ from season to season, but jasmine, cannas, pomegranate and osmanthus flowers must always be included. With the large numbers of seeds in the pomegranate, the hope for a child at an early date is expressed. Since "osmanthus" and "fortune" are homophones in Chinese, wishes for riches and honor are given form through the inclusion of this flower. Jasmine, on the other hand, has the power to dispel evils, according to legend, so that its role is to guarantee the couple a peaceful and harmonious life. With regard to cannas, the Chinese name *meirenjiao* (beauty plant) carries the implication that the newlyweds are handsome. When the bride enters the bridal chamber, she hangs her bouquet high above the mosquito net, suggesting added joy on the wedding night.

The next day the bride's brother visits the bridal chamber on behalf of his parents bearing flowers of the season in a red lacquer vase on the outside of which is written the Chinese character for happiness. In autumn, the choice is usually chrysanthemums, which suggest a wish for health and conjugal bliss for the bridal pair.

Funerals here are also special. Hearing of someone's death, friends, relatives and fellow villagers immediately go to express their condolences with flowers. On the third day, when the remains is buried, the custom is to gather up all the flowers lying around the coffin into four huge wreaths and place them on the grave. Then when the Qingming Festival comes and they go to sweep the weeds off the graves, they are also supposed to bring bouquets of flowers for the dead, who in life were almost certainly flower growers in this province of flowers.

Flower Growers Live Long Lives; Flower Sellers Are Lucky

Throughout my stay at Baihua Village, I woke up to the chirping of birds at dawn every day. I always found that my old landlord was already long up and was busily spraying clean water over the flowers picked the previous afternoon and moving potted flowers into large bamboo baskets. Then carrying the flowers on his shoulders, he got on his way for the morning fair in Zhangzhou— a half hour's brisk walk for him. Just after midday, he came back beaming, baskets empty. Anybody could see he did a good business. With his strong body and agile movements, the man did not look his seventy-four years. I only knew how old he was because I asked.

According to the Chinese national population census of July 1982, of the 3,370 people of Baihua Village, 182 were over 70 of whom 51 were over 80. The 99-year-old Lin Chuang was the oldest "Star of Longevity" of the village. The day we went to visit her, we saw this old lady sitting by the door doing needlework and looking after her great great grandchild in a bamboo cradle at the same time. I was told that for decades she had been getting up early every morning to sweep the courtyard, feed her pigs, and take care of the flowers.

"Flower growers are favored with longevity and sellers with good fortune and happiness" is a common saying among the local flower growers.

The founder of Baihua Village, according to legend, was Zhu Maolin, who came to the area some 580 years ago with his political refugee father, discovered an abundance of strange flowers and plants all over the fields and hills. In a dream his father saw and heard flower fairies playing music and singing and dancing for him, which he regarded as a sufficiently auspicious omen to settle down here. Thus it was that he began a new life as a florist and at his death left the wish that "flower growers be favored with longevity and sellers with good fortune and happiness," and asked his son to continue the tradition of flower growing in their family. So this is the "history" of the founding of Baihua Village. Of course the story about the appearance of fairies in a dream is itself a fairy tale, and the fact that flowers grow here so well depends mainly on the unique cli-

326

mate and other natural conditions but also on the industry and skill of the growers down through the generations.

Drinking *Gongfu* Tea

The people of Fujian and Guangdong, both of which lie in the subtropics, are passionately fond of tea. Their way of drinking it differs from any other place. Because of a whole set of *gongfu* (skills) required in its making and drinking, it is known as *gongfu* tea.

We were invited into the sitting room by our host who waved us to the rattan and bamboo chairs near the tea table. Offering us candies and cake, he proceeded to make tea for us.

Items in the tea set were incredibly small: the china pot only as big as a fist, the cups the size of wineglasses. First he poured boiling water over the whole pot, a washing which was said to serve three purposes— cleaning the tea service, taking away the old tea smell left in the pot, and heating up the pot to make it easy to make fresh tea. After performing this ritual, our host poured out a big handful of tea leaves and dropped them into the pot and raising the water pitcher high above the pot, poured in the water until it was just a bit too full. I was told that in this way the foam over the tea would be washed away, thus guaranteeing the original taste. When the cover of the teapot was replaced, hot water was poured all over the outside of the pot to quicken the swelling of the tea leaves inside.

A moment later when the flavor of the tea had fully permeated the water, our host placed the cups in a small circle on the tray and poured us round after round. As this was happening, the little mouth of the pot was kept ever so close to the cups lest the tea spill out. It was truly wonderful to watch— so agile and skillful was our host, so graceful and respectful his presentation.

As I received the first elegant little cup he presented to me and looked into it, I found the tea a rather dark yellow, transparent and clear. Its refreshing aroma reminded me of the fragrance of orchids. Then taking a sip, I found it slightly bitter in the first moments, but as I went on sipping I began to find it a little sweet, almost like honey. I looked at the tea leaves that had been fully soaked and noticed red rings around them. Ah, that was *Tieguanyin*, a type of oolong tea. To me it was a particular pleasure to enjoy such first-class *Tieguanyin* tea in its native home.

People in Beijing usually drink *huacha* (flower-scented tea). *Huacha* is scented with particularly fragrant flowers, usually jasmine or cymbidium. Fujian produces much scented tea, but local inhabitants rarely drink it. They prefer oolong. Half-fermented oolong tea, because of its pure and strong taste like that of black tea and its sweet refreshing flavor like that of green tea, leaves a very pleasant aftertaste. Besides, oolong tea has medicinal properties. Some research suggests that it can prevent cancer— other research that it alleviates arteriosclerosis. The Japanese have come to be prime consumers of oolong tea, believing that it promotes both beauty and health.

A folk tale provides a fanciful version of the origin of oolong tea:

Long long ago there was a hunter named Wuliang, who made his living by picking tea leaves as well as stalking game in the mountains of Anxi County in southern Fujian. One day he went up into the mountains as usual with his tea basket and a hunting rifle on his shoulder. After picking about two kilos, he suddenly caught sight of a river deer and took aim after a bit of a chase. The bullet found its mark, which meant that the night was taken up with slaughtering instead of processing into green tea the leaves that had been picked earlier. The next day when he looked into the basket, he found that because they had been kept in this warm place for too long after they had been shaken and rubbed against each other during the chase, the tea leaves were half fermented. However, when he processed them, he found to his surprise that the bitter taste of the normal green tea had disappeared. Thereafter, Wuliang introduced this new technique to the other villagers. People who drank this new type of tea all spoke highly of it, naming it "Wuliang Tea." Since "liang" and "long" were homophones in the dialect of southern Fujian, it was later called "Wulong tea," and then "oolong tea," as it came to be generally known outside China.

328

Research has shown that the Chinese began to drink tea over four thousand years ago. At first it was regarded as a medicine. Not until after the Tang Dynasty did it come to be associated with entertaining visitors. It gradually spread to other countries, first to Korea and then to Japan, where during the past five centuries it is used in a ceremony which has long been an integral part of the culture.

Meanwhile, the Chinese tea service has been growing in simplicity. At the moment the artistic way of appreciating *gongfu* tea is only found in two of China's southern provinces: Fujian and Guangdong. While traveling in Fujian, from time to time we saw in the living room of local homes a tiny kettle over a small stove boiling away on one side of the room while on the other side sat two or more close friends enjoying their hot fragrant tea in cups as small as a thumb while they chatted, occasionally bursting into song as the spirit moved them, with or without musical accompaniment.

Home-made Lychee Wine

As I strolled about the village one day I noticed an exceptionally big lychee tree in front of the home of an obviously dedicated flower grower, a tree with an enormous crown of thick, large leaves and with a trunk too big around for even two people to encircle with their arms. Spying the owner in the yard I asked him how much fruit the tree yields every year.

"Not just sure," the owner admitted. "Altogether maybe half a ton from all three trees I have."

Lychees, longans, oranges, bananas and pineapples grow everywhere in Fujian. One day we defied a drizzle to climb Fenghuang Mountains in the suburbs of Zhangzhou. Looking down from the summit, we could see row upon row of lychee trees shading the peasant houses. Our host observed regretfully, "Too bad you didn't come in June when the lychees were all ripe. All those trees covered with bright red fruit are gorgeous from up here. And the fruit itself is tops in quality. You could have had your fill."

Traditionally, lychees have been hailed as "King of All Fruits." Nonetheless, they are at the same time fragile. They tend

329

to rot quickly once they are picked. As Tang Dynasty poet Bai Juyi noted: once lychees are picked, their color begins to fade in a day, their fragrance in two days, and their taste in three. In four or five days their original color, fragrance and taste are completely lost. The story about the emperor of the Tang Dynasty, Tang Xuanzong, who employed express horses to carry lychees to his favorite concubine Yang Yuhuan, is known throughout China. Yang had been born in the South where she had learned to love lychees, and so the Emperor saw to it that horses would run between stations around the clock to fetch and return supplies of the tasty fruit to the Tang capital, Chang'an, today's Xi'an. The weary riders are reputed to have covered four hundred kilometers a day. Du Mu, another poet of the Tang Dynasty, told the tale in his own way:

> Looking back from our capital Chang'an
> You find many beautiful scenes in view;
> The gates of the palace on the mountain
> Slowly open two by two.
>
> At sight of a horse running in red dust,
> The face of Yang was wreathed in smiles;
> No one could know any better than she
> That the lychees had come many hundreds of miles.

Fujian produces an abundance of lychees every year. Besides the quantity needed to satisfy the demand within the province itself, much of the fresh fruit is transported to northern cities. The local people also convert much of it into dried fruit or lychee wine.

Making lychee wine is not difficult. You put the pulp into a wine jar— first a layer of the fruit pulp, then one of sugar— until the jar is filled. Then you add in some white spirits and seal the mouth of the container. Four months later the sweet wine is ready. Once you open the jar, a fragrance fills the whole house. However, such wine is actually overly sweet and will be drinkable only if mixed with rice wine.

Before we left Baihua Village our host prepared a dinner

for us. What we drank that night was the home-made lychee wine that he had prepared long before. It was as good as its reputation. In truth it was the best fruit wine I have ever tasted.

Fujian also produces a great quantity of honey every year, with that produced from lychee flowers counting as the sweetest, most fragrant and most nutritious.

So flowers not only enrich the lives of the local people but provide many means of making a living.

QUANZHOU — HOME OF OVERSEAS CHINESE

Living Examples of the Ancient Chinese Language

Upon my arrival in Fujian, I could not understand anything the local people said. Their dialect sounded just like a foreign language to me. I remember the first day I was in Quanzhou the receptionist said to me, "*Dongji, jiabeng luo!*" Lu Huang and I looked at each other blankly. If our guide had not interpreted for us, we would never have known that we were being told: "Comrades, it's time for dinner."

Being a country with a vast territory and a history long predating nationhood, China has many regional dialects which have little in common with one another. For example, the word *qifan* (here a meal) in Shanghai dialect is pronounced in Cantonese *sefan*, and in Hakka *shifan*. Although pronunciation varies greatly among these dialects, it is possible for a Mandarin speaker to catch on and understand. That is to say they are not as difficult as the dialect spoken in Quanzhou, which shuts the door to comprehension. It might as well be a totally foreign language.

The proverb goes: "When in Rome do as the Romans do." In Chinese we have a somewhat similar saying: "Learn about its customs on entering a new land but always start with its dialect." I began to learn a few sentences, noting some of the characters in *pinyin* (English spelling and standard pronunciation of Chinese): "*wo* (I)" — *wa*, "*zuo* (take a bus, etc;)" — *ze*, "*shu* (tree)" — *qiu*, "*hua* (flower)" — *hui*, "*yusan* (umbrella)" — *housuan*, etc.

Having learned a few sentences, I sometimes even tried to show off, ending up only making a fool of myself. One day our guide said to us (naturally in his dialect): "*Wa ze kaqia ke.*" ("I'll go there by truck or by bike.") Thinking that he was going there by truck, I answered immediately, "I don't think that's a good idea. It's too much trouble to take a truck."

"Who said anything about a truck?" he laughed. "I'm riding my bike!" In the local dialect a *bike* is a *kataqia*, or *kaqia*, while a truck is a *kaqia*. Quanzhou and its neighboring cities, including Xiamen and Zhangzhou among others, are known as Minnan, or Southern Fujian. (*Min* is the short name for Fujian Province, whose ancestors made the snake their totem.) Accordingly, linguists call the dialect of these places the Minnan dialect, which is one of the seven major Chinese dialects. Altogether there are fifty million people speaking this dialect, including people in Shantou Prefecture, in Guangdong Province, in Taiwan, and many overseas Chinese. The Minnan is in fact one branch of the Min dialect, which also includes the Puxian and Mindong dialects.

The other six major Chinese dialects are: the Northern, spoken in north and southwest China; the Wu, mainly used in Shanghai, Jiangsu, and Zhejiang; the Xiang, found in Hunan Province; the Gan, spoken in Jiangxi Province; Hakka, spoken in some of the regions in Guangdong, Guangxi, Fujian, and Jiangxi; and Cantonese, used in the central and western parts of Guangdong and the southeastern part of Guangxi.

The dialects in Fujian count as the most complicated in China. The twenty-six million people in the province speak the Minnan dialect and the Puxian, Mindong, Minbei, and Hakka dialects, among over thirty minor ones. As for the different dialects within each county, they are simply too many to count. A friend from Fujian told me that once when somebody in his village got married, he was asked to go and borrow some dishes from a neighbor living in a village 1.5 kilometers away separated only by a hill and could neither understand nor make himself understood. Only after elaborate pantomiming was he finally able to make his meaning clear and come away with the dishes.

When Professor Huang Diancheng at Xiamen University, a well-known linguist in China, talked about his own dialect, he remarked, "You find many ancient Chinese words and expressions in the Minnan dialect really living examples of the ancient Chinese language."

Some of this linguistic history is revealed on inscriptions carved on bones and tortoise shells that date back three thousand years. Of course it has been easier to find words and expressions with the same meaning in the Chinese spoken during the Han Dynasty. In 1972 archaeologists excavated large quantities of cultural relics from the Han Dynasty tombs of 2,100 years ago which link the Minnan dialect to characters from that time. Said Professor Huang: "If the historians Sima Qian and Ban Gu of the Han Dynasty and the poets Li Bai and Du Fu of the Tang Dynasty were still alive today they would find it quite easy to converse and chant poems with the people in Quanzhou." He points out that *The Revised Rhyming Dictionary of the Song Dynasty* includes 26,194 characters which are divided into 206 rhymes with four tones. In today's Beijing dialect, there are only 36 vowels. The only dialect that comes close to distinguishing the 206 vowels is the Minnan dialect.

But why is it that the Minnan dialect spoken in the Southeast today includes words and expressions of the ancient Chinese spoken in the Central Plains?

In ancient China, Fujian was inhabited by the people of the Baiyue nationality, a minority nationality in the South. After unifying China in 221 B.C., Emperor Qinshihuang set up a Minzhong (Central Min) Prefecture here. At the same time he sent large numbers of immigrants and soldiers into this new region. In this way the language of the Central Plains began to spread to this area. During the last years of the Jin Dynasty, due to the long years of wars and natural disasters, many of the northerners moved to the South. The refugees who came to Min also brought with them the official language used in the Central Plains at that time.

In the next thousand years wars broke out frequently and national migrations occurred all over the land, with the result that the language of the Central Plains also changed rapidly. By

333

contrast, because of the mountains in between, Fujian had very little contact with the Central Plains, so its dialect remained unchanged on the whole. That is why it still includes many ancient Chinese words and expressions dating back to the Han and Tang dynasties.

I myself happen to know some Japanese, and I've noticed that when you first listen to the Minnan dialect, you find many words such as "Japan," "pen," "school," "translation" and "bitter," among others, bearing about the same pronunciation as their Japanese equivalents. Why should this be?

The explanation lies in the frequent cultural exchanges starting with the Tang Dynasty envoys to Japan and Jian Zhen's frequent visits to Japan. Borrowing the Chinese cursive script style, the Japanese created their *hiragana*, and based upon the Chinese radicals in the regular script style, they created their *katakana*. These have both been used up until now as the alphabetic letters of the Japanese language. It is because the Japanese letters borrowed the phonetics of the Chinese language used during the Tang Dynasty that Japanese and the Minnan dialect came to be similar in pronunciation.

Some Taboos

Why the first lunar month in Quanzhou should be distinguished by so many taboos puzzles visitors from other places. One morning we visited a family who ran a small restaurant. No sooner had we taken our seats in his central room than our hospitable host Lao Lin brought us oranges, candies, cake and candied fruit. The local people offer these sweets to whatever visitors they have through the Spring Festival season. When Lao Lin saw me sitting without eating anything, he peeled an orange and gave it to me. Later I learned that in offering visitors "sweets" and "oranges" (a homonym of "good luck" in Chinese), they expressed their very best wishes.

A while later our hostess prepared a bowl of eggs with sugar and jujubes added. (Fujian produces sugar itself, and its citizens all love sweet food; they even add sugar to fried salty vegetables.) The local people call this dish "sweet eggs." By offering such a treat on holidays, they extend to them their warm welcome and best wishes.

Deciding that it would be better to flatter my hostess by eating what she had given rather than simply being polite and respectful, I finished the four eggs in the bowl in one gulp. But when I glanced at our guide Lao Huang, I was surprised to see that he had left two eggs untouched. When I asked him why I learned that because of the homonyms in the local dialect, the visitors wish their host family a year of good fortune by leaving two eggs in the bowl. During the Spring Festival season, visitors who are familiar with the local customs just drink the soup when sweet eggs are offered them. Eating the eggs is generally considered a breach of etiquette.

I apologized to my host — a man in his late fifties — for my ignorance of their customs, but he just laughed. "I long ago gave up all that old stuff," he chuckled, confiding that in the old society his visitors always left eggs in the bowls he presented to them, but he couldn't remember living through one single year of good luck and bliss in all that time. It was only after the founding of the People's Republic of China, he said, that his life began to change gradually. Four years before, he and his wife and daughters had set up this small restaurant. Since he was a skilled cook, whatever food he prepared was tasty and because the price was also right, the place was always crowded with diners. When asked about his monthly income, he answered, "Not much, a thousand *yuan* a month." One thousand, it should be noted, is equal to a whole year's income of a skilled worker.

Talking about taboos at the dining table, Lao Huang told me one I hadn't heard: when you have finished the meat of the upper half of a fish at a banquet, you must never turn the other half over. He said that this taboo was closely related to the life of the local men, who make their living by fishing. Turning the fish over courts the danger of capsizing.

Quanzhou was a famous harbor in ancient China. During the prosperous Song and Yuan dynasties, it had commercial links with about a hundred countries. In the 13th century, when the Italian traveler Marco Polo set sail for home from this city, he wrote in his travel notes that with its large numbers of boats coming and going and its goods piled up like hills, Quanzhou rivaled Alexandria of Egypt for the title of the largest harbor in the world. In 1974, when a wooden boat that had sunk seven hundred years ago was dug out from Quanzhou Bay, its hold still contained spices and other goods shipped from Southeast Asia. Because it was mostly spices that were shipped to Quanzhou in those years, the route came to be called the "Spice Route." Exported from the port then were chinaware, silks and tea. The route remained busy until after the 15th century when the governments of the Ming and Qing dynasties placed a ban on maritime trade. Nonetheless since ancient times Quanzhou has been seen as a cosmopolitan city. Ironically in modern times so many natives have been unable to make a living here that it has come to be known as the hometown of overseas Chinese.

In the years of sailing vessels a trip across the sea was always a risk. The boats often capsized when encountering a rain or wind storm. Praying for safety on the sea became an important rite for all sea travelers and their relatives and friends. Whenever someone was going abroad, his fellow villagers would hold a farewell feast for him called a *songshunfeng* to wish him a safe journey at which a whole fish was served. Turning the fish over came to be associated with capsizing and thus was strictly forbidden.

A five-storied stone pagoda stands on top of the Baogai Mountains at Quanzhou Bay. On top of the pagoda stand statues of a man and two women whose story I soon learned. The legend of the "Gusao Pagoda" (*sao* means one's elder brother's wife; *gu* means one's wife's husband's sister) goes that more than eight hundred years ago there lived a peasant family at the foot of the mountains whose straitened circumstances demanded that the elder brother leave home to seek his fortune abroad. Before his departure he promised his wife and his younger sister that three years later he would come home by boat with a silk belt fluttering from the masthead. But though the date for his return came and went, he never did show and neither his wife nor his sister ever heard from him. And so together they began to climb to the top of the Baogai Mountains every day, and each day they would build up their standing place by adding one stone so that they could more easily look across the sea to discern the promised silk belt streaming from the mast. The days turned into weeks and the months into years into years until their stones rose into a tall pagoda and still their loved one did not return. Finally the grief-stricken pair died on the pagoda and the sympathetic villagers erected a statue uniting the three at last.

For eight hundred years this stone pagoda has been a place where the local people greet their relatives coming back from abroad. Whenever a returning overseas Chinese standing at the bow of a ship catches sight of the distant Gusao Pagoda, he will be sure to shed a few tears, for it appears to be his own loved ones on the lookout for him.

I was told about a strange rule having to do with these re-unions. The returning voyager must not see his parents or wife and children upon his arrival. Instead he will be received by his aunts. Only after he has taken a short break and eaten a bowl of sweet eggs can he meet those closest to him.

This traditional practice makes sense when one thinks about it carefully. First of all, that a returnee first meets more distant relatives, fits in with the general etiquette. It can be argued that those having high blood pressure or heart trouble will be benefitted by a short rest after a long sail— that it can be good for anyone to have a chance to calm down a bit. Such a respite also gives the aunts time to inform the returnee of any unhappy events that might have taken place in the family. Thus he will be prepared for anything, cushioned against shocks that could spoil the joy of reuniting with his loved ones.

Lantern Festival Celebrations

It happened to be the Lantern Festival the 15th of the 1st lunar month — while we were in Quanzhou. Since the villagers were still free from farming responsibilities and still in a mood for enjoying themselves started by the Spring Festival activities, they were in high spirits on this night that saw the first full moon of the new year. The Lantern Festival, Spring

Festival, Dragon Boat Festival and Mid-Autumn Festival together constitute the four major traditional festivals in China.

According to traditional practice, the Lantern Festival is not a festival for paying homage to the full moon but rather a night for appreciating lanterns. Houses are all decorated with red lanterns, while children play with lanterns of various colors and designs outdoors. Lantern sheds are set up at street corners and at public squares attracting people of all ages. That is why this traditional festival, which is actually known as the *Yuanxiao* Festival in Chinese, is called the "Lantern Festival."

According to history, the Lantern Festival originated at the time of the Western Han Dynasty over two thousand years ago: on the 15th of the 1st lunar month every year, Emperor Hanwu had lighted lanterns hung in the palace throughout the night to accompany prayers to God Taiyi for good weather for all crops, peace for the whole country, and happiness for all the people. In the Tang Dynasty, the imperial government connected the lighting of lanterns with people's belief in Buddhism, making this activity of keeping lighted lanterns on the 15th of the 1st lunar month a kind of official etiquette and an annual practice for the whole nation. Later, Tang Xuanzong turned this one-night practice into a three-night festival, holding lantern fairs inside the Forbidden City in Chang'an, setting up lantern towers, and planting at the top of the hills 25-meter-high multibranched lantern trees. People within a distance of fifty kilometers could see these bright lanterns that flickered like stars in the sky.

Celebrating the Lantern Festival is a common practice in China. The lanterns, however, differ from place to place owing to the various ways and the materials they are made of. Villagers in Northern Shaanxi, for example, tie lantern frames with sorghum stalks split into strips, then cover them up with red paper, thus making "pumpkin lanterns," "cotton lanterns," and "lamb lanterns." They either mold flour dough into small containers or cut potatoes into little bowls; then by filling them with oil and putting in wicks, they turn them into red lamps. The villagers hang these red lanterns in the cave

338

dwellings, storerooms, stables, and over the main entrances to their houses. They also decorate date trees and scholartrees with colored paper and with lanterns, charging their names temporarily "lantern trees."

The annual Lantern Festival in the ancient capital of Beijing saw large numbers of palace lanterns hung up all over the imperial palace. The making of palace lanterns combined into one the plastic arts of silk tying, papering, weaving, carving, and painting. The frames are generally made up of small carved wooden sticks, usually lacquered, then covered up with silk or glass, and finally painted with landscapes, human figures, flowers and birds or other designs. Besides hanging lanterns, there are hand lanterns, wall lanterns, table lanterns, and lanterns for honor guards. Beijing's folk Lantern Festival celebrations in ancient times were very rich and full of ceremony. And their design and workmanship were clearly the best to be found anywhere in the country. Today's Dengshikou near Wangfujing was once the marketplace where lanterns were sold in those years.

Games are always a prime feature of the Lantern Festival, with riddles at the top of the list. They are either written on the coverings of lanterns or on strips of paper hung over the lanterns. Prizes are awarded those who come up with correct answers.

Ha'erbin, capital of Heilongjiang Province, which lies at the northern frontier of China, is known as "Ice City." The lanterns used at the Lantern Festival in this city are translucent ice lanterns which glitter wonderously in the light as well as the dark.

The Lantern Festival celebrations I saw in Quanzhou were quite different. Because of the frequent rains in this province, the colorful lanterns were all hung under the *qilou*. (*Qilou* refers to the passageway on the left side of the first floors of buildings on both sides of the streets, found only in southern cities.) The large numbers of beautiful lanterns, thousands in all, turned the long streets into "Lantern Streets."

Appreciating their traditional lanterns under the *qilou*, I noticed that they were made in the shape of animals, birds, insects

339

and fish, flowers and plants.... However, representations of "oranges," "lychees," "pineapples," "fingered citrons" and other rare southern fruits reminded us of where we were. Exceptionally attractive were several dozen of "ball lanterns" made of thin plastic sheets hanging from the third to the ground floor, resembling the "flag lanterns" found in the army camps of ancient China. Representations of today's rockets, satellites and other modern things introduce novelty to the scene.

Suddenly I became aware of the scent of especially fragrant incense. Tracing the aroma, I found that it came from an octagonal palace lantern. It turned out that burning inside the lantern were two coils of precious sandal incense.

People in Quanzhou have the custom of sending friends and relatives lanterns as gifts. On the 2nd of the 1st lunar month every newly married couple will go to pay the young wife's parents a New Year visit bearing gifts. In return, her parents will give them a pair of lotus lanterns joined together by one string and two whole sugarcanes with roots and leaves, to wish the young couple a life as sweet as the sugarcanes.

As for the pair of lotus lanterns, one of which is red and the other white, they are to be hung over the bed on the night of the Lantern Festival only. Husband and wife, each lighting one of the two candles of the lanterns at the same time, wait to see whose candle burns out first. If the white lantern does, it means they will have a boy; and of course if the red one does, they will have a girl.

In the old society, Chinese men and women did not meet together openly, so the Lantern Festival, when people gathered to watch the full moon and enjoy the lanterns, offered a young people a chance to pair off. In Fujian a love story is told which has the Lantern Festival as its background. Chen San, son of a Quanzhou official, attended the Lantern Festival celebrations in Chaozhou, Guangdong Province, which he met Huang Wuniang, daughter of a wealthy local family, with whom he fell in love at first sight and she with him. Huang's father, a socially ambitious man had ideas that did not include Chen San. He decided to marry off his daughter to Lin Da, son of a rich and influential family. Being informed of these plans, Chen San took on the guise of a craftsman and got himself hired to polish a valuable mirror for the Huang family. As he went about his task, Chen broke the mirror deliberately and to pay for it he sold himself as a slave to the Huang family in order to be able to be near his sweetheart, meeting secretly, plotted to flee to Quanzhou where they were married and lived in permanent bliss. The local opera *Chen San and Wuniang* adapted from this story is performed at the Lantern Festival here every year. The film version is also shown again and again in the Southeast Asia and never lacks for audiences.

Paying Homage to Ancestors by Making Sacrifices

Traditionally, every family should have a meal of *yuanxiao* (round dumplings made of glutinous rice flour with sweet stuffing) during the Lantern Festival.

Making of *yuanxiao* is actually quite easy. People in Beijing use the "rolling method": they first mix with sugar the shelled peanuts, walnuts, and sesames that have been previously fried and ground into pieces and after kneading well, shape the mixture into small balls. After that, they put the balls into glutinous rice flour, shaking them as they continuously spray water over the rice flour until the little balls become as big as pingpong balls. Then they drop the *yuanxiao* into a pot of boiling water and when they float to the top, they are ready to serve.

Southerners have a more complicated way of making *yuanxiao*. They first grind the glutinous rice into flour which they mix with enough water to knead it into half balls, then fill in the stuffing and seal up the opening. This is called "the stuffing method." Besides sweet stuffing, they prepare salty fillings made from a mixture of shrimp, ground meat and ham.

We spent the Lantern Festival at a friend's house that day. It took no more than twenty minutes for our hostess to prepare the *yuanxiao*. Offering the steaming bowl to us, she said, "Have some *yuanxiao*. We wish you a pleasant traveling and your whole family happiness!" I learned that on the Lantern Festival by having *yuanxiao*, which not only looked round but also was pronounced "round" in Chinese, they implied a wish for a fine reunion of friends and relatives. This also reminds me of the Taiwan folk song popularly sung in the mainland "Selling *Tangyuan*" (round dumplings made of glutinous rice flour served in soup, another form of *yuanxiao*):

> *Tangyuan*, *tangyuan*, selling *tangyuan*—
> Xiao Er's *tangyuan* are *yuan*, *yuan*, *yuan* (round)!
> Now come and enjoy my *tangyuan*,
> Then go home for a happy reunion....

The Lantern Festival is also a time for making sacrificial offerings to ancestors. On that day the Huangs' Ancestral Hall in the suburbs of Quanzhou housed crowds upon crowds of people setting off deafening rounds of firecrackers inside. All the households with the Huang surname brought with them chickens, meats, fish, fruit and other offerings. After placing them on the sacrificial table, they burnt joss sticks, prostrating themselves before a color portrait of the founder of their village, that was hung in the hall.

The color lanterns hung inside flickered through the smoke in the dark hall. All of them had been sent by families which had acquired infant boys in the previous year. In the local dialect, "lantern" and "man" share the same pronunciation. According to their custom, such a family should send one color lantern to the hall at Lantern Festival time, when the traditional offerings are made to their ancestors, so as to make known to the public that a man-to-be has been born. The elders told me that besides those from the local villagers, there were also lanterns sent by overseas Chinese and families living in Taiwan.

Most of the ancestors of the Hans in Taiwan were from Fujian or Guangdong, many of whom went to Taiwan after the Ming Dynasty. In 1661 when Zheng Chenggong and his royal army of about thirty thousand drove out the Dutch aggressors and recovered Taiwan, they set up villages and towns and began to develop the province. Several centuries later the descendants still remember their ancestors and speak the dialect of their native home. As regards building houses, holding wedding or funeral ceremonies and practicing religious beliefs, they also have kept to the traditions and customs found on the mainland of China.

Baijiao Village in Minnan has a Ciji Temple and so does Xuejia Town in Taiwan. A deity worshipped here is "Emperor Baosheng," who was in fact a country doctor by the name of Wu Tao who went to Taiwan with Zheng Chenggong and his royal army, including the men of Baijiao Village. Before they left for Taiwan, they made sacrificial offerings at the Ciji Temple, wrapping up a little handful of incense ashes to show that they would never forget their home village. On the 11th of the 3rd lunar month, the men of Baijiao Village landed at Xuejia. After that they built another Ciji Temple there. On the 11th of the 3rd lunar month every year, people in Xuejia hold a memorial ceremony they call "going to Baijiao" to homage to the Ciji Temple in Baijiao on the other side of the straits; they also draw water from the rivulet with small clay pots, then respectfully place the pots of water in front of the sacrificial altar to demonstrate that they always remember their home village.

In recent years, more and more Taiwan compatriots are seeking their roots, trying to discover when and from where their ancestors came to Taiwan and what relatives they still have on the mainland. According to such research, the roots of the Huang clan can be traced to the Huaxia Clans living along the Yellow River. The first ancestor of the Huangs was Emperor Huangdi (Xuanyuan) of over four thousand years ago. With regard to the famous clan of the Yingchuan Chens in Fujian and Taiwan, their number one ancestor was Chen Shi (104-186), descendant of the 81st generation of Yu Shun.

Simple Folk Dances

With all its lights on the night of the Lantern Festival, Quanzhou became ablaze with lights. The citizens all left their homes, happy swarming into the streets, parks, and squares to watch special performances and the grand show of lanterns.

The recreational organizations from schools, factories,

governmental departments, department stores and villages one by one, marched into the central square of the city to put on their performances. Among these the "Beating-Chest Dance" presented by the peasants of the suburbs was the most impressive. Several dozen men stripped to the waist, straw rings around their heads, dance barefoot, beating their shoulders, chests, arms and thighs accompanied by drumbeats, as they kept changing formations. Though its steps were simple and its style broad, this primitive dance was irresistible to those watching, most of whom swayed in response to its vigor and mesmerizing drumbeats.

There are different versions of the origins of the "Beating-Chest Dance." One has it that ancient farmers, impelled by the need to relieve the tired muscles and stiffness caused by long hours of bending down during harvest times, invented the dance during breaks in their field work. Because of the lack of props and musical instruments, they wove straw into ropes which they put atop their heads, inserting ears of unhusked rice as ornaments. With their bodies stripped to the waist, they beat their chests and thighs, dancing and shouting at the same time, thus not only expressing their joy over a bountiful harvest, but limbering up their muscles and joints at the same time.

Next came the "Fire-Pot Dance" — a humorous re-enactment of the scenes: a pair of made-up newlyweds, looking very shy; they were accompanied by the best man and the bridesmaid. The parents-in-law of the bride walking in the front were carrying a fiery pot, or rather a pot of roaring charcoal fire, shouting and dancing at the same time. There was also a "matchmaker" who was carrying a clay pot of salt mixed with bran. From time to time she threw handfuls of the salt and bran into the fiery pot, making cracking sounds to add joy to the festive atmosphere. She blessed the audience as she spread the salt and bran, "All's red and prosperous!" Her funny performance set all the audience to hearty laughter.

Everybody tried to elbow to the front, hoping that the "matchmaker" would spread her blessing salt and bran over his head. I was told that in the old days, when the "Fire-Pot Dancers" were giving their performances, the villagers would crowd along the roads with torches in hand. They would elbow their way to the fire pot to light their torches, then carry them home, believing that they had brought back the tinder of happiness. Thus, in no time the "Fire-Pot Dance" would change into a torch procession going through all the villages in the country.

"There come the dragon lanterns!" In the cheers of the heavy crowds two huge green dragons jumped into the square.

The dragons were forty-eight meters long. Each consisted of a head, a body of nine sections and a tail, all of which were tied up with bamboo strips, then clothed with gauze painted as scales. Beneath every section of the body was a wooden stick held by a strong young man for the group dance. The dragon head, in particular, weighed more than ten kilos, but with the pulling force resulting from the dancing became the equivalent of thirty. Leading in the front was another man dancing with a dragon pearl. All the dancers were very active and vigorous. Following the dragon pearl, they jumped high up into the sky, then dived downward as if they were diving into the sea. With the background presented the lively fish, shrimps, turtles and clams, they brought to mind the magnificent scene in the legend about the Dragon King's seething in the sea.

Finally, the dancers lighted the fireworks hidden in the dragon heads and in the mouths of the marine animals. All of a sudden, flames scattered all over the place, filling the sky with smoke. Thus, the folk Lantern Festival celebrations ended in the cheers of the excited audience "The dragons are spitting fire now!"

The dragon is of course a purely mythical being, a totem of ancient clans. Probably the dragon dance first appeared as a kind of ceremony at celebrations of happy events and sacrificial rites. Back in the Han Dynasty over two thousand years ago, peasants already had the habit of holding dragon dances when worshipping Tianzu, god of land, and when praying for rains. Dragons of the Song Dynasty were made of straw covered with blue curtains. In the old days, the annual dragon dance was a kind of competition, through every village or town tried to beat the others by making the largest dragon and performing the best dance. Such spontaneous competitions helped to develop this folk dance over time. According to their custom, the dragon dancers also beat drums and gongs and fired off firecrackers in order to prevent misfortunes from befalling the people and bringing them good luck instead. Today, as part of the repertoire, the dragon dance often is performed on holidays and other occasions for celebration, always drawing large numbers of spectators.

FISHERMEN'S UNIQUE CUSTOMS

Peculiar Ways of Dressing

Although Hui'an County is no more than thirty kilometers from Quanzhou, the clothes worn by the women of its fishing villages differ strikingly from those seen on the streets of their urban neighbors. The standard blue blouse is so short it leaves the abdomen completely bare. Yet the black silk trousers the women wear are large and loose and usually caught at the waist by three or four belts. And the brightly colored scarves that tightly cover their heads allow only eyes, noses and mouths to be seen while yellow bamboo hats cast shadows on their mostly hidden faces. The irony of so much concealment contrasted with exposed abdomens causes outsiders to remark on the women's "feudally hidden faces but democratically exposed bellies."

Why should the women of Hui'an expose their bellies in public? Folklorists explain it in terms of their notions of what is beautiful. The bright belts they wear are their most conspicuous adornments. Especially prized among them is the silver belt given them by their husbands on their wedding day. On that day they not only wear exceptionally short blouses but tie their belts even lower than usual, the better to display their bellies. Indeed, this part of them is exposed even on the coldest winter days, since they would rather smear frostbite preventive salve on their bellies than cover them.

Generally speaking, each local woman has thirty to forty scarves which are worn in rotation according to the seasons. In summer they prefer light flowers on a white background while white flowers on a blue background are favored for winter. Girls who go to town seldom fail to buy bright-colored cotton prints with new designs if they run into any. Back home they embroider them and trim them with lace. Visitors from afar who bring their hostesses' scarves with fresh designs are especially welcome.

There are many different versions of the costume's origins. One traces it to the Baiyue people, ancestors of Hui'an County. Since the ancients stubbornly kept to their old ways, the costume worn in this remote region was handed down from generation to generation.

The aesthetic tastes of the ancients were closely related to their work, as were those of the women of the fishing villages in Hui'an. One afternoon, while we were strolling along the seashore, we noticed women carrying fresh water to the fishing boats. Despite their heavy buckets, they walked briskly against the sea breeze across the white sand. Approaching the sampans, they grasped their carrying poles with one hand and pulled up their trouser legs with the other and carried their pails onto the boats. Now we could see why the trouser legs were kept loose.

The Chinese have been wearing bamboo hats for a good long time. Although the hats vary in shape and size from place to place. The women here wear a wide-brimmed peaked one in all weather both indoors and out. Its practicality for outdoor work is immediately apparent, but why they keep it on inside remains obscure— perhaps even to them. A woman seems to feel undressed without her bamboo hat and her waist belt. Indeed, a new bamboo hat is a sign of a newly married woman.

According to our guide, Chongwu native Lao Cai, a man in his late fifties, such costumes have survived in only about a dozen villages in the Chongwu and Xiaozuo Peninsulas, with a total population today of no more than sixty thousand.

Typhoon-resistant Stone Houses

With the rocky hills behind and the sea gulf in front, Gangqian of the Chongwu Peninsula has a splendid little natural harbor. But it's first and foremost a fishing village as

347

was clear to us at first glance. Fishing boats of all sizes were berthed everywhere, the air was filled with a strong fishy smell, and nets glistened in the sun in front of all the houses. The 1,300 houses, located near the sea or on the hilly slopes, were all granite structures, everything of stone except for the wooden doors and window lattices: stone walls, roofs, door and window frames. Even the water vat in the kitchen was made of stone— in this case slabs joined with cement. Also, the walls of the courtyards, their dikes, and roads were all built of stone. Lying in the open fields along the road were still more neatly cut stone slabs.

The villagers of Gangqian made the best use of the building material available to them, getting stone from the quarry on the hills behind their village. Accompanied by the ringing sounds of their hammer and rods, the masons turned what they got from nature into beautiful building materials, which of course did not cost much. Eight bamboo-hatted women were carrying stone slabs in rhythmic step toward the building site of a new house. Watching these small, slender women carrying such heavy burdens so easily and listening to the soft, musical voices that belied their lives of hardship, I marveled at their resilience in adapting to such hard labor while retaining the gentleness we Chinese so like to see in women.

In times when they can't engage in fishing, almost all the men leave home to work as stonemasons or bricklayers. Naturally they leave all the heavy household chores to the women. Thus, the women have to carry water, do the cooking and washing, feed the pigs, repair the fishnets, and take care of the children. When their men's boats return from the sea, they are there to meet them and immediately carry the fish to town for sale. Before their husbands go out to fish, they must carry onto the boats fresh water, firewood, foodstuffs and ice needed in the freezing of marine animals. No wonder so many people call this fishing village "a Kingdom of Women"!

Delicious Local Food

We had arrived to visit the family of Lao Cai's cousin, Zhang Hongjiu: a tall, vigorous man of over fifty, an honest man of few words. All his hospitality was shown through actions. On hearing that "these journalists from Beijing are on their way — could you prepare some local food for them?" he at once set his wife to work in the kitchen.

To these folks fish and shrimps were commonplace, but I found the fish cubes braised in brown sauce prepared by our hostess extraordinarily delicious and her fried shrimps exceptionally tasty and crisp — dishes I find it hard to find in Beijing, especially cooked the way she did them.

The staple is "potato starch," which has a unique local flavor. In preparing it, you first add water to sweet potato starch and mix it well, then put in peanuts and cook the mixture with peeled taros. When it's done, you add in various ingredients as well as rice noodles and continue cooking until it turns into porridge. Though it looks like ordinary food, this local dish contains not only shelled shrimps and dry cuttlefish but also fresh celery and garlic seedlings. With the smooth, tasty potato starch added in, it was a most appetizing dish. While I was eating, I told my host that the dish had been poorly named and we should call it "Potato Starch Prepared with Seafood and Peanuts" instead. But the straightforward host disagreed. "It's not that good," he protested mildly. "'Potato starch' suits it just fine. No need for so many words."

Fujian is a province that turns out large quantities of rice every year. But because of its special soil texture and the quality of its water, Hui'an County produces mainly peanuts and potatoes instead. The big sweet potatoes grown here become yellow when steamed — soft and sweet and truly delicious. Because they are the main food of the local people, Hui'an is often referred to as "Sweet Potato County." With their richness in sugar, starch and vitamins, they are given credit for the robust health of the local people — sharing the honors with fish, also consumed in quantity here.

As I was helping my hostess in her kitchen, I couldn't help but pay admiring notice to the stove, especially its striking inlay of red bricks. In other places the chimney is usually at the back of the stove, where it draws out the smoke directly, but here chimneys are fixed above the stove's mouth, reaching up-

349

ward in stairsteps. At first sight I thought that the smoke might find its way into the house, but throughout the cooking — nearly an hour — it drew up all the smoke easily, not allowing even a bit to escape.

I was told that saving firewood was the first merit of this stove. From their long years of experience, the local people had discovered a way to design a stove so that the fire will smoke most at the back and then move to the front before it goes out the chimney. In this way the fire lasts longer and creates more heat. The stair-like chimney has the dual function of providing storage space for bottles or small jars containing oil, sauce, salt and vinegar.

Newlyweds Sleep Separately

The Zhangs were a family of eight living in a compound of five rooms, one of which was a central living room which doubled as kitchen-dining room. The eastern rooms were occupied by the parents and their daughter respectively, while the western rooms were reserved for 22-year-old Haidong, the middle-aged couple's newly married son. The marriage couplet remained in place on the door of the bridal room:

Celebrating marriage day and night —
Receiving the bride with happy delight.

Haidong was a sailor on a trawler, an occupation which had left its mark on his permanently sun- and wind-burned face and had made him into a strong, bold, proud man. Just three weeks before, he had married Zhang Yaya, a girl from his own village.

Entering the bridal room, I found all the furniture inside brand-new: desk, wardrobe, sewing machine, etc. Red papercuts of the character: " 囍 " (double happiness) decorated the full-length mirror and a framed photograph. Set against the wall was a wooden bed carved with traditional designs — the headboard a garden of flowers and plants shared with birds and animals. Fixed on the corners were four posts on which mosquito net was hung. On a shelf over the bed inside the mosquito net were two brand-new shiny leather suitcases on which

350

were pasted lists of names in red ink, obviously the givers. New suitcases are a "must" for newlyweds throughout China.

"You'll sleep with Haidong in this room tonight," our host informed us. I was taken aback and refused without hesitation. How could we usurp the bed of a honeymooning couple? Impossible!

"The bride has returned to her parents' home and will not come back for a year or so," our host explained. Later I learned that the daughter who slept in one of the east rooms had been married recently to a man from a neighboring village. She, too, had returned to her parents' home after the wedding. Had they all had a falling out? Not at all, I was told. Living away from their husbands right after marriage is the way it's done in Chongwu and Xiaozuo.

When they are still small children, their parents begin to look for husbands for their daughters. Their spouses are to be chosen only among the dozen or so nearby villages that share the same customs. The ceremony of engagement is actually quite simple; all they do is buy some candy and cake and distribute small shares to neighbors, relatives and friends. Nonetheless, such an engagement bears the effect of law.

We saw one marriage ceremony in Gangqian which we found rather strange. The troop that went to escort the bride walked all the way to fetch her. Carrying the bride's dowry in the front— including suitcases, clothes and a sewing machine— were a group of young girls. Next came the matchmaker carrying gifts: ornaments that the bride would give her mother-in-law and sisters-in-law and cakes to be presented to her father-in-law and brothers-in-law. Although the bride's head and face were tightly covered with a cloth, she further hid her face with a cloth umbrella. The result was that she could walk only with the aid of her two attendants. Bringing up the rear were a group of relatives, the bride's friends (all females) who were seeing her to her new home, and a small boy and girl. In the old days when people had little knowledge of physiology, they thought that it was the gods who determined child bearing; so they festooned the children with masses of flowers so that they would seem to have been sent by the immortals, the point of

351

the entire ritual being to express and help along the wish that the bride would give birth to a child at the earliest possible time.

The bride showed up amid the rat-a-tat of popping firecrackers. When she entered the yard, people threw salt on the fire in front of the house and when it crackled loudly enough, directed the bride to go around the fire once to dispel all evils and devils that might have come along with her. In order to avoid overwhelming the shy bride, her parents-in-law and her brothers- and sisters-in-law had all hidden themselves before she entered the house. The bridegroom received her by himself, unveiling her with the arm of a steelyard, whereupon he showed her into the bridal room. After that a wedding feast was served to all the relatives, friends and other wellwishers.

All these customs were known to me or were variations on a theme. Nothing out of the way, that is. But that the young couples here could not sleep together after the wedding night games were played, that they weren't even allowed to sleep under the same roof! In the 1980s? I wasn't ready for this!

The tradition that the brides and bridegrooms should not sleep together on their wedding night dates back to antiquity. The bride either begs a place to sleep from a neighboring granny or asks girlfriends to stay with her in the bridal room. Or she might even sit by her dressing table throughout the night. The bridegroom at the wedding we attended went to the best man's home for the night.

The next day, fulfilling traditional practice, the bride went to the central room of the house to kowtow to the ancestors of the family and her parents-in-law. There she also presented her "gifts for the first meeting" to the seniors, ancestors, relatives and friends. Early on the third morning, led by her little sister-in-law, the bride went to fetch her first load of water from the well, known locally as "exploring the well." Finally, after enduring five long days of tedious formalities, the bride was free to return to her own parents' home to continue her free life as before.

However, the wife must return to her husband for three

days at the time of the Spring Festival. If she fails to come back, her husband has the right to abandon her, and even her own parents will blame her for any misfortunes that may occur in the new year, believing any and all to be caused by her disobedience. Moreover, she should return to her husband for the Qingming Festival to pay homage and make offerings to his ancestors at their tombs. Acting in accordance with the legend that people on earth and the moon in the sky reunite in midautumn, she also has to join her husband then. For all the other days, the young wife stays with her parents until her first child is about to be born.

Research shows that a woman staying away from her husband after her marriage is a custom surviving from the primitive matriarchal society. This custom is also still observed by some of the national minorities in China. With regard to its origin, one school of thought holds that it was a natural result of the bride's longing for the continuation of a girl's life and of her worry about getting pregnant right away. She well knew that once she gave birth to a child, she could no longer live the life she had known with her own parents and sisters and brothers; nor could she work to repay her parents for all they had done in bringing her up or participate in the upbringing of her younger brothers and sisters.

For the same reason perhaps, in the old days people here also carried on the questionable practice of separating husbands and wives from each other. For example, when a man and his wife met in public they were supposed to act as if they were strangers and not speak to one another. A wife who stayed at her parents' could entertain any visitor except her own husband. Once he came, she had to go into hiding. In addition, girls of the same village often solemnly swore to each other that they would postpone child bearing as long as they possibly could. Anyone who broke her promise would earn the ridicule of her friends.

Having stayed with Haidong for some days now, I felt comfortable speaking to him personally. So I plunged ahead. "When you run into your wife, you dare not even speak to her," I said. "Do you think that's a good thing?"

"Not at all," he said firmly. "It would be much better for my wife and me — for all couples — to live together and speak to each other openly in public like people do everywhere else."

It's clear that the young and the old differ greatly on these matters. Actually, in Chongwu many young people no longer accept the primitive customs of their village and instead go by the national marriage law, exercising free will in the choice of their spouses.

Mazu: Goddess of the Sea

Fine weather came at last and the fishing village became noisy with activity even before daybreak. Men and women with oars on their shoulders and fishnets in their hands crowded around the harbor. A few women who had come to see off their men shouted at the top of their lungs: "Eat a good breakfast now!" "Be sure to dress warmly enough!"

As soon as they got on the boats, the fishermen all took off their regular clothes and donned oversized outfits with cotton buttons affixed below the right armpit. The jackets and shirts they wore on land that had buttons in the front might easily get caught on fishnets, which could cause not only inconvenience but even lead to their being dragged into the sea. These strips of cotton fasteners — placed, as they were, under the right arm — would not hook on anything; and since the men pulled up their nets from the right to the left, they were safe from getting tangled up. All the canvas, the fishnets, and these special work outfits were the same reddish brown, the color of the longan bark used to dye them. Practice had long ago established this dye as especially resistant to the corrosion of salt water.

The sun was rising slowly in the east, turning the vast sea a vivid scarlet and causing glittering ripples to follow all the boats. Besides working the inland sea, the men go out with their trawlnets to the Taiwan Straits or to the Zhoushan Archipelagoes of Zhejiang Province to fish for hairtails and to Shantou, Guangdong Province, in search of squid.

Haidong was working on his fishing boat with his mates.

354

From a distance his heavily lacquered boat, with its two round eyes fixed on either side of the bow, looked like a yellow dragon taking its ease on the beach.

This way of decorating boats goes way back. In the old days people believed that the sea was ruled over by the Dragon King and all the marine animals — fish, shrimps, turtles, crabs — were in his thrall. Fishermen especially sought to stay on the good side of the Dragon King, for the sea was fraught with dangers. Take the matter of sharks. No sensible fisherman liked them, for they not only scared away their potential catch — they were behind any number of disasters or thought to be. Boats painted like dragons, then, were believed to have the ability to intimidate sharks.

To my surprise I discovered large red scrolls tacked up all over Haidong's boat. On the mast of the middle sail hung the saying: "All's Well Everywhere." Over the first sail I read: "Good Luck at First Sight." Above the bow a scroll said: "The Sea Is All at Peace." Over the rudder I saw: "Commander of All Troops" — on the fish cabin: "Bursting with Fishes" — on the fresh water bucket: "Dragon Water and Sweet Spring."

The chief boatman explained that this was a regular custom of the fishermen. Every year before the Spring Festival the fishermen's wives put up couplets everywhere — on doors, granaries, stoves — saying things like: "Each voyage brings tons and tons of fish/Every catch brings good cheer to all." The chief boatman told me that he himself leads the men to the boat in a kind of procession to put up their own couplets. "The fishing boat is our lifeblood," he explained. "We want to see it taking on a new look for the New Year, and we like to think the couplets bring us luck."

Knowing that every household sets off firecrackers to welcome the arrival of the Lunar New Year, I asked Haidong if they did the same on the boat during the Spring Festival.

"We're always back home for the Festival," he told me, "so we wait till then." Then he hesitated. "Of course, when the boat is fixed, we do have to set off a few firecrackers when we go through the Sanguan-Xiongji Pass for the first time,

355

so we have to have some set aside for that."

"Sanguan" and "Xiongji" are two huge rocks, the first of which has three towering peaks while the other looks like a crowing cock. The channel between the two rocks is the only passage possible for fishing boats to take in and out of the harbor. According to a traditional practice that nobody seems able to trace, new boats, or those that have just been repaired, or boats that are making their first voyage, all must burn joss sticks and paper that resembles money while requesting Mazu for safe passage on the sea and for help in bringing home abundant catches.

The day a boat returns home safe and sound, the chief boatman's wife goes to the Mazu temple in the neighboring village with a pig's head, a yellow croaker, some duck eggs, candies, cake and fruit as offerings to Mazu. When the rite is completed, the wife returns home with these same offerings and prepares a dinner with them for all the boatmen to celebrate their triumphal return.

Mazu is the goddess of the sea worshipped along the southeast coast of China. Originally named Lin Moniang, she was born in the year 960 on the nearby Meizhou Island of Putian County. Because she was not heard to cry during her first month of life, she was named Moniang or "Silent Girl." An unusually intelligent and sensitive child, she was taught to walk on the surface of the sea by a pious monk. At the age of fifteen having heard that a wreck had occurred near Meizhou Harbor where there were submerged reefs and vortexes, she rowed there without hesitation in her small boat and directed boatmen in a successful rescue of those threatened with drowning.

Late one night when she was twenty-eight she heard that a boat which was returning to the harbor had capsized in a sudden storm. Immediately she set forth. Walking back and forth on the sea carrying a half-drowned fisherman, often two at a time, she saw them all to safety. She herself, however, died of exhaustion soon after returning to shore. To honor this heroine who had devoted her life to rescue, the villagers built a temple and erected a statue of her there renaming her the Goddess

Mazu and calling the temple after her.

As time went on more and more stories about how Mazu blessed this person and that spread around, stories which became ever more fanciful. The classic *Anecdotes of the Sea* reports:

Every prayer-maker received blessings from Mazu, seeing immortal soldiers either protecting them or helping and rescuing them.... On a stormy night when the sea was pitch-dark, a supernatural light appeared above the masts to direct the sea routes for the fishermen.... Fishermen called it "Mazu Light."

Most of these tales are simply that— tales that have been handed down from ancient times and improved on in the telling over time. Today, thanks to the achievements made in navigation, as well as in oceanography and many technologies, the secrets of the vast oceans have been unfolding. We don't need Mazus and Dragon Kings to protect us but rather science and technology. Still the stories of Mazu demonstrate the aspirations and lofty morality of the ancient fishermen and their yearning to conquer nature. Unsurprisingly, the tales are still popular among the fishermen in southeast China. Indeed the chief boatman told me that he often sees pictures of Mazu above the bridges of boats from Taiwan. Before they go to sea, he said, fishermen from Taiwan always burn joss sticks and kowtow in front of shrines. And when they are attacked by windstorms they still pray to Mazu for deliverance.

This belief in Mazu shared by the fishermen of Taiwan and Fujian is said to have started some 300 years ago when the villagers from Putian who went to settle in Taiwan brought with them pictures of Mazu. Today the Mazu temples found all over Taiwan are crowded with worshippers every day. There appears to be among Fujian natives an element of yearning for home in their fealty to Mazu. The folk song goes: "*Bai Mazu, huai gutu.*" (Worship Mazu and yearn for our native home.)

Music Played for Dying Elders

After supper our host said, "One of the elders in our village is dying. All the villagers are keeping watch at his bedside. Why not go and have a look?"

The ancestral hall, ablaze with lights in the center of the village, was crowded with people. On the temporary bed set up in the eastern part of the hall lay 79-year-old Zhang Tufa, his eyes closed. I was told that he had not eaten anything for six days and nights and had scarcely one more breath to breathe. According to the old way of looking at things, anybody over age fifty dying of a serious disease is considered to be dying a natural death. He must be moved to the ancestral hall to be watched over by all the villagers until his death.

When they first heard the news that old Zhang was near death, about two hundred people — relatives, friends and fellow villagers — rushed to the hall to help look after the old man, some even through the night. Shijin and Yaguo, sons of the old man, were the busiest of all, for they not only had to care for their father but entertain the others with tea and cigarettes. Still when I expressed my sympathy to them, they were quick with their thanks. "So good of you to come; you must think so much of us!"

When a dying old person was moved to the ancestral hall, there would be many villagers available to help look after him. And once he died, the funeral could be held right there. The way things were happening now in the case of Zhang Tufa made it clear that he was someone who enjoyed a good deal of respect and affection. The entire event was considered to redound to his credit and glory.

The strains of music suddenly were heard from one side of the hall. A close look revealed several village musicians playing Fujian music. A woman began to sing to their accompaniment beating time with a pair of castanets.

Fujian music, or *nanyin* as it's called in Chinese, is one kind of ancient folk music popular among the people of south Fujian, Taiwan and the Chinese living in Southeast Asia. Musicologists have described it as "music...with elegant melody originating from Emperor Tang Xuanzong of the Tang Dynasty." If that is true, then *nanyin* has a history of at least 1,200 years.

Zhao Puchu, chairman of China's Buddhism Association, traces orchestral *nanyin* to the Tang and Song dynasties. It certainly is to be regretted that this palace music, which spread to the common people of ancient times, could not have survived in its entirety. However, parts of the Tang music, which was brought to Fujian by eunuchs, refugees and commercial travelers, do survive and we're the better for it. Absorbing the style of local operas and of India's Buddhist music, it gradually evolved its own style. Of the *nanyin* melodies of today, more than two thousand in number, some are elegantly simple, others passionate and abandoned, still others very sentimental. When night falls here, friends who play musical instruments often gather to while away the evening hours playing and singing *nanyin* melodies as they burn joss sticks and drink tea.

What I wanted to know was: why did they play music and sing, apparently for pleasure, when the old man lay mortally ill? After the first melody, when the musicians were taking a break, I asked them why. I found it was simply their custom. Playing music and singing at the deathbed of an aged person was actually part of the entire funeral process, and it also served as a means to comfort members of his family.

"This old gentleman is himself an accomplished singer of *nanyin*. We're all his students," said a *pipa* player. "Now our revered teacher lies on his deathbed. It comforts us to play for him. This way we can express some of our love and gratitude for all he did for us." He spoke fervently. No one could have doubted his sincerity.

The traditional practice of relatives and friends coming to comfort dying old people is one of their ways of showing respect for aged. It is also tied to the custom of coming to the aid of people when they are in trouble. Applied in these circumstances, it clearly means a lot to the survivors, especially those whose men have long been away from home — fishing on the sea, for example.

The next evening when the old man died, the ancestral hall was immediately turned into a mourning hall. The coffin was made and thus a regular funeral was able to start formally.

The aged villager's stay in the ancestral hall together with the funeral lasted about two weeks. During this time, Shijin and Yaguo could not go fishing and what's more had to spend money for the funeral. The unwritten law of the village provided that for the days the sons were not able to go to sea the other fishermen would donate a share of the money they made through the sale of their fish.

CHAPTER XIV

GUANGDONG— Home Province to Most Overseas Chinese

PECULIAR FOODS AND A SPRING FESTIVAL FLOWER MARKET

Guangzhou is a beautiful old city of south China. As legend tells it, one day back in ancient times five immortal beings dressed in different colors, each riding a goat with its own special color, came to Guangzhou from the South Sea. All these immortal beings presented local inhabitants with a head of rice as a symbol of their blessing and wish for bumper harvests here way into the future. And that's how Guangzhou earned the nickname "Yangcheng" (City of Goats) and "Suishi" (City of Grains). And it's also how the statue of five goats happened to find its home on the Yuexiu Hills that lie in the city center and to become the emblem of Guangzhou.

Cats, Rats, Snakes and Monkeys: Guangzhou Delicacies All

It was early spring as I walked along the streets of Guangzhou admiring its endless rows of vegetable stalls under lush banyans. The dewy green kale, rape with its yellow flowers, and the blood red tomatoes looked ever so appealing to me, fresh as I was from freezing Beijing where now markets were selling mostly cabbages covered with heavy cotton-padded quilts. That evening when a cousin who worked here invited me to dinner, I accepted without hesitation, and when asked for requests, quickly came up with kale and rape. Sure enough, when I got there, next to the roast goose, braised chicken with dry mushrooms, steamed carp and spiced sausages were platters of

361

bright green kale fried with beef and sauteed rape cooked with dry mushrooms.

But first came tomato soup with eggs. Before the wine was offered, my cousin's wife ladled half a bowl for me, urging, "Of course you'll have a bit of soup first." This sequence was in marked contrast to the way it would be done in Beijing where the soup is the last dish to come. The weather in Guangzhou is hot most of the year, so having soup before other food enables the local people to clear their throats, moisten their lungs and increase their appetites. And this is just what it does, for the belief helps to make it so.

My favorite besides the green vegetables was the roast goose bought already cooked from a stall. With its crisp golden skin and tender meat — rich yet not greasy — it rivaled Beijing's own roast duck, justifiably famous throughout the world. But those neatly piled leaves of kale and rape were the real masterpieces of the table to my mind — as green and fresh as if they had just come in from the fields. And, oh, so wonderfully crisp and tender! I asked my hostess why she had not cut them into shorter pieces and she explained that they were "suburb greens" and the way to cook them originated with their growers. Whole pieces of vegetables whose roots are cut off are dipped into boiling water for some seconds. When properly parboiled, they are plucked from the water. The other ingredients and seasonings are added as they are turned over for another second in the pot. Finally they are arranged in those special piles and then set out. Prepared this way the vegetables not only keep their original bright green color and their full store of vitamins, but they are lovely to look at and stay fresh and crisp.

Wandering into a vegetable market I found it bursting with customers, for it was the Spring Festival season. What had attracted me were the fish stands on one side of it. There I noticed an old man saying something to a woman seller, whereupon she picked up a live silver carp from her large basin, scraping all its scales off with an iron tool full of punches. Then she chopped off the head and peeled up one side of the skin which she then cut into slices. It had taken no more than two minutes for the old man to have his fish slices for lunch. Guangzhou people are known for liking sea and river foods. They don't eat a great deal, but what they do eat they insist must be fresh and tasty. Unlike Beijingers, they do not care for frozen "salty water fishes," as translates a local term.

My photographer companion, Xiao Lu, was visiting Guangzhou for the first time. He couldn't get over the sight of an elderly woman eagerly buying the fish head that the old man had left behind. Fish heads are often thrown into the garbage in Beijing, but here they are cherished as gourmet food.

Guangzhou cooks can turn all manner of bits and pieces discarded elsewhere into delicacies. On the menu of one famous Guangzhou restaurant which lists over a thousand courses, there are such specialties as chicken claws, taroes and any number of cheap items transformed by the restaurant's chefs. The boned chicken claws that are first fried in boiling oil and then braised in thick spiced soup are called "Phoenix Claws."

I asked the old woman who had grabbed up the fish head how she was going to cook it. "First you cut it in two and spread spring onions and ginger on it. Then you pour vegetable oil and cooking wine over it and steam it. That's all." Then she added with an air of conspiracy: "Fish heads are not only delicious — they make you smart!"

Guangzhou cooks are also concerned about nourishment and the medicinal properties of certain foods. They're given to adding medicinal herbs to some stewed dishes according to the season. Some of these are: quick-boiled pork liver with Chinese wolfberry leaves — to enrich the blood and sharpen the eyes; stewed pork hearts with seeds of Oriental arborvitae — to nourish the heart and calm the mind; duck cooked with winter melon and seeds of puncture vines and Job's tears — to build up *yin* and minimize the ill effects of summer heat and wetness.

Winter is the best season for healthful nourishment because of the cold weather. Some people stuff Chinese angelica and *dangshen* into a cleaned chicken and steam it — a combination which nourishes *yin* and invigorates the kidneys. Others stew dog meat with sweet potatoes, which invigorates *yang* and benefits vital energy. Feeble old people normally find lean pork simmered with lotus seed and lilies strengthening. Women who suffer from anemia benefit from mutton stewed with ginger and Chinese angelica. Upon the arrival of winter, restaurants put up advertisements of various nourishing "mugs" such as chicken stewed with fruit of Chinese wolfberry and *huaishan*, doves stewed with the root of membranous milk vetch and *dangshen*. Since the "mugs," which cost only one or two *yuan*, (half a dollar) are cheap as well as nutritious, they normally attract long lines of buyers.

Lured on by their adventurous palates, Guangzhou citizens turn all manner of creatures not thought to be edible elsewhere into food for the table: sparrows, partridges, musk civets, pangolins, dogs, cats, rats, turtles, monkeys. For that reason, astonished outsiders have been known to taunt: "The Cantonese will eat anything except planes in the sky, ships on the sea and benches on the land!"

I had long heard the praises sung of the Snake Restaurant located on Jianglan Road of the busy western district, and so I made a point of stopping by. I found there a middle-aged man who had come to sample "snake bile wine." A 23-year-old employee by the name of Liu Yanyun at once moved in and out of a cage of snakes, grasping a cobra in his bare hands. One foot on the snake's head and the other on its tail, he slit its belly open and drew out its gallbladder. Cutting open the sac, he mixed the bile with some rice wine and offered it to the customer, who drank it down in one gulp.

"Is the bile bitter?" I asked.

"No, it's sweet," he answered, smacking his lips as he left.

It is said that snake bile can dispel "wind-evil" and "wet-evil," stop coughing and eliminate phlegm, sharpen the eyes and benefit the liver. For these curative effects, people suffering from such illnesses as arthritis and asthma as well as handicapped people confined to wheelchairs come here in droves for "snake bile wine."

Having rid it of its poison and fangs, the worker skillfully chopped off the snake's head, stripped off its skin, and removed the meat, which he sent off to the kitchen immediately.

Half an hour later a large bowl of thick soup was brought out. The snow-white thin shreds of snake meat tasted tender, fresh and delicious when prepared with shreds of cat meat and chicken, shredded lemon leaves and chrysanthemum petals. Somehow, because the term "snake soup" did not sound too appealing, the restaurant dubbed it "Hodgepodge of Chrysanthemums, Dragons, Tigers and Phoenixes." Of course, the snake does resemble the dragon and the cat is related to the tiger and the chicken to the phoenix.

The custom of dining on snake meat is not only found in today's Guangzhou. Liu An wrote in his book *Huainanzi* over two thousand years ago: "The Yue people consider snake meat a delicacy." But in recent years, through adding the meat of chicken and cat and other ingredients, the Cantonese have acquired fame for their preparation of snake meat. Manager Wu told me that in the prime season of autumn when snakes are fat they serve a thousand to two thousand diners a day. Some timid ones keep their eyes closed at their first "go," but they soon come around. One of these applauded as he finished and declared, "To go to Guangzhou without trying snake soup would be like visiting Beijing and missing out on roast duck."

Teahouses and Snack Bars

At daybreak friends in groups began to descend on the nearby teahouses for breakfast. There they found their own seats and ordered according to the advice of the menu: "One tea with two items."

"One tea" originally referred to a cup of tea for each diner. In the old days, as in Sichuan today, an individual tea setting consisted of a teacup, a cover, and a saucer. Tea drinkers naturally found it convenient. However, because the waiters had to uncover the cups, fill them with tea, pour in hot water and then cover them again one by one, they complained of too many steps to serve their customers well. That is why the small tea service was later replaced by the large one, and the dainty cups eliminated.

"Two items" refers to two kinds of food. Different from teahouses in other places that provide tea only, Guangzhou's teahouses prepare all manner of light food for the customers at the same time. In Guangzhou waiters and waitresses go to each table carrying choices in open containers. The customers choose whatever they like and pay finally according to the number of cups, yet today's teahouses serve many courses offered by larger restaurants. So when a Cantonese says, "Let's go for some tea," he's actually inviting you to dinner.

That day, while in the Lianxianglou Restaurant, I not only had delicious *lianrongbao* (steamed buns stuffed with lotus seed paste), but also tasted some *baiqieji* (unspiced steamed chicken), roast piglet and several other Cantonese specialties. That crisp and tender roast pig in particular was so delicious I can still taste it.

While we were eating, we suddenly heard the popping of firecrackers from the entrance of the restaurant. Somebody said that a wedding feast was being served upstairs and the firecrackers had been the signal to start. In the old days, to avoid disputes among teahouses and restaurants, an unwritten law held sway in Guangzhou that teahouses should not serve feasts and restaurants should not sell crisp cake. But since living standards have improved over the past three decades or so, none of the six hundred or more restaurants and teahouses in Guangzhou is lacking for customers. So they no longer pay attention to old rules about what they should or should not serve. Or sell.

Of course, teahouses are still teahouses; they mainly do serve tea, after all. Etiquette can't be totally disregarded. So when your friends or the waiters pour tea for you, you should thank them by making your forefinger and middle finger kneel toward them on the table. I was told that this was an adaptation of the old custom that tea drinkers had to stand up to bow to their friends in thanks for the tea poured for them. That got in the way of the fun, having to stop eating and stand up from time to time, and so the hand bow was invented. But if they happened to be picking up food with their chopsticks when the hand bow was indicated, this, too, could be inconvenient. So the shorthand of the knock on the table was born.

While teahouses in Sichuan are usually small in size and

366

their tables and chairs rather low, teahouses in Guangzhou, a city with hot weather, are usually quite elevated and grand. Rooms are spacious, the tables often round, the chairs high. These well-ventilated teahouses have become places where people like to spend their leisure time, read newspapers, chat, meet friends, even conduct business negotiations. In the past, people from different fields had their own teahouses in Guangzhou: artists of Cantonese opera went to Tao Tao Ju to talk opera or organize actors and actresses for new programs; journalists would go to Ju Feng Yuan to talk shop and pursue tips. So it went.

On street corners or the corners of residential buildings, groups of young people often put up a tent, install a stove, put up a few tables and chairs and proceed to lure customers to try their "fast food." Such snack bars in Guangzhou are simply too many to count.

One day Lu Huang and I had to catch an early plane in the morning, so we stopped at one of these street snack bars for breakfast. A girl spread a very thin layer of liquid rice paste on a square flat metal container, placed some beef slices on it and moved it into her steamer. Before long she drew out the shallow container and rolled up the steamed contents into the shape of a section of intestine. The local people have come to call this *Changfen* (Intestine Rice Sheet). I ordered two pieces and found them fresh, tender and utterly delightful.

An elderly person was enjoying some soft cake and thin porridge at a nearby table. Noting that the porridge was scarcely thicker than water, I asked our guide in a low voice, "Why do they cook such thin porridge?"

"Well, that's what they call 'milk porridge,'" he told me. "It helps to increase the appetite, so it's especially good for feeble old people." He went on to explain that there are a hundred types of porridge in Guangzhou. Named after the ingredient it is cooked with, there are: "fish-slice porridge," "chicken porridge," "pig blood porridge," and so on and on. A well-known type is named "boat porridge," which offers not only a typical local flavor but also a bit of drama. You sit on a boat on the Pearl River while enjoying boatman's porridge, which is cooked with many different kinds of seafood.

Another interesting treat was "pot rice." Pressed together over fires were small clay pots with rice mixed with such ingredients as hearts of rape and sausages inside. As customers made their choices, the cook would immediately send the pots over gripped in tongs. When the cover of the pot was removed, the steaming contents would send up a mouth-watering aroma. Hearing me speak highly of the pot food, an elderly diner added in Cantonese, "With the rice, meat and vegetables cooked in one pot, it is clean, and you eat it hot, which makes it very good for you. But once it is cold, it's not much good." He was speaking rapidly, making it impossible for Lu Huang to make out what he was saying. Since I knew a little Cantonese I could interpret for him. This visit made me treasure the little knowledge I did have. They say that a little knowledge is a dangerous thing, but when it comes to a language, it's always better than nothing — as most lovers of travel discover over and over.

Cantonese— a Combination of Ancient Mandarin and an Aboriginal Dialect

Cantonese, also known as the Guangdong dialect, is one of the seven major dialects in China. It is spoken in central and southeastern Guangdong Province and in southeastern Guangxi, in about a hundred counties all told with a total population of about fifty million.

Guangdong Province is called "Yue" for short (粤 and also 越). Research reveals that the regions where Cantonese is spoken were once inhabited by the Baiyue people of ancient times. The aboriginal dialect spoken by these ancients belonged to the Zhuang-dong language family. In the beginning of the Warring States Period, Chu State sent an army commanded by Wu Qi to the South and conquered the Baiyue people. Thereafter Hans from the Central Plains began to move to the conquered areas, Qin State contributing the largest number — some 500,000. Then during the troubled last years of the Western Jin and the Southern Song dynasties, large numbers of Han war victims fled their homes for Yue. The fact that people of various nationalities were living together here led to the birth of a mixed dialect—Cantonese. It was natural that the new dialect, which combined the Han of the Central Plains with the aboriginal one of Yue would differ greatly from Mandarin.

Cantonese is difficult to understand because it contains a lot of slang and colloquialisms. Typical examples are: " 佢 " — "he" or "she;" " 嘢 " — "things;" " 乜 " — "what;" " 点 " — "how;" " 搵 " — "look for;" " 咁 " — "like this," "so;" " 捻 " — "think carefully;" " 靓 " — "beautiful," etc. Most likely these are sample of slang left by the ancient Yue people.

As a dialect that combined the aboriginal language and ancient and transportation was not convenient in those years by the way, it is only natural that such ancient Chinese words as " 睇 " (look at), " 企 " (stand on tiptoe). and " 衫裤 " (clothes) are found in Cantonese. These words, however, are strange to today's northerners, in whose native tongue they had originated. Besides, the natural environment of the South also has added local color to the Cantonese dialect. For instance, because it never snows in Guangzhou, the Cantonese can hardly distinguish the difference between snow and ice. Accordingly, they call an "ice-lolly" "snow-lolly," "refrigerator" "ice-box," and "skates" "snow-shoes."

Guangzhou has long been a harbor for external trade, and its citizens have borrowed many foreign words to enrich their own dialect through their frequent contacts with foreigners. Examples include " 士担 " — "stamp," " 菲林 " — "film," and " 波 " — "ball." Among all the dialects in China, Cantonese has borrowed the biggest number of foreign words.

In addition, the normal order of standard Chinese is often changed in Cantonese. One example is that in standard Chinese people always say "You go first," but Cantonese will say, "You first go" instead, which is something hardly found in

Mandarin.

Cantonese has nine different tones. Tones and vowels may also be changed for the sake of emphasis. Women with soft voices speak rhythmically with prolonging tunes. Their talking sounds as pleasant to the ear as singing, yet they do have quite a bit of trouble when they have to communicate with outsiders. And it is because of this that the Chinese Government has been trying to popularize Mandarin throughout China since the birth of the People's Republic, hoping that Chinese living in all parts of the country will come to the point that they can communicate among themselves. With regard to the younger people, more and more of them are able to speak Mandarin as time goes on.

"Flower Street" on the Eve of Spring Festival

The Spring Festival flower markets in Guangzhou are well-known throughout China. The one on Jiaoyu Road which I visited was one of the six major ones of the city. Stretching from the intersection down the roads in four directions, there was an endless garden of gorgeous blossoms everywhere you looked interspersed with potted landscapes and other plants.

Spring Festival is a time when flowers are of course much in evidence. But since early spring in the North is still cold, they cannot grow or survive outdoors. So a compromise is struck and potted flowers are displayed in homes and public places indoors, and flower replicas — flower vegetable bouquets, for example — abound. Girls in the countryside with clever fingers cut peach and plum blossoms out of red paper and paste them on windows. They may also tie flowers made of red velvet to their hair coils and pigtails. But Guangzhou, the "Flower City," enjoys beautiful weather all year round, so each season has its blooms. The annual flower market there originated from the Ming Dynasty, and a unique southern custom gradually developed. The local people feel ever so strongly that a trip to the flower market is a "must" as part of the Spring Festival celebrations. In the past the flower fair was held on New Year's Eve only, but because more and more people bring flowers to the fair, the night is no longer enough to satisfy everybody. So florists begin to set up shelves and sell flowers four or five days before the Eve.

While rambling through the "flower streets," one should buy a pot of kumquats and a mixed bouquet, according to tradition, to put in the sitting room at home. People feel that these flowers and plants will help to assure health and good fortune in the coming year. Kumquats stand for wealth, "Four-season Mandarins" for safety and good luck, and chrysanthemums for longevity, while *liangtianchi* (ruler measuring heaven) cactus stands for steady progress. Some people hang scarlet mandarins over their beds to invite blessings from "Stars Shining Above." If one has not bought any flowers when the market is over and the New Year has arrived, he's sure to feel dejected. What's more, he'll really hate himself if he runs into trouble in the new year.

Among the heavy crowds that were buying or admiring the flowers were men who carried potted mandarins with green leaves and golden fruit, and elders and girls, all smiles, holding bouquets high above their heads. Two young men, each carrying a budding peach branch, were walking toward me. The saying goes, "A flower in blossom brings wealth and good fortune." The peach branch would bloom continuously for a full month when it was planted in a pot, while theoretically they get richer and richer. But actually the fact that these young men and girls like to buy peach branches does not mean they are burning to get rich. Instead, borrowing the hidden meaning of the Chinese expression "Chinese blossom luck," they are more likely to wish for a sweetheart in the new year.

Fish Ponds and Fish Raising

Like people in other parts of China, the Cantonese prepare one whole fish for the dinner that falls on the eve of the Spring Festival. Yet they do not eat the fish at dinner. Instead they put it on the rice container and have it only after the Festival is over. This is a practice based on the Chinese homophones "fish" and "things to spare." After saving the fish for the "next year," they believe they will enhance their chances of having money and food to spare in the new year. Still more superstitious families prepare *facai* (a type of hair-like seaweed soup) to help them get rich in the new year, for *facai* and "get rich" are another pair of homophones.

"Rather eat without meat than without fish," goes a local saying, which tells us how much the Cantonese like fish. It so happens that there is a river in the suburbs of Guangzhou where fish are raised all year round. Thus it is possible for the city people to cook whatever fish courses they want.

Longjiang, a district in Shunde County particularly well known for fish raising, lies sixty kilometers southwest of Guangzhou. What we saw of the plain of the Pearl River Delta on our way to Longjiang that day was pretty as a picture: rivers and their branches crisscrossing in the distance, ripples flickering in the clear fish ponds, small country residential buildings facing rivers or seas looking like elegant villas. From time to time a boat passed, leaving behind laps that stirred up the reflections of the banana and sugarcane groves.

There are 134 rivers or river branches in Longjiang district. Of its 69,000 *mu* (1 *mu*=0.0667 hectares) of farmland, 37,000 are occupied by fish ponds, 21,000 by sugarcane, mulberry or banana. The local peasants cleverly knitted together the fish ponds, mulberry, sugarcane and banana fields, calling the result "mulberry-diked fish ponds."

Driving along the river, we finally got to our goal, Changtang Village, where fish ponds lay side by side divided by earth dikes. Planted on the dikes were mulberries or sugarcanes and bananas so that they were called either "mulberry dikes" or "fruit dikes."

"The good thing about this fish pond is that the water and land, the plants and animals — all make the best possible use of each other," said our guide Lao Zuo. Mulberries that absorb the rich light, heat, water and fertilizer of the South are especially lush. You feed silkworms the mulberry leaves, and the silkworms produce cocoons and excrement so that the mulberry leaf residue becomes good for the fish in the pond. The excrement of the fish and the organic substance in turn change into sludge, becoming manure for the mulberries. Thus, good ecologic circulation is occurring: luxuriant mulberries — strong

372

silkworms — fat fish — good sludge — rich and abundant mulberries again.

The average fish pond here is about two meters deep. The farmers raise in the same pond different fishes living at different water levels: grass carp, silver carp, variegated carp and dace, which they call "stereoscopic fish raising." In this way silkworm excrement and various feeds thrown into the pond are first consumed by grass carp at the upper level. The excrement of the grass carp and the residue of the food are then dissolved by the microbes in the water, turning it into nutrients for aquatic plants and plankton, which become good food for the silver carp and variegated carp living at the middle level. Finally the excrement of the silver and the variegated carp, in addition to the leftovers of their food, become feed for the carp, dace and crustaceans at the bottom. Making use of each other in this circulating way makes for abundant yields of both fish and silkworms.

Catching sight of some people carrying fish through the mulberry trees, our guide said, "Come on, let's go and watch them scraping fish." Falling in step behind him, we saw more than a dozen men dressed in rubber boots and jackets fishing in the pond. Divided into two groups, one on the left and the other on the right, they towed a long net which nearly touched bottom from one side of the pond to the other. What they were doing was "scraping." All varieties of carp and dace were flopping around inside the net. The men sorted them out, putting different types of fish into different wooden buckets. These they carried to the boats — special boats with small holes drilled on both sides which were used only for shipping fish. As the boat sailed, water from the river came in through the holes to keep the fish alive.

The owner of the fish pond was a forceful, middle-aged man named Li Qiang who told us that his pond, which covered an area of six *mu*, yielded more than five tons of fish a year. When the money he got for the silk cocoons, sugarcane and other fruit was added on, his yearly income was pretty impressive. I was told that Shunde County produced one hundred thousand tons of fish annually, which makes it number one in

China, and its output of sugar and silk is the highest in Guangdong Province.

Of course, raising fish is a very hard job. Starting from the day when the fry are released in the pond, you have to keep close watch, feeding the fish and getting rid of the weeds on both banks. In summer when they eat more and grow faster, you have to provide them with extra grass. In September, when the little dace begin to put on weight and speed up in their growth, they also must be provided with extra food. If they don't get enough, they won't reach the standard size and weight and you'll lose money. That is why fish raisers hold to the saying: "The old should not want for money and a fish pond must have sufficient food in September."

Most terrifying of all dangers to the fish pond owner, however, are the fish diseases. In the rainy spring, plankton grows rapidly, consuming far too much of the water's oxygen, which often causes rotten gills in grass carp. In summer, when these fish become greedy eaters, they must be provided with equal amounts of food regularly to protect them from enteritis. Another scourge is "red skin" trouble, when the skins of the fish turn red, scales fall off, and their bellies putrefy. Fish that catch this disease can die overnight.

In the old days when people lacked knowledge about science, their only recourse was to make offerings and seek blessings when the fish they depended on for a living fell ill. The moment their fish ponds got into trouble, the old women would slaughter chickens and buy meat. Then armed with fake paper money and joss sticks, they would go to the pond's entrance to present offerings to the "god of the lake," who was believed to have the power to dispel all evils and protect the fish. Every Spring Festival and Lantern Festival, the old women would pay a visit to the temples where through the drawing of lots provided by the fortune tellers, they would find out how good their harvests of fish and silk cocoons would be. Then they would be prepared to make their sacrificial offerings.

Nowadays, the government's department of fisheries is introducing methods that can prevent fish diseases. Since the fry, feed and the water in the ponds are sterilized and the fragile

374

grass carp are injected with inoculations, the rate of illness among the fish is greatly diminished. Even if any is present, the fish raisers can effectively control it by giving the fish granular feed mixed with medicine. The result is that fewer and fewer of the younger people believe in the god of the lake anymore.

HAKKA HOUSES, FAMILY AND VILLAGE RULES

Having been away from my hometown of Jiaoling County for many years, I welcomed the chance to go back as a reporter. It could be fascinating to view my friends and relatives in the role of the outsider I'd been trying to play. Would I be able to be objective? We would see.

Our bus started out from Guangzhou before daybreak taking us along the winding roads eastward to arrive at the county town after nightfall. Waiting at the bus station was Huang Kunquan of the Propaganda Department of Jiaoling County to see to our comfort. After settling us in our rooms, he fetched buckets of hot water and while I washed away the dust and fatigue of my journey, he made me a pot of oolong tea. Already refreshed by the washing up, I was wholly rejuvenated once I finished off a couple of cups of that wonderfully strong brew. Huang's warm reception put me in mind of the common Chinese saying: "Dear are the folks of your hometown and sweet is the water of your own land."

I got to my home village of Lanfang after nightfall the next day to be met and fussed over by any number of folks whose mission it was to let me know that the whole community had missed me and wanted me to feel welcome. This was according to the general custom that saves the close relatives for the last — like dessert. My parents, brothers, uncles and cousins had to wait in line! Once together we made the most of it, talking and laughing far into the night.

Weiwu Compound Houses Accommodate Modern Clans

Ancestral Pomei House in my village is actually a hundred-year-old apartment house with a design that continues to suit today's residents, descendants of the original Qiu Pomei.

A rectangular structure, the main entrance opens onto a

375

vestibule facing a square courtyard which opens onto the principal hall. Corridors run along either side of the two buildings linking both courtyards, vestibules, principal halls and indeed the more than forty rooms that make up this enduring residential Compound. Of course, this is not the only compound of its kind. They're called *Weiwu* hereabouts.

In addition to its livability, Pomei House is notable for its lovely natural setting. Gentle hills rise behind it covered with pines, Chinese firs and orange trees. In front lies a semicircular pond in which are reflected the gray buildings, the green hills, blue sky and white clouds—at least on a sunny day and I can testify to the likelihood of such days in this my native village. The pond holds the drainage from the three yards and provides a place to raise fish, wash clothes, and get water for the vegetable fields. In case of fire, of course, it would be put to immediate use. When I was a boy I often sat by this pond with my friends on hot summer nights trying to stay cool and often singing:

> On a fair moon-lit night
> A girl scholar rides a horse
> Right across a lotus pond.
> Growing there above the pond
> Are chives — some graceful, some coarse:
> All blossoming within sight.
>
> She picks a man for her spouse;
> In front of her darling's house
> Lies a pond teeming with carp:
> The longer ones for eating,
> The rest sold to pay for schooling.

Shortly before Spring Festival when I was a boy the pond would be partially drained for a kind of community fishing spree. Adults and children together would roll up their trouser legs and wade in to catch fish with their bare hands. Though we were usually hot and covered all over with dirt, that didn't diminish the thrill of catching something.

In addition to those rectangular houses in my home village, there are other unique styles of compound in the area: round and semicircular. The Luos building of Suba Village, Guangfu District, is the latter type. It lies off by itself in the fields, one house crowding upon another, so that it looks rather like three coiled dragons. Some imaginative citizen way back when may have noticed this and said, "How about calling these coiling dragon compounds?" Anyway the name stuck.

In the middle of the compound we visited lies a grand ancestral hall known as *Erjin Gaotang* among the locals. On either side of the hall are two rows of houses and behind are three other rows in a semicircle. The huge structure, which is enclosed with an arched gate, has through corridors between the houses so that it's convenient to go in and out, and it's safe inside, too. Architects call this type of compound one of the five major types of traditional houses in China. The other four, by the way, are the *siheyuan* in Beijing, the dwelling caves in Shaanxi, the "railing" house in Guangxi, and the "one seal" structure in Yunnan.

According to Luo Zhiwen, a villager of nearly sixty, the walls of *weiwu* compounds were rammed of mud, so that as long as they used short molding boards, they could easily pound up circular walls. This compound consists of a total of about three hundred rooms—including kitchens, bedrooms, storerooms, rooms for sundries, stables and toilets—occupied by fifty families.

Between the houses of the compound are narrow open yards good for sunning things on sunny days and for catching water on rainy days. They not only bring in light and fresh air to the houses, but also serve as fire preventive corridors (in case of fire, they would help contain it or provide escape in other circumstances). Because the houses lie in the west but face the east, in winter they are free from the direct attacks of northern cold winds and get the warm sun. And in summer southern winds that blow through the lanes cool the houses. That is why since the first row of *weiwu* houses was built 170 years ago, this residential compound has been expanded twice, two other rows having been set up with funds collected from the members of the clan in accordance with tradition.

The hall which displays tablets of the ancestors is the "heart" of the compound. During festivals and on other traditional holidays the families of the clan all come to pay homage to their ancestors with all manner of offerings. When a man gets married, custom decrees that he must kowtow to his ancestors in the hall and hold his wedding feast there. When a girl marries somebody outside the clan, she must go to the hall and say good-bye to the ancestors. Only then can she put on her face veiling, step onto the large round inscribed board that symbolizes reunion and get on her way to the bridegroom's home. When an old person dies, the hall becomes a place of mourning. So it is this ancestral hall that binds together this large clan, enabling them to share their happy times as well as their sorrows. No wonder outsiders say that these *weiwu* houses, which provide room for living, animal breeding, storage, sunning and processing things, and which are also safe inside and free from the usual dangers of fire, express the way of life of the Hakkas.

The Birth of the Hakkas and Their Customs

The name "Hakka," or *kejia* (families from strange places) in Chinese, was chosen to distinguish Han migrants from the natives in places where they settled. Today there are about forty million of their descendants living in Guangdong, Fujian, Jiangxi, Hunan, Guangxi and Sichuan provinces and in Taiwan.

The migrations started in the last years of the Eastern Han Dynasty when the Three Kingdoms (220-280) — Wei, Shu and Wu — were at war and continued in the last years of the Western Jin Dynasty (265-316) when all the states were fighting among themselves. People of Shanxi, Hebei and Henan deserted their wartorn homes and crossed the Yellow River in hordes. First they came to Anhui, then crossed the Yangtze River, heading toward northern Jiangxi. Together these movements of people are called the first major migration of the Hakkas.

Then during the late Tang Dynasty (618-907), the northern Hans who had already settled in Anhui and northern

Jiangxi had to move southward again. Once more driven to escape local wars, they settled in the south of Jiangxi and the west of Fujian. In the Song Dynasty (960-1279), to distinguish these newer residents from the locals, the government began calling the natives *Zhu* (host) and the migrants *Ke* (guest) when the households were registered. And that is, more specifically, how the name *Kejia* or *Hakka* came into being.

The third major migration occurred during the late Southern Song Dynasty (1127-1279). When the Mongolian cavalry in the north swept southward, the incompetent imperial family of the Song Dynasty fled to Guangdong immediately. Now the Hakkas living in Jiangxi and Fujian moved further to the south, swarming into eastern and northern Guangdong.

The final dynasty of imperial China— Qing (1644-1911) —saw Hakkas moving in great numbers to western Guangdong, Hunan, Guangxi, Sichuan, Taiwan and Hainan because of a fast increase of population and fighting between Hakkas and natives, a migration that actually took place at two different times. Some scholars maintain that an outline of the history of Chinese migration in a general sense can easily be drawn by tracing the route and process of the Hakkas' movements.

Hakkas who settled in the South did not forget their original homes and passed this love and loyalty down through the generations. On the doors of their ancestral halls they inscribed their family names or the names of the places they had come from— "Hebei Hall" (the Xus), for example, or "Henan Hall" (the Qius). Or they might put up couplets like "Families from Yingchuan/Descendants of Guishui" (the Chens), and "Children of Gaoyang/Descendants of Luoshui" (the Xus). Thus they tried to see to it that the younger generations would not forget where they, or actually their family line, had come from. And since they continued to speak their own language and keep their own culture, and because they had little contact with the local people as a result of the isolation caused by the high mountains, their customs continued to develop in a way that set them apart.

On holidays and festivals, for example, a course of bean

curd stuffed with meat is always present on the Hakka dining table. To prepare this typical dish, you first cut a lump of bean curd open in the middle, fill in the meat stuffing, and then fry it in boiling oil until it turns yellowish, when it is stewed. And why this instead of *jiaozi* (dumplings), usually associated with holidays? It is believed that when the first migrants arrived in the South there was a shortage of wheat flour. So this was the nearest thing to *jiaozi* they could come up with, and it stuck.

The Hakka dialect is one of the seven major dialects in China. Compared with the other two important ones in Guangdong—Cantonese and Minnan—it's much closer to Mandarin. What's more, Han opera, which is popular throughout the Hakka areas, is still performed in the northern dialect, which cannot be said about local operas in Guangdong. Of course, the Hakka dialect still keeps many ancient words from the old Central Plains and a lot of slang which today's northerners can hardly understand at first hearing.

The Hakka regions are traditionally known as the — "Home of Mountain Folk Songs." Young people of both sexes often sing to each other as they gather firewood in the mountains, work in the fields, or put down their heavy loads on the roads for a rest. Making up the words as they go along, they sing of the scenery of their hometown, work and life. Here are two of their favorite songs:

1) A pair of swans glide on the pond,
   Gently swaying from left to right;
   Like two devoted lovers,
   In antiphony they sing with delight.

2) Climbing the mountains, I see vines
      twisting around trees;
   Leaving the mountains, I see trees
      clinging to vines.
   Even when the trees all die of disease,
   The vines still cling to them as if fast bound.
   Even when all the vines are deceased,

Still the trees cling to them
As when first found.

Research has revealed that the poetic convention of the comparison and the repeating of lines and words found in Hakka folk songs may be traced to the same source as those known as "*Shiwu Guofeng*" in Confucius' *Book of Songs* from such provinces as Shanxi, Hebei, and Henan and also the folk songs that have come down from the Han Dynasty.

At noon that day I happened to see the celebration of the rebuilding of the ancestral hall of the Huangs in Fengkou Village. Members of the clan living within ten square kilometers of the hall came for the ceremony, each bearing a load of offerings. As soon as the rounds of firecrackers were spent, every family retrieved the offerings they had brought and left in haste with their burning lanterns since traditional belief had it that the faster they walked and the sooner they reached home to hang their lanterns on their own doors, the better luck would be theirs. As the saying goes: "The sooner you go, the sooner you prosper."

The Hakkas also have special funeral rites. Most Hans put the remains of the deceased in wooden coffins and after burial set up tombstones in front of the graves. Hakka custom, however, dictates that on the first of the 8th lunar month, after the remains have been kept underground for three or five years, once the ceremony of making offerings with burning joss sticks is over, the members of the deceased's family will dig up the coffin, open it, and signal a special artisan who has been invited to the graveside for this purpose to pick up the bones. Then shaded by an umbrella while at work, the artisan will clean the bones with tea-seed oil as part of the ceremony known as "pulling up the dead." This accomplished, he will arrange the bones according to anatomical structure and bending them so that they will fit, place them in a clay jar known as a "gold container" locally. Then choosing a new "lucky spot," the relatives will place the remains in their final and permanent resting place. Folklorists refer to this custom as "second burial," tracing it to the Hakkas' migration to the south. Whenever they migrated, the men always carried along the bones of their ancestors. Only when they felt they were settled permanently in a strange land would they bury the bones again.Thus they would not have to go back to their distant native place to pay respects to their ancestors, hardly possible in any case.

One morning more than a hundred men and women, accompanied by drumbeats and gongs, lanterns high above their heads, danced the lion dance on their way to the ancestral tombs of the Xus in the suburbs of the town. Carrying the whole carcasses of pigs and sheep among their sacrifices, many in the procession were snapping pictures, others were making recordings. These would be sent to relatives overseas who keenly felt the distance between themselves and their hometown and ancestors. Indeed, many of the overseas Hakkas who have continued to follow the customs of their hometown exact promises from their children to bring back their bones one day for the second burial.

Nowadays, of course, the Hakkas for the most part are engaged in productive work and enjoy a reasonable standard of living. They no longer have to pull up stakes to look for these things elsewhere. Therefore, anybody who sticks to the old ways and digs up buried remains for second burials will be regarded as a waster of land, not to mention labor and money. And any fight that might erupt over "lucky spots" will be despised as an act harmful to social peace and security.

Because their ancestral memory encompasses so much displacement, the longing for the home that had to be abandoned and the desire to find a new and permanent place at last would be sure to find expression in the customs that grew up. I found just such expression when I attended the wedding of a young man of Shizhai Village. I suddenly caught sight of a bunch of wild grass tied with a red thread inside a bamboo basket hung above the bed in the bridal room. When I asked about it, I was told that this was "longevity grass" brought by the bride to be planted in the vegetable garden of her new family on this day. The symbolism was clear. In planting the grass she would be saying that here she would stay for the rest of her life and the prayer that she would never have to move anywhere else. Over the head of the bed had been placed a branch of China fir which had been held by the bride's brother to brush the way for his sister as she made her way to the home of her bridegroom. Called "pulling the green" by the locals — a homophone for "giving birth" in the Hakka dialect — this part of the ceremony expressed the wish that the couple have a child at the earliest possible date.

The Organization of Clans and Village Rules and Regulations

A village surrounded by mountains, Shizhai Village's rectangular three-storeyed adobe multiple family dwellings looked like watchtowers more than the apartment houses they actually were. Their original dual purpose explains why. Built by the forefathers of today's Guos some four hundred years ago to guard against attacks by bandits and other enemies, their outer earthen walls are one meter thick; their narrow first-storey windows doubled as gun holes; their two far-stretching watchtowers were the places where residents could be vigilant to avoid approaching dangers. Above the ten-centimeter-thick wooden doors, four "protective holes" imbedded in the bamboo tubes provided passages for missiles or boiling oil aimed at attackers. In the open yard a well had been dug so that water would be easily available in case of encirclement.

Many shortcomings would be apparent to any current visitor. For example, the narrow windows meant dark and stuffy interiors, and it isn't hard to imagine the stench and filth of bygone times when pigs were raised in huts around the yard. Residents had to wait until the founding of the People's Republic of China for all the bandits to disappear and the locals and Hakkas to stop fighting each other. And as social security and peace came to be taken for granted, the villagers began to build separate small houses outside the old residence.

Although the twenty-two households with over a hundred people living in the same residence were all descended from the same forefather, they were not necessarily always one big happy family. Like extended families the world over, they were quite capable of quarreling among themselves. "Children quarrel a lot," Guo Huirong pointed out, "and grown-ups are known to have their battles. But here once one of the Seniors of the clan tells them to stop it, it's like magic. The fight stops just like that." And he chopped the air with his flattened palm.

"Senior" was a title of respect reserved for a clan chief in ancient times: a clan being a loose organization of blood relations from the closest to the comparatively distant. Except for criminals who had been expelled from the clan, everyone who lived in the residence was a member of one large family. Through history the mobile Hakkas had had to depend on wise chiefs in selecting new sites for their homes or when they were forced to take up arms against the natives. Consequently they developed a strong belief in the patriarchal clan and the cohesive family.

Nonetheless, the title "Senior" could not be inherited, nor were these chiefs ever appointed by any local government. Rather they were elected from among the common people, who usually settled on men known for their courage who were versed both in letters and martial arts and who had proved themselves disinterested in personal gain throughout long lives. Shizhai, a village of more than four hundred households which shared the family name Guo had over a dozen Seniors, all of whom, like other villagers, were engaged in the daily work of farming. Only when the clan was going to make sacrificial offerings to their ancestors in the ancestral hall or in the graveyard, when a wedding or funeral was about to take place, or when the village needed to build a school, a bridge, a road or an irrigation works would the Seniors get together formally. Of course they would come forth to adjudicate or work out countermeasures should any of the clan members break village rules and regulations or should the village find itself in disputes with neighboring villages.

The local inhabitants all had unwritten rules and regulations which effectively guaranteed peace and security in the area. In Shizhai Village, for example, each household in the same residence had the right to build a stove or store things in front of its own rooms but none could infringe on anyone else's space. During the season when rice seedlings were transplanted, in order to enable everyone to finish his farm work in time, the water must be equally shared. If anyone whose land was espec-

384

ially close to the irrigation canals dammed up the water for himself, the Seniors had the right to reroute it to serve the fields of others. Should anybody get hurt in a dispute over irrigation water, the wrong side not only had to pay for the other side's medical treatment but also had to ask forgiveness of the abused member's family by setting off a string of firecrackers in front of the family's house. Then when the rice was ripening, the Seniors would put up posters forbidding anyone to drive ducks and chickens into the paddies. The animals of violators could be killed, cooked and eaten in front of the sacred altar of the village by anyone who caught them eating grain in the fields. And since the woods that covered the mountains were the main source of the village's income, anybody who stole wood from there must pay the full price for whatever he had cut down. Those who caused a fire in the woods through their carelessness had to cover the financial loss and in addition prepare a rich dinner for the neighboring villagers who had come to help put out the fire.

A Chinese saying states that "a country has laws and a family has domestic disciplines." Family rules of the Hakkas forbade stealing, robbery, prostitution and gambling. Inevitably then the Hakkas tended to be an industrious and thrifty people, honest and simple, who always helped each other and were united as one. Anybody who committed adultery or any other offense would be severely punished by the Seniors. For example, when one of the Seniors in Shizhai Village found his son gambling, he tied him up, dragged him to the ancestral hall and whipped him publicly before the memorial tablets. Finally he drove him out of the village, writing in the Public Book that this shameful descendant was not to be given any share of his parents' properties when the other sons became eligible to claim their inheritance.

When the sons of a family who left their parents to found independent families of their own wanted to divide the houses, fields, trees and other properties, it was the Seniors who worked out who was to get what. On the day when the new households were founded, the parents-in-law of the newly married sons sent each some rice, some firewood and a pair of water buckets early in the morning after setting off some firecrackers. In the buckets were usually kitchenware, steamed cake, onions and heads of garlic and celery. On the one hand these items carried wishes for a happy new life; on the other hand, through the homophonic Chinese meanings of celery=industrious, onion=intelligent, and garlic=witty, they were intended to encourage the newlyweds to work hard and try to be clever. The steamed cake carried with it the wish for prosperity and a future that would keep getting better and better, and the firewood expressed hopes for riches.

Still the sons never did divide up all the properties of the family. Instead, they kept some of the land, woods and fish ponds as properties of the family, calling them "public properties." For the sake of good relations between brothers and between uncles and nephews and the unity of the extended family, the "public" fields and mountain land were to be worked by the descendants by turns. Whatever income resulted would go to pay for sacrificial offerings to their ancestors in the same year, be given to members of the clan who were in need, or spent on their young people's education away from home. Another use might be for public facilities.

In the old days prices went up and down rapidly. On *Lixia*, or the beginning of summer, every year the Seniors would gather at the marketplace to calculate, based upon a price slightly lower than that of the market that day, the "public" annual income and expenses. That is what they called the "*Lixia* Price" — the price fixed on the first day of summer.

After the founding of New China, the political organizations of the villages and the districts of the People's Government replaced the Seniors, and new laws and regulations took the place of the old family rules. However, the simple clan rules and regulations can still play a positive role in upholding the unity of the villages and developing the spirit of the Chinese nation.

The National Spirit of Striving for the Future
Following the canal bringing water to the hydroelectric

power station of Shizhai Village, we went into the mountains to get in touch with more local customs. In the years when the local villagers had no electricity, they had to use split bamboo on the walls for lighting. When they put on an opera or a puppet show, they would have to hang up two huge tung oil lamps in the village hall. By the time the show was over, the faces of the villagers would be pitch black from the smoke of the lamps. This is just one example of the many nuisances villagers had to put up with as a result of their lack of electricity. Today they are enjoying the results of twenty years of cleaving cliffs, digging tunnels through mountains, and channeling water from rivers to build six small hydroelectric power stations. Today Jiaoling County is one of the hundred experimental counties in China that has spread electrification to the countryside.

Along the heavily forested paths of the high mountains we saw slender, graceful bamboo trees; tall, straight China firs; and majestic broadleaf trees of several varieties. The light of the sky could show through but dimly in such dense woods. The sighing of the wind in the pines chiming in with the birdsong made for an enchanting mountain-forest symphony. The Chinese saying goes: "Those living on the mountain live off the mountain," and here the villagers fell trees, process wood, hoop baskets, carve ladles and make bamboo beds and chairs. They also tap the pine trees for their resin and make charcoal.

The charcoal smoke curling up to the sky led us to the charcoal kilns. About twenty villagers had set up simple thatched huts here, building domelike kilns inside. They had carried here on their shoulders what they had felled and sawed it into neat logs all about the same length. After piling up the logs in a kiln, they shut up the entrance tight and lighted the wood through the hole on the side wall. Then when the wood was fully lighted, they stopped up the fire hole, leaving the wood burning from top to bottom inside. Finally they covered the chimney, extinguishing the fire to make the wood change into charcoal. In the evening they split bamboo strips and wove baskets into which they put the charcoal. Watching them laboring away such long hard hours, I felt a sense of pride that in actuality I was one of them, having been born a Hakka myself.

387

Not flinching from difficulties and hardships has been a characteristic of the Hakkas historically. When the forefathers of the Hakkas first came to Guangdong, the plains and fertile land were already occupied. They were forced to move into the remote mountains with their families. Actually that's how the saying was born: "Where there is a mountain, there are Hakkas." (The second translated meaning is: "Where there is a mountain, there are people.") Braving harsh winds and rainstorms, accepting the challenge of fierce animals and poisonous snakes, the Hakkas went through the severest adversities on the way to setting up new homes for themselves.

In modern times, perhaps as an outcome of the epic struggles of their own people, many individual Hakkas have written their own brilliant chapters in the history of the Chinese nation, particularly in the Taiping Revolution, which shook to its foundations the feudal society that had held sway in China for thousands of years. Its leader Hong Xiuquan, its prominent generals, and the core members of the Charcoal Party were all Hakkas from Guangdong or Guangxi. The ancestors of the great Dr. Sun Yat-sen and of Soong Ching-Ling were Hakkas from Meixian, Guangdong; the contemporary proletarian revolutionary Ye Jianying was a Hakka from Meixian; and Zhu De, Marshal of the People's Republic of China and ex-chairman of the Standing Committee of the People's Congress was a Hakka from Sichuan Province.

"Strong women plow like robust men," observed poet Guo Moruo when he visited Meixian. And it certainly is true that Hakka women are remarkable for their industry and endurance. They never did bind their feet or breasts to any significant degree and have always been known as strong, capable people. Throughout a history marked by their husbands' leavetaking because of the difficulties in eking out a living in mountains where farmland was in short supply, the women have taken up the multiple tasks of farming, running the household, looking after the elders and educating the children.

The Tradition of Respecting Teachers and Elders
On the second day of my visit to my hometown I dropped

in on Luo Wanquan at Lanfang Middle School — my teacher of thirty years ago. I noticed that his hair was graying but I heard more talk of the future from him than the past. In reply to my effusive expressions of gratitude for his years of devoted teaching he was self-deprecating. "It is the government and the people of your hometown you should thank," he told me. "They are the ones who have been supporting the school." And now the school was on the verge of expansion — ready to build more classrooms, dormitories and playing fields. The higher authorities had allotted special funds to the school and the local government had provided free land and wood needed in the construction. In addition, over thirty overseas Hakkas had been generous with their donations.

I thought back to the years when I studied here, when it was a primary school — not a middle school also — which had been rebuilt from an old temple. In those days it was the traditional practice for pupils to take turns bringing vegetables to the teacher for his table. When my day came up, my mother would pick the tenderest greens, wash them and hand them to me as she said, "Be sure to tell the teacher we are sorry we have nothing better to offer him."

The Hakkas have always had a reputation for respecting teachers and placing a high value on education. The local saying puts it that "he who cannot read or write is like a person with eyes but no sight." As long as the children study hard, Hakka parents will do everything in their power to see to it that they get as much education as they can absorb. Traditionally, it was the duty of the seniors of the family to support education with whatever money they could get from the "public" land and woods from the mountains. A rule of the Guos of Shizhai Village provided that any middle school graduate was entitled to receive a hectoliter of unhusked rice every year for life. Moreover, many villages set up what were in effect their own scholarship funds through local organizations with such names as The Association of Polite Letters or The Mutual Aid Society.

Nowadays respecting teachers and valuing education are even more the order of the day in Jiaoling County. I learned from Liu Jijun, Director of the Education Bureau there, that 137 schools of the county had received donations from overseas Chinese and compatriots in Hong Kong and Macao as well as from individuals in the community. The result has been enormous building activity, with classrooms, science halls, libraries and residential buildings for teachers and students going up one after another. An anecdote illustrates the spirit behind all this exertion.

An old man from a mountain village who was not able to contribute when he learned that his village was collecting money for the school went up high into the mountains and gathered a load of firewood which he sold for five *yuan* and contributed the entire amount to the school fund. Though five *yuan* could hardly be considered a large sum, it represented the old man's commitment to doing his part for the village's future.

The fact that the story about the firewood involves an old man is a strong reason for its popularity, for respect of the elderly is well known as a virtue of the Chinese nation and one held in particularly high esteem by the Hakkas, as I myself was reminded of during this recent hometown visit that combined business and pleasure. One evening as my mother and I were walking home from a friend's house carrying bags on our shoulders heavy enough to make us pant a bit as we made our way down the road, two young girls from a neighboring village noticed our straining and caught up with us. "Do let us carry your bags for you," they pled and grabbed for them before I knew what was happening. They walked us the rest of the way home and left us as soon as we got there, refusing to pause even for a cup of water. Their children in the future would do the same, I reflected, for that is the Hakka way — indeed the Chinese way.

INDEX

391

397

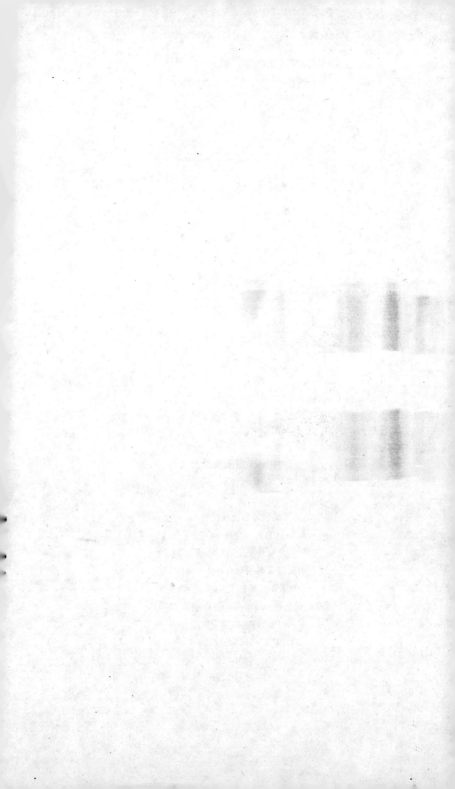

中国民俗采英录

丘桓兴著

*

新世界出版社出版

（北京百万庄路 24 号）

北京外文印刷厂印刷

中国国际图书贸易总公司发行

（中国北京车公庄西路 35 号）

北京邮政信箱第 399 号　邮政编码 100044

1993（英文）第一版

ISBN 7—80005—192—7

03900

17—E—2778P